Praise for
WebGL Programmi

"WebGL provides one of the final features for creating applications that deliver 'the desktop application experience' in a web browser, and the *WebGL Programming Guide* leads the way in creating those applications. Its coverage of all aspects of using WebGL—JavaScript, OpenGL ES, and fundamental graphics techniques—delivers a thorough education on everything you need to get going. Web-based applications are the wave of the future, and this book will get you ahead of the curve!"

Dave Shreiner, Coauthor of *The OpenGL Programming Guide, Eighth Edition*; Series Editor, *OpenGL Library* (Addison Wesley)

"HTML5 is evolving the Web into a highly capable application platform supporting beautiful, engaging, and fully interactive applications that run portably across many diverse systems. WebGL is a vital part of HTML5, as it enables web programmers to access the full power and functionality of state-of-the-art 3D graphics acceleration. WebGL has been designed to run securely on any web-capable system and will unleash a new wave of developer innovation in connected 3D web-content, applications, and user interfaces. This book will enable web developers to fully understand this new wave of web functionality and leverage the exciting opportunities it creates."

Neil Trevett, Vice President Mobile Content, NVIDIA; President, The Khronos Group

"With clear explanations supported by beautiful 3D renderings, this book does wonders in transforming a complex topic into something approachable and appealing. Even without denying the sophistication of WebGL, it is an accessible resource that beginners should consider picking up before anything else."

Evan Burchard, Author, *Web Game Developer's Cookbook* (Addison Wesley)

"Both authors have a strong OpenGL background and transfer this knowledge nicely over to WebGL, resulting in an excellent guide for beginners as well as advanced readers."

Daniel Haehn, Research Software Developer, Boston Children's Hospital

"*WebGL Programming Guide* provides a straightforward and easy-to-follow look at the mechanics of building 3D applications for the Web without relying on bulky libraries or wrappers. A great resource for developers seeking an introduction to 3D development concepts mixed with cutting-edge web technology."

Brandon Jones, Software Engineer, Google

"This is more great work from a brilliant researcher. Kouichi Matsuda shows clear and concise steps to bring the novice along the path of understanding WebGL. This is a complex topic, but he makes it possible for anyone to start using this exciting new web technology. And he includes basic 3D concepts to lay the foundation for further learning. This will be a great addition to any web designer's library."

Chris Marrin, WebGL Spec. Editor

"*WebGL Programming Guide* is a great way to go from a WebGL newbie to a WebGL expert. WebGL, though simple in concept, requires a lot of 3D math knowledge, and *WebGL Programming Guide* helps you build this knowledge so you'll be able to understand and apply it to your programs. Even if you end up using some other WebGL 3D library, the knowledge learned in *WebGL Programming Guide* will help you understand what those libraries are doing and therefore allow you to tame them to your application's specific needs. Heck, even if you eventually want to program desktop OpenGL and/or DirectX, *WebGL Programming Guide* is a great start as most 3D books are outdated relative to current 3D technology. *WebGL Programming Guide* will give you the foundation for fully understanding modern 3D graphics."

Gregg Tavares, An Implementer of WebGL in Chrome

WebGL Programming Guide

WebGL Programming Guide:
Interactive 3D Graphics Programming with WebGL

Kouichi Matsuda
Rodger Lea

♠ Addison-Wesley

Upper Saddle River, NJ • Boston • Indianapolis • San Francisco
New York • Toronto • Montreal • London • Munich • Paris • Madrid
Cape Town • Sydney • Tokyo • Singapore • Mexico City

The publisher offers excellent discounts on this book when ordered in quantity for bulk purchases or special sales, which may include electronic versions and/or custom covers and content particular to your business, training goals, marketing focus, and branding interests. For more information, please contact:

U.S. Corporate and Government Sales
(800) 382-3419
corpsales@pearsontechgroup.com

For sales outside the United States, please contact:

International Sales
international@pearsoned.com

Visit us on the Web: informit.com/aw

Library of Congress Control Number: 2013936083

ISBN-13: 978-0-321-90292-4
ISBN-10: 0-321-90292-0

Text printed in the United States on recycled paper at Edwards Brothers Malloy in Ann Arbor, Michigan

First printing: June 2013

Editor-in-Chief
Mark Taub

Executive Editor
Laura Lewin

Development Editor
Sheri Cain

Managing Editor
Krista Hansing

Senior Project Editor
Lori Lyons

Copy Editor
Gill Editorial Services

Senior Indexer
Cheryl Lenser

Proofreader
Paula Lowell

Technical Reviewers
Jeff Gilbert
Daniel Haehn
Rick Rafey

Editorial Assistant
Olivia Basegio

Interior Designer
Mark Shirar

Cover Designer
Chuti Prasertsith

Senior Compositor
Gloria Schurick

Graphics
Laura Robbins

Manufacturing Buyer
Dan Uhrig

Thoughts are filled along with time, the distant days will not return,
and time passed is like a spiral of semiprecious stones...
—Kouichi Matsuda

To my wife, family, and friends—for making life fun.
—Rodger Lea

Contents

6. The OpenGL ES Shading Language (GLSL ES)   191

8. Lighting Objects

291

9. Hierarchical Objects

323

10. Advanced Techniques

Preface

WebGL is a technology that enables drawing, displaying, and interacting with sophisticated interactive three-dimensional computer graphics ("3D graphics") from within web browsers. Traditionally, 3D graphics has been restricted to high-end computers or dedicated game consoles and required complex programming. However, as both personal computers and, more importantly, web browsers have become more sophisticated, it has become possible to create and display 3D graphics using accessible and well-known web technologies. This book provides a comprehensive overview of WebGL and takes the reader, step by step, through the basics of creating WebGL applications. Unlike other 3D graphics technologies such as OpenGL and Direct3D, WebGL applications can be constructed as web pages so they can be directly executed in the browsers without installing any special plug-ins or libraries. Therefore, you can quickly develop and try out a sample program with a standard PC environment; because everything is web based, you can easily publish the programs you have constructed on the web. One of the promises of WebGL is that, because WebGL applications are constructed as web pages, the same program can be run across a range of devices, such as smart phones, tablets, and game consoles, through the browser. This powerful model means that WebGL will have a significant impact on the developer community and will become one of the preferred tools for graphics programming.

Who the Book Is For

We had two main audiences in mind when we wrote this book: web developers looking to add 3D graphics to their web pages and applications, and 3D graphics programmers wishing to understand how to apply their knowledge to the web environment. For web developers who are familiar with standard web technologies such as HTML and JavaScript and who are looking to incorporate 3D graphics into their web pages or web applications, WebGL offers a simple yet powerful solution. It can be used to add 3D graphics to enhance web pages, to improve the user interface (UI) for a web application by using a 3D interface, and even to develop more complex 3D applications and games that run in web browsers.

The second target audience is programmers who have worked with one of the main 3D application programming interfaces (APIs), such as Direct3D or OpenGL, and who are interested in understanding how to apply their knowledge to the web environment. We would expect these programmers to be interested in the more complex 3D applications that can be developed in modern web browsers.

However, the book has been designed to be accessible to a wide audience using a step-by-step approach to introduce features of WebGL, and it assumes no background in 2D or 3D graphics. As such, we expect it also to be of interest to the following:

- General programmers seeking an understanding of how web technologies are evolving in the graphics area

- Students studying 2D and 3D graphics because it offers a simple way to begin to experiment with graphics via a web browser rather than setting up a full programming environment

- Web developers exploring the "bleeding edge" of what is possible on mobile devices such as Android or iPhone using the latest mobile web browsers

What the Book Covers

This book covers the WebGL 1.0 API along with all related JavaScript functions. You will learn how HTML, JavaScript, and WebGL are related, how to set up and run WebGL applications, and how to incorporate sophisticated 3D program "shaders" under the control of JavaScript. The book details how to write vertex and fragment shaders, how to implement advanced rendering techniques such as per-pixel lighting and shadowing, and basic interaction techniques such as selecting 3D objects. Each chapter develops a number of working, fully functional WebGL applications and explains key WebGL features through these examples. After finishing the book, you will be ready to write WebGL applications that fully harness the programmable power of web browsers and the underlying graphics hardware.

How the Book Is Structured

This book is organized to cover the API and related web APIs in a step-by-step fashion, building up your knowledge of WebGL as you go.

Chapter 1—Overview of WebGL

This chapter briefly introduces you to WebGL, outlines some of the key features and advantages of WebGL, and discusses its origins. It finishes by explaining the relationship of WebGL to HTML5 and JavaScript and which web browsers you can use to get started with your exploration of WebGL.

Chapter 2—Your First Step with WebGL

This chapter explains the `<canvas>` element and the core functions of WebGL by taking you, step-by-step, through the construction of several example programs. Each example is written in JavaScript and uses WebGL to display and interact with a simple shape on a web page. The example WebGL programs will highlight some key points, including: (1) how WebGL uses the `<canvas>` element object and how to draw on it; (2) the linkage between HTML and WebGL using JavaScript; (3) simple WebGL drawing functions; and (4) the role of shader programs within WebGL.

Chapter 3—Drawing and Transforming Triangles

This chapter builds on those basics by exploring how to draw more complex shapes and how to manipulate those shapes in 3D space. This chapter looks at: (1) the critical role of triangles in 3D graphics and WebGL's support for drawing triangles; (2) using multiple triangles to draw other basic shapes; (3) basic transformations that move, rotate, and scale triangles using simple equations; and (4) how matrix operations make transformations simple.

Chapter 4—More Transformations and Basic Animation

In this chapter, you explore further transformations and begin to combine transformations into animations. You: (1) are introduced to a matrix transformation library that hides the mathematical details of matrix operations; (2) use the library to quickly and easily combine multiple transformations; and (3) explore animation and how the library helps you animate simple shapes. These techniques provide the basics to construct quite complex WebGL programs and will be used in the sample programs in the following chapters.

Chapter 5—Using Colors and Texture Images

Building on the basics described in previous chapters, you now delve a little further into WebGL by exploring the following three subjects: (1) besides passing vertex coordinates, how to pass other data such as color information to the vertex shader; (2) the conversion from a shape to fragments that takes place between the vertex shader and the fragment shader, which is known as the rasterization process; and (3) how to map images (or textures) onto the surfaces of a shape or object. This chapter is the final chapter focusing on the key functionalities of WebGL.

Chapter 6—The OpenGL ES Shading Language (GLSL ES)

This chapter takes a break from examining WebGL sample programs and explains the core features of the OpenGL ES Shading Language (GLSL ES) in detail. You will cover: (1) data, variables, and variable types; (2) vector, matrix, structure, array, and sampler; (3) operators, control flow, and functions; (4) attributes, uniforms, and varyings; (5) precision qualifier; and (6) preprocessor and directives. By the end of this chapter you will have a good understanding of GLSL ES and how it can be used to write a variety of shaders.

Chapter 7—Toward the 3D World

This chapter takes the first step into the 3D world and explores the implications of moving from 2D to 3D. In particular, you will explore: (1) representing the user's view into the 3D world; (2) how to control the volume of 3D space that is viewed; (3) clipping; (4) foreground and background objects; and (5) drawing a 3D object—a cube. All these issues have a significant impact on how the 3D scene is drawn and presented to viewers. A mastery of them is critical to building compelling 3D scenes.

Chapter 8—Lighting Objects

This chapter focuses on lighting objects, looking at different light sources and their effects on the 3D scene. Lighting is essential if you want to create realistic 3D scenes because it helps to give the scene a sense of depth.

The following key points are discussed in this chapter: (1) shading, shadows, and different types of light sources including point, directional, and ambient; (2) reflection of light in the 3D scene and the two main types: diffuse and ambient reflection; and (3) the details of shading and how to implement the effect of light to make objects look three-dimensional.

Chapter 9—Hierarchical Objects

This chapter is the final chapter describing the core features and how to program with WebGL. Once completed, you will have mastered the basics of WebGL and will have enough knowledge to be able to create realistic and interactive 3D scenes. This chapter focuses on hierarchical objects, which are important because they allow you to progress beyond single objects like cubes or blocks to more complex objects that you can use for game characters, robots, and even modeling humans.

Chapter 10—Advanced Techniques

This chapter touches on a variety of important techniques that use what you have learned so far and provide you with an essential toolkit for building interactive, compelling 3D graphics. Each technique is introduced through a complete example, which you can reuse when building your own WebGL applications.

Appendix A—No Need to Swap Buffers in WebGL

This appendix explains why WebGL programs don't need to swap buffers.

Appendix B—Built-In Functions of GLSL ES 1.0

This appendix provides a reference for all the built-in functions available in the OpenGL ES Shading Language.

Appendix C—Projection Matrices

This appendix provides the projection matrices generated by `Matrix4.setOrtho()` and `Matrix4.setPerspective()`.

Appendix D—WebGL/OpenGL: Left or Right Handed?

This appendix explains how WebGL and OpenGL deal internally with the coordinate system and clarify that technically, both WebGL and OpenGL are agnostic as to handedness.

Appendix E—The Inverse Transpose Matrix

This appendix explains how the inverse transpose matrix of the model matrix can deal with the transformation of normal vectors.

Appendix F—Loading Shader Programs from Files

This appendix explains how to load the shader programs from files.

Appendix G—World Coordinate System Versus Local Coordinate System

This appendix explains the different coordinate systems and how they are used in 3D graphics.

Appendix H—Web Browser Settings for WebGL

This appendix explains how to use advanced web browser settings to ensure that WebGL is displayed correctly, and what to do if it isn't.

WebGL-Enabled Browsers

At the time of writing, WebGL is supported by Chrome, Firefox, Safari, and Opera. Sadly, some browsers, such as IE9 (Microsoft Internet Explorer), don't yet support WebGL. In this book, we use the Chrome browser released by Google, which, in addition to WebGL supports a number of useful features such as a console function for debugging. We have checked the sample programs in this book using the following environment (Table P.1) but would expect them to work with any browser supporting WebGL.

Table P.1 PC Environment

Browser	Chrome (25.0.1364.152 m)
OS	Windows 7 and 8
Graphics boards	NVIDIA Quadro FX 380, NVIDIA GT X 580, NVIDIA GeForce GTS 450, Mobile Intel 4 Series Express Chipset Family, AMD Radeon HD 6970

Refer to the www.khronos.org/webgl/wiki/BlacklistsAndWhitelists for an updated list of which hardware cards are known to cause problems.

To confirm that you are up and running, download Chrome (or use your preferred browser) and point it to the companion website for this book at https://sites.google.com/site/webglbook/

Navigate to Chapter 3 and click the link to the sample file `HelloTriangle.html`. If you can see a red triangle as shown in Figure P.1 in the browser, WebGL is working.

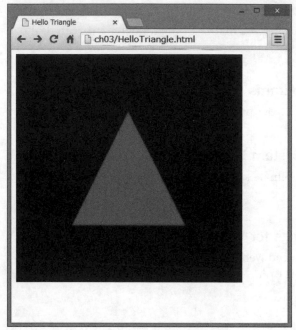

Figure P.1   Loading `HelloTriangle` results in a red triangle

If you don't see the red triangle shown in the figure, take a look at Appendix H, which explains how to change your browser settings to load WebGL.

Sample Programs and Related Links

All sample programs in this book and related links are available on the companion websites. The official site hosted by the publisher is www.informit.com/title/9780321902924 and the author site is hosted at https://sites.google.com/site/webglbook/.

The latter site contains the links to each sample program in this book. You can run each one directly by clicking the links.

If you want to modify the sample programs, you can download the zip file of all the samples, available on both sites, to your local disk. In this case, you should note that the sample program consists of both the HTML file and the associated JavaScript file in the same folder. For example, for the sample program `HelloTriangle`, you need both `HelloTriangle.html` and `HelloTriangle.js`. To run `HelloTriangle`, double-click `HelloTriangle.html`.

Style Conventions

These style conventions are used in this book:

- **Bold**—First occurrences of key terms and important words

- *Italic*—Parameter names and names of references

- `Monospace`—Code examples, methods, functions, variables, command options, JavaScript object names, filenames, and HTML tags

Acknowledgments

We have been fortunate to receive help and guidance from many talented individuals during the process of creating this book, both with the initial Japanese version and the subsequent English one.

Takafumi Kanda helped by providing numerous code samples for our support libraries and sample programs; without him, this book could not have been realized. Yasuko Kikuchi, Chie Onuma, and Yuichi Nishizawa provided valuable feedback on early versions of the book. Of particular note, one insightful comment by Ms. Kikuchi literally stopped the writing, causing a reevaluation of several sections and leading to a much stronger book. Hiroyuki Tanaka and Kazsuhira Oonishi (iLinx) gave excellent support with the sample programs, and Teruhisa Kamachi and Tetsuo Yoshitani supported the writing of sections on HTML5 and JavaScript. The WebGL working group, especially Ken Russell (Google), Chris Marin (Apple), and Dan Ginsburg (AMD), have answered many technical questions. We have been privileged to receive an endorsement from the president of the Khronos Group, Neil Trevett, and appreciate the help of Hitoshi Kasai (Principal, MIACIS Associates) who provided the connection to Mr. Trevett and the WebGL working group. In addition, thank you to Xavier Michel and Makoto Sato (Sophia University), who greatly helped with the translation of the original text and issues that arose during the translation. For the English version, Jeff Gilbert, Rick Rafey, and Daniel Haehn reviewed this book carefully and gave us excellent technical comments and feedback that greatly improved the book. Our thanks also to Laura Lewin and Olivia Basegio from Pearson, who have helped with organizing the publication and ensuring the whole process has been as smooth and as painless as possible.

We both owe a debt of gratitude to the authors of the "Red Book" (OpenGL Programming Guide) and the "Gold Book" (OpenGL ES 2.0 Programming Guide) both published by Pearson, without which this book would not have been possible. We hope, in some small way, that this book repays some of that debt.

About the Authors

Dr. Kouichi Matsuda has a broad background in user interface and user experience design and its application to novel multimedia products. His work has taken him from product development, through research, and back to development, having spent time at NEC, Sony Corporate Research, and Sony Computer Science Laboratories. He is currently a chief distinguished researcher focused on user experience and human computer interaction across a range of consumer electronics. He was the designer of the social 3D virtual world called "PAW" (personal agent-oriented virtual world), was involved in the development of the VRML97 (ISO/IEC 14772-1:1997) standard from the start, and has remained active in both VRML and X3D communities (precursors to WebGL). He has written 15 books on computer technologies and translated a further 25 into Japanese. His expertise covers user experiences, user interface, human computer interaction, natural language understanding, entertainment-oriented network services, and interface agent systems. Always on the lookout for new and exciting possibilities in the technology space, he combines his professional life with a love of hot springs, sea in summer, wines, and MANGA (at which he dabbles in drawing and illustrations). He received his Ph.D. (Engineering) from the Graduate School of Engineering, University of Tokyo, and can be reached via WebGL.prog.guide@gmail.com.

Dr. Rodger Lea is an adjunct professor with the Media and Graphics Interdisciplinary Centre at the University of British Columbia, with an interest in systems aspects of multimedia and distributed computing. With more than 20 years of experience leading research groups in both academic and industrial settings, he has worked on early versions of shared 3D worlds, helped define VRML97, developed multimedia operating systems, prototyped interactive digital TV, and led developments on multimedia home networking standards. He has published more than 60 research papers and three books, and he holds 12 patents. His current research explores the growing "Internet of Things," but he retains a passion for all things media and graphics.

Chapter 1

Overview of WebGL

WebGL is a technology that enables drawing, displaying, and interacting with sophisticated interactive three-dimensional computer graphics ("3D graphics") from within web browsers. Traditionally, 3D graphics has been restricted to high-end computers or dedicated game consoles and has required complex programming. However, as both personal computers and, more importantly, web browsers, have become more sophisticated, it has become possible to create and display 3D graphics using accessible and well-known web technologies. WebGL, when combined with HTML5 and JavaScript, makes 3D graphics accessible to web developers and will play an important role in the development of next generation, easy-to-use and intuitive user interfaces and web content. Some examples of this are shown in Figure 1.1. Over the next few years, you can expect to see WebGL used on a range of devices from standard PCs to consumer electronics, smart phones, and tablets.

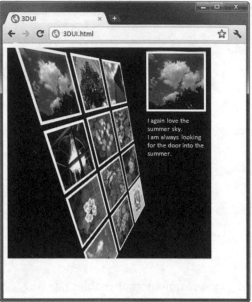

Figure 1.1 Complex 3D graphics within a browser. © 2011 Hiromasa Horie (left), 2012 Kouichi Matsuda (right)

HTML5, the latest evolution of the HTML standard, expands traditional HTML with features covering 2D graphics, networking, and local storage access. With the advent of HTML5, browsers are rapidly evolving from simple presentation engines to sophisticated application platforms. With this evolution comes a need for interface and graphics capabilities beyond 2D. WebGL has been designed for that central role of creating the visual layer for new browser-based 3D applications and experiences.

Traditionally, creating compelling 3D graphics required you to create a stand-alone application using a programming language such as C or C++ along with dedicated computer graphics libraries such as OpenGL and Direct3D. However, with WebGL, you can now realize 3D graphics as part of a standard web page using familiar HTML and JavaScript— with a little extra code for the 3D graphics.

Importantly, because WebGL is supported as the browser's default built-in technology for rendering 3D graphics, you can use WebGL directly without having to install special plug-ins or libraries. Better still, because it's all browser based, you can run the same WebGL applications on various platforms, from sophisticated PCs down to consumer electronics, tablets, and smart phones.

This chapter briefly introduces you to WebGL, outlines some of the key features and advantages of WebGL, and discusses its origins. It also explains the relationship of WebGL to HTML5 and JavaScript and the structure of WebGL programs.

Advantages of WebGL

As HTML has evolved, web developers have been able to create increasingly sophisticated web-based applications. Originally, HTML offered only static content, but the introduction of scripting support like JavaScript enabled more complex interactions and dynamic content. HTML5 introduced further sophistication, including support for 2D graphics via the canvas tag. This allowed a variety of graphical elements on a web page, ranging from dancing cartoon characters to map animations that respond to user input by updating the maps in real time.

WebGL takes this one step further, enabling the display and manipulation of 3D graphics on web pages by using JavaScript. Using WebGL, it becomes possible to create rich user interfaces and 3D games and to use 3D to visualize and manipulate a variety of information from the Internet. Although the technical capabilities of WebGL are impressive, it is perhaps the ease of use and accessibility that differentiate it from other technologies and that will ensure its impact. In particular:

- You can start developing 3D graphics applications using only a text editor and browser.

- You can easily publish the 3D graphics applications using standard web technologies, making them available to your friends or other web users.

- You can leverage the full functionality of the browser.

- Learning and using WebGL is easy because a lot of material is already available for study and development.

You Can Start Developing 3D Graphics Applications Using Only a Text Editor

One handy and convenient point in developing applications using WebGL is that you don't need to set up an application developing environment for WebGL. As explained earlier, because WebGL is built into the browser, there is no need for special application development tools such as compilers and linkers to create 3D graphics applications. As a minimum, to view the sample programs explained in this book, you only need a WebGL-enabled browser. If you want to edit them or create your own, a standard text editor (for example, Notepad or TextEdit) is enough. In Figure 1.2, you can see a WebGL application running in Chrome and the HTML file opened in Notepad. The JavaScript file (RotateObject.js) that uses WebGL is loaded by the HTML file and could also be edited using a simple text editor.

Browser (Chrome)   Notepad

Figure 1.2   The only tools needed for developing 3D graphics applications using WebGL

Publishing Your 3D Graphics Applications Is Easy

Traditionally, 3D graphics applications have been developed using a programming language such as C or C++ and then compiled into an executable binary for a specific platform. This meant, for example, the version for a Macintosh wouldn't work on Windows or Linux. Additionally, users often needed to install not only the applications themselves but also libraries required by the applications to run, which meant another level of complexity when you wanted to share your work.

In contrast, because WebGL applications are composed of HTML and JavaScript files, they can be easily shared by simply putting them on a web server just like standard web pages or distributing the HTML and JavaScript files via email. For example, Figure 1.3 shows some sample WebGL applications published by Google and available at http://code. google.com/p/webglsamples/.

Figure 1.3   WebGL sample applications published by Google (with the permission of Gregg Tavares, Google)

You Can Leverage the Full Functionality of the Browser

Because WebGL applications are created as part of a web page, you can utilize the full functionality of the browser such as arranging buttons, displaying dialog boxes, drawing text, playing video or audio, and communicating with web servers. These advanced features come for free, whereas in traditional 3D graphics applications they would need to be programmed explicitly.

Learning and Using WebGL Is Easy

The specification of WebGL is based on the royalty-free open standard, OpenGL, which has been widely used in graphics, video games, and CAD applications for many years. In one sense, WebGL is "OpenGL for web browsers." Because OpenGL has been used in a variety of platforms over the past 20 years, there are many reference books, materials, and sample programs using OpenGL, which can be used to better understand WebGL.

Origins of WebGL

Two of the most widely used technologies for displaying 3D graphics on personal computers are Direct3D and OpenGL. Direct3D, which is part of Microsoft's DirectX technologies, is the 3D graphics technology primarily used on Windows platforms and is a proprietary application programming interface (API) that Microsoft controls. An alternative, OpenGL has been widely used on various platforms due to its open and royalty-free nature. OpenGL is available for Macintosh, Linux, and a variety of devices such as smart phones, tablet computers, and game consoles (PlayStation and Nintendo). It is also well supported on Windows and provides an alternative to Direct3D.

OpenGL was originally developed by Silicon Graphics Inc. and published as an open standard in 1992. OpenGL has evolved through several versions since 1992 and has had a profound effect on the development of 3D graphics, software product development, and even film production over the years. The latest version of OpenGL at the time of writing is version 4.3 for desktop PCs. Although WebGL has its roots in OpenGL, it is actually derived from a version of OpenGL designed specifically for embedded computers such as smart phones and video game consoles. This version, known as OpenGL ES (for Embedded Systems), was originally developed in 2003–2004 and was updated in 2007 (ES 2.0) and again in 2012 (ES 3.0). WebGL is based on the ES 2.0 version. In recent years, the number of devices and processors that support the specification has rapidly increased and includes smart phones (iPhone and Android), tablet computers, and game consoles. Part of the reason for this successful adoption has been that OpenGL ES added new features but also removed many unnecessary or old-fashioned features from OpenGL, resulting in a lightweight specification that still had enough visual expressive power to realize attractive 3D graphics.

Figure 1.4 shows the relationship among OpenGL, OpenGL ES 1.1/2.0/3.0, and WebGL. Because OpenGL itself has continued to evolve from 1.5, to 2.0, to 4.3, OpenGL ES have been standardized as a subset of specific versions of OpenGL (OpenGL 1.5 and OpenGL 2.0).

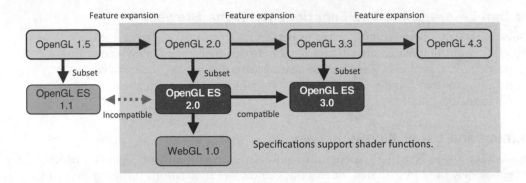

Figure 1.4 Relationship among OpenGL, OpenGL ES 1.1/2.0/3.0, and WebGL

As shown in Figure 1.4, with the move to OpenGL 2.0, a significant new capability, **programmable shader functions**, was introduced. This capability has been carried through to OpenGL ES 2.0 and is a core part of the WebGL 1.0 specification.

Shader functions or **shaders** are computer programs that make it possible to program sophisticated visual effects by using a special programming language similar to C. This book explains shader functions in a step-by-step manner, allowing you to quickly master the power of WebGL. The programming language that is used to create shaders is called a **shading language**. The shading language used in OpenGL ES 2.0 is based on the **OpenGL shading language** (GLSL) and referred to as **OpenGL ES shading language** (GLSL ES). Because WebGL is based on OpenGL ES 2.0, it also uses GLSL ES for creating shaders.

The Khronos Group (a non-profit industry consortium created to develop, publish, and promote various open standards) is responsible for the evolution and standardization of OpenGL. In 2009, Khronos established the WebGL working group and then started the standardization process of WebGL based on OpenGL ES 2.0, releasing the first version of WebGL in 2011. This book is written based primarily on that specification and, where needed, the latest specification of WebGL published as an Editor's Draft. For more information, please refer to the specification.[1]

Structure of WebGL Applications

In HTML, dynamic web pages can be created by using a combination of HTML and JavaScript. With the introduction of WebGL, the shader language GLSL ES needs to be added to the mix, meaning that web pages using WebGL are created by using three

---

[1] WebGL 1.0: www.khronos.org/registry/webgl/specs/1.0/ and Editor's draft: www.khronos.org/registry/webgl/specs/latest/

languages: HTML5 (as a Hypertext Markup Language), JavaScript, and GLSL ES. Figure 1.5 shows the software architecture of traditional dynamic web pages (left side) and web pages using WebGL (right side).

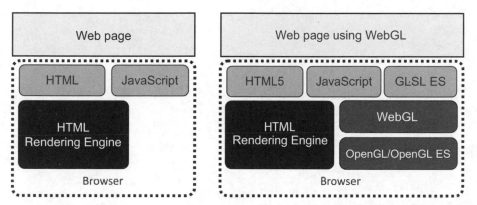

Figure 1.5 The software architecture of dynamic web pages (left) and web pages using WebGL (right)

However, because GLSL ES is generally written within JavaScript, only HTML and JavaScript files are actually necessary for WebGL applications. So, although WebGL does add complexity to the JavaScript, it retains the same structure as standard dynamic web pages, only using HTML and JavaScript files.

Summary

This chapter briefly overviewed WebGL, explained some key features, and outlined the software architecture of WebGL applications. In summary, the key takeaway from this chapter is that WebGL applications are developed using three languages: HTML5, JavaScript, and GLSL ES—however, because the shader code (GLSL ES) is generally embedded in the JavaScript, you have exactly the same file structure as a traditional web page. The next chapter explains how to create applications using WebGL, taking you step by step through a set of simple WebGL examples.

Chapter 2

Your First Step with WebGL

As explained in Chapter 1, "Overview of WebGL," WebGL applications use both HTML and JavaScript to create and draw 3D graphics on the screen. To do this, WebGL utilizes the new `<canvas>` element, introduced in HTML5, which defines a drawing area on a web page. Without WebGL, the `<canvas>` element only allows you to draw two-dimensional graphics using JavaScript. With WebGL, you can use the same element for drawing three-dimensional graphics.

This chapter explains the `<canvas>` element and the core functions of WebGL by taking you, step-by-step, through the construction of several example programs. Each example is written in JavaScript and uses WebGL to display and interact with a simple shape on a web page. Because of this, these JavaScript programs are referred to as **WebGL applications**.

The example WebGL applications will highlight some key points, including:

- How WebGL uses the `<canvas>` element and how to draw on it

- The linkage between HTML and WebGL using JavaScript

- Simple WebGL drawing functions

- The role of shader programs within WebGL

By the end of this chapter, you will understand how to write and execute basic WebGL applications and how to draw simple 2D shapes. You will use this knowledge to explore further the basics of WebGL in Chapters 3, "Drawing and Transforming Triangles," 4, "More Transformations and Basic Animation," and 5, "Using Colors and Texture Images."

What Is a Canvas?

Before HTML5, if you wanted to display an image in a web page, the only native HTML approach was to use the `<img>` tag. This tag, although a convenient tool, is restricted to still images and doesn't allow you to dynamically draw and display the image on the fly. This is one of the reasons that non-native solutions such as Flash Player have been used.

However, HTML5, by introducing the `<canvas>` tag, has changed all that, offering a convenient way to draw computer graphics dynamically using JavaScript.

In a similar manner to the way artists use paint canvases, the `<canvas>` tag defines a drawing area on a web page. Then, rather than using brush and paints, you can use JavaScript to draw anything you want in the area. You can draw points, lines, rectangles, circles, and so on by using JavaScript methods provided for `<canvas>`. Figure 2.1 shows an example of a drawing tool that uses the `<canvas>` tag.

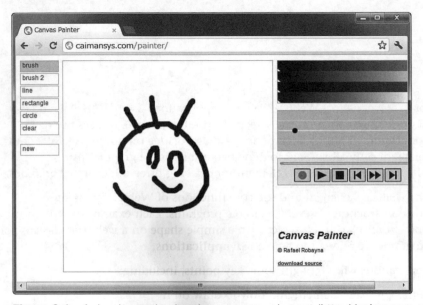

Figure 2.1   A drawing tool using the <canvas> element (http://caimansys.com/painter/)

This drawing tool runs within a web page and allows you to interactively draw lines, rectangles, and circles and even change their colors.

Although you won't be creating anything as sophisticated just yet, let's look at the core functions of `<canvas>` by using a sample program, `DrawRectangle`, which draws a filled blue rectangle on a web page. Figure 2.2 shows `DrawRectangle` when it's loaded into a browser.

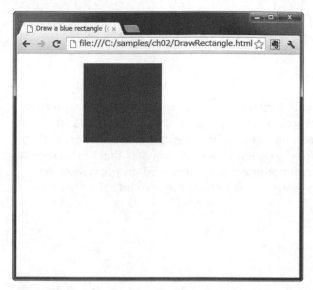

Figure 2.2 DrawRectangle

Using the <canvas> Tag

Let's look at how DrawRectangle works and explain how the <canvas> tag is used in the HTML file. Listing 2.1 shows DrawingTriangle.html. Note that all HTML files in this book are written in HTML5.

Listing 2.1 DrawRectangle.html

```
1   <!DOCTYPE html>
2   <html lang="en">
3     <head>
4       <meta charset="utf-8" />
5       <title>Draw a blue rectangle (canvas version)</title>
6     </head>
7
8     <body onload="main()">
9       <canvas id="example" width="400" height="400">
10      Please use a browser that supports "canvas"
11      </canvas>
12      <script src="DrawRectangle.js"></script>
13    </body>
14  </html>
```

The `<canvas>` tag is defined at line 9. This defines the drawing area as a 400 × 400 pixel region on a web page using the `width` and `height` attributes in the tag. The canvas is given an identifier using the `id` attribute, which will be used later:

```
<canvas id="example" width="400" height="400"></canvas>
```

By default, the canvas is invisible (actually transparent) until you draw something into it, which we'll do with JavaScript in a moment. That's all you need to do in the HTML file to prepare a `<canvas>` that the WebGL program can use. However, one thing to note is that this line only works in a `<canvas>`-enabled browser. However, browsers that don't support the `<canvas>` tag will ignore this line, and nothing will be displayed on the screen. To handle this, you can display an error message by adding the message into the tag as follows:

```
 9     <canvas id="example" width="400" height="400">
10     Please use a browser that supports "canvas"
11     </canvas>
```

To draw into the canvas, you need some associated JavaScript code that performs the drawing operations. You can include that JavaScript code in the HTML or write it as a separate JavaScript file. In our examples, we use the second approach because it makes the code easier to read. Whichever approach you take, you need to tell the browser where the JavaScript code starts. Line 8 does that by telling the browser that when it loads the separate JavaScript code it should use the function `main()` as the entry point for the JavaScript program. This is specified for the `<body>` element using its `onload` attribute that tells the browser to execute the JavaScript function `main()` after it loads the `<body>` element:

```
8     <body onload="main()">
```

Line 12 tells the browser to import the JavaScript file `DrawRectangle.js` in which the function `main()` is defined:

```
12     <script src="DrawRectangle.js"></script>
```

For clarity, all sample programs in this book use the same filename for both the HTML file and the associated JavaScript file, which is imported in the HTML file (see Figure 2.3).

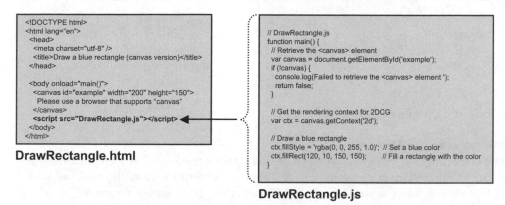

```
<!DOCTYPE html>
<html lang="en">
 <head>
  <meta charset="utf-8" />
  <title>Draw a blue rectangle (canvas version)</title>
 </head>

 <body onload="main()">
  <canvas id="example" width="200" height="150">
   Please use a browser that supports "canvas"
  </canvas>
  <script src="DrawRectangle.js"></script>
 </body>
</html>
```

DrawRectangle.html

```
// DrawRectangle.js
function main() {
  // Retrieve the <canvas> element
  var canvas = document.getElementById('example');
  if (!canvas) {
    console.log(Failed to retrieve the <canvas> element ');
    return false;
  }

  // Get the rendering context for 2DCG
  var ctx = canvas.getContext('2d');

  // Draw a blue rectangle
  ctx.fillStyle = 'rgba(0, 0, 255, 1.0)';  // Set a blue color
  ctx.fillRect(120, 10, 150, 150);         // Fill a rectangle with the color
}
```

DrawRectangle.js

Figure 2.3   DrawRectangle.html and DrawRectangle.js

DrawRectangle.js

DrawRectangle.js is a JavaScript program that draws a blue rectangle on the drawing area defined by the <canvas> element (see Listing 2.2). It has only 16 lines, which consist of the three steps required to draw two-dimensional computer graphics (2D graphics) on the canvas:

1. Retrieve the <canvas> element.

2. Request the rendering "context" for the 2D graphics from the element.

3. Draw the 2D graphics using the methods that the context supports.

These three steps are the same whether you are drawing a 2D or a 3D graphic; here, you are drawing a simple 2D rectangle using standard JavaScript. If you were drawing a 3D graphic using WebGL, then the rendering context in step (2) at line 11 would be for a 3D rendering context; however, the high-level process would be the same.

Listing 2.2   DrawRectangle.js

```
1   // DrawRectangle.js
2   function main() {
3    // Retrieve <canvas> element                              <- (1)
4     var canvas = document.getElementById('example');
5     if (!canvas) {
6       console.log('Failed to retrieve the <canvas> element');
7       return;
8     }
9
10   // Get the rendering context for 2DCG                      <- (2)
11    var ctx = canvas.getContext('2d');
```

```
12
13   // Draw a blue rectangle                                    <- (3)
14   ctx.fillStyle = 'rgba(0, 0, 255, 1.0)';  // Set a blue color
15   ctx.fillRect(120, 10, 150, 150); // Fill a rectangle with the color
16   }
```

Let us look at each step in order.

Retrieve the <canvas> Element

To draw something on a <canvas>, you must first retrieve the <canvas> element from the HTML file in the JavaScript program. You can get the element by using the method docu-ment.getElementById(), as shown at line 4. This method has a single parameter, which is the string specified in the attribute id in the <canvas> tag in our HTML file. In this case, the string is 'example' and it was defined back in DrawRectangle.html at line 9 (refer to Listing 2.1).

If the return value of this method is not null, you have successfully retrieved the element. However, if it is null, you have failed to retrieve the element. You can check for this condition using a simple if statement like that shown at line 5. In case of error, line 6 is executed. It uses the method console.log() to display the parameter as a string in the browser's console.

Note   In Chrome, you can show the console by going to Tools, JavaScript Console or pressing Ctrl+Shift+J (see Figure 2.4); in Firefox, you can show it by going to Tools, Web Developer, Web Console or pressing Ctrl+Shift+K.

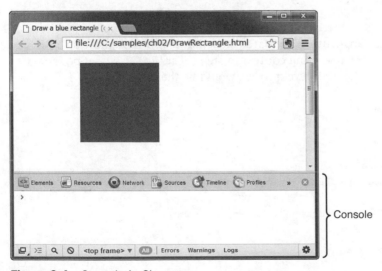

Figure 2.4   Console in Chrome

Get the Rendering Context for the 2D Graphics by Using the Element

Because the `<canvas>` is designed to be flexible and supports both 2D and 3D, it does not provide drawing methods directly and instead provides a mechanism called a **context**, which supports the actual drawing features. Line 11 gets that context:

```
11    var ctx = canvas.getContext('2d');
```

The method `canvas.getContext()` has a parameter that specifies which type of drawing features you want to use. In this example you want to draw a 2D shape, so you must specify 2d (case sensitive).

The result of this call, the context, is stored in the variable `ctx` ready for use. Note, for brevity we haven't checked error conditions, which is something you should always do in your own programs.

Draw the 2D Graphics Using the Methods Supported by the Context

Now that we have a drawing context, let's look at the code for drawing a blue rectangle, which is a two-step process. First, set the color to be used when drawing. Second, draw (or fill) a rectangle with the color.

Lines 14 and 15 handle these steps:

```
13    // Draw a blue rectangle                        <- (3)
14    ctx.fillStyle = 'rgba(0, 0, 255, 1.0)';  // Set color to blue
15    ctx.fillRect(120, 10, 150, 150); // Fill a rectangle with the color
```

The `rgba` in the string `rgba(0, 0, 255, 1.0)` on line 14 indicate r (red), g (green), b (blue), and a (alpha: transparency), with each RGB parameter taking a value from 0 (minimum value) to 255 (maximum value) and the alpha parameter from 0.0 (transparent) to 1.0 (opaque). In general, computer systems represent a color by using a combination of red, green, and blue (light's three primary colors), which is referred to as **RGB format**. When alpha (transparency) is added, the format is called **RGBA format**.

Line 15 then uses the `fillStyle` property to specify the fill color when drawing the rectangle. However, before going into the details of the arguments on line 15, let's look at the coordinate system used by the `<canvas>` element (see Figure 2.5).

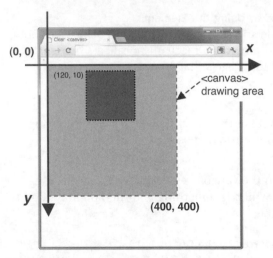

Figure 2.5 The coordinate system of <canvas>

As you can see in the figure, the coordinate system of the <canvas> element has the horizontal direction as the x-axis (right-direction is positive) and the vertical direction as the y-axis (down-direction is positive). Note that the origin is located at the upper-left corner and the down direction of the y-axis is positive. The rectangle drawn with a dashed line is the original <canvas> element in our HTML file (refer to Listing 2.1), which we specified as being 400 by 400 pixels. The dotted line is the rectangle that the sample program draws.

When we use ctx.fillRect() to draw a rectangle, the first and second parameters of this method are the position of the upper-left corner of the rectangle within the <canvas>, and the third and fourth parameters are the width and height of the rectangle (in pixels):

```
15   ctx.fillRects(120, 10, 150, 150);// Fill a rectangle with the color
```

After loading DrawRectangle.html into your browser, you will see the rectangle that was shown in Figure 2.2.

So far, we've only looked at 2D graphics. However, WebGL also utilizes the same <canvas> element to draw 3D graphics on a web page, so let's now enter into the WebGL world.

The World's Shortest WebGL Program: Clear Drawing Area

Let's start by constructing the world's shortest WebGL program, HelloCanvas, which simply clears the drawing area specified by a <canvas> tag. Figure 2.6 shows the result of loading the program, which clears (by filling with black) the rectangular area defined by a <canvas>.

Figure 2.6   HelloCanvas

The HTML File (HelloCanvas.html)

Take a look at `HelloCanvas.html`, as shown in Figure 2.7). Its structure is simple and starts by defining the drawing area using the `<canvas>` element at line 9 and then importing `HelloCanvas.js` (the WebGL program) at line 16.

Lines 13 to 15 import several other JavaScript files, which provide useful convenience functions that help WebGL programming. These will be explained in more detail later. For now, just think of them as libraries.

```
 1 <!DOCTYPE html>
 2 <html lang="en">
 3 <head>
 4   <meta charset="utf-8" />
 5   <title>Clear canvas</title>
 6 </head>
 7
 8 <body onload="main()">
 9   <canvas id="webgl" width="400" height="400">          <canvas> into which
10     Please use the browser supporting "canvas"           WebGL draws shapes
11   </canvas>
12
13   <script src="../lib/webgl-utils.js"></script>         JavaScript files
14   <script src="../lib/webgl-debug.js"></script>         containing convenient
15   <script src="../lib/cuon-utils.js"></script>          functions for WebGL
16   <script src="HelloCanvas.js"></script>               JavaScript file drawing
17 </body>                                                 shapes into the <canvas>
18 </html>
```

Figure 2.7 HelloCanvas.html

You've set up the canvas (line 9) and then imported the HelloCanvas JavaScript file (line 16), which actually uses WebGL commands to access the canvas and draw your first 3D program. Let us look at the WebGL program defined in HelloCanvas.js.

JavaScript Program (HelloCanvas.js)

HelloCanvas.js (see Listing 2.3) has only 18 lines, including comments and error handling, and follows the same steps as explained for 2D graphics: retrieve the <canvas> element, get its rendering context, and then begin drawing.

Listing 2.3 HelloCanvas.js

```
 1 // HelloCanvas.js
 2 function main() {
 3   // Retrieve <canvas> element
 4   var canvas = document.getElementById('webgl');
 5
 6   // Get the rendering context for WebGL
 7   var gl = getWebGLContext(canvas);
 8   if (!gl) {
 9     console.log('Failed to get the rendering context for WebGL');
10     return;
11   }
```

```
12
13    // Specify the color for clearing <canvas>
14    gl.clearColor(0.0, 0.0, 0.0, 1.0);
15
16    // Clear <canvas>
17    gl.clear(gl.COLOR_BUFFER_BIT);
18  }
```

As in the previous example, there is only one function, main(), which is the link between the HTML and the JavaScript and set at <body> element using its onload attribute (line 8) in HelloCanvas.html (refer to Figure 2.7).

Figure 2.8 shows the processing flow of the main() function of our WebGL program and consists of four steps, which are discussed individually next.

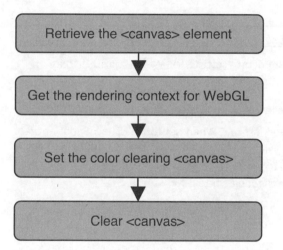

Figure 2.8   The processing flow of the main() function

Retrieve the <canvas> Element

First, main() retrieves the <canvas> element from the HTML file. As explained in DrawRectangle.js, it uses the document.getElementById() method specifying webgl as the argument. Looking back at HelloCanvas.html (refer to Figure 2.7), you can see that attribute id is set at the <canvas> tag at line 9:

```
9    <canvas id="webgl" width="400" height="400">
```

The return value of this method is stored in the canvas variable.

Get the Rendering Context for WebGL

In the next step, the program uses the variable `canvas` to get the rendering context for WebGL. Normally, we would use `canvas.getContext()` as described earlier to get the rendering context for WebGL. However, because the argument specified in `canvas.getContext()` varies between browsers,[1] we have written a special function `getWebGLContext()` to hide the differences between the browsers:

```
7        var gl = getWebGLContext(canvas);
```

This is one of the convenience functions mentioned earlier that was written specially for this book and is defined in `cuon-utils.js`, which is imported at line 15 in `HelloCanvas.html`. The functions defined in the file become available by specifying the path to the file in the attribute `src` in the `<script>` tag and loading the file. The following is the specification of `getWebGLContext()`.

`getWebGLContext(element [, debug])`

Get the rendering context for WebGL, set the debug setting for WebGL, and display any error message in the browser console in case of error.

Parameters	element	Specifies `<canvas>` element to be queried.
	debug (optional)	Default is `true`. When set to `true`, JavaScript errors are displayed in the console. Note: Turn off after debugging; otherwise, performance is affected.
Return value	non-null	The rendering context for WebGL.
	null	WebGL is not available.

The processing flow to retrieve the `<canvas>` element and use the element to get the rendering context is the same as in `DrawRectangle.js` shown earlier, where the rendering context was used to draw 2D graphics on the `<canvas>`.

In a similar way, WebGL uses the rendering context returned by `getWebGLContext()` to draw on the `<canvas>`. However, now the context is for 3D rather than 2D, so 3D (that is, WebGL) methods are available. The program stores the context in the variable `gl` at line 7. You can use any name for the variable. We have intentionally used `gl` throughout this book, because it aligns the names of the WebGL-related methods to that of OpenGL ES 2.0, which is the base specification of WebGL. For example, `gl.clearColor()` at line 14 corresponds to `glClearColor()` in OpenGL ES 2.0 or OpenGL:

```
14   gl.clearColor(0.0, 0.0, 0.0, 1.0);
```

---

[1] Although most browsers are settling on "experimental-webgl" for this argument, not all do. Additionally, over time, this will evolve to plain 'webgl,' so we have chosen to hide this.

This book explains all WebGL-related methods assuming that the rendering context is held in the variable `gl`.

Once you have the rendering context for WebGL, the next step is to use the context to set the color for clearing the drawing area specified by the `<canvas>`.

Set the Color for Clearing the <canvas>

In the previous section, `DrawRectangle.js` set the drawing color before drawing the rectangle. In a similar way, with WebGL you need to set the color before actually clearing the drawing area. Line 14 uses `gl.clearColor()` to set the color in RGBA format.

`gl.clearColor``(red, green, blue, alpha)`

Specify the clear color for a drawing area:

Parameters	red	Specifies the red value (from 0.0 to 1.0).
	green	Specifies the green value (from 0.0 to 1.0).
	blue	Specifies the blue value (from 0.0 to 1.0).
	alpha	Specifies an alpha (transparency) value (from 0.0 to 1.0).
		0.0 means transparent and 1.0 means opaque.
		If any of the values of these parameters is less than 0.0 or more than 1.0, it is truncated into 0.0 or 1.0, respectively.
Return value	None	
Errors[2]	None	

The sample program calls `gl.clearColor(0.0, 0.0, 0.0, 1.0)` at line 14, so black is specified as the clear color. The followings are examples that specify other colors:

```
(1.0, 0.0, 0.0, 1.0)     red
(0.0, 1.0, 0.0, 1.0)     green
(0.0, 0.0, 1.0, 1.0)     blue
(1.0, 1.0, 0.0, 1.0)     yellow
(1.0, 0.0, 1.0, 1.0)     purple
(0.0, 1.0, 1.0, 1.0)     light blue
(1.0, 1.0, 1.0, 1.0)     white
```

---

[2] In this book, the item "errors" is shown for all specifications of WebGL-related methods. This indicates errors that cannot be represented by the return value of the method when the method will result in as error. By default, the errors are not displayed, but they can be displayed in a JavaScript console by specifying `true` as the second argument of `getWebGLContext()`.

You might have noticed that in our 2D programming example in this chapter, `DrawRectangle`, each value for color is specified from 0 to 255. However, because WebGL is based on OpenGL, it uses the traditional OpenGL values from 0.0 to 1.0. The higher the value is, the more intense the color becomes. Similarly, for the alpha parameter (fourth parameter), the higher the value, the less transparent the color.

Once you specify the clear color, the color is retained in the **WebGL system** and not changed until another color is specified by a call to `gl.clearColor()`. This means you don't need to specify the clear color again if at some point in the future you want to clear the area again using the same color.

Clear <canvas>

Finally, you can use `gl.clear()` to clear the drawing area with the specified clear color:

```
17    gl.clear(gl.COLOR_BUFFER_BIT);
```

Note that the argument of this method is `gl.COLOR_BUFFER_BIT`, not, as you might expect, the `<canvas>` element that defines the drawing area to be cleared. This is because the WebGL method `gl.clear()` is actually relying on OpenGL, which uses a more sophisticated model than simple canvases, instead using multiple underlying buffers. One such buffer, the color buffer, is used in this example. By using `gl.COLOR_BUFFER_BIT`, you are telling WebGL to use the color buffer when clearing the canvas. WebGL uses a number of buffers in addition to the color buffer, including a depth buffer and a stencil buffer. The color buffer will be covered in detail later in this chapter, and you'll see the depth buffer in action in Chapter 7, "Toward the 3D World." The stencil buffer will not be covered in this book because it is seldom used.

Clearing the color buffer will actually cause WebGL to clear the `<canvas>` area on the web page.

`gl.clear(buffer)`

Clear the specified buffer to preset values. In the case of a color buffer, the value (color) specified by `gl.clearColor()` is used.

Parameters	buffer	Specifies the buffer to be cleared. Bitwise OR (|) operators are used to specify multiple buffers.
		`gl.COLOR_BUFFER_BIT` — Specifies the color buffer.
		`gl.DEPTH_BUFFER_BIT` — Specifies the depth buffer.
		`gl.STENCIL_BUFFER_BIT` — Specifies the stencil buffer.
Return value	None	
Errors	INVALID_VALUE	*buffer* is none of the preceding three values.

If no color has been specified (that is, you haven't made a call to gl.clearColor()), then the following default value is used (see Table 2.1).

Table 2.1 Default Values to Clear Each Buffer and Associated Methods

Buffer Name	Default Value	Setting Method
Color buffer	(0.0, 0.0, 0.0, 0.0)	gl.clearColor(red, green, blue, alpha)
Depth buffer	1.0	gl.clearDepth(depth)
Stencil buffer	0	gl.clearStencil(s)

Now that you've read through and understand this simple WebGL example, you should load HelloCanvas into your browser to check that the drawing area is cleared to black. Remember, you can run all the examples in the book directly from the companion website. However, if you want to experiment with any, you need to download the examples from the book's website to a location on your local disk. If you've done that, to load the example, navigate to that location on your disk and load HelloCanvas.html into your browser.

Experimenting with the Sample Program

Let's experiment a little with the sample program to become familiar with the way you specify colors in WebGL by trying some other colors for the clear operation. Using your favorite editor, rewrite Line 14 of HelloCanvas.js as follows and save your modification back to the original file:

```
14    gl.clearColor(0.0, 0.0, 1.0, 1.0);
```

After reloading HelloCanvas.html into your browser, HelloCanvas.js is also reloaded, and then main() is executed to clear the drawing area to blue. Try to use other colors and check the result. For example, gl.clearColor(0.5, 0.5, 0.5, 1.0) clears the area to gray.

Draw a Point (Version 1)

In the previous section, you saw how to initialize WebGL and use some simple WebGL-related methods. In this section, you are going to go one step further and construct a sample program to draw the simplest shape of all: a point. The program will draw a red point using 10 pixels at (0.0, 0.0, 0.0). Because WebGL deals with three-dimensional graphics, three coordinates are necessary to specify the position of the point. You'll be introduced to coordinates later, but for now simply accept that a point drawn at (0.0, 0.0, 0.0) is displayed at the center of the <canvas> area.

The sample program name is `HelloPoint1` and, as shown in Figure 2.9, it draws a red point (rectangle) at the center of the `<canvas>`, which has been cleared to black.[3] You will actually be using a filled rectangle as a point instead of a filled circle because a rectangle can be drawn faster than a circle. (We will deal with how to draw a rounded point in Chapter 9, "Hierarchical Objects.")

Figure 2.9 HelloPoint1

Just like clearing the color in the previous section, the color of a point must be specified in RGBA. For red, the value of R is 1.0, G is 0.0, B is 0.0, and A is 1.0. You will remember that `DrawRectangle.js` earlier in the chapter specifies the drawing color and then draws a rectangle as follows:

```
ctx.fillStyle='rgba(0, 0, 255, 1.0)';
ctx.fillRect(120, 10, 150, 150);
```

So you are probably thinking that WebGL would do something similar, perhaps something like this:

```
gl.drawColor(1.0, 0.0, 0.0, 1.0);
gl.drawPoint(0, 0, 0, 10); // The position of center and the size of point
```

---

[3] The sample programs in Chapter 2 are written in the simplest way possible so the reader can focus on understanding the functionality of shaders. In particular, they don't use "buffer objects" (see Chapter 3), which are generally used in WebGL. Although this helps by simplifying the explanation, some browsers (especially Firefox) expect buffer objects and may fail to display correctly any examples without them. In later chapters, and in actual application development, this will not cause problems because you will be using "buffer objects." However, if you are having problems, try another browser. You can switch back in the next chapter.

Unfortunately, this is not possible. WebGL relies on a new type of drawing mechanism called a **shader**, which offers a flexible and powerful mechanism for drawing 2D and 3D objects and must be used by all WebGL applications. Shaders, although powerful, are more complex, and you can't just specify a simple draw command.

Because the shader is a critical core mechanism in WebGL programming that you will use throughout this book, let's examine it one step at a time so that you can understand it easily.

HelloPoint1.html

Listing 2.4 shows `HelloPoint1.html`, which is functionally equivalent to `HelloCanvas.html` (refer to Figure 2.7). The title of the web page and the JavaScript filename were changed (lines 5 and 16), but everything else remains the same. From now on, unless the HTML file is different from this example, we'll skip showing the HTML files for the examples.

Listing 2.4 HelloPoint1.html

```
1   <!DOCTYPE html>
2   <html lang="en">
3     <head>
4       <meta charset="utf-8" />
5       <title>Draw a point (1)</title>
6     </head>
7
8     <body onload="main()">
9       <canvas id="webgl" width="400" height="400">
10      Please use the browser supporting "canvas".
11      </canvas>
12
13      <script src="../libs/webgl-utils.js"></script>
14      <script src="../libs/webgl-debug.js"></script>
15      <script src="../libs/cuon-utils.js"></script>
16      <script src="HelloPoint1.js"></script>
17    </body>
18  </html>
```

HelloPoint1.js

Listing 2.5 shows `HelloPoint1.js`. As you can see from the comments in the listing, two "shader programs" are prepended to the JavaScript (lines 2 to 13). Glance through the shader programs, and then go to the next section, where you'll see more detailed explanations.

Listing 2.5 HelloPoint1.js

```
1  // HelloPoint1.js
2  // Vertex shader program
3  var VSHADER_SOURCE =
4    'void main() {\n' +
5    '  gl_Position = vec4(0.0, 0.0, 0.0, 1.0);\n' + // Coordinates
6    '  gl_PointSize = 10.0;\n' +            // Set the point size
7    '}\n';
8
9  // Fragment shader program
10 var FSHADER_SOURCE =
11   'void main() {\n' +
12   '  gl_FragColor = vec4(1.0, 0.0, 0.0, 1.0);\n' + // Set the color
13   '}\n';
14
15 function main() {
16   // Retrieve <canvas> element
17   var canvas = document.getElementById('webgl');
18
19   // Get the rendering context for WebGL
20   var gl = getWebGLContext(canvas);
21   if (!gl) {
22     console.log('Failed to get the rendering context for WebGL');
23     return;
24   }
25
26   // Initialize shaders
27   if (!initShaders(gl, VSHADER_SOURCE, FSHADER_SOURCE)) {
28     console.log('Failed to initialize shaders.');
29     return;
30   }
31
32   // Set the color for clearing <canvas>
33   gl.clearColor(0.0, 0.0, 0.0, 1.0);
34
35   // Clear <canvas>
36   gl.clear(gl.COLOR_BUFFER_BIT);
37
38   // Draw a point
39   gl.drawArrays(gl.POINTS, 0, 1);
40 }
```

What Is a Shader?

`HelloPoint1.js` is our first WebGL program that uses shaders. As mentioned earlier, shader programs are necessary when you want to draw something on the screen in WebGL. Essentially, shader programs are "embedded" in the JavaScript file and, in this case, set up at the start. This seems at first sight to be complicated, but let's take it one step at a time.

WebGL needs the following two types of shaders, which you saw at line 2 and line 9:

- **Vertex shader:** Vertex shaders are programs that describe the traits (position, colors, and so on) of a vertex. The **vertex** is a point in 2D/3D space, such as the corner or intersection of a 2D/3D shape.

- **Fragment shader:** A program that deals with per-fragment processing such as lighting (see Chapter 8, "Lighting Objects"). The **fragment** is a WebGL term that you can consider as a kind of pixel (picture element).

You'll explore shaders in more detail later, but simply put, in a 3D scene, it's not enough just to draw graphics. You have to also account for how they are viewed as light sources hit them or the viewer's perspective changes. Shading does this with a high degree of flexibility and is part of the reason that today's 3D graphics are so realistic, allowing them to use new rendering effects to achieve stunning results.

The shaders are read from the JavaScript and stored in the WebGL system ready to be used for drawing. Figure 2.10 shows the basic processing flow from a JavaScript program into the WebGL system, which applies the shader programs to draw shapes that the browser finally displays.

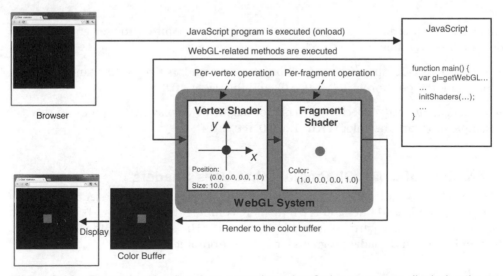

Figure 2.10 The processing flow from executing a JavaScript program to displaying the result in a browser

You can see two browser windows on the left side of the figure. These are the same; the upper one shows the browser before executing the JavaScript program, and the lower one shows the browser after execution. Once the WebGL-related methods are called from the JavaScript program, the vertex shader in the WebGL system is executed, and the fragment shader is executed to draw the result into the color buffer. This is the clear part—that is, step 4 in Figure 2.8, described in the original HelloCanvas example. Then the content in the color buffer is automatically displayed on the drawing area specified by the <canvas> in the browser.

You'll be seeing this figure frequently in the rest of this book. So we'll use a simplified version to save space (see Figure 2.11). Note that the flow is left to right and the right-most component is a color buffer, not a browser, because the color buffer is automatically displayed in the browser.

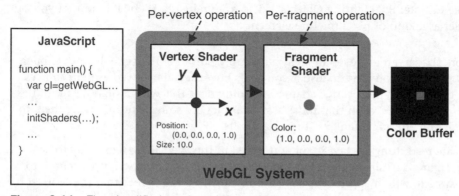

Figure 2.11 The simplified version of Figure 2.9

Getting back to our example, the goal is to draw a 10-pixel point on the screen. The two shaders are used as follows:

- The vertex shader specifies the position of a point and its size. In this sample program, the position is (0.0, 0.0, 0.0), and the size is 10.0.

- The fragment shader specifies the color of fragments displaying the point. In this sample program, the color is red (1.0, 0.0, 0.0, 1.0).

The Structure of a WebGL Program that Uses Shaders

Based on what you've learned so far, let's look at HelloPoint1.js again (refer to Listing 2.5). This program has 40 lines and is a little more complex than HelloCanvas.js (18 lines). It consists of three parts, as shown in Figure 2.12. The main() function in JavaScript starts from line 15, and shader programs are located from lines 2 to 13.

```
 1 // HelloPint1.js
 2 // Vertex shader program
 3 var VSHADER_SOURCE =
 4  'void main() {\n' +
 5  '  gl_Position = vec4(0.0, 0.0, 0.0, 1.0);\n' +
 6  '  gl_PointSize = 10.0;\n' +
 7  '}\n';
 8
 9 // Fragment shader program
10 var FSHADER_SOURCE =
11  'void main() {\n' +
12  '  gl_FragColor = vec4(1.0, 0.0, 0.0, 1.0);\n' +
13  '}\n';
14
15 function main() {
16   // Retrieve <canvas> element
17   var canvas = document.getElementById('webgl');
18
19   // Get the rendering context for WebGL
20   var gl = getWebGLContext(canvas);
            ...
26   // Initialize shaders
27   if (!initShaders(gl, VSHADER_SOURCE, ...
            ...
32   // Set the color for clearing <canvas>
33   gl.clearColor(0.0, 0.0, 0.0, 1.0);
            ...
35   // Clear <canvas>
36   gl.clear(gl.COLOR_BUFFER_BIT);
37
38   // Draw a point
39   gl.drawArrays(gl.POINTS, 0, 1);
40 }
```

Vertex shader program
(Language: GLSL ES)

Fragment shader program
(Language: GLSL ES)

Main program
(Language: JavaScript)

Figure 2.12 The basic structure of a WebGL program with embedded shader programs

The vertex shader program is located in lines 4 to 7, and the fragment shader is located in lines 11 to 13. These programs are actually the following shader language programs but written as a JavaScript string to make it possible to pass the shaders to the WebGL system:

```
// Vertex shader program
void main() {
  gl_Position = vec4(0.0, 0.0, 0.0, 1.0);
  gl_PointSize = 10.0;
}
// Fragment shader program
void main() {
  gl_FragColor = vec4(1.0, 0.0, 0.0, 1.0);
}
```

As you learned in Chapter 1, shader programs must be written in the **OpenGL ES shading language (GLSL ES)**, which is similar to the C language. Finally, GLSL ES comes onto the stage! You will get to see the details of GLSL ES in Chapter 6, "The OpenGL ES Shading Language (GLSL ES)," but in these early examples, the code is simple and should be understandable by anybody with a basic understanding of C or JavaScript.

Because these programs must be treated as a single string, each line of the shader is concatenated using the + operator into a single string. Each line has \n at the end because the line number is displayed when an error occurs in the shader. The line number is helpful to check the source of the problem in the codes. However, the \n is not mandatory, and you could write the shader without it.

At lines 3 and 10, each shader program is stored in the variables VSHADER_SOURCE and FSHADER_SOURCE as a string:

```
 2 // Vertex shader program
 3 var VSHADER_SOURCE =
 4   'void main() {\n' +
 5   '  gl_Position = vec4(0.0, 0.0, 0.0, 1.0);\n' +
 6   '  gl_PointSize = 10.0;\n' +
 7   '}\n';
 8
 9 // Fragment shader program
10 var FSHADER_SOURCE =
11   'void main() {\n' +
12   '  gl_FragColor = vec4(1.0, 0.0, 0.0, 1.0);\n' +
13   '}\n';
```

If you are interested in loading the shader programs from files, refer to Appendix F, "Loading Shader Programs from Files."

Initializing Shaders

Before looking at the details of each shader, let's examine the processing flow of main() that is defined from line 15 in the JavaScript (see Figure 2.13). This flow, shown in Figure 2.13, is the basic processing flow of most WebGL applications. You will see the same flow throughout this book.

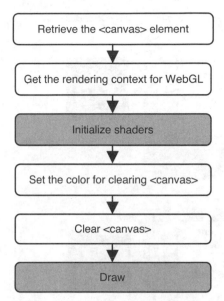

Figure 2.13   The processing flow of a WebGL program

This flow is similar to that shown in Figure 2.8 except that a third step ("Initialize Shaders") and a sixth step ("Draw") are added.

The third step "Initialize Shaders" initializes and sets up the shaders that are defined at line 3 and line 10 within the WebGL system. This step is done using the convenience function `initShaders()` that is defined in `cuon-util.js`. Again, this is one of those special functions we have provided for this book.

`initShaders(gl, vshader, fshader)`

Initialize shaders and set them up in the WebGL system ready for use:

Parameters	gl	Specifies a rendering context.
	vshader	Specifies a vertex shader program (string).
	fshader	Specifies a fragment shader program (string).
Return value	true	Shaders successfully initialized.
	false	Failed to initialize shaders.

Figure 2.14 shows how the convenience function `initShaders()` processes the shaders. You will examine in detail what this function is doing in Chapter 8. For now, you just need to understand that it sets up the shaders in the WebGL system and makes them ready for use.

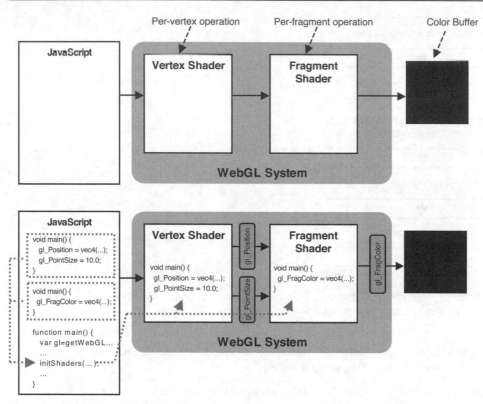

Figure 2.14 Behavior of initShaders()

As you can see in the upper figure in Figure 2.14, the WebGL system has two containers: one for a vertex shader and one for a fragment shader. This is actually a simplification, but helpful at this stage. We return to the details in Chapter 10. By default, the contents of these containers are empty. To make the shader programs, written as JavaScript strings and ready for use in the WebGL system, we need something to pass these strings to the system and then set them up in the appropriate containers; initShaders() performs this operation. Note that the shader programs are executed within the WebGL system, not the JavaScript program.

The lower portion in Figure 2.14 shows that after executing initShaders(), the shader programs that are passed as a string to the parameters of initShaders() are set up in the containers in the WebGL system and then made ready for use. The lower figure schematically illustrates that a vertex shader is passing gl_Position and gl_PointSize to a fragment shader and that just after assigning values to these variables in the vertex shader, the fragment shader is executed. In actuality, the fragments that are generated after processing these values are passed to the fragment shader. Chapter 5 explains this mechanism in detail, but for now you can consider the attributes to be passed.

The important point here is that *WebGL applications consist of a JavaScript program executed by the browser and shader programs that are executed within the WebGL system.*

Now, having completed the explanation of the second step "Initialize Shaders" in Figure 2.13, you are ready to see how the shaders are actually used to draw a simple point. As mentioned, we need three items of information for the point: its position, size, and color, which are used as follows:

- The vertex shader specifies the position of a point and its size. In this sample program, the position is (0.0, 0.0, 0.0), and the size is 10.0.

- The fragment shader specifies the color of the fragments displaying the point. In this sample program, they are red (1.0, 0.0, 0.0, 1.0).

Vertex Shader

Now, let us start by examining the vertex shader program listed in `HelloPoint1.js` (refer to Listing 2.5), which sets the position and size of the point:

```
2   // Vertex shader program
3   var VSHADER_SOURCE =
4     'void main() {\n' +
5     '  gl_Position = vec4(0.0, 0.0, 0.0, 1.0);\n' +
6     '  gl_PointSize = 10.0;\n' +
7     '}\n';
```

The vertex shader program itself starts from line 4 and must contain a single `main()` function in a similar fashion to languages such as C. The keyword `void` in front of `main()` indicates that this function does not return a value. You cannot specify other arguments to `main()`.

Just like JavaScript, we can use the `=` operator to assign a value to a variable in a shader. Line 5 assigns the position of the point to the variable `gl_Position`, and line 6 assigns its size to the variable `gl_PointSize`. These two variables are built-in variables available only in a vertex shader and have a special meaning: `gl_Position` specifies a position of a vertex (in this case, the position of the point), and `gl_PointSize` specifies the size of the point (see Table 2.2).

Table 2.2 Built-In Variables Available in a Vertex Shader

Type and Variable Name	Description
vec4 `gl_Position`	Specifies the position of a vertex
float `gl_PointSize`	Specifies the size of a point (in pixels)

Note that `gl_Position` should always be written. If you don't specify it, the shader's behavior is implementation dependent and may not work as expected. In contrast, `gl_PointSize` is only required when drawing points and defaults to a point size of 1.0 if you don't specify anything.

For those of you mostly familiar with JavaScript, you may be a little surprised when you see "type" specified in Table 2.2. Unlike JavaScript, GLSL ES is a "typed" programming language; that is, it requires the programmer to specify what type of data a variable holds. C and Java are examples of typed languages. By specifying "type" for a variable, the system can easily understand what type of data the variable holds, and then it can optimize its processing based on that information. Table 2.3 summarizes the "type" in GLSL ES used in the shaders in this section.

Table 2.3 Data Types in GLSL ES

Type	Description
float	Indicates a floating point number
vec4	Indicates a vector of four floating point numbers

float	float	Float	float

Note that an error will occur when the type of data that is assigned to the variable is different from the type of the variable. For example, the type of `gl_PointSize` is float, and you must assign a floating point number to it. So, if you change line 6 from

```
gl_PointSize = 10.0;
```

to

```
gl_PointSize = 10;
```

it will generate an error simply because `10` is interpreted as an integer number, whereas `10.0` is a floating point number in GLSL ES.

The type of the variable `gl_Position`, the built-in variable for specifying the position of a point, is `vec4`; `vec4` is a vector made up of three floats. However, you only have three floats (0.0, 0.0, 0.0) representing X, Y, and Z. So you need to convert these to a `vec4` somehow. Fortunately, there is a built-in function, `vec4()`, that will do this for you and return a value of type `vec4` –, which is just what you need!

`vec4 vec4(v0, v1, v2, v3)`

Construct a `vec4` object from *v0*, *v1*, *v2*, and *v3*.

Parameters	v0, v1, v2, v3	Specifies floating point numbers.
Return value	A `vec4` object made from *v0*, *v1*, *v2*, and *v3*.	

In this sample program, `vec4()` is used at line 5 as follows:

```
gl_Position = vec4(0.0, 0.0, 0.0, 1.0);
```

Note that the value that is assigned to `gl_Position` has 1.0 added as a fourth component. This four-component coordinate is called a **homogeneous coordinate** (see the boxed article below) and is often used in 3D graphics for processing three-dimensional information efficiently. Although the homogeneous coordinate is a four-dimensional coordinate, if the last component of the homogeneous coordinate is 1.0, the coordinate indicates the same position as a three-dimensional one. So, you can supply 1.0 as the last component if you need to specify four components as a vertex coordinate.

Homogeneous Coordinates

The homogeneous coordinates use the following coordinate notation: (x, y, z, w). The homogeneous coordinate (x, y, z, w) is equivalent to the three-dimensional coordinate (x/w, y/w, z/w). So, if you set w to 1.0, you can utilize the homogeneous coordinate as a three-dimensional coordinate. The value of w must be greater than or equal to 0. If w approaches zero, the coordinates approach infinity. So we can represent the concept of infinity in the homogeneous coordinate system. Homogeneous coordinates make it possible to represent vertex transformations described in the next chapter as a multiplication of a matrix and the coordinates. These coordinates are often used as an internal representation of a vertex in 3D graphics systems.

Fragment Shader

After specifying the position and size of a point, you need to specify its color using a fragment shader. As explained earlier, a **fragment** is a pixel displayed on the screen, although technically the fragment is a pixel along with its position, color, and other information.

The fragment shader is a program that processes this information in preparation for displaying the fragment on the screen. Looking again at the fragment shader listed in `HelloPoint1.js` (refer to Listing 2.5), you can see that just like a vertex shader, a fragment shader is executed from `main()`:

```
9  // Fragment shader program
10 var FSHADER_SOURCE =
11   'void main() {\n' +
12   '  gl_FragColor = vec4(1.0, 0.0, 0.0, 1.0);\n' +
13   '}\n';
```

The job of the shader is to set the color of the point as its per-fragment operation, which is carried out at line 12. `gl_FragColor` is a built-in variable only available in a fragment shader; it controls the color of a fragment, as shown in Table 2.4.

Table 2.4 The Built-In Value Available in a Fragment Shader

Type and Variable Name	Description
vec4 gl_FragColor	Specify the color of a fragment (in RGBA)

When we assign a color value to the built-in variable, the fragment is displayed using that color. Just like the position in the vertex shader, the color value is a `vec4` data type consisting of four floating point numbers representing the RGBA values. In this sample program, a red point will be displayed because you assign (1.0, 0.0, 0.0, 1.0) to the variable.

The Draw Operation

Once you set up the shaders, the remaining task is to draw the shape, or in our case, a point. As before, you need to clear the drawing area in a similar way to that described in `HelloCanvas.js`. Once the drawing area is cleared, you can draw the point using `gl.drawArrays()`, as in line 39:

```
39 gl.drawArrays(gl.POINTS, 0, 1);
```

`gl.drawArrays()` is a powerful function that is capable of drawing a variety of basic shapes, as detailed in the following box.

`gl.drawArrays(mode, first, count)`

Execute a vertex shader to draw shapes specified by the *mode* parameter.

Parameters	mode	Specifies the type of shape to be drawn. The following symbolic constants are accepted: `gl.POINTS`, `gl.LINES`, `gl.LINE_STRIP`, `gl.LINE_LOOP`, `gl.TRIANGLES`, `gl.TRIANGLE_STRIP`, and `gl.TRIANGLE_FAN`.
	first	Specifies which vertex to start drawing from (integer).
	count	Specifies the number of vertices to be used (integer).
Return value	None	
Errors	INVALID_ENUM *mode* is none of the preceding values.	
	INVALID_VALUE *first* is negative or *count* is negative.	

In this sample program, because you are drawing a point, you specify `gl.POINTS` as the *mode* in the first parameter. The second parameter is set to 0 because you are starting from the first vertex. The third parameter, *count*, is 1 because you are only drawing 1 point in this sample program.

Now, when the program makes a call to `gl.drawArrays()`, the vertex shader is executed *count* times, each time working with the next vertex. In this sample program, the shader is executed once (*count* is set to 1) because we only have one vertex: our point. When the shader is executed, the function `main()` in the shader is called, and then each line in the function is executed sequentially, resulting in (0.0, 0.0, 0.0, 1.0) being assigned to `gl_Position` (line 5) and then 10.0 assigned to `gl_PointSize` (line 6).

Once the vertex shader executes, the fragment shader is executed by calling its `main()` function which, in this example, assigns the color value (red) to `gl_FragColor` (line 12). As a result, a red point of 10 pixels is drawn at (0.0, 0.0, 0.0, 1.0), or the center of the drawing area (see Figure 2.15).

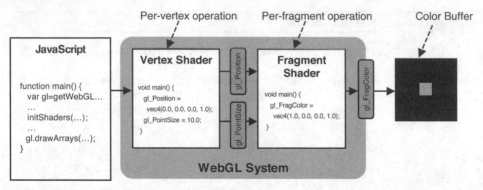

Figure 2.15   The behavior of shaders

At this stage, you should have a rough understanding of the role of a vertex shader and a fragment shader and how they work. In the rest of this chapter, you'll build on this basic understanding through a series of examples, allowing you to become more accustomed to WebGL and shaders. However, before that, let's quickly look at how WebGL describes the position of shapes using its coordinate system.

The WebGL Coordinate System

Because WebGL deals with 3D graphics, it uses a three-dimensional coordinate system along the x-, y-, and z-axis. This coordinate system is easy to understand because our world has the same three dimensions: width, height, and depth. In any coordinate system, the direction of each axis is important. Generally, in WebGL, when you face the computer screen, the horizontal direction is the x-axis (right direction is positive), the vertical direction is the y-axis (up direction is positive), and the direction from the screen to the viewer is the z-axis (the left side of Figure 2.16). The viewer's eye is located at the origin (0.0, 0.0, 0.0), and the line of sight travels along the negative direction of the z-axis, or from you into the screen (see the right side of Figure 2.16). This coordinate system is also called the **right-handed coordinate system** because it can be expressed using the right hand (see Figure 2.17) and is the one normally associated with WebGL. Throughout this book, we'll use the right-handed coordinate system as the default for WebGL. However, you should note that it's actually more complex than this. In fact, WebGL is neither left handed nor right handed. This is explained in detail in Appendix D, "WebGL/OpenGL: Left or Right Handed?," but it's safe to treat WebGL as right handed for now.

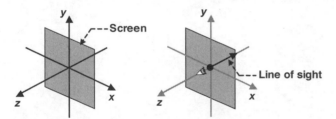

Figure 2.16   WebGL coordinate system

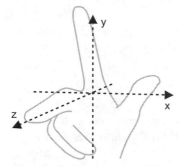

Figure 2.17 The right-handed coordinate system

As you have already seen, the drawing area specified for a <canvas> element in JavaScript is different from WebGL's coordinate system, so a mapping is needed between the two. By default, as you see in Figure 2.18, WebGL maps the coordinate system to the area as follows:

- The center position of a <canvas>: (0.0, 0.0, 0.0)

- The two edges of the x-axis of the <canvas>: (–1.0, 0.0, 0.0) and (1.0, 0.0, 0.0)

- The two edges of the y-axis of the <canvas>: (0.0, –1.0, 0.0) and (0.0, 1.0, 0.0)

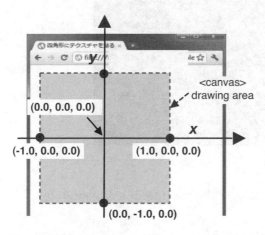

Figure 2.18 The <canvas> drawing area and WebGL coordinate system

As previously discussed, this is the default. It's possible to use another coordinate system, which we'll discuss later, but for now this default coordinate system will be used. Additionally, to help you stay focused on the core functionality of WebGL, the example programs will mainly use the x and y coordinates and not use the z or depth coordinate. Therefore, until Chapter 7, the z-axis value will generally be specified as 0.0.

Experimenting with the Sample Program

First, you can modify line 5 to change the position of the point and gain a better understanding of the WebGL coordinate system. For example, let's change the x coordinate from 0.0 to 0.5 as follows:

```
5     '  gl_Position = vec4(0.5, 0.0, 0.0, 1.0);\n' +
```

Save the modified `HelloPoint1.js` and click the Reload button on your browser to reload it. You will see that the point has moved and is now displayed on the right side of the `<canvas>` area (see Figure 2.19, left side).

Now change the y coordinate to move the point toward the top of the `<canvas>` as follows:

```
5     '  gl_Position = vec4(0.0, 0.5, 0.0, 1.0);\n' +
```

Again, save the modified `HelloPoint1.js` and reload it. This time, you can see the point has moved and is displayed in the upper part of the canvas (see Figure 2.19, right side).

Figure 2.19   Modifying the position of the point

As another experiment, let's try changing the color of the point from red to green by modifying line 12, as follows:

```
12    '  gl_FragColor = vec4(0.0, 1.0, 0.0, 1.0);\n' +
```

Let's conclude this section with a quick recap. You've been introduced to the two basic shaders we use in WebGL—the vertex shader and the fragment shader—and seen how, although they use their own language, they can be executed from within JavaScript. You've also seen that the basic processing flow of a WebGL application using shaders is the same as in other types of WebGL applications. A key lesson from this section is that a WebGL program consists of a JavaScript program executing in conjunction with shader programs.

For those of you with experience in using OpenGL, you may feel that something is missing; there is no code to swap color buffers. One of the significant features of WebGL is that it does not need to do that. For more information, see Appendix A, "No Need to Swap Buffers in WebGL."

Draw a Point (Version 2)

In the previous section, you explored drawing a point and the related core functions of shaders. Now that you understand the fundamental behavior of a WebGL program, let's examine how to pass data between JavaScript and the shaders. HelloPoint1 always draws a point at the same position because its position is directly written ("hard-coded") in the vertex shader. This makes the example easy to understand, but it lacks flexibility. In this section, you'll see how a WebGL program can pass a vertex position from JavaScript to the vertex shader and then draw a point at that position. The name of the program is HelloPoint2, and although the result of the program is the same as HelloPoint1, it's a flexible technique you will use in future examples.

Using Attribute Variables

Our goal is to pass a position from the JavaScript program to the vertex shader. There are two ways to pass data to a vertex shader: attribute variable and uniform variable (see Figure 2.20). The one you use depends on the nature of the data. The **attribute variable** passes data that differs for each vertex, whereas the **uniform variable** passes data that is the same (or uniform) in each vertex. In this program, you will use the attribute variable because each vertex generally has different coordinates.

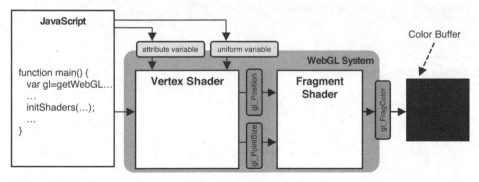

Figure 2.20 Two ways to pass data to a vertex shader

The attribute variable is a GLSL ES variable which is used to pass data from the world outside a vertex shader into the shader and is only available to vertex shaders.

To use the attribute variable, the sample program involves the following three steps:

1. Prepare the attribute variable for the vertex position in the vertex shader.

2. Assign the attribute variable to the gl_Position variable.

3. Pass the data to the attribute variable.

Let's look at the sample program in more detail to see how to carry out these steps.

Sample Program (HelloPoint2.js)

In HelloPoint2 (see Listing 2.6), you draw a point at a position the JavaScript program specifies.

Listing 2.6   HelloPoint2.js

```
 1 // HelloPoint2.js
 2 // Vertex shader program
 3 var VSHADER_SOURCE =
 4   'attribute vec4 a_Position;\n' +
 5   'void main() {\n' +
 6   '  gl_Position = a_Position;\n' +
 7   '  gl_PointSize = 10.0;\n' +
 8   '}\n';
 9
10 // Fragment shader program
   ... snipped because it is the same as HelloPoint1.js
15
16 function main() {
17   // Retrieve <canvas> element
18   var canvas = document.getElementById('webgl');
19
20   // Get the rendering context for WebGL
21   var gl = getWebGLContext(canvas);
       ...
26
27   // Initialize shaders
28   if (!initShaders(gl, VSHADER_SOURCE, FSHADER_SOURCE)) {
         ...
31   }
32
33   // Get the storage location of attribute variable
34   var a_Position = gl.getAttribLocation(gl.program, 'a_Position');
35   if (a_Position < 0) {
36     console.log('Failed to get the storage location of a_Position');
37     return;
```

```
38   }
39
40   // Pass vertex position to attribute variable
41   gl.vertexAttrib3f(a_Position, 0.0, 0.0, 0.0);
42
43   // Set the color for clearing <canvas>
44   gl.clearColor(0.0, 0.0, 0.0, 1.0);
45
46   // Clear <canvas>
47   gl.clear(gl.COLOR_BUFFER_BIT);
48
49   // Draw a point
50   gl.drawArrays(gl.POINTS, 0, 1);
51   }
```

As you can see, the attribute variable is prepared within the shader on line 4:

```
4    'attribute vec4 a_Position;\n' +
```

In this line, the keyword attribute is called a **storage qualifier**, and it indicates that the following variable (in this case, a_Position) is an attribute variable. This variable must be declared as a global variable because data is passed to it from outside the shader. The variable must be declared following a standard pattern <Storage Qualifier> <Type> <Variable Name>, as shown in Figure 2.21.

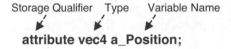

Figure 2.21   The declaration of the attribute variable

In line 4, you declare a_Position as an attribute variable with data type vec4 because, as you saw in Table 2.2, it will be assigned to gl_Position, which always requires a vec4 type.

Note that throughout this book, we have adopted a programming convention in which all attribute variables have the prefix a_, and all uniform variables have the prefix u_ to easily determine the type of variables from their names. Obviously, you can use your own convention when writing your own programs, but we find this one simple and clear.

Once a_Position is declared, it is assigned to gl_Position at line 6:

```
6    '  gl_Position = a_Position;\n' +
```

At this point, you have completed the preparation in the shader for receiving data from the outside. The next step is to pass the data to the attribute variable from the JavaScript program.

Getting the Storage Location of an Attribute Variable

As you saw previously, the vertex shader program is set up in the WebGL system using the convenience function `initShaders()`. When the vertex shader is passed to the WebGL system, the system parses the shader, recognizes it has an attribute variable, and then prepares the location of its attribute variable so that it can store data values when required. When you want to pass data to `a_Position` in the vertex shader, you need to ask the WebGL system to give you the location it has prepared, which can be done using `gl.getAttribLocation()`, as shown in line 34:

```
33    // Get the location of attribute variable
34    var a_Position = gl.getAttribLocation(gl.program, 'a_Position');
35    if (a_Position < 0) {
36      console.log('Fail to get the storage location of a_Position');
37      return;
38    }
```

The first argument of this method specifies a **program object** that holds the vertex shader and the fragment shader. You will examine the program object in Chapter 8, but for now, you can just specify `gl.program` as the argument here. Note that you should use `gl.program` only after `initShaders()` has been called because `initShaders()` assigns the program object to the variable. The second parameter specifies the attribute variable name (in this case `a_Position`) whose location you want to know.

The return value of this method is the storage location of the specified attribute variable. This location is then stored in the JavaScript variable, `a_Position`, at line 34 for later use. Again, for ease of understanding, this book uses JavaScript variable names for attribute variables, which are the same as the GLSL ES attribute variable name. You can, of course, use any variable name.

The specification of `gl.getAttribLocation()` is as follows:

`gl.getAttribLocation(program, name)`

Retrieve the storage location of the attribute variable specified by the *name* parameter.

Parameters	program	Specifies the program object that holds a vertex shader and a fragment shader.
	name	Specifies the name of the attribute variable whose location is to be retrieved.
Return value	greater than or equal to 0	The location of the specified attribute variable.
	-1	The specified attribute variable does not exist or its name starts with the reserved prefix `gl_` or `webgl_`.

Errors	INVALID_OPERATION	*program* has not been successfully linked (See Chapter 9.)
	INVALID_VALUE	The length of *name* is more than the maximum length (256 by default) of an attribute variable name.

Assigning a Value to an Attribute Variable

Once you have the attribute variable location, you need to set the value using the `a_Position` variable. This is performed at line 41 using the `gl.vertexAttrib3f()` method.

```
40    // Set vertex position to attribute variable
41    gl.vertexAttrib3f(a_Position, 0.0, 0.0, 0.0);
```

The following is the specification of `gl.vertexAtrrib3f()`.

`gl.vertexAttrib3f(location, v0, v1, v2)`

Assign the data (*v0*, *v1*, and *v2*) to the attribute variable specified by *location*.

Parameters	location	Specifies the storage location of an attribute variable to be modified.
	v0	Specifies the value to be used as the first element for the attribute variable.
	v1	Specifies the value to be used as the second element for the attribute variable.
	v2	Specifies the value to be used as the third element for the attribute variable.
Return value	None	
Errors	INVALID_OPERATION	There is no current program object.
	INVALID_VALUE	*location* is greater than or equal to the maximum number of attribute variables (8, by default).

The first argument of the method call specifies the location returned by `gl.getAttribLocation()` at line 34. The second, third, and fourth arguments specify the floating point number to be passed to `a_Position` representing the x, y, and z coordinates of the point. After calling the method, these three values are passed as a group to `a_Position`, which was prepared at line 4 in the vertex shader. Figure 2.22 shows the processing flow of getting the location of the attribute variable and then writing a value to it.

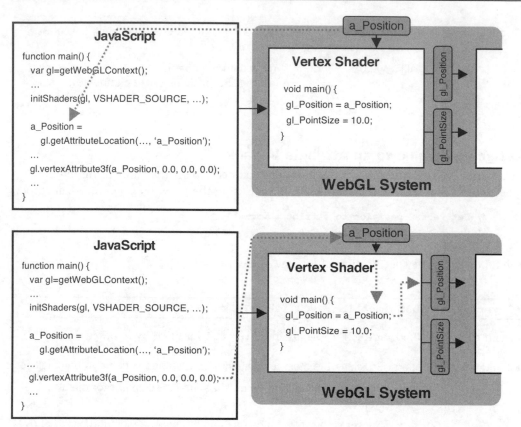

Figure 2.22 Getting the storage location of an attribute variable and then writing a value to the variable

`a_Position` is then assigned to `gl_Position` at line 6 in the vertex shader, in effect passing the x, y, and z coordinates from your JavaScript, via the attribute variable into the shader, where it's written to `gl_Position`. So the program has the same effect as `HelloPoint1`, where `gl_Position` is used as the position of a point. However, `gl_Position` has now been set dynamically from JavaScript rather than statically in the vertex shader:

```
4    'attribute vec4 a_Position;\n' +
5    'void main() {\n' +
6    '  gl_Position = a_Position;\n' +
7    '  gl_PointSize = 10.0;\n' +
8    '}\n';
```

Finally, you clear the `<canvas>` using `gl.clear()` (line 47) and draw the point using `gl.drawArrays()` (line 50) in the same way as in `HelloPoint1.js`.

As a final note, you can see `a_Position` is prepared as `vec4` at line 4 in the vertex shader. However, `gl.vertexAttrib3f()` at line 41 specifies only three values (x, y, and z), not four. Although you may think that one value is missing, this method automatically supplies the value 1.0 as the fourth value (see Figure 2.23). As you saw earlier, a default fourth value of 1.0 for a color ensures it is fully opaque, and a default fourth value of 1.0 for a homogeneous coordinate maps a 3D coordinate into a homogenous coordinate, so essentially the method is supplying a "safe" fourth value.

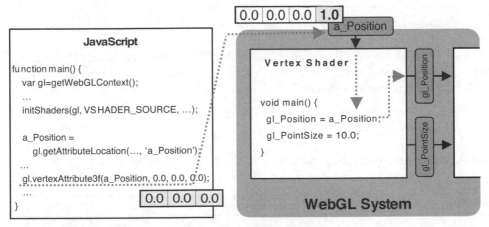

Figure 2.23 The missing data is automatically supplied

Family Methods of gl.vertexAttrib3f()

`gl.vertexAttrib3f()` is part of a family of methods that allow you to set some or all of the components of the attribute variable. `gl.vertexAttrib1f()` is used to assign a single value (v0), `glvertexAttrib2f()` assigns two values (v0 and v1), and `gl.vertexAttrib4f()` assigns four values (v0, v1, v2, and v3).

```
gl.vertexAttrib1f(location, v0)
gl.vertexAttrib2f(location, v0, v1)
gl.vertexAttrib3f(location, v0, v1, v2)
gl.vertexAttrib4f(location, v0, v1, v2, v3)
```

Assign data to the attribute variable specified by *location*. `gl.vertexAttrib1f()` indicates that only one value is passed, and it will be used to modify the first component of the attribute variable. The second and third components will be set to 0.0, and the fourth component will be set to 1.0. Similarly, `gl.vertexAttrib2f()` indicates that values are provided for the first two components, the third component will be set to 0.0, and the fourth component will be set to 1.0. `gl.vertexAttrib3f()` indicates that values are provided for the first three components, and the fourth component will be set to 1.0, whereas `gl.vertexAttrib4f()` indicates that values are provided for all four components.

Parameters	location	Specifies the storage location of the attribute variable.
	v0, v1, v2, v3	Specifies the values to be assigned to the first, second, third, and fourth components of the attribute variable.
Return value	None	
Errors	INVALID_VALUE	*location* is greater than or equal to the maximum number of attribute variables (8 by default).

The vector versions of these methods are also available. Their name contains "v" (vector), and they take a typed array (see Chapter 4) as a parameter. The number in the method name indicates the number of elements in the array. For example,

```
var position = new Float32Array([1.0, 2.0, 3.0, 1.0]);
gl.vertexAttrib4fv(a_Position, position);
```

In this case, 4 in the method name indicates that the length of the array is 4.

The Naming Rules for WebGL-Related Methods

You may be wondering what 3f in gl.vertexAttrib3f() actually means. WebGL bases its method names on the function names in OpenGL ES 2.0, which as you now know, is the base specification of WebGL. The function names in OpenGL comprise the three components: <base function name> <number of parameters> < parameter type>. The name of each WebGL method also uses the same components: <base method name> <number of parameters> <parameter type> as shown in Figure 2.24.

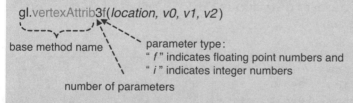

Figure 2.24 The naming rules of WebGL-related methods

As you can see in the example, in the case of gl.vertexAttrib3f(), the base method name is vertexAttrib, the number of parameters is 3, and the parameter type is f (that is, float or floating point number). This method is a WebGL version of the function glVertexAttrib3f() in OpenGL. Another character for the parameter type is i, which indicates integer. You can use the following notation to represent all methods from gl.vertexAttrib1f() to gl.vertexAttrib4f(): gl.vertexAttrib[1234]f().

Where [] indicates that one of the numbers in it can be selected.

When v is appended to the name, the methods take an array as a parameter. In this case, the number in the method name indicates the number of elements in the array.

```
var positions = new Float32Array([1.0, 2.0, 3.0, 1.0]);
gl.vertexAttrib4fv(a_Position, positions);
```

Experimenting with the Sample Program

Now that you have the program to pass the position of a point from a JavaScript program to a vertex shader, let's change that position. For example, if you wanted to display a point at (0.5, 0.0, 0.0), you would modify the program as follows:

```
33    gl.vertexAttrib3f(a_Position, 0.5, 0.0, 0.0);
```

You could use other family methods of `gl.vertexAttrib3f()` to perform the same task in the following way:

```
gl.vertexAttrib1f(a_Position, 0.5);
gl.vertexAttrib2f(a_Position, 0.5, 0.0);
gl.vertexAttrib4f(a_Position, 0.5, 0.0, 0.0, 1.0);
```

Now that you are comfortable using attribute variables, let's use the same approach to change the size of the point from within your JavaScript program. In this case, you will need a new attribute variable for passing the size to the vertex shader. Following the naming rule used in this book, let's use `a_PointSize`. As you saw in Table 2.2, the type of `gl_PointSize` is `float`, so you need to prepare the variable using the same type as follows:

```
attribute float a_PointSize;
```

So, the vertex shader becomes:

```
2   // Vertex shader program
3   var VSHADER_SOURCE =
4     'attribute vec4 a_Position;\n' +
5     'attribute float a_PointSize; \n' +
6     'void main() {\n' +
7     '  gl_Position = a_Position;\n' +
8     '  gl_PointSize = a_PointSize;\n' +
9     '}\n';
```

Then, after you get the storage location of `a_PointSize`, to pass the size of the point to the variable, you can use `gl.vertexAttrib1f()`. Because the type of `a_PointSize` is `float`, you can use `gl.vertexAttrib1f()` as follows:

```
33  // Get the storage location of attribute variable
34  var a_Position = gl.getAttribLocation(gl.program, 'a_Position');
    ...
```

```
39   var a_PointSize = gl.getAttribLocation(gl.program, 'a_PointSize');
40   // Set vertex position to attribute variable
41   gl.vertexAttrib3f(a_Position, 0.0, 0.0, 0.0);
42   gl.vertexAttrib1f(a_PointSize, 5.0);
```

At this stage, you might want to experiment a little with the program and make sure you understand how to use these attribute variables and how they work.

Draw a Point with a Mouse Click

The previous program HelloPoint2 can pass the position of a point to a vertex shader from a JavaScript program. However, the position is still hard-coded, so it is not so different from HelloPoint1, in which the position was also directly written in the shader.

In this section, you add a little more flexibility, exploiting the ability to pass the position from a JavaScript program to a vertex shader, to draw a point at the position where the mouse is clicked. Figure 2.25 shows the screen shot of ClickedPoint.[4]

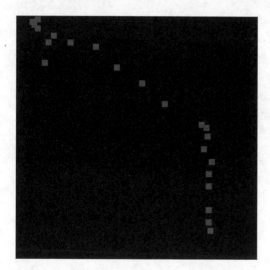

Figure 2.25   ClickedPoint

This program uses an event handler to handle mouse-related events, which will be familiar to those of you who have written JavaScript programs.

Sample Program (ClickedPoints.js)

Listing 2.7 shows ClickedPoints.js. For brevity, we have removed code sections that are the same as the previous example and replaced these with ....

---

[4] © 2012 Marisuke Kunnya

Listing 2.7 ClickedPoints.js

```
1  // ClickedPoints.js
2  // Vertex shader program
3  var VSHADER_SOURCE =
4    'attribute vec4 a_Position;\n' +
5    'void main() {\n' +
6    '  gl_Position = a_Position;\n' +
7    '  gl_PointSize = 10.0;\n' +
8    '}\n';
9
10 // Fragment shader program
   ...
16 function main() {
17   // Retrieve <canvas> element
18   var canvas = document.getElementById('webgl');
19
20   // Get the rendering context for WebGL
21   var gl = getWebGLContext(canvas);
   ...
27   // Initialize shaders
28   if (!initShaders(gl, VSHADER_SOURCE, FSHADER_SOURCE)){
   ...
31   }
32
33   // Get the storage location of a_Position variable
34   var a_Position = gl.getAttribLocation(gl.program, 'a_Position');
   ...
40   // Register function (event handler) to be called on a mouse press
41   canvas.onmousedown = function(ev) { click(ev, gl, canvas, a_Position); };
   ...
47   gl.clear(gl.COLOR_BUFFER_BIT);
48 }
49
50 var g_points = []; // The array for a mouse press
51 function click(ev, gl, canvas, a_Position) {
52   var x = ev.clientX; // x coordinate of a mouse pointer
53   var y = ev.clientY; // y coordinate of a mouse pointer
54   var rect = ev.target.getBoundingClientRect();
55
56   x = ((x - rect.left) - canvas.height/2)/(canvas.height/2);
57   y = (canvas.width/2 - (y - rect.top))/(canvas.width/2);
58   // Store the coordinates to g_points array
59   g_points.push(x); g_points.push(y);
60
```

```
61    // Clear <canvas>
62    gl.clear(gl.COLOR_BUFFER_BIT);
63
64    var len = g_points.length;
65    for(var i = 0; i < len; i+=2) {
66      // Pass the position of a point to a_Position variable
67      gl.vertexAttrib3f(a_Position, g_points[i], g_points[i+1], 0.0);
68
69      // Draw a point
70      gl.drawArrays(gl.POINTS, 0, 1);
71    }
72  }
```

Register Event Handlers

The processing flow from lines 17 to 39 is the same as `HelloPoint2.js`. These lines get the WebGL context, initialize the shaders, and then retrieve the location of the attribute variable. The main differences from `HelloPoint2.js` are the registration of an event handler (line 41) and the definition of the function `click()` as the handler (from line 51).

An event handler is an asynchronous callback function that handles input on a web page from a user, such as mouse clicks or key presses. This allows you to create a dynamic web page that can change the content that's displayed according to the user's input. To use an event handler, you need to register the event handler (that is, tell the system what code to run when the event occurs). The `<canvas>` supports special properties for registering event handlers for a specific user input, which you will use here.

For example, when you want to handle mouse clicks, you can use the `onmousedown` property of the `<canvas>` to specify the event handler for a mouse click as follows:

```
40    // Register function (event handler) to be called on a mouse press
41    canvas.onmousedown = function(ev) { click(ev, gl, canvas, a_Position); };
```

Line 41 uses the statement `function(){ ... }` to register the handler:

```
function(ev){ click(ev, gl, canvas, a_Position); }
```

This mechanism is called an **anonymous function**, which, as its name suggests, is a convenient mechanism when you define a function that does not need to have a name.

For those of you unfamiliar with this type of function, let's explain the mechanism using an example. Next, we define the variable `thanks` as follows using the form:

```
var thanks = function () { alert(' Thanks a million!'); }
```

We can execute the variable as a function as follows:

```
thanks(); // 'Thanks a million!' is displayed
```

You can see that the variable `thanks` can be operated as a function. These lines can be rewritten as follows:

```
function thanks() { alert('Thanks a million!'); }
thanks(); // 'Thanks a million!' is displayed
```

So why do you need to use an anonymous function? Well, when you draw a point, you need the following three variables: `gl`, `canvas`, and `a_Position`. These variables are local variables that are prepared in the function `main()` in the JavaScript program. However, when a mouse click occurs, the browser will automatically call the function that is registered to the `<canvas>`'s `onmousedown` property with a **predefined single parameter** (that is, an event object that contains information about the mouse press. Therefore, usually, you will register the event handler and define the function for it as follows:

```
canvas.onmousedown = mousedown; // Register "mousedown" as event handler
...
function mousedown(ev) { // Event handler: It takes one parameter "ev"

  ...

}
```

However, if you define the function in this way, it cannot access the local variables `gl`, `canvas`, and `a_Position` to draw a point. The anonymous function at line 41 provides the solution to make it possible to access them:

```
41    canvas.onmousedown = function(ev) { click(ev, gl, canvas, a_Position); };
```

In this code, when a mouse click occurs, the anonymous function `function(ev)` is called first. Then it calls `click(ev, gl, canvas, a_Position)` with the local variables defined in `main()`. Although this may seem a little complicated, it is actually quite flexible and avoids the use of global variables, which is always good. Take a moment to make sure you understand this approach, because you will often see this way of registering event handlers in this book.

Handling Mouse Click Events

Let's look at what the function `click()` is doing. The processing flow follows:

1. Retrieve the position of the mouse click and then store it in an array.

2. Clear `<canvas>`.

3. For each position stored in the array, draw a point.

```
50  var g_points = [];  // The array for mouse click positions
51  function click(ev, gl, canvas, a_Position) {
52    var x = ev.clientX; // x coordinate of a mouse pointer
53    var y = ev.clientY; // y coordinate of a mouse pointer
54    var rect = ev.target.getBoundingClientRect();
```

```
55
56    x = ((x - rect.left) - canvas.height/2)/(canvas.height/2);
57    y = (canvas.width/2 - (y - rect.top))/(canvas.width/2);
58    // Store the coordinates to a_points array                      <- (1)
59    g_points.push(x); g_points.push(y);
60
61    // Clear <canvas>
62    gl.clear(gl.COLOR_BUFFER_BIT);                                  <- (2)
63
64    var len = g_points.length;
65    for(var i = 0; i < len; i+=2) {
66      // Pass the position of a point to a_Position variable        <- (3)
67      gl.vertexAttrib3f(a_Position, g_points[i], g_points[i+1], 0.0);
68
69      // Draw a point
70      gl.drawArrays(gl.POINTS, 0, 1);
71    }
72  }
```

The information about the position of a mouse click is stored as an event object and passed by the browser using the argument ev to the function click(). ev holds the position information, and you can get the coordinates by using ev.clientX and ev.clientY, as shown in lines 52 and 53. However, you cannot use the coordinates directly in this sample program for two reasons:

1. The coordinate is the position in the "client area" in the browser, not in the <canvas> (see Figure 2.26).

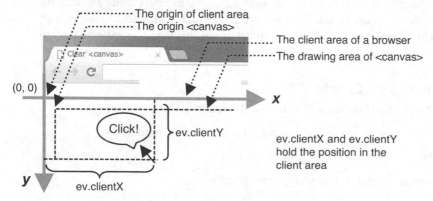

Figure 2.26 The coordinate system of a browser's client area and the position of the <canvas>

2. The coordinate system of the <canvas> is different from that of WebGL (see Figure 2.27) in terms of their origin and the direction of the y-axis.

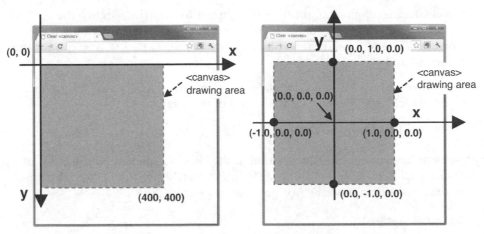

Figure 2.27 The coordinate system of <canvas> (left) and that of WebGL on <canvas> (right)

First you need to transform the coordinates from the browser area to the canvas, and then you need to transform them into coordinates that WebGL understands. Let's look at how to do that.

These transformations are performed at lines 56 and 57 in the sample program:

```
52    var x = ev.clientX;
53    var y = ev.clientY;
54    var rect = ev.target.getBoundingClientRect();
55    ...
56    x = ((x - rect.left) - canvas.width/2)/(canvas.width/2);
57    y = (canvas.height/2 - (y - rect.top))/(canvas.height/2);
```

Line 54 gets the position of the <canvas> in the client area. The rect.left and rec.top indicate the position of the origin of the <canvas> in the browser's client area (refer to Figure 2.26). So, (x - rect.left) at line 56 and (y - rect.top) at line 57 slide the position (x, y) in the client area to the correct position on the <canvas> element.

Next, you need to transform the <canvas> position into the WebGL coordinate system shown in Figure 2.27. To perform the transformation, you need to know the center position of the <canvas>. You can get the size of the <canvas> by canvas.height (in this case, 400) and canvas.width (in this case, 400). So, the center of the element will be (canvas.height/2, canvas.width/2).

Next, you can implement this transformation by sliding the origin of the <canvas> into the origin of the WebGL coordinate system located at the center of <canvas>. The ((x - rect.left) - canvas.width/2) and (canvas.height/2 - (y -rect.top)) perform the transformation.

Finally, as shown in Figure 2.27, the range of the x-axis in the <canvas> goes from 0 to canvas.width (400), and that of the y-axis goes from 0 to canvas.height (400). Because the axes in WebGL range from –1.0 to 1.0, the last step is to map the range of the `<canvas>` coordinate system to that of the WebGL coordinate system by dividing the x coordinate by `canvas.width/2` and the y coordinate by `canvas.height/2`. You can see this division in lines 56 and 57.

Line 59 stores the resulting position of the mouse click in the array `g_points` using the `push()` method, which appends the data to the end of the array:

```
59    g_points.push(x); g_points.push(y);
```

So every time a mouse click occurs, the position of the click is appended to the array, as shown in Figure 2.28. (The length of the array is automatically stretched.) Note that the index of an array starts from 0, so the first position is `g_points[0]`.

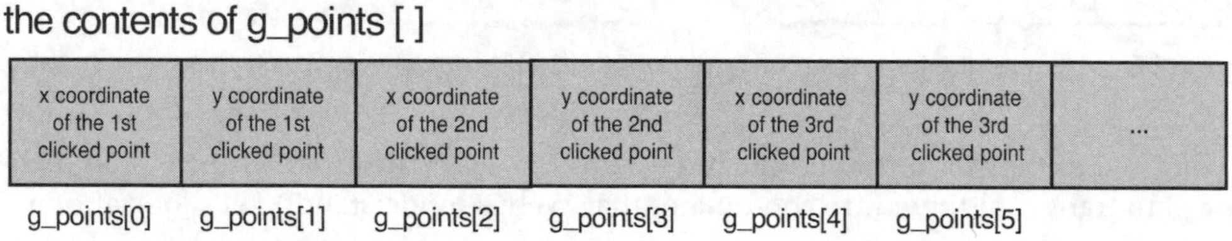

the contents of g_points [ ]

x coordinate of the 1st clicked point	y coordinate of the 1st clicked point	x coordinate of the 2nd clicked point	y coordinate of the 2nd clicked point	x coordinate of the 3rd clicked point	y coordinate of the 3rd clicked point	...
g_points[0]	g_points[1]	g_points[2]	g_points[3]	g_points[4]	g_points[5]	

Figure 2.28   The content of g_points

You may be wondering why you need to store all the positions rather than just the most recent mouse click. This is because of the way WebGL uses the color buffer. You will remember from Figure 2.10 that in the WebGL system, first the drawing operation is performed to the color buffer, and then the system displays its content to the screen. After that, the color buffer is reinitialized and its content is lost. (This is the default behavior, which you'll investigate in the next section.) Therefore, it is necessary to save all the positions of the clicked points in the array, so that on each mouse click, the program can draw all the previous points as well as the latest. For example, the first point is drawn at the first mouse click. The first and second points are drawn at the second mouse click. The first, second, and third points are drawn on the third click, and so on.

Returning to the program, the `<canvas>` is cleared at line 62. After that, the `for` statement at line 65 passes each position of the point stored in `g_points` to `a_Position` in the vertex shader. Then `gl.drawArrays()` draws the point at that position:

```
65    for(var i = 0; i < len; i+=2) {
66      // Pass the position of a point to a_Position variable
67      gl.vertexAttrib3f(a_Position, g_points[i], g_points[i+1], 0.0);
```

Just like in `HelloPoint2.js`, you will use `gl.vertexAttrib3f()` to pass the point position to the attribute variable `a_Position`, which was passed as the fourth parameter of `click()` at line 51.

The array g_points holds the x coordinate and y coordinate of the clicked points, as shown in Figure 2.28. Therefore, g_points[i] holds the x coordinate, and g_points[i+1] holds the y coordinate, so the loop index i in the for statement at line 65 is incremented by 2 using the convenient + operator.

Now that you have completed the preparations for drawing the point, the remaining task is just to draw it using gl.drawArrays():

```
69    // Draw a point
70    gl.drawArrays(gl.POINTS, 0, 1);
```

Although it's a little complicated, you can see that the use of event handlers combined with attribute variable provides a flexible and generic means for user input to change what WebGL draws.

Experimenting with the Sample Program

Now let's experiment a little with this sample program ClickedPoints. After loading ClickedPoints.html in your browser, every time you click, it draws a point at the clicked position, as shown in Figure 2.26.

Let's examine what will happen when you stop clearing the <canvas> at line 62. Comment out the line as follows, and then reload the modified file into your browser.

```
61    // Clear <canvas>
62    // gl.clear(gl.COLOR_BUFFER_BIT);
63
64    var len = g_points.length;
65    for(var i = 0; i < len; i+=2) {
66      // Pass the position of a point to a_Position variable
67      gl.vertexAttrib3f(a_Position, g_points[i], g_points[i+1], 0.0);
68
69      // Draw a point
70      gl.drawArrays(gl.POINTS, 0, 1);
71    }
72  }
```

After running the program, you initially see a black background, but at the first click, you see a red point on a white background. This is because WebGL reinitializes the color buffer to the default value (0.0, 0.0, 0.0, 0.0) after drawing the point (refer to Table 2.1). The alpha component of the default value is 0.0, which means the color is transparent. Therefore, the color of the <canvas> becomes transparent, so you see the background color of the web page (white, in this case) through the <canvas> element. If you don't want this behavior, you should use gl.clearColor() to specify the clear color and then always call gl.clear() before drawing something.

Another interesting experiment is to look at how to simplify the code. In `ClickedPoints.js`, the x and y coordinates are stored separately in the `g_points` array. However, you can store the x and y coordinates as a group into the array as follows:

```
58    // Store the coordinates to a_points array          <- (1)
59    g_points.push([x, y]);
```

In this case, the new two-element array `[x, y]` is stored as an element in the array `g_points`. Conveniently, JavaScript can store an array in an array.

You can retrieve the x and y coordinates from the array as follows. First, you retrieve an element from the array by specifying its index (line 66). Because the element itself is an array containing (x, y), you can retrieve the first element and the second element as the x and y coordinate of each point from the array (line 67):

```
65   for(var i = 0; i < len; i++) {
66     var xy = g_points[i];
67     gl.vertexAttrib3f(a_Position, xy[0], xy[1], 0.0);
       . . .
71   }
```

In this way, you can deal with the x and y coordinates as a group, simplifying your program and increasing the readability.

Change the Point Color

By now you should have a good feel for how the shaders work and how to pass data to them from your JavaScript program. Let's build on your understanding by constructing a more complex program that draws points whose colors vary depending on their position on the `<canvas>`.

You already studied how to change the color of a point when you looked at `HelloPoint1`. In that example, you modified the fragment shader program directly to embed the color value into the shader. In this section, let's construct the program so that you can specify the color of a point from JavaScript. This is similar to `HelloPoint2` earlier, where you passed the position of a point from a JavaScript program to the vertex shader. However, in this sample program, you need to pass the data to a "fragment shader," not to a vertex shader.

The name of the sample program is `ColoredPoints`. If you load the example into your browser, the result is the same as `ClickedPoints` except that each point's color varies depending on its position (see Figure 2.29).

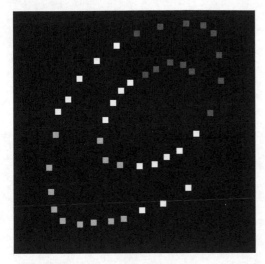

Figure 2.29 ColoredPoints

To pass data to a fragment shader, you can use a uniform variable and follow the same steps that you used when working with attribute variables. However, this time the target is a fragment shader, not a vertex shader:

1. Prepare the uniform variable for the color in the fragment shader.

2. Assign the uniform variable to the gl_FragColor variable.

3. Pass the color data to the uniform variable from the JavaScript program.

Let's look at the sample program and see how these steps are programmed.

Sample Program (ColoredPoints.js)

The vertex shader of this sample program is the same as in ClickedPoints.js. However, this time, the fragment shader plays a more important role because the program changes the color of the point dynamically and, as you will remember, fragment shaders handle colors. Listing 2.8 shows ColoredPoints.js.

Listing 2.8 ColoredPoints.js

```
1 // ColoredPoints.js
2 // Vertex shader program
3 var VSHADER_SOURCE =
4   'attribute vec4 a_Position;\n' +
5   'void main() {\n' +
6   ' gl_Position = a_Position;\n' +
7   ' gl_PointSize = 10.0;\n' +
```

```
 8    '}\n';
 9
10  // Fragment shader program
11  var FSHADER_SOURCE =
12    'precision mediump float;\n' +
13    'uniform vec4 u_FragColor;\n' + // uniform variable            <- (1)
14    'void main() {\n' +
15    '  gl_FragColor = u_FragColor;\n' +                            <- (2)
16    '}\n';
17
18  function main() {
    ...
29    // Initialize shaders
30    if (!initShaders(gl, VSHADER_SOURCE, FSHADER_SOURCE)) {
    ...
33    }
34
35    // Get the storage location of a_Position variable
36    var a_Position = gl.getAttribLocation(gl.program, 'a_Position');
    ...
42    // Get the storage location of u_FragColor variable
43    var u_FragColor = gl.getUniformLocation(gl.program, 'u_FragColor');
    ...
49    // Register function (event handler) to be called on a mouse press
50    canvas.onmousedown = function(ev){ click(ev, gl, canvas, a_Position,
                                          ➥u_FragColor) };
    ...
56    gl.clear(gl.COLOR_BUFFER_BIT);
57  }
58
59  var g_points = [];  // The array for a mouse press
60  var g_colors = [];  // The array to store the color of a point
61  function click(ev, gl, canvas, a_Position, u_FragColor) {
62    var x = ev.clientX; // x coordinate of a mouse pointer
63    var y = ev.clientY; // y coordinate of a mouse pointer
64    var rect = ev.target.getBoundingClientRect();
65
66    x = ((x - rect.left) - canvas.width/2)/(canvas.width/2);
67    y = (canvas.height/2 - (y - rect.top))/(canvas.height/2);
68
69    // Store the coordinates to g_points array
70    g_points.push([x, y]);
71    // Store the color to g_colors array
72    if(x >= 0.0 && y >= 0.0) {            // First quadrant
73      g_colors.push([1.0, 0.0, 0.0, 1.0]);  // Red
```

```
74    } else if(x < 0.0 && y < 0.0) {        // Third quadrant
75      g_colors.push([0.0, 1.0, 0.0, 1.0]);  // Green
76    } else {                      // Others
77      g_colors.push([1.0, 1.0, 1.0, 1.0]);  // White
78    }
79
80    // Clear <canvas>
81    gl.clear(gl.COLOR_BUFFER_BIT);
82
83    var len = g_points.length;
84    for(var i = 0; i < len; i++) {
85      var xy = g_points[i];
86      var rgba = g_colors[i];
87
88      // Pass the position of a point to a_Position variable
89      gl.vertexAttrib3f(a_Position, xy[0], xy[1], 0.0);
90      // Pass the color of a point to u_FragColor variable
91      gl.uniform4f(u_FragColor, rgba[0],rgba[1],rgba[2],rgba[3]);    <-(3)
92      // Draw a point
93      gl.drawArrays(gl.POINTS, 0, 1);
94    }
95  }
```

Uniform Variables

You likely remember how to use an attribute variable to pass data from a JavaScript program to a vertex shader. Unfortunately, the attribute variable is only available in a vertex shader, and when using a fragment shader, you need to use a uniform variable. There is an alternative mechanism, a varying variable (bottom of Figure 2.30); however, it is more complex, so you won't use it until Chapter 5.

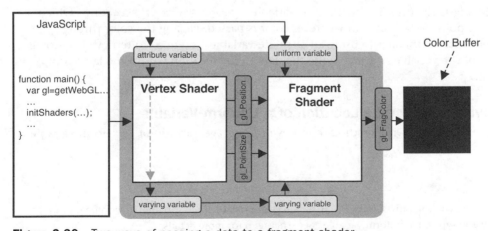

Figure 2.30 Two ways of passing a data to a fragment shader

When you were introduced to attribute variables, you saw that a uniform variable is a variable for passing "uniform" (nonvariable) data from a JavaScript program to all vertices or fragments in the shader. Let's now use that property.

Before using a uniform variable, you need to declare the variable using the form <Storage Qualifier> <Type> <Variable name> in the same way (see Figure 2.31) as declaring an attribute variable. (See the section "Sample Program (HelloPoint2.js).")[5]

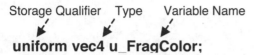

Figure 2.31 The declaration of the uniform variable

In this sample program, the uniform variable u_FragColor is named after the variable gl_FragColor because you will assign the uniform variable to the gl_FragColor later. The u_ in u_FragColor is part of our programming convention and indicates that it is a uniform variable. You need to specify the same data type as gl_FragColor for u_FragColor because you can only assign the same type of variable to gl_FragColor. Therefore, you prepare u_FragColor at line 13, as follows:

```
10  // Fragment shader program
11  var FSHADER_SOURCE =
12    'precision mediump float;\n' +
13    'uniform vec4 u_FragColor;\n' + // uniform variable
14    'void main() {\n' +
15    '  gl_FragColor = u_FragColor;\n' +
16    '}\n';
```

Note that line 12 specifies the range and precision of variables by using a **precision qualifier**, in this case medium precision, which is covered in detail in Chapter 5.

Line 15 assigns the color in the uniform variable u_FragColor to gl_FragColor, which causes the point to be drawn in whatever color is passed. Passing the color through the uniform variable is similar to using an attribute variable; you need to retrieve the storage location of the variable and then write the data to the location within the JavaScript program.

Retrieving the Storage Location of a Uniform Variable

You can use the following method to retrieve the storage location of a uniform variable.

---

[5] In GLSL ES, you can only specify float data types for an attribute variable; however, you can specify any type for a uniform variable. (See Chapter 6 for more details.)

`gl.getUniformLocation(program, name)`	

Retrieve the storage location of the uniform variable specified by the *name* parameter.

Parameters	program	Specifies the program object that holds a vertex shader and a fragment shader.
	name	Specifies the name of the uniform variable whose location is to be retrieved.
Return value	non-null	The location of the specified uniform variable.
	null	The specified uniform variable does not exist or its name starts with the reserved prefix `gl_` or `webgl_`.
Errors	INVALID_OPERATION	*program* has not been successfully linked (See Chapter 9.)
	INVALID_VALUE	The length of *name* is more than the maximum length (256 by default) of a uniform variable.

The functionality and parameters of this method are the same as in `gl.getAttribLocation()`. However, the return value of this method is `null`, not –1, if the uniform variable does not exist or its name starts with a reserved prefix. For this reason, unlike attribute variables, you need to check whether the return value is `null`. You can see this error checking line 44. In JavaScript, `null` can be treated as `false` when checking the condition of an `if` statement, so you can use the `!` operator to check the result:

```
42    // Get the storage location of uniform variable
43    var u_FragColor = gl.getUniformLocation(gl.program, 'u_FragColor');
44    if (!u_FragColor) {
45      console.log('Failed to get u_FragColor variable');
46      return;
47    }
```

Assigning a Value to a Uniform Variable

Once you have the location of the uniform variable and the WebGL method, `gl.uniform4f()` is used to write data to it. It has the same functionality and parameters as those of `gl.vertexAttrib[1234]f()`.

gl.uniform4f(location, v0, v1, v2, v3)		

Assign the data specified by *v0*, *v1*, *v2*, and *v3* to the uniform variable specified by *location*.

Parameters	location	Specifies the storage location of a uniform variable to be modified.
	v0	Specifies the value to be used as the first element of the uniform variable.
	v1	Specifies the value to be used as the second element of the uniform variable.
	v2	Specifies the value to be used as the third element of the uniform variable.
	v3	Specifies the value to be used as the fourth element of the uniform variable.
Return value	None	
Errors	INVALID_OPERATION	There is no current program object.
		location is an invalid uniform variable location.

Let's look at the portion of the sample program where the `gl.uniform4f()` method is used to assign the data (line 91). As you can see, several processing steps are needed in advance:

```
71    // Store the color to g_colors array
72    if(x >= 0.0 && y >= 0.0) {            // First quadrant
73      g_colors.push([1.0, 0.0, 0.0, 1.0]);  // Red
74    } else if(x < 0.0 && y < 0.0) {       // Third quadrant
75      g_colors.push([0.0, 1.0, 0.0, 1.0]);  // Green
76    } else {                              // Other quadrants
77      g_colors.push([1.0, 1.0, 1.0, 1.0]);  // White
78    }
      ...
83    var len = g_points.length;
84    for(var i = 0; i < len; i++) {
85      var xy = g_points[i];
86      var rgba = g_colors[i];
        ...
91      gl.uniform4f(u_FragColor, rgba[0], rgba[1], rgba[2], rgba[3]);
```

To understand this program logic, let's return to the goal of this program, which is to vary the color of a point according to where on the <canvas> the mouse is clicked. In the first quadrant, the color is set to red; in the third quadrant, the color is green; in the other quadrants, the color is white (see Figure 2.32).

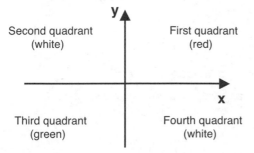

Figure 2.32 The name of each quadrant in a coordinate system and its drawing colors

The code from lines 72 to 78 simply determines which quadrant the mouse click was in and then, based on that, writes the appropriate color into the array g_colors. Finally, at line 84, the program loops through the points, passing the correct color to the uniform variable u_FragColor at line 91. This causes WebGL to write all the points stored so far to the color buffer, which then results in the browser display being updated.

Before finishing this chapter, let's take a quick look at the rest of the family methods for gl.uniform[1234]f().

Family Methods of gl.uniform4f()

gl.uniform4f() also has a family of methods. gl.uniform1f() is a method to assign a single value (v0), gl.uniform2f() assigns two values (v0 and v1), and gl.uniform3f() assigns three values (v0, v1, and v2).

```
gl.uniform1f(location, v0)
gl.uniform2f(location, v0, v1)
gl.uniform3f(location, v0, v1, v2)
gl.uniform4f(location, v0, v1, v2, v3)
```

Assign data to the uniform variable specified by *location*. gl.uniform1f() indicates that only one value is passed, and it will be used to modify the first component of the uniform variable. The second and third components will be set to 0.0, and the fourth component will be set to 1.0. Similarly, gl.uniform2f() indicates that values are provided for the first two components, the third component will be set to 0.0, and the fourth component will be set to 1.0. gl.uniform3f() indicates that values are provided for the first three components and the fourth component will be set to 1.0, whereas gl.unifrom4f() indicates that values are provided for all four components.

Parameters	location	Specifies the storage location of a uniform variable.
	v0, v1, v2, v3	Specifies the values to be assigned to the first, second, third, and fourth component of the uniform variable.
Return value	None	
Errors	INVALID_OPERATION	There is no current program object.
		location is an invalid uniform variable location.

Summary

In this chapter, you saw the core functions of WebGL and how to use them. In particular, you learned about shaders, which are the main mechanism used in WebGL to draw graphics. Based on this, you constructed several sample programs starting with a simple program to draw a red point, and then you added complexity by changing its position based on a mouse click and changed its color. In both cases, these examples helped you understand how to pass data from a JavaScript program to the shaders, which will be critical for future examples.

The shapes found in this chapter were still just two-dimensional points. However, you can apply the same knowledge of the use of the core WebGL functions and shaders to more complex shapes and to three-dimensional objects.

A key learning point in this chapter is this: A vertex shader performs per-vertex operations, and a fragment shader performs per-fragment operations. The following chapters explain some of the other functions of WebGL, while slowly increasing the complexity of the shapes that you manipulate and display on the screen.

Chapter 3

Drawing and Transforming Triangles

Chapter 2, "Your First Step with WebGL," explained the basic approach to drawing WebGL graphics. You saw how to retrieve the WebGL context and clear a <canvas> in preparation for drawing your 2D/3DCG. You then explored the roles and features of the vertex and fragment shaders and how to actually draw graphics with them. With this basic structure in mind, you then constructed several sample programs that drew simple shapes composed of points on the screen.

This chapter builds on those basics by exploring how to draw more complex shapes and how to manipulate those shapes in 3D space. In particular, this chapter looks at

- The critical role of triangles in 3DCG and WebGL's support for drawing triangles

- Using multiple triangles to draw other basic shapes

- Basic transformations that move, rotate, and scale triangles using simple equations

- How matrix operations make transformations simple

By the end of this chapter, you will have a comprehensive understanding of WebGL's support for drawing basic shapes and how to use matrix operations to manipulate those shapes. Chapter 4, "More Transformations and Basic Animation," then builds on this knowledge to explore simple animations.

Drawing Multiple Points

As you are probably aware, 3D models are actually made from a simple building block: the humble triangle. For example, looking at the frog in Figure 3.1, the figure on the right side shows the triangles used to make up the shape, and in particular the three vertices that make up one triangle of the head. So, although this game character has a complex shape, its basic components are the same as a simple one, except of course for many more triangles and their associated vertices. By using smaller and smaller triangles, and therefore more and more vertices, you can create more complex or smoother objects. Typically, a complex shape or game character will consist of tens of thousands of triangles and their associated vertices. Thus, multiple vertices used to make up triangles are pivotal for drawing 3D objects.

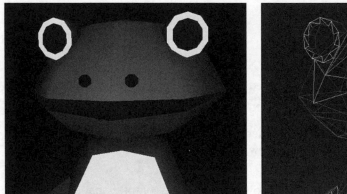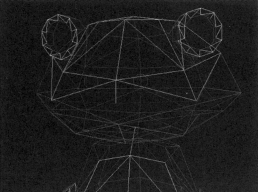

Figure 3.1 Complex characters are also constructed from multiple triangles

In this section, you explore the process of drawing shapes using multiple vertices. However, to keep things simple, you'll continue to use 2D shapes, because the technique to deal with multiple vertices for a 2D shape is the same as dealing with them for a 3D object. Essentially, if you can master these techniques for 2D shapes, you can easily understand the examples in the rest of this book that use the same techniques for 3D objects.

As an example of handling multiple vertices, let's create a program, `MultiPoint`, that draws three red points on the screen; remember, three points or vertices make up the triangle. Figure 3.2 shows a screenshot from `Multipoint`.

Figure 3.2 `MultiPoint`

In the previous chapter, you created a sample program, `ClickedPoints`, that drew multiple points based on mouse clicks. `ClickedPoints` stored the position of the points in a JavaScript array (`g_points[]`) and used the `gl.drawArrays()` method to draw each point (Listing 3.1). To draw multiple points, you used a loop that iterated through the array, drawing each point in turn by passing one vertex at a time to the shader.

Listing 3.1 Drawing Multiple Points as Shown in ClickedPoints.js (Chapter 2)

```
65    for(var i = 0; i<len; i+=2) {
66      // Pass the position of a point to a_Position variable
67      gl.vertexAttrib3f(a_Position, g_points[i], g_points[i+1], 0.0);
68
69      // Draw a point
70      gl.drawArrays(gl.POINTS, 0, 1);
71    }
```

Obviously, this method is useful only for single points. For shapes that use multiple vertices, you need a way to simultaneously pass multiple vertices to the vertex shader so that you can draw shapes constructed from multiple vertices, such as triangles, rectangles, and cubes.

WebGL provides a convenient way to pass multiple vertices and uses something called a **buffer object** to do so. A buffer object is a memory area that can store multiple vertices in the WebGL system. It is used both as a staging area for the vertex data and a way to simultaneously pass the vertices to a vertex shader.

Let's examine a sample program before explaining the buffer object so you can get a feel for the processing flow.

Sample Program (MultiPoint.js)

The processing flowchart for `MultiPoint.js` (see Figure 3.3) is basically the same as for `ClickedPoints.js` (Listing 2.7) and `ColoredPoints.js` (Listing 2.8), which you saw in Chapter 2. The only difference is a new step, setting up the positions of vertices, which is added to the previous flow.

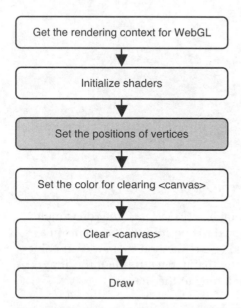

Figure 3.3   Processing flowchart for MultiPoints.js

This step is implemented at line 34, the function `initVertexBuffers()`, in Listing 3.2.

Listing 3.2   MultiPoint.js

```
1 // MultiPoint.js
2 // Vertex shader program
3 var VSHADER_SOURCE =
4   'attribute vec4 a_Position;\n' +
5   'void main() {\n' +
6   ' gl_Position = a_Position;\n' +
7   ' gl_PointSize = 10.0;\n' +
8   '}\n';
9
10 // Fragment shader program
   ...
15
16 function main() {
   ...
```

```
20   // Get the rendering context for WebGL
21   var gl = getWebGLContext(canvas);
       ...
27   // Initialize shaders
28   if (!initShaders(gl, VSHADER_SOURCE, FSHADER_SOURCE)) {
       ...
31   }
32
33   // Set the positions of vertices
34   var n = initVertexBuffers(gl);
35   if (n < 0) {
36     console.log('Failed to set the positions of the vertices');
37     return;
38   }
39
40   // Set the color for clearing <canvas>
       ...
43   // Clear <canvas>
...
46   // Draw three points
47   gl.drawArrays(gl.POINTS, 0, n); // n is 3
48 }
49
50 function initVertexBuffers(gl) {
51   var vertices = new Float32Array([
52     0.0, 0.5,   -0.5, -0.5,   0.5, -0.5
53   ]);
54   var n = 3; // The number of vertices
55
56   // Create a buffer object
57   var vertexBuffer = gl.createBuffer();
58   if (!vertexBuffer) {
59     console.log('Failed to create the buffer object ');
60     return -1;
61   }
62
63   // Bind the buffer object to target
64   gl.bindBuffer(gl.ARRAY_BUFFER, vertexBuffer);
65   // Write date into the buffer object
66   gl.bufferData(gl.ARRAY_BUFFER, vertices, gl.STATIC_DRAW);
67
68   var a_Position = gl.getAttribLocation(gl.program, 'a_Position');
     ...
73   // Assign the buffer object to a_Position variable
74   gl.vertexAttribPointer(a_Position, 2, gl.FLOAT, false, 0, 0);
```

```
75
76    // Enable the assignment to a_Position variable
77    gl.enableVertexAttribArray(a_Position);
78
79    return n;
80 }
```

The new function `initVertexBuffers()` is defined at line 50 and used at line 34 to set up the vertex buffer object. The function stores multiple vertices in the buffer object and then completes the preparations for passing it to a vertex shader:

```
33 // Set the positions of vertices
34   var n = initVertexBuffers(gl);
```

The return value of this function is the number of vertices being drawn, stored in the variable n. Note that in case of error, n is negative.

As in the previous examples, the drawing operation is carried out using a single call to `gl.drawArrays()` at Line 48. This is similar to `ClickedPoints.js` except that n is passed as the third argument of `gl.drawArrays()` rather than the value 1:

```
46    // Draw three points
47    gl.drawArrays(gl.POINTS, 0, n); // n is 3
```

Because you are using a buffer object to pass multiple vertices to a vertex shader in `init-VertexBuffers()`, you need to specify the number of vertices in the object as the third parameter of `gl.drawArrays()` so that WebGL then knows to draw a shape using all the vertices in the buffer object.

Using Buffer Objects

As indicated earlier, a buffer object is a mechanism provided by the WebGL system that provides a memory area allocated in the system (see Figure 3.4) that holds the vertices you want to draw. By creating a buffer object and then writing the vertices to the object, you can pass multiple vertices to a vertex shader through one of its attribute variables.

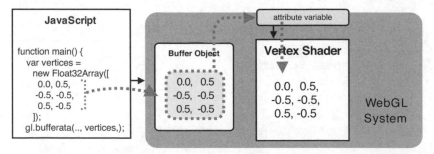

Figure 3.4 Passing multiple vertices to a vertex shader by using a buffer object

In the sample program, the data (vertex coordinates) written into a buffer object is defined as a special JavaScript array (Float32Array) as follows. We will explain this special array in detail later, but for now you can think of it as a normal array:

```
51    var vertices = new Float32Array([
52      0.0, 0.5,    -0.5, -0.5,    0.5, -0.5
53    ]);
```

There are five steps needed to pass multiple data values to a vertex shader through a buffer object. Because WebGL uses a similar approach when dealing with other objects such as texture objects (Chapter 4) and framebuffer objects (Chapter 8, "Lighting Objects"), let's explore these in detail so you will be able to apply the knowledge later:

1. Create a buffer object (gl.createBuffer()).

2. Bind the buffer object to a target (gl.bindBuffer()).

3. Write data into the buffer object (gl.bufferData()).

4. Assign the buffer object to an attribute variable (gl.vertexAttribPointer()).

5. Enable assignment (gl.enableVertexAttribArray()).

Figure 3.5 illustrates the five steps.

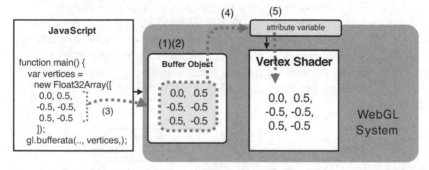

Figure 3.5   The five steps to pass multiple data values to a vertex shader using a buffer object

The code performing the steps in the sample program in Listing 3.2 is as follows:

```
56    // Create a buffer object                              <- (1)
57    var vertexBuffer = gl.createBuffer();
58    if (!vertexBuffer) {
59      console.log('Failed to create a buffer object');
60      return -1;
61    }
62
63    // Bind the buffer object to a target                  <- (2)
```

```
64    gl.bindBuffer(gl.ARRAY_BUFFER, vertexBuffer);
65    // Write date into the buffer object                      <- (3)
66    gl.bufferData(gl.ARRAY_BUFFER, vertices, gl.STATIC_DRAW);
67
68    var a_Position = gl.getAttribLocation(gl.program, 'a_Position');
      ...
73    // Assign the buffer object to a_Position variable         <- (4)
74    gl.vertexAttribPointer(a_Position, 2, gl.FLOAT, false, 0, 0);
75
76    // Enable the assignment to a_Position variable            <- (5)
77    gl.enableVertexAttribArray(a_Position);
```

Let's start with the first three steps (1–3), from creating a buffer object to writing data (vertex coordinates in this example) to the buffer, explaining the methods used within each step.

Create a Buffer Object (gl.createBuffer())

Before you can use a buffer object, you obviously need to create the buffer object. This is the first step, and it's carried out at line 57:

```
57    var vertexBuffer = gl.createBuffer();
```

You use the `gl.createBuffer()` method to create a buffer object within the WebGL system. Figure 3.6 shows the internal state of the WebGL system. The upper part of the figure shows the state before executing the method, and the lower part is after execution. As you can see, when the method is executed, it results in a single buffer object being created in the WebGL system. The keywords `gl.ARRAY_BUFFER` and `gl.ELEMENT_ARRAY_BUFFER` in the figure will be explained in the next section, so you can ignore them for now.

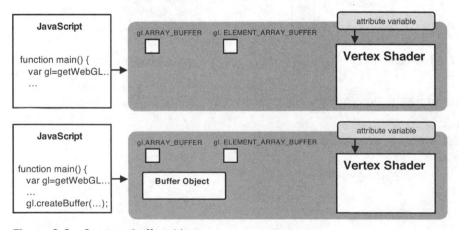

Figure 3.6   Create a buffer object

The following shows the specification of `gl.createBuffer()`.

`gl.createBuffer()`

Create a buffer object.

Return value	non-null	The newly created buffer object.
	null	Failed to create a buffer object.
Errors	None	

The corresponding method `gl.deleteBuffer()` deletes the buffer object created by `gl.createBuffer()`.

`gl.deleteBuffer(buffer)`

Delete the buffer object specified by *buffer*.

Parameters	buffer	Specifies the buffer object to be deleted.
Return Value	None	
Errors	None	

Bind a Buffer Object to a Target (gl.bindBuffer())

After creating a buffer object, the second step is to bind it to a "target." The target tells WebGL what type of data the buffer object contains, allowing it to deal with the contents correctly. This binding process is carried out at line 64 as follows:

```
64 gl.bindBuffer(gl.ARRAY_BUFFER, vertexBuffer);
```

The specification of `gl.bindBuffer()` is as follows.

`gl.bindBuffer(target, buffer)`

Enable the buffer object specified by *buffer* and bind it to the *target*.

Parameters	Target can be one of the following:
	`gl.ARRAY_BUFFER`	Specifies that the buffer object contains vertex data.

	gl.ELEMENT_ ARRAY_BUFFER	Specifies that the buffer object contains index values pointing to vertex data. (See Chapter 6, "The OpenGL ES Shading Language [GLSL ES].)
	buffer	Specifies the buffer object created by a previous call to gl.createBuffer().
		When null is specified, binding to the *target* is disabled.
Return Value	None	
Errors	INVALID_ENUM	*target* is none of the above values. In this case, the current binding is maintained.

In the sample program in this section, gl.ARRAY_BUFFER is specified as the *target* to store vertex data (positions) in the buffer object. After executing line 64, the internal state in the WebGL system changes, as shown in Figure 3.7.

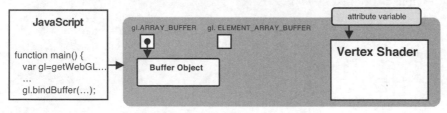

Figure 3.7 Bind a buffer object to a target

The next step is to write data into the buffer object. Note that because you won't be using the gl.ELEMENT_ARRAY_BUFFER until Chapter 6, it'll be removed from the following figures for clarity.

Write Data into a Buffer Object (gl.bufferData())

Step 3 allocates storage and writes data to the buffer. You use gl.bufferData() to do this, as shown at line 66:

```
66   gl.bufferData(gl.ARRAY_BUFFER, vertices, gl.STATIC_DRAW);
```

This method writes the data specified by the second parameter (vertices) into the buffer object bound to the first parameter (gl.ARRAY_BUFFER). After executing line 66, the internal state of the WebGL system changes, as shown in Figure 3.8.

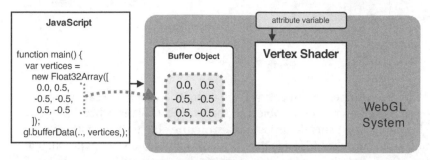

Figure 3.8 Allocate storage and write data into a buffer object

You can see in this figure that the vertex data defined in your JavaScript program is written to the buffer object bound to gl.ARRAY_BUFFER. The following table shows the specification of gl.bufferData().

---

gl.bufferData(target, data, usage)

Allocate storage and write the data specified by *data* to the buffer object bound to *target*.

Parameters	target	Specifies gl.ARRAY_BUFFER or gl.ELEMENT_ARRAY_BUFFER.
	data	Specifies the data to be written to the buffer object (typed array; see the next section).
	usage	Specifies a hint about how the program is going to use the data stored in the buffer object. This hint helps WebGL optimize performance but will not stop your program from working if you get it wrong.
	gl.STATIC_DRAW	The buffer object data will be specified once and used many times to draw shapes.
	gl.STREAM_DRAW	The buffer object data will be specified once and used a few times to draw shapes.
	gl.DYNAMIC_DRAW	The buffer object data will be specified repeatedly and used many times to draw shapes.
Return value	None	
Errors	INVALID_ENUM	*target* is none of the preceding constants

Now, let us examine what data is passed to the buffer object using gl.bufferData(). This method uses the special array vertices mentioned earlier to pass data to the vertex shader. The array is created at line 51 using the new operator with the data arranged as <x coordinate and y coordinate of the first vertex>, <x coordinate and y coordinate of the second vertex>, and so on:

```
51   var vertices = new Float32Array([
52     0.0, 0.5,   -0.5, -0.5,   0.5, -0.5
53   ]);
54   var n = 3; // The number of vertices
```

As you can see in the preceding code snippet, you are using the `Float32Array` object instead of the more usual JavaScript `Array` object to store the data. This is because the standard array in JavaScript is a general-purpose data structure able to hold both numeric data and strings but isn't optimized for large quantities of data of the same type, such as `vertices`. To address this issue, the typed array, of which one example is `Float32Array`, has been introduced.

Typed Arrays

WebGL often deals with large quantities of data of the same type, such as vertex coordinates and colors, for drawing 3D objects. For optimization purposes, a special type of array (**typed array**) has been introduced for each data type. Because the type of data in the array is known in advance, it can be handled efficiently.

`Float32Array` at line 51 is an example of a typed array and is generally used to store vertex coordinates or colors. It's important to remember that a typed array is expected by WebGL and is needed for many operations, such as the second parameter *data* of `gl.bufferData()`.

Table 3.1 shows the different typed arrays available. The third column shows the corresponding data type in C as a reference for those of you familiar with the C language.

Table 3.1 Typed Arrays Used in WebGL

Typed Array	Number of Bytes per Element	Description (C Types)
Int8Array	1	8-bit signed integer (signed char)
Uint8Array	1	8-bit unsigned integer (unsigned char)
Int16Array	2	16-bit signed integer (signed short)
Uint16Array	2	16-bit unsigned integer (unsigned short)
Int32Array	4	32-bit signed integer (signed int)
Uint32Array	4	32-bit unsigned integer (unsigned int)
Float32Array	4	32-bit floating point number (float)
Float64Array	8	64-bit floating point number (double)

Like JavaScript, these typed arrays have a set of methods, a property, and a constant available that are shown in Table 3.2. Note that, unlike the standard `Array` object in JavaScript, the methods `push()` and `pop()` are not supported.

Table 3.2 Methods, Property, Constant of Typed Arrays

Methods, Properties, and Constants	Description
get(index)	Get the *index*-th element
set(index, value)	Set *value* to the *index*-th element
set(array, offset)	Set the elements of *array* from *offset*-th element
length	The length of the array
BYTES_PER_ELEMENT	The number of bytes per element in the array

Just like standard arrays, the new operator creates a typed array and is passed the array data. For example, to create Float32Array vertices, you could pass the array [0.0, 0.5, -0.5, -0.5, 0.5, -0.5], which represents a set of vertices. Note that the only way to create a typed array is by using the new operator. Unlike the Array object, the [] operator is not supported:

```
51    var vertices = new Float32Array([
52      0.0, 0.5,   -0.5, -0.5,   0.5, -0.5
53    ]);
```

In addition, just like a normal JavaScript array, an empty typed array can be created by specifying the number of elements of the array as an argument. For example:

```
var vertices = new Float32Array(4);
```

With that, you've completed the first three steps of the process to set up and use a buffer (that is, creating a buffer object in the WebGL system, binding the buffer object to a target, and then writing data into the buffer object). Let's now look at how to actually use the buffer, which takes place in steps 4 and 5 of the process.

Assign the Buffer Object to an Attribute Variable (gl.vertexAttribPointer())

As explained in Chapter 2, you can use gl.vertexAttrib[1234]f() to assign data to an attribute variable. However, these methods can only be used to assign a single data value to an attribute variable. What you need here is a way to assign an array of values—the vertices in this case—to an attribute variable.

gl.vertexAttribPointer() solves this problem and can be used to assign a buffer object (actually a reference or handle to the buffer object) to an attribute variable. This can be seen at line 74 when you assign a buffer object to the attribute variable a_Position:

```
74    gl.vertexAttribPointer(a_Position, 2, gl.FLOAT, false, 0, 0);
```

The specification of gl.vertexAttribPointer() is as follows.

```
gl.vertexAttribPointer(location, size, type, normalized, stride,
offset)
```

Assign the buffer object bound to `gl.ARRAY_BUFFER` to the attribute variable specified by *location*.

Parameters	location	Specifies the storage location of an attribute variable.
	size	Specifies the number of components per vertex in the buffer object (valid values are 1 to 4). If *size* is less than the number of components required by the attribute variable, the missing components are automatically supplied just like `gl.vertexAttrib[1234]f()`.
		For example, if *size* is 1, the second and third components will be set to 0, and the fourth component will be set to 1.
	type	Specifies the data format using one of the following:

`gl.UNSIGNED_BYTE`	unsigned byte	for `Uint8Array`
`gl.SHORT`	signed short integer	for `Int16Array`
`gl.UNSIGNED_SHORT`	unsigned short integer	for `Uint16Array`
`gl.INT`	signed integer	for `Int32Array`
`gl.UNSIGNED_INT`	unsigned integer	for `Uint32Array`
`gl.FLOAT`	floating point number	for `Float32Array`

	normalized	Either `true` or `false` to indicate whether nonfloating data should be normalized to [0, 1] or [−1, 1].
	stride	Specifies the number of bytes between different vertex data elements, or zero for default stride (see Chapter 4).
	offset	Specifies the offset (in bytes) in a buffer object to indicate what number-th byte the vertex data is stored from. If the data is stored from the beginning, *offset* is 0.

Return value	None	
Errors	INVALID_OPERATION	There is no current program object.
	INVALID_VALUE	*location* is greater than or equal to the maximum number of attribute variables (8, by default). *stride* or *offset* is a negative value.

So, after executing this fourth step, the preparations are nearly completed in the WebGL system for using the buffer object at the attribute variable specified by *location*. As you can see in Figure 3.9, although the buffer object has been assigned to the attribute variable, WebGL requires a final step to "enable" the assignment and make the final connection.

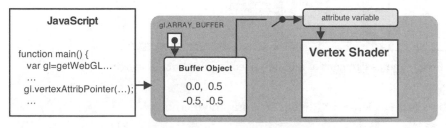

Figure 3.9　Assign a buffer object to an attribute variable

The fifth and final step is to enable the assignment of the buffer object to the attribute variable.

Enable the Assignment to an Attribute Variable (gl.enableVertexAttribArray())

To make it possible to access a buffer object in a vertex shader, we need to enable the assignment of the buffer object to an attribute variable by using `gl.enableVertexAttrib-Array()` as shown in line 77:

```
77    gl.enableVertexAttribArray(a_Position);
```

The following shows the specification of `gl.enableVertexAttribArray()`. Note that we are using the method to handle a buffer even though the method name suggests it's only for use with "vertex arrays." This is not a problem and is simply a legacy from OpenGL.

gl.enableVertexAttribArray(location)		
Enable the assignment of a buffer object to the attribute variable specified by *location*.		
Parameters	location	Specifies the storage location of an attribute variable.
Return value	None	
Errors	INVALID_VALUE	*location* is greater than or equal to the maximum number of attribute variables (8 by default).

When you execute `gl.enableVertexAttribArray()` specifying an attribute variable that has been assigned a buffer object, the assignment is enabled, and the unconnected line is connected as shown in Figure 3.10.

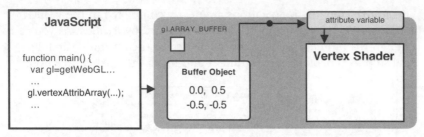

Figure 3.10 Enable the assignment of a buffer object to an attribute variable

You can also break this assignment (disable it) using the method
`gl.disableVertexAttribArray()`.

gl.disableVertexAttribArray(location)

Disable the assignment of a buffer object to the attribute variable specified by *location*.

Parameters	location	Specifies the storage location of an attribute variable.
Return Value	None	
Errors	INVALID_VALUE	*location* is greater than or equal to the maximum number of attribute variables (8 by default).

Now, everything is set! All you need to do is run the vertex shader, which draws the points using the vertex coordinates specified in the buffer object. As in Chapter 2, you will use the method `gl.drawArrays`, but because you are drawing multiple points, you will actually use the second and third parameters of `gl.drawArrays()`.

Note that after enabling the assignment, you can no longer use `gl.vertexAttrib[1234]` `f()` to assign data to the attribute variable. You have to explicitly disable the assignment of a buffer object. You can't use both methods simultaneously.

The Second and Third Parameters of gl.drawArrays()

Before entering into a detailed explanation of these parameters, let's take a look at the specification of `gl.drawArrays()` that was introduced in Chapter 2. Following is a recap of the method with only the relevant parts of the specification shown.

Execute a vertex shader to draw shapes specified by the *mode* parameter.

Parameters   mode   Specifies the type of shape to be drawn. The following symbolic constants are accepted: gl.POINTS, gl.LINES, gl.LINE_STRIP, gl. LINE_LOOP, gl.TRIANGLES, gl.TRIANGLE_STRIP, and gl.TRIANGLE_ FAN.

              first   Specifies what number-th vertex is used to draw from (integer).

           count   Specifies the number of vertices to be used (integer).

In the sample program this method is used as follows:

```
47   gl.drawArrays(gl.POINTS, 0, n); // n is 3
```

As in the previous examples, because you are simply drawing three points, the first parameter is still gl.POINTS. The second parameter *first* is set to 0 because you want to draw from the first coordinate in the buffer. The third parameter *count* is set to 3 because you want to draw three points (in line 47, n is 3).

When your program runs line 47, it actually causes the vertex shader to be executed *count* (three) times, sequentially passing the vertex coordinates stored in the buffer object via the attribute variable into the shader (Figure 3.11).

Note that for each execution of the vertex shader, 0.0 and 1.0 are automatically supplied to the z and w components of a_Position because a_Position requires four components (vec4) and you are supplying only two.

Remember that at line 74, the second parameter *size* of gl.vertexAttribPointer() is set to 2. As just discussed, the second parameter indicates how many coordinates per vertex are specified in the buffer object and, because you are only specifying the x and y coordinates in the buffer, you set the size value to 2:

```
74   gl.vertexAttribPointer(a_Position, 2, gl.FLOAT, false, 0, 0);
```

After drawing all points, the content of the color buffer is automatically displayed in the browser (bottom of Figure 3.11), resulting in our three red points, as shown in Figure 3.2.

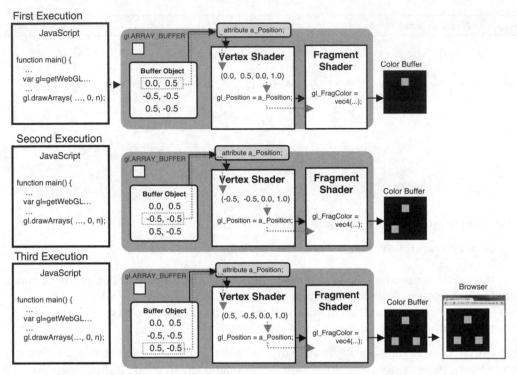

Figure 3.11 How the data in a buffer object is passed to a vertex shader during execution

Experimenting with the Sample Program

Let's experiment with the sample program to better understand how gl.drawArrays() works by modifying the second and third parameters. First, let's specify 1 as the third argument for *count* at line 47 instead of our variable n (set to 3) as follows:

```
47  gl.drawArrays(gl.POINTS, 0, 1);
```

In this case, the vertex shader is executed only once, and a single point is drawn using the first vertex in the buffer object.

If you now specify 1 as the second argument, only the second vertex is used to draw a point. This is because you are telling WebGL that you want to start drawing from the second vertex and you only want to draw one vertex. So again, you will see only a single point, although this time it is the second vertex coordinates that are shown in the browser:

```
47  gl.drawArrays(gl.POINTS, 1, 1);
```

This gives you a quick feel for the role of the parameters *first* and *count*. However, what will be happen if you change the first parameter *mode*? The next section explores the first parameter in more detail.

Hello Triangle

Now that you've learned the basic techniques to pass multiple vertex coordinates to a vertex shader, let's try to draw other shapes using multiple vertex coordinates. This section uses a sample program HelloTriangle, which draws a single 2D triangle. Figure 3.12 shows a screenshot of HelloTriangle.

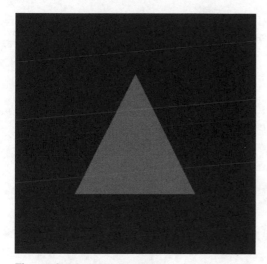

Figure 3.12　HelloTriangle

Sample Program (HelloTriangle.js)

Listing 3.3 shows HelloTriangle.js, which is almost identical to MultiPoint.js used in the previous section with two critical differences.

Listing 3.3　HelloTriangle.js

```
1 // HelloTriangle.js
2 // Vertex shader program
3 var VSHADER_SOURCE =
4   'attribute vec4 a_Position;\n' +
5   'void main() {\n' +
6   '  gl_Position = a_Position;\n' +
7   '}\n';
8
```

```
 9 // Fragment shader program
10 var FSHADER_SOURCE =
11   'void main() {\n' +
12   '  gl_FragColor = vec4(1.0, 0.0, 0.0, 1.0);\n' +
13   '}\n';
14
15 function main() {
   ...
19   // Get the rendering context for WebGL
20   var gl = getWebGLContext(canvas);
   ...
26   // Initialize shaders
27   if (!initShaders(gl, VSHADER_SOURCE, FSHADER_SOURCE)) {
   ...
30   }
31
32   // Set the positions of vertices
33   var n = initVertexBuffers(gl);
...
39   // Set the color for clearing <canvas>
   ...
45   // Draw a triangle
46   gl.drawArrays(gl.TRIANGLES, 0, n);
47 }
48
49 function initVertexBuffers(gl) {
50   var vertices = new Float32Array([
51     0.0, 0.5,   -0.5, -0.5,   0.5, -0.5
52   ]);
53   var n = 3; // The number of vertices
   ...
78   return n;
79 }
```

The two differences from `MultiPoint.js` are

- The line to specify the size of a point `gl_PointSize = 10.0;` has been removed from the vertex shader. This line only has an effect when you are drawing a point.

- The first parameter of `gl.drawArrays()` has been changed from `gl.POINTS` to `gl.TRIANGLES` at line 46.

The first parameter, *mode,* of `gl.drawArrays()` is powerful and provides the ability to draw various shapes. Let's take a look.

Basic Shapes

By changing the argument we use for the first parameter, *mode,* of `gl.drawArrays()`, we can change the meaning of line 46 into "execute the vertex shader three times (n is 3), and draw a triangle using the three vertices in the buffer, starting from the first vertex coordinate":

```
46   gl.drawArrays(gl.TRIANGLES, 0, n);
```

In this case, the three vertices in the buffer object are no longer individual points, but become three vertices of a triangle.

The WebGL method `gl.drawArrays()` is both powerful and flexible, allowing you to specify seven different types of basic shapes as the first argument. These are explained in more detail in Table 3.3. Note that v0, v1, v2 ... indicates the vertices specified in a buffer object. The order of vertices affects the drawing of the shape.

The shapes in the table are the only ones that WebGL can draw directly, but they are the basics needed to construct complex 3D graphics. (Remember the frog at the start of this chapter.)

Table 3.3 Basic Shapes Available in WebGL

Basic Shape	Mode	Description
Points	`gl.POINTS`	A series of points. The points are drawn at v0, v1, v2 ...
Line segments	`gl.LINES`	A series of unconnected line segments. The individual lines are drawn between vertices given by (v0, v1), (v2, v3), (v4, v5)... If the number of vertices is odd, the last one is ignored.
Line strips	`gl.LINE_STRIP`	A series of connected line segments. The line segments are drawn between vertices given by (v0, v1), (v1, v2), (v2, v3), ... The first vertex becomes the start point of the first line, the second vertex becomes the end point of the first line and the start point of the second line, and so on. The *i*-th (*i*> 1) vertex becomes the start point of the *i*-th line and the end point of the *i-1*-th line. (The last vertex becomes the end point of the last line.)
Line loops	`gl.LINE_LOOP`	A series of connected line segments. In addition to the lines drawn by `gl.LINE_STRIP`, the line between the last vertex and the first vertex is drawn. The line segments drawn are (v0, v1), (v1, v2), ..., and (vn, v0). vn is the last vertex.
Triangles	`gl.TRIANGLES`	A series of separate triangles. The triangles given by vertices (v0, v1, v2), (v3, v4, v5), ... are drawn. If the number of vertices is not a multiple of 3, the remaining vertices are ignored.

Basic Shape	Mode	Description
Triangle strips	gl.TRIANGLE_ STRIP	A series of connected triangles in strip fashion. The first three vertices form the first triangle and the second triangle is formed from the next vertex and one of the sides of the first triangle. The triangles are drawn given by (v0, v1, v2), (v2, v1, v3), (v2, v3, v4) ... (Pay attention to the order of vertices.)
Triangle fans	gl.TRIANGLE_ FAN	A series of connected triangles sharing the first vertex in fan-like fashion. The first three vertices form the first triangle and the second triangle is formed from the next vertex, one of the sides of the first triangle, and the first vertex. The triangles are drawn given by (v0, v1, v2), (v0, v2, v3), (v0, v3, v4), ...

Figure 3.13 shows these basic shapes.

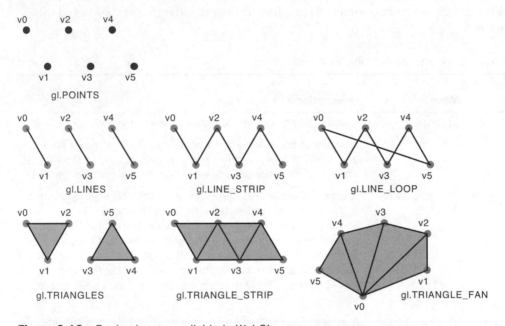

Figure 3.13 Basic shapes available in WebGL

As you can see from the figure, WebGL can draw only three types of shapes: a point, a line, and a triangle. However, as explained at the beginning of this chapter, spheres to cubes to 3D monsters to humanoid characters in a game can be constructed from small triangles. Therefore, you can use these basic shapes to draw anything.

Experimenting with the Sample Program

To examine what will happen when using gl.LINES, gl.LINE_STRIP, and gl.LINE_LOOP, let's change the first argument of gl.drawArrays() as shown next. The name of each sample program is HelloTriangle_LINES, HelloTriangle_LINE_STRIP, and HelloTriangle_LINE_LOOP, respectively:

```
46    gl.drawArrays(gl.LINES, 0, n);
46    gl.drawArrays(gl.LINE_STRIP, 0, n);
46    gl.drawArrays(gl.LINE_LOOP, 0, n);
```

Figure 3.14 shows a screenshot of each program.

Figure 3.14   gl.LINES, gl.LINE_STRIP, and gl.LINE_LOOP

As you can see, gl.LINES draws a line using the first two vertices and does not use the last vertex, whereas gl.LINE_STRIP draws two lines using the first three vertices. Finally, gl.LINE_LOOP draws the lines in the same manner as gl.LINE_STRIP but then "loops" between the last vertex and the first vertex and makes a triangle.

Hello Rectangle (HelloQuad)

Let's use this basic way of drawing triangles to draw a rectangle. The name of the sample program is HelloQuad, and Figure 3.15 shows a screenshot when it's loaded into your browser.

Figure 3.16 shows the vertices of the rectangle. Of course, the number of vertices is four because it is a rectangle. As explained in the previous section, WebGL cannot draw a rectangle directly, so you need to divide the rectangle into two triangles (v0, v1, v2) and (v2, v1, v3) and then draw each one using gl.TRIANGLES, gl.TRIANGLE_STRIP, or gl.TRIANGLE_FAN. In this example, you'll use gl.TRIANGLE_STRIP because it only requires you to specify four vertices. If you were to use gl.TRIANGLES, you would need to specify a total of six.

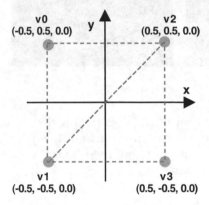

Figure 3.15 HelloQuad

Figure 3.16 The four vertex coordinates of the rectangle

Basing the example on `HelloTriangle.js`, you need to add an extra vertex coordinate at line 50. Pay attention to the order of vertices; otherwise, the draw command will not execute correctly:

```
50   var vertices = new Float32Array([
51      -0.5, 0.5,   -0.5, -0.5,   0.5, 0.5,   0.5, -0.5
52   ]);
```

Because you've added a fourth vertex, you need to change the number of vertices from 3 to 4 at line 53:

```
53   var n = 4; // The number of vertices
```

Then, by modifying line 46 as follows, your program will draw a rectangle in the browser:

```
46    gl.drawArrays(gl.TRIANGLE_STRIP, 0, n);
```

Experimenting with the Sample Program

Now that you have a feel for how to use `gl.TRIANGLE_STRIP`, let's change the first parameter of `gl.drawArrays()` to `gl.TRIANGLE_FAN`. The name of the sample program is `HelloQuad_FAN`:

```
46    gl.drawArrays(gl.TRIANGLE_FAN, 0, n);
```

Figure 3.17 show a screenshot of `HelloQuad_FAN`. In this case, we can see the ribbon-like shape on the screen.

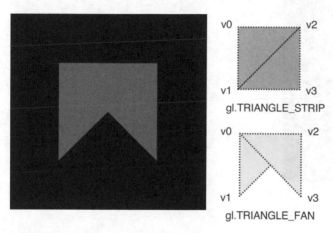

Figure 3.17   HelloQuad_FAN

Looking at the order of vertices and the triangles drawn by `gl.TRIANGLE_FAN` shown on the right side of Figure 3.17, you can see why the result became a ribbon-like shape. Essentially, `gl.TRIANGLE_FAN` causes WebGL to draw a second triangle that shares the first vertex (v0), and this second triangle overlaps the first, creating the ribbon-like effect.

Moving, Rotating, and Scaling

Now that you understand the basics of drawing shapes like triangles and rectangles, let's take another step and try to move (translate), rotate, and scale the triangle and display the results on the screen. These operations are called **transformations (affine transformations)**. This section introduces some math to explain each transformation and help you to understand how each operation can be realized. However, when you write your own programs, you don't need the math; instead, you can use one of several convenient libraries, explained in the next section, that handle the math for you.

If you find reading this section and in particular the math too much on first read, it's okay to skip it and return later. Or, if you already know that transformations can be written using a matrix, you can skip this section as well.

First, let's write a sample program, `TranslatedTriangle`, that moves a triangle 0.5 units to the right and 0.5 units up. You can use the triangle you drew in the previous section. The right direction means the positive direction of the x-axis, and the up direction means the positive direction of the y-axis. (See the coordinate system in Chapter 2.) Figure 3.18 shows `TranslatedTriangle`.

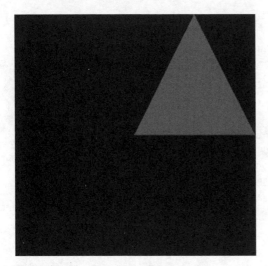

Figure 3.18   TranslatedTriangle

Translation

Let us examine what kind of operations you need to apply to each vertex coordinate of a shape to translate (move) the shape. Essentially, you just need to add a translation distance for each direction (x and y) to each component of the coordinates. Looking at Figure 3.19, the goal is to translate the point p (x, y, z) to the point p' (x', y', z'), so the translation distance for the x, y, and z direction is Tx, Ty, and Tz, respectively. In this figure, Tz is 0.

To determine the coordinates of p', you simply add the T values, as shown in Equation 3.1.

Equation 3.1

$$x' = x + Tx$$

$$y' = y + Ty$$

$$z' = z + Tz$$

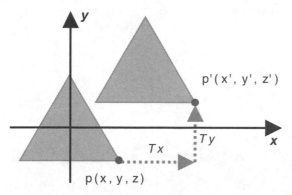

Figure 3.19 Calculating translation distances

These simple equations can be implemented in a WebGL program just by adding each constant value to each vertex coordinate. You've probably realized already that because they are a **per-vertex operation**, you need to implement the operations in a vertex shader. Conversely, they clearly aren't a per-fragment operation, so you don't need to worry about the fragment shader.

Once you understand this explanation, implementation is easy. You need to pass the translation distances Tx, Ty, and Tz to the vertex shader, apply Equation 3.1 using the distances, and then assign the result to gl_Position. Let's look at a sample program that does this.

Sample Program (TranslatedTriangle.js)

Listing 3.4 shows TranslatedTriangle.js, in which the vertex shader is partially modified to carry out the translation operation. However, the fragment shader is the same as in HelloTriangle.js in the previous section. To support the modification to the vertex shader, some extra code is added to the main() function in the JavaScript.

Listing 3.4   TranslatedTriangle.js

```
1 // TranslatedTriangle.js
2 // Vertex shader program
3 var VSHADER_SOURCE =
4    'attribute vec4 a_Position;\n' +
5    'uniform vec4 u_Translation;\n' +
6    'void main() {\n' +
7    '  gl_Position = a_Position + u_Translation;\n' +
8    '}\n';
9
10 // Fragment shader program
   ...
```

```
16 // The translation distance for x, y, and z direction
17 var Tx = 0.5, Ty = 0.5, Tz = 0.0;
18
19 function main() {
   ...
23   // Get the rendering context for WebGL
24   var gl = getWebGLContext(canvas);
   ...
30   // Initialize shaders
31   if (!initShaders(gl, VSHADER_SOURCE, FSHADER_SOURCE)) {
   ...
34   }
35
36   // Set the positions of vertices
37   var n = initVertexBuffers(gl);
   ...
43   // Pass the translation distance to the vertex shader
44   var u_Translation = gl.getUniformLocation(gl.program, 'u_Translation');
   ...
49   gl.uniform4f(u_Translation, Tx, Ty, Tz, 0.0);
50
51   // Set the color for clearing <canvas>
   ...
57   // Draw a triangle
58   gl.drawArrays(gl.TRIANGLES, 0, n);
59 }
60
61 function initVertexBuffers(gl) {
62   var vertices = new Float32Array([
63     0.0.0, 0.5,   -0.5, -0.5,   0.5, -0.5
64   ]);
65   var n = 3; // The number of vertices
   ...
90   return n;
93 }
```

First, let's examine `main()` in JavaScript. Line 17 defines the variables for each translation distance of Equation 3.1:

```
17 var Tx = 0.5, Ty = 0.5, Tz = 0.0;
```

Because `Tx`, `Ty`, and `Tz` are fixed (uniform) values for all vertices, you use the uniform variable `u_Translation` to pass them to a vertex shader. Line 44 retrieves the storage location of the uniform variable, and line 49 assigns the data to the variable:

```
44    var u_Translation = gl.getUniformLocation(gl.program, 'u_Translation');
      ...
49    gl.uniform4f(u_Translation, Tx, Ty, Tz, 0.0);
```

Note that gl.uniform4f() requires a homogenous coordinate, so we supply a fourth argument (w) of 0.0. This will be explained in more detail later in this section.

Now, let's take a look at the vertex shader that uses this translation data. As you can see, the uniform variable u_Translation in the shader, to which the translation distances are passed, is defined as type vec4 at line 5. This is because you want to add the components of u_Translation to the vertex coordinates passed to a_Position (as defined by Equation 3.1) and then assign the result to the variable gl_Position, which has type vec4. Remember, per Chapter 2, that the assignment operation in GLSL ES is only allowed between variables of the same types:

```
4    'attribute vec4 a_Position;\n' +
5    'uniform vec4 u_Translation;\n' +
6    'void main() {\n' +
7    '  gl_Position = a_Position + u_Translation;\n' +
8    '}\n';
```

After these preparations have been completed, the rest of tasks are straightforward. To calculate Equation 3.1 within the vertex shader, you just add each translation distance (Tx, Ty, Tz) passed in u_Translation to each vertex coordinate (x, y, z) passed in a_Position.

Because both variables are of type vec4, you can use the + operator, which will actually add the four components simultaneously (see Figure 3.20). This easy addition of vectors is a feature of GLSL ES and will be explained in more detail in Chapter 6.

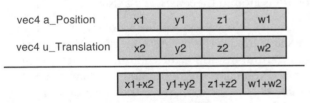

Figure 3.20 Addition of vec4 variables

Now, we'll return to the fourth element, (w), of the vector. As explained in Chapter 2, you need to specify the homogeneous coordinate to gl_Position, which is a four-dimensional coordinate. If the last component of the homogeneous coordinate is 1.0, the coordinate indicates the same position as the three-dimensional coordinate. In this case, because the last component is w1+w2 to ensure that w1+w2 is 1.0, you need to specify 0.0 to the value of w (the fourth parameter of gl.uniform4f()).

Finally, at line 58, `gl.drawArrays(gl.TRIANGLES, 0, n)` executes the vertex shader. For each execution, the following three steps are performed:

1. Each vertex coordinate set is passed to `a_Position`.

2. `u_Translation` is added to `a_Position`.

3. The result is assigned to `gl_Position`.

Once executed, you've achieved your goal because each vertex coordinate set is modified (translated), and then the translated shape (in this case, a triangle) is displayed on the screen. If you now load `TranslatedTriangle.html` into your browser, you will see the translated triangle.

Now that you've mastered translation (moving), the next step is to look at rotation. The basic approach to realize rotation is the same as translation, requiring you to manipulate the vertex coordinates in the vertex shader.

Rotation

Rotation is a little more complex than translation because you have to specify multiple items of information. The following three items are required:

- Rotation axis (the axis the shape will be rotated around)
- Rotation direction (the direction: clockwise or counterclockwise)
- Rotation angle (the number of degrees the shape will be rotated through)

In this section, to simplify the explanation, you can assume that the rotation is performed around the z-axis, in a counterclockwise direction, and for β degrees. You can use the same approach to implement other rotations around the x-axis or y-axis.

In the rotation, if β is positive, the rotation is performed in a counterclockwise direction around the rotation axis looking at the shape toward the negative direction of the z-axis (see Figure 3.21); this is called **positive rotation**. Just as for the coordinate system, your hand can define the direction of rotation. If you take your right hand and have your thumb follow the direction of the rotation axis, your fingers show the direction of rotation. This is called the **right-hand-rule rotation**. As we discussed in Chapter 2, it's the default we are using for WebGL in this book.

Now let's find the expression to calculate the rotation in the same way that you did for translation. As shown in Figure 3.22, we assume that the point p' (x', y', z') is the β degree rotated point of p (x, y, z) around the z-axis. Because the rotation is around the z-axis, the z coordinate does not change, and you can ignore it for now. The explanation is a little mathematical, so let's take it a step at a time.

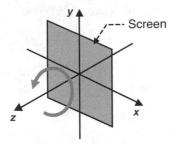

Figure 3.21 Positive rotation around the z-axis

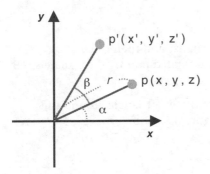

Figure 3.22 Calculating rotation around the z-axis

In Figure 3.22, r is the distance from the origin to the point p, and α is the rotation angle from the x-axis to the point. You can use these items of information to represent the coordinates of p, as shown in Equation 3.2.

Equation 3.2

$$x = r \cos \alpha$$

$$y = r \sin \alpha$$

Similarly, you can find the coordinate of p' by using r, α, and β as follows:

$$x' = r \cos (\alpha + \beta)$$

$$y' = r \sin (\alpha + \beta)$$

Then you can use the addition theorem of trigonometric functions[1] to get the following:

$$x' = r\ (\cos \alpha \cos \beta - \sin \alpha \sin \beta)$$

$$y' = r\ (\sin \alpha \cos \beta + \cos \alpha \sin \beta)$$

Finally, you get the following expressions (Equation 3.3) by assigning Equation 3.2 to the previous expressions and removing r and α.

Equation 3.3

$$x' = x \cos \beta - y \sin \beta$$

$$y' = x \sin \beta + y \cos \beta$$

$$z' = z$$

So by passing the values of $\sin \beta$ and $\cos \beta$ to the vertex shader and then calculating Equation 3.3 in the shader, you get the coordinates of the rotated point. To calculate $\sin \beta$ and $\cos \beta$, you can use the methods of the JavaScript `Math` object.

Let's look at a sample program, `RotatedTriangle`, which rotates a triangle around the z-axis, in a counterclockwise direction, by 90 degrees. Figure 3.23 shows `RotatedTriangle`.

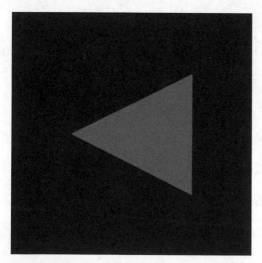

Figure 3.23 RotatedTriangle

---

[1] $\sin(a \pm b) = \sin a \cos b \mp \cos a \sin b$
$\cos(a \pm b) = \cos a \cos b \mp \sin a \sin b$

Sample Program (RotatedTriangle.js)

Listing 3.5 shows RotatedTriangle.js which, in a similar manner to TranslatedTriangle.js, modifies the vertex shader to carry out the rotation operation. The fragment shader is the same as in TranslatedTriangle.js and, as usual, is not shown. Again, to support the shader modification, several processing steps are added to main() in the JavaScript program. Additionally, Equation 3.3 is added in the comments from lines 4 to 6 to remind you of the calculation needed.

Listing 3.5 RotatedTriangle.js

```
1   // RotatedTriangle.js
2   // Vertex shader program
3   var VSHADER_SOURCE =
4   // x' = x cos b - y sin b
5   // y' = x sin b + y cos b                          Equation 3.3
6   // z' = z
7   'attribute vec4 a_Position;\n' +
8   'uniform float u_CosB, u_SinB;\n' +
9   'void main() {\n' +
10  '  gl_Position.x = a_Position.x * u_CosB - a_Position.y *u_SinB;\n'+
11  '  gl_Position.y = a_Position.x * u_SinB + a_Position.y * u_CosB;\n'+
12  '  gl_Position.z = a_Position.z;\n' +
13  '  gl_Position.w = 1.0;\n' +
14  '}\n';
15
16  // Fragment shader program
    ...
22  // Rotation angle
23  var ANGLE = 90.0;
24
25  function main() {
      ...
42    // Set the positions of vertices
43    var n = initVertexBuffers(gl);
      ...
49    // Pass the data required to rotate the shape to the vertex shader
50    var radian = Math.PI * ANGLE / 180.0; // Convert to radians
51    var cosB = Math.cos(radian);
52    var sinB = Math.sin(radian);
53
54    var u_CosB = gl.getUniformLocation(gl.program, 'u_CosB');
55    var u_SinB = gl.getUniformLocation(gl.program, 'u_SinB');
      ...
```

```
60   gl.uniform1f(u_CosB, cosB);
61   gl.uniform1f(u_SinB, sinB);
62
63    // Set the color for clearing <canvas>
        ...
69    // Draw a triangle
70    gl.drawArrays(gl.TRIANGLES, 0, n);
71  }
72
73  function initVertexBuffers(gl) {
74    var vertices = new Float32Array([
75       0.0, 0.5,    -0.5, -0.5,    0.5, -0.5
76    ]);
77    var n = 3; // The number of vertices
        ...
105    return n;
106  }
```

Let's look at the vertex shader, which is straightforward:

```
2   // Vertex shader program
3   var VSHADER_SOURCE =
4    // x' = x cos b - y sin b
5    // y' = x sin b + y cos b
6    // z' = z
7    'attribute vec4 a_Position;\n' +
8    'uniform float u_CosB, u_SinB;\n' +
9    'void main() {\n' +
10   '  gl_Position.x = a_Position.x * u_CosB - a_Position.y * u_SinB;\n'+
11   '  gl_Position.y = a_Position.x * u_SinB + a_Position.y * u_CosB;\n'+
12   '  gl_Position.z = a_Position.z;\n' +
13   '  gl_Position.w = 1.0;\n' +
14   '}\n';
```

Because the goal is to rotate the triangle by 90 degrees, the sine and cosine of 90 need to be calculated. Line 8 defines two uniform variables for receiving these values, which are calculated in the JavaScript program and then passed to the vertex shader.

You could pass the rotation angle to the vertex shader and then calculate the values of sine and cosine in the shader. However, because they are identical for all vertices, it is more efficient to do it once in the JavaScript.

The name of these uniform variables, u_CosB and u_SinB, are defined following the naming rule used throughout this book. As you will remember, you use the uniform variable because the values of these variables are uniform (unchanging) per vertex.

As in the previous sample programs, x, y, z, and w are passed in a group to the attribute variable a_Position in the vertex shader. To apply Equation 3.3 to x, y, and z, you need to access each component in a_Position separately. You can do this easily using the. operator, such as a_Position.x, a_Position.y, and a_Position.z (see Figure 3.24 and Chapter 6).

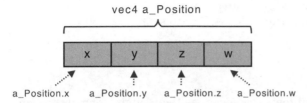

Figure 3.24 Access methods for each component in a vec4

Handily, you can use the same operator to access each component in gl_Position to which the vertex coordinate is written, so you can calculate x' = x cos β – y sin β from Equation 3.3 as shown at line 10:

```
10   '  gl_Position.x = a_Position.x * u_CosB - a_Position.y * u_SinB;\n'+
```

Similarly, you can calculate y' as follows:

```
11   '  gl_Position.y = a_Position.x * u_SinB + a_Position.y * u_CosB;\n'+
```

According to Equation 3.3, you just need to assign the original z coordinate to z' directly at line 12. Finally, you need to assign 1.0 to the last component w[2]:

```
12   '  gl_Position.z = a_Position.z;\n' +
13   '  gl_Position.w = 1.0;\n' +
```

Now look at main() in the JavaScript code, which starts from line 25. This code is mostly the same as in TranslatedTriangle.js. The only difference is passing cos β and sin β to the vertex shader. To calculate the sine and cosine of β, you can use the JavaScript Math. sin() and Math.cos() methods. However, these methods expect parameters in radians, not degrees, so you need to convert from degrees to radians by multiplying the number of degrees by pi and then dividing by 180. You can utilize Math.PI as the value of pi as shown at line 50, where the variable ANGLE is defined as 90 (degrees) at line 23:

```
50   var radian = Math.PI * ANGLE / 180.0; // Converts degrees to radians
```

---

[2] In this program, you can also write gl_Position.w = a_Position.w; because a_Position.w is 1.0.

Once you have the angle in radians, lines 51 and 52 calculate cos β and sin β, and then lines 60 and 61 pass them to the uniform variables in the vertex shader:

```
51    var cosB = Math.cos(radian);
52    var sinB = Math.sin(radian);
53
54    var u_CosB = gl.getUniformLocation(gl.program, 'u_CosB');
55    var u_SinB = gl.getUniformLocation(gl.program, 'u_SinB');
      ...
60    gl.uniform1f(u_CosB, cosB);
61    gl.uniform1f(u_SinB, sinB);
```

When you load this program into your browser, you can see the triangle, rotated through 90 degrees, on the screen. If you specify a negative value to ANGLE, you can rotate the triangle in the opposite direction (clockwise). You can also use the same equation. For example, to rotate the triangle in the clockwise direction, you can specify –90 instead of 90 at line 23, and Math.cos() and Math.sin() will deal with the remaining tasks for you.

For those of you concerned with speed and efficiency, the approach taken here (using two uniform variables to pass the values of cos β and sin β) isn't optimal. To pass the values as a group, you can define the uniform variable as follows:

```
uniform vec2 u_CosBSinB;
```

and then pass the values by:

```
gl.uniform2f(u_CosBSinB,cosB, sinB);
```

Then in the vertex shader, you can access them using u_CosBSinB.x and u_CosBSinB.y.

Transformation Matrix: Rotation

For simple transformations, you can use mathematical expressions. However, as your needs become more complex, you'll quickly find that applying a series of equations becomes quite complex. For example a "translation after rotation" as shown in Figure 3.25 can be realized by using Equations 3.1 and 3.3 to find the new mathematical expressions for the transformation and then implementing them in a vertex shader.

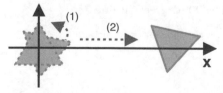

Figure 3.25 Rotate first and then translate a triangle

However, it is time consuming to determine the mathematical expressions every time you need a new set of transformation and then implement them in a vertex shader. Fortunately, there is another tool in the mathematical toolbox, the **transformation matrix**, which is excellent for manipulating computer graphics.

As shown in Figure 3.26, a matrix is a rectangular array of numbers arranged in rows (in the horizontal direction) and columns (in the vertical direction). This notation makes it easy to write the calculations explained in the previous sections. The brackets indicate that these numbers are a group.

$$\begin{bmatrix} 8 & 3 & 0 \\ 4 & 3 & 6 \\ 3 & 2 & 6 \end{bmatrix}$$

Figure 3.26 Example of a matrix

Before explaining the details of how to use a transformation matrix to replace the equations used here, you need to make sure you understand the multiplication of a matrix and a vector. A vector is an object represented by an n-tuple of numbers, such as the vertex coordinates (0.0, 0.5, 1.0).

The multiplication of a matrix and a vector can be written as shown in Equation 3.4. (Although the multiply operator × is often omitted, we explicitly write the operator in this book for clarity.) Here, our new vector (on the left) is the result of multiplying a matrix (in the center) by our original vector (on the right). Note that matrix multiplication is noncommutative. In other words, A × B is not the same as B × A. We discuss this further in Chapter 6.

Equation 3.4

$$\begin{bmatrix} x' \\ y' \\ z' \end{bmatrix} = \begin{bmatrix} a & b & c \\ d & e & f \\ g & h & i \end{bmatrix} \times \begin{bmatrix} x \\ y \\ z \end{bmatrix}$$

This matrix has three rows and three columns and is called a 3×3 matrix. The rightmost part of the equation is a vector composed of x, y, and z. (In the case of a multiplication of a matrix and vector, the vector is written vertically, but it has the same meaning as when it is written horizontally.) This vector has three elements, so it is called a three-dimensional vector. Again, the brackets on both sides of the array of numbers (vector) are also just notation for recognizing that these numbers are a group.

In this case, x', y', and z' are defined using the elements of the matrix and the vector, as shown by Equation 3.5. Note that the multiplication of a matrix and vector can be defined only if the number of columns in a matrix matches the number of rows in a vector.

Equation 3.5

$$x' = ax + by + cz$$

$$y' = dx + ey + fz$$

$$z' = gx + hy + iz$$

Now, to understand how to use a matrix instead of our original equations, let's compare the matrix equations and Equation 3.3 (shown again as Equation 3.6).

Equation 3.6

$$x' = x \cos \beta - y \sin \beta$$

$$y' = x \sin \beta + y \cos \beta$$

$$z' = z$$

For example, compare the equation for x':

$$x' = ax + by + cz$$

$$x' = x \cos \beta - y \sin \beta$$

In this case, if you set a = cos β, b = -sin β, and c = 0, the equations become the same. Similarly, let us compare the equation for y':

$$y' = dx + ey + fz$$

$$y' = x \sin \beta + y \cos \beta$$

In this case, if you set d = sin β, e = cos β, and f = 0, you get the same equation. The last equation about z' is easy. If you set g = 0, h = 0, and i = 1, you get the same equation.

Then, by assigning these results to Equation 3.4, you get Equation 3.7.

Equation 3.7

$$\begin{bmatrix} x' \\ y' \\ z' \end{bmatrix} = \begin{bmatrix} \cos\beta & -\sin\beta & 0 \\ \sin\beta & \cos\beta & 0 \\ 0 & 0 & 1 \end{bmatrix} \times \begin{bmatrix} x \\ y \\ z \end{bmatrix}$$

This matrix is called a **transformation matrix** because it "transforms" the right-side vector (x, y, z) to the left-side vector (x', y', z'). The transformation matrix representing a rotation is called a **rotation matrix**.

You can see that the elements of the matrix in Equation 3.7 are an array of coefficients in Equation 3.6. Once you become accustomed to matrix notation, it is easier to write and use matrices than to have to deal with a set of transformation equations.

As you would expect, because matrices are used so often in 3DCG, multiplication of a matrix and a vector is easy to implement in shaders. However, before exploring how, let's quickly look at other types of transformation matrices, and then we will start to use them in shaders.

Transformation Matrix: Translation

Obviously, if we can use a transformation matrix to represent a rotation, we should be able to use it for other types of transformation, such as translation. For example, let us compare the equation for x' in Equation 3.1 to that in Equation 3.5 as follows:

x' = ax + by + cz   --- from Equation (3.5)

$x' = x + T_x$ --- from Equation (3.1)

Here, the second equation has the constant term T_x, but the first one does not, meaning that you cannot deal with the second one by using the 3×3 matrix of the first equation. To solve this problem, you can use a 4×4 matrix and the fourth components of the coordinate, which are set to 1 to introduce the constant terms. That is to say, we assume that the coordinates of point p are (x, y, z, 1), and the coordinates of the translated point p (p') are (x', y', z', 1). This gives us Equation 3.8.

Equation 3.8

$$\begin{bmatrix} x' \\ y' \\ z' \\ 1 \end{bmatrix} = \begin{bmatrix} a & b & c & d \\ e & f & g & h \\ i & j & k & l \\ m & n & o & p \end{bmatrix} \times \begin{bmatrix} x \\ y \\ z \\ 1 \end{bmatrix}$$

This multiplication is defined as follows:

Equation 3.9

$$x' = ax + by + cz + d$$

$$y' = ex + fy + gz + h$$

$$z' = ix + jy + kz + l$$

$$1 = mx + ny + oz + p$$

From the equation $1 = mx + ny + oz + p$, it is easy to find that the coefficients are $m = 0$, $n = 0$, $o = 0$, and $p = 1$. In addition, these equations have the constant terms d, h, and l, which look helpful to deal with Equation 3.1 because it also has constant terms. Let us compare Equation 3.9 and Equation 3.1 (translation), which is reproduced again:

$$x' = x + T_x$$

$$y' = y + T_y$$

$$z' = z + T_z$$

When you compare the x' component of both equations, you can see that a=1, b=0, c=0, and d=T_x. Similarly, when comparing y' from both equations, you find e = 0, f = 1, g = 0, and h = T_y; when comparing z' you see i=0, j=0, k=1, and l=T_z. You can use these results to write a matrix that represents a translation, called a **translation matrix**, as shown in Equation 3.10.

Equation 3.10

$$\begin{bmatrix} x' \\ y' \\ z' \\ 1 \end{bmatrix} = \begin{bmatrix} 1 & 0 & 0 & Tx \\ 0 & 1 & 0 & Ty \\ 0 & 0 & 1 & Tz \\ 0 & 0 & 0 & 1 \end{bmatrix} \times \begin{bmatrix} x \\ y \\ z \\ 1 \end{bmatrix}$$

Rotation Matrix, Again

At this stage you have successfully created a rotation and a translation matrix, which are equivalent to the two equations you used in the example programs earlier. The final step is to combine these two matrices; however, the rotation matrix (3×3 matrix) and transformation matrix (4×4 matrix) have different numbers of elements. Unfortunately, you cannot combine matrices of different sizes, so you need a mechanism to make them the same size.

To do that, you need to change the rotation matrix (3×3 matrix) into a 4×4 matrix. This is straightforward and requires you to find the coefficient of each equation in Equation 3.9 by comparing it with Equation 3.3. The following shows both equations:

$$x' = x \cos \beta - y \sin \beta$$

$$y' = x \sin \beta + y \cos \beta$$

$$z' = z$$

$$x' = ax + by + cz + d$$

$$y' = ex + fy + gz + h$$

$$z' = ix + iy + kz + l$$

$$1 = mx + ny + oz + p$$

For example, when you compare x' = x cos β – y sin β with x' = ax + by + cz +d, you find a = cos β, b = –sin β, c = 0, and d = 0. In the same way, after comparing in terms of y and z, you get the rotation matrix shown in Equation 3.11:

Equation 3.11

$$\begin{bmatrix} x' \\ y' \\ z' \\ 1 \end{bmatrix} = \begin{bmatrix} \cos\beta & -\sin\beta & 0 & 0 \\ \sin\beta & \cos\beta & 0 & 0 \\ 0 & 0 & 1 & 0 \\ 0 & 0 & 0 & 1 \end{bmatrix} \times \begin{bmatrix} x \\ y \\ z \\ 1 \end{bmatrix}$$

This allows you to represent both a rotation matrix and translation matrix in the same 4×4 matrix, achieving the original goal!

Sample Program (RotatedTriangle_Matrix.js)

Having constructed a 4×4 rotation matrix, let's go ahead and use this matrix in a WebGL program by rewriting the sample program RotatedTriangle, which rotates a triangle 90 degrees around the z-axis in a counterclockwise direction, using the rotation matrix. Listing 3.6 shows RotatedTriangle_Matrix.js, whose output will be the same as Figure 3.23 shown earlier.

Listing 3.6 RotatedTriangle_Matrix.js

```
1  // RotatedTriangle_Matrix.js
2  // Vertex shader program
3  var VSHADER_SOURCE =
4    'attribute vec4 a_Position;\n' +
5    'uniform mat4 u_xformMatrix;\n' +
6    'void main() {\n' +
7    '  gl_Position = u_xformMatrix * a_Position;\n' +
8    '}\n';
9
10 // Fragment shader program
   ...
16 // Rotation angle
17 var ANGLE = 90.0;
```

```
18
19   function main() {
         ...
36       // Set the positions of vertices
37       var n = initVertexBuffers(gl);
         ...
43       // Create a rotation matrix
44     var radian = Math.PI * ANGLE / 180.0; // Convert to radians
45     var cosB = Math.cos(radian), sinB = Math.sin(radian);
46
47       // Note: WebGL is column major order
48     var xformMatrix = new Float32Array([
49        cosB,  sinB,  0.0, 0.0,
50       -sinB,  cosB,  0.0, 0.0,
51        0.0,   0.0,   1.0, 0.0,
52        0.0,   0.0,   0.0, 1.0
53     ]);
54
55     // Pass the rotation matrix to the vertex shader
56       var u_xformMatrix = gl.getUniformLocation(gl.program, 'u_xformMatrix');
         ...
61     gl.uniformMatrix4fv(u_xformMatrix, false, xformMatrix);
62
63       // Set the color for clearing <canvas>
         ...
69       // Draw a triangle
70       gl.drawArrays(gl.TRIANGLES, 0, n);
71   }
72
73   function initVertexBuffers(gl) {
74       var vertices = new Float32Array([
75          0.0, 0.5,   -0.5, -0.5,    0.5, -0.5
76       ]);
77       var n = 3; // Number of vertices
         ...
105      return n;
106  }
```

First, let us examine the vertex shader:

```
2   // Vertex shader program
3   var VSHADER_SOURCE =
4      'attribute vec4 a_Position;\n' +
5      'uniform mat4 u_xformMatrix;\n' +
```

```
6    'void main() {\n' +
7    '  gl_Position = u_xformMatrix * a_Position;\n' +
8    '}\n';
```

At line 7, u_xformMatrix, containing the rotation matrix described in Equation 3.11, and a_Position, containing the vertex coordinates (this is the right-side vector in Equation 3.11), are multiplied, literally implementing Equation 3.11.

In the sample program TranslatedTriangle, you were able to implement the addition of two vectors in one line (gl_Position = a_Position + u_Translation). In the same way, a multiplication of a matrix and vector can be written in one line in GLSL ES. This is convenient, allowing the calculation of the four equations (Equation 3.9) in one line. Again, this shows how GLSL ES has been designed specifically for 3D computer graphics by supporting powerful operations like this.

Because the transformation matrix is a 4×4 matrix and GLSL ES requires the data type for all variables, line 5 declares u_xformMatrix as type mat4. As you would expect, mat4 is a data type specifically for holding a 4×4 matrix.

Within the main JavaScript program, the rest of the changes just calculate the rotation matrix from Equation 3.11 and then pass it to u_xformMatrix. This part starts from line 44:

```
43    // Create a rotation matrix
44    var radian = Math.PI * ANGLE / 180.0; // Convert to radians
45    var cosB = Math.cos(radian), sinB = Math.sin(radian);
46
47    // Note: WebGL is column major order
48    var xformMatrix = new Float32Array([
49       cosB, sinB, 0.0, 0.0,
50      -sinB, cosB, 0.0, 0.0,
51        0.0,  0.0, 1.0, 0.0,
52        0.0,  0.0, 0.0, 1.0
53    ]);
54
55    // Pass the rotation matrix to the vertex shader
      ...
61    gl.uniformMatrix4fv(u_xformMatrix, false, xformMatrix);
```

Lines 44 and 45 calculate the values of cosine and sine, which are required in the rotation matrix. Then line 48 creates the matrix xformMatrix using a Float32Array. Unlike GLSL ES, because JavaScript does not have a dedicated object for representing a matrix, you need to use the Float32Array. One question that arises is in which order you should store the elements of the matrix (which is arranged in rows and columns) in the elements of the array (which is arranged in a line). There are two possible orders: **row major order** and **column major order** (see Figure 3.27).

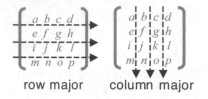

row major   column major

Figure 3.27 Row major order and column major order

WebGL, just like OpenGL, requires you to store the elements of a matrix in the elements of an array in column major order. So, for example, the matrix shown in Figure 3.27 is stored in an array as follows: [*a, e, i, m, b, f, j, n, c, g, k, o, d, h, l, p*]. In the sample program, the rotation matrix is stored in the `Float32Array` in this order in lines 49 to 52.

The array created is then passed to the uniform variable `u_xformMatrix` by using `gl.uniformMatrix4fv()` at line 61. Note that the last letter of this method name is `v`, which indicates that the method can pass multiple data values to the variable.

`gl.uniformMatrix4fv``(location, transpose, array)`

Assign the 4×4 matrix specified by *array* to the uniform variable specified by *location*.

Parameters	location	Specifies the storage location of the uniform variable.
	Transpose	Must be `false` in WebGL.[3]
	array	Specifies an array containing a 4×4 matrix in column major order (typed array).
Return value	None	
Errors	INVALID_OPERATION	There is no current program object.
	INVALID_VALUE	*transpose* is not `false`, or the length of *array* is less than 16.

If you load and run the sample program in your browser, you'll see the rotated triangle. Congratulations! You have successfully learned how to use a transformation matrix to rotate a triangle.

---

[3] This parameter specifies whether to transpose the matrix or not. The transpose operation, which exchanges the column and row elements of the matrix (see Chapter 7), is not supported by WebGL's implementation of this method and must always be set to `false`.

Reusing the Same Approach for Translation

Now, as you have seen with Equations 3.10 and 3.11, you can represent both a translation and a rotation using the same type of 4×4 matrix. Both equations use the matrices in the form <new coordinates> = <transformation matrix> * <original coordinates>. This is coded in the vertex shader as follows:

```
7      '  gl_Position = u_xformMatrix * a_Position;\n' +
```

This means that if you change the elements of the array xformMatrix from those of a rotation matrix to those of a translation matrix, you will be able to apply the translation matrix to the triangle to achieve the same result as shown earlier but which used an equation (Figure 3.18).

To do that, change line 17 in RotatedTriangle_Matrix.js using the translation distances from the previous example:

```
17  varTx = 0.5, Ty = 0.5, Tz = 0.0;
```

You need to rewrite the code for creating the matrix, remembering that you need to store the elements of the matrix in column major order. Let's keep the same name for the array variable, xformMatrix, even though it's now being used to hold a translation matrix, because it reinforces the fact that we are using essentially the same code. Finally, you are not using the variable ANGLE, so lines 43 to 45 are commented out:

```
43   // Create a rotation matrix
44   // var radian = Math.PI * ANGLE / 180.0; // Convert to radians
45   // var cosB = Math.cos(radian), sinB = Math.sin(radian);
46
47    // Note: WebGL is column major order
48    var xformMatrix = new Float32Array([
49       1.0, 0.0, 0.0, 0.0,
50       0.0, 1.0, 0.0, 0.0,
51       0.0, 0.0, 1.0, 0.0,
52       Tx, Ty, Tz, 1.0
53    ]);
```

Once you've made the changes, run the modified program, and you will see the same output as shown in Figure 3.18. By using a transformation matrix, you can apply various transformations using the same vertex shader. This is why the transformation matrix is such a convenient and powerful tool for 3D graphics, and it's why we've covered it in detail in this chapter.

Transformation Matrix: Scaling

Finally, let's define the transformation matrix for scaling using the same assumption that the original point is p and the point after scaling is p'.

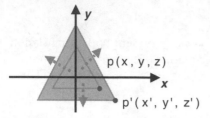

Figure 3.28 A scaling transformation

Assuming the scaling factor for the x-axis, y-axis, and z-axis is S_x, S_y, and S_z respectively, you obtain the following equations:

$$x' = S_x \times x$$

$$y' = S_y \times y$$

$$z' = S_z \times z$$

The following transformation matrix can be obtained by comparing these equations with Equation 3.9.

$$\begin{bmatrix} x' \\ y' \\ z' \\ 1 \end{bmatrix} = \begin{bmatrix} Sx & 0 & 0 & 0 \\ 0 & Sy & 0 & 0 \\ 0 & 0 & Sz & 0 \\ 0 & 0 & 0 & 1 \end{bmatrix} \times \begin{bmatrix} x \\ y \\ z \\ 1 \end{bmatrix}$$

As with the previous example, if you store this matrix in xformMatrix, you can scale the triangle by using the same vertex shader you used in RotatedTriangle_Matrix.js. For example, the following sample program will scale the triangle by a factor of 1.5 in a vertical direction, as shown in Figure 3.29:

```
17  varSx = 1.0, Sy = 1.5, Sz = 1.0;
    ...
47    // Note: WebGL is column major order
48    var xformMatrix = new Float32Array([
49       Sx,  0.0,  0.0,  0.0,
50       0.0,  Sy,  0.0,  0.0,
51       0.0,  0.0,  Sz,  0.0,
52       0.0,  0.0,  0.0,  1.0
53    ]
```

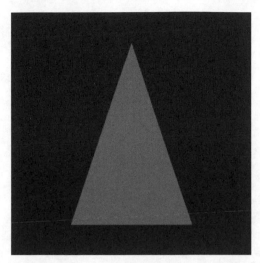

Figure 3.29 Triangle scaled in a vertical direction

Note that if you specify 0.0 to sx, sy, or sz, the scaled size will be 0.0. If you want to keep the original size, specify 1.0 as the scaling factor.

Summary

In this chapter, you explored the process of passing multiple items of information about vertices to a vertex shader, the different types of shapes available to be drawn using that information, and the process of transforming those shapes. The shapes dealt with in this chapter changed from a point to a triangle, but the method of using shaders remained the same, as in the examples in the previous chapter. You were also introduced to matrices and learned how to use transformation matrices to apply translation, rotation, or scaling to 2D shapes. Although it's a little complicated, you should now have a good understanding of the math behind calculating the individual transformation matrices.

In the next chapter, you'll explore more complex transformations but will use a handy library to hide the details, allowing you to focus on the higher-level tasks.

Summary

Chapter 4

More Transformations and Basic Animation

Chapter 3, "Drawing and Transforming Triangles," explained how to use the buffer object to draw more complex shapes and how to transform them using simple equations. Because this approach is cumbersome for multiple transformations, you were then introduced to matrices and their use to simplify transformation operations. In this chapter, you explore further transformations and begin to combine transformations into animations. In particular, you will

- Be introduced to a matrix transformation library that hides the mathematical details of matrix operations

- Use the library to quickly and easily combine multiple transformations

- Explore animation and how the library helps you animate simple shapes

These techniques provide the basics to construct complex WebGL programs and will be used in the sample programs in the following chapters.

Translate and Then Rotate

As you saw in Chapter 3, although transformations such as translation, rotation, and scaling can be represented as a 4×4 matrix, it is time consuming to specify each matrix by hand whenever you write WebGL programs. To simply the task, most WebGL developers use a convenient library that automates creating these matrices and hides the details. There are several public matrix libraries for WebGL, but in this section, you'll use a library created for this book and will see how the library can be used to combine multiple transformations to achieve results such as "translate and then rotate a triangle."

Transformation Matrix Library: cuon-matrix.js

In OpenGL, the parent specification of WebGL, there's no need to specify by hand each element of the transformation matrix when you use it. Instead, OpenGL supports a set of handy functions that make it easy to construct the matrices. For example, `glTranslatef()`, when called with translation distances for the x-, y-, and z-axes as arguments, will create a translation matrix internally and then set up the matrix needed to translate a shape (see Figure 4.1).

$$
\text{glTranslatef(5, 80, 30);} \quad \longrightarrow \quad
\begin{bmatrix}
1 & 0 & 0 & 5 \\
0 & 1 & 0 & 80 \\
0 & 0 & 1 & 30 \\
0 & 0 & 0 & 1
\end{bmatrix}
$$

Figure 4.1 An example of glTranslatef() in OpenGL

Unfortunately, WebGL doesn't provide these functions, so if you wanted to use this approach you'd need to look for or write them yourself. Because these functions are useful, we've created a JavaScript library for you, `cuon-matrix.js`, which allows you to create transformation matrices in a similar way to those specified in OpenGL. Although this library was written specifically for this book, it is general purpose, and you are free to use it in your own applications.

As you saw in Chapter 3, JavaScript provides the sine and cosine function as methods of the `Math` object. In the same way, the functions for creating transformation matrices are provided as methods of the `Matrix4` object defined in `cuon-matrix.js`.

`Matrix4` is a new object, defined by the library, and as the name suggests, deals with 4×4 matrices. Internally, these are represented using a typed array, `Float32Array`, which you saw in Chapter 3.

To get a feel for the library, let's rewrite `RotatedTriangle_Matrix` using the `Matrix4` object and its methods. The program for this example is called `RotatedTriangle_Matrix4`.

Because the `Matrix4` object is defined in the library `cuon-matrix.js`, you need to load it into your HTML file before using the object. To do this, you simply use the `<script>` tag, as shown in Listing 4.1.

Listing 4.1 RotatedTriangle_Matrix4.html (The Codes for Loading the Library)

```
13    <script src="../lib/webgl-debug.js"></script>
14    <script src="../lib/cuon-utils.js"></script>
15    <script src="../lib/cuon-matrix.js"></script>
16    <script src="RotatedTriangle_Matrix4.js"></script>
```

Once loaded, let's examine how to use it by comparing the previous `RotatedTriangle_Matrix.js` with `RotatedTriangle_Matrix4.js`, which uses the new `Matrix4` object.

Sample Program (RotatedTriangle_Matrix4.js)

This sample program is almost the same as `RotatedTriangle_Matrix.js` used in Chapter 3 except for the new steps that create the transformation matrix and pass it to `u_xformMatrix` in the vertex shader.

In `RotatedTriangle_Matrix.js`, you created the transformation matrix as follows:

```
1   // RotatedTriangle_Matrix.js
    ...
43    // Create a rotation matrix
44    var radian = Math.PI * ANGLE / 180.0; // Convert to radians
45    varcosB = Math.cos(radian), sinB = Math.sin(radian);
46
47    // Note: WebGL is column major order
48    var xformMatrix = new Float32Array([
49      cosB, sinB, 0.0, 0.0,
50     -sinB, cosB, 0.0, 0.0,
51       0.0,  0.0, 1.0, 0.0,
52       0.0,  0.0, 0.0, 1.0
53    ]);
    ...
61    gl.uniformMatrix4fv(u_xformMatrix, false, xformMatrix);
```

In this sample program, you need to rewrite this part using a `Matrix4` object and utilize its method `setRotate()` to calculate a rotation matrix. The following code snippet shows the rewritten part from `RotatedTriangle_Matrix4.js`:

```
1   // RotatedTriangle_Matrix4.js
    ...
47    // Create Matrix4 object for a rotation matrix
48    var xformMatrix = new Matrix4();
49    // Set the rotation matrix to xformMatrix
50    xformMatrix.setRotate(ANGLE, 0, 0, 1);
    ...
56    // Pass the rotation matrix to the vertex shader
57    gl.uniformMatrix4fv(u_xformMatrix, false, xformMatrix.elements);
```

You can see that the basic processing flow to create a matrix (line 48 and 50) and then pass it to the uniform variable is the same as in the previous sample. A `Matrix4` object is created using the `new` operator in the same way that an `Array` or `Date` object is created in JavaScript. Line 48 creates the `Matrix4` object, and then line 50 uses `setRotate()` to calculate the rotation matrix and write it to the `xformMatrix` object.

The `setRotate()` method takes four parameters: a rotation angle (specified in degrees, not radians) and the rotation axis around which the rotation will take place. The rotation axis, specified by x, y, and z, and associated direction are defined by the line drawn from

(0, 0, 0) to (x, y, z). As you will remember from Chapter 3 (Figure 3.21), the angle is positive if the rotation is performed in the clockwise direction around the rotation axis. In this example, because the rotation is performed around the z-axis, the axis is set to (0, 0, 1):

```
50    xformMatrix.setRotate(ANGLE, 0, 0, 1);
```

Similarly, for the x-axis, you can specify x = 1, y =0, and z = 0 and for the y-axis, x = 0, y = 1, and z = 0. Once you have set up the rotation matrix in the variable xformMatrix, all you need to do is to pass the matrix to the vertex shader using the same method gl.uniformMatrix4fv() as before. Note that you cannot pass a Matrix4 object directly as the last argument of this method because a typed array is required for the parameter. However, you can retrieve the elements of the Matrix4 object as a typed array by using its property elements, which you can then pass as shown at line 57:

```
57    gl.uniformMatrix4fv(u_xformMatrix, false, xformMatrix.elements);
```

The Matrix4 object supports the methods and properties shown in Table 4.1.

Table 4.1 The Methods and Properties Supported by Matrix4

Methods and Properties	Description
Matrix4.setIdentity()	Initialize a matrix (to the identity matrix*).
Matrix4.setTranslate(x, y, z)	Set Matrix4 to the translation matrix, which translates *x* units in the direction of the x-axis, *y* units in the direction of the y-axis, and *z* units in the direction of the z-axis.
Matrix4.setRotate(angle, x, y, z)	Set Matrix4 to the rotation matrix, which rotates *angle* degrees around the rotation axis (*x*, *y*, *z*). The (*x*, *y*, *z*) coordinates do not need to be **normalized**. (See Chapter 8, "Lighting Objects.")
Matrix4.setScale(x, y, z)	Set Matrix4 to the scaling matrix with scaling factors *x*, *y*, and *z*.
Matrix4.translate (x, y, z)	Multiply the matrix stored in Matrix4 by the translation matrix, which translates *x* units in the direction of the x-axis, *y* units in the direction of the y-axis, and *z* units in the direction of the z-axis, storing the result back into Matrix4.
Matrix4.rotate(angle, x, y, z)	Multiply the matrix stored in Matrix4 by the rotation matrix, which rotates *angle* degrees around the rotation axis (*x*, *y*, *z*), storing the results back into Matrix4. The (*x*, *y*, *z*) coordinates do not need to be normalized. (See Chapter 8.)
Matrix4.scale(x, y, z)	Multiply the matrix stored in Matrix4 by the scaling matrix, with scaling factors *x*, *y*, and *z*, storing the results back into Matrix4.

Methods and Properties	Description
Matrix4.set(m)	Set the matrix m to Matrix4. m must be a Matrix4 object.
Matrix4.elements	The typed array (Float32Array) containing the elements of the matrix stored in Matrix4.

* The identity matrix is a matrix that behaves for matrix multiplication like the scalar value 1 does for scalar multiplication. Multiplying by the identity matrix has no effect on the other matrix. The identity matrix has 1.0 in its diagonal elements.

As can be seen from the table, there are two types of methods supported by Matrix4: those whose names include set, and those that don't. The set methods calculate the transformation matrix using their parameters and then set or write the resulting matrix to the Matrix4 object. In contrast, the methods without set multiply the matrix already stored in the Matrix4 object by the matrix calculated using the parameters and then store the result back in the Matrix4 object.

As you can see from the table, these methods are both powerful and flexible. More importantly, it makes it easy to quickly change transformations. For example, if you wanted to translate the triangle instead of rotating, you could just rewrite line 50 as follows:

```
50    xformMatrix.setTranslate( 0.5, 0.5, 0.0);
```

The example uses the variable name xformMatrix to represent a generic transformation. Obviously, you can use an appropriate variable name for the transformations within your applications (such as rotMatrix, as was used in Chapter 3).

Combining Multiple Transformation

Now that you are familiar with the basics of the Matrix4 object, let's see how it can be used to combine two transformations: a translation followed by a rotation. The sample program RotatedTranslatedTriangle does just that, resulting in Figure 4.2. Note that the example uses a smaller triangle so that you can easily understand the effect of the transformation.

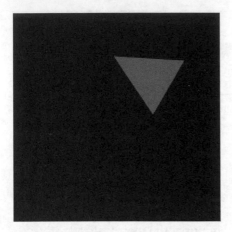

Figure 4.2 RotatedTranslatedTriangle

Obviously, this example consists of the following two transformations, shown in Figure 4.3:

1. Translate the triangle along the x-axis.

2. Rotate the triangle translated by (1).

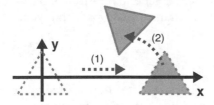

Figure 4.3 The triangle translated and then rotated

Based on the explanations so far, we can write the equation of the translated triangle from (1) as follows:

Equation 4.1

$$\langle "translated" \ coordinates \rangle = \\ \langle translation \ matrix \rangle \times \langle original \ coordinates \rangle$$

Then you just need to rotate the < *"translated" coordinates* > as follows:

Equation 4.2

$$\langle "translated \ and \ then \ rotated" \ coordinates \rangle = \\ \langle rotation \ matrix \rangle \times \langle translated \ coordinates \rangle$$

You can calculate these equations separately, but they can be combined by substituting Equation 4.1 into Equation 4.2.

Equation 4.3

$$\langle\textit{"translated and then rotated" coordinates}\rangle =$$
$$\langle\textit{rotation matrix}\rangle \times (\langle\textit{translation matrix}\rangle \times \langle\textit{original coordinates}\rangle)$$

Where

$$\langle\textit{rotation matrix}\rangle \times (\langle\textit{translation matrix}\rangle \times \langle\textit{original coordinates}\rangle)$$

is equal to

$$(\langle\textit{rotation matrix}\rangle \times \langle\textit{translation matrix}\rangle) \times \langle\textit{original coordinates}\rangle$$

This final step, calculating $\langle\textit{rotation matrix}\rangle \times \langle\textit{translation matrix}\rangle$, can be carried out in a JavaScript program and the result passed to the vertex shader. The combination of multiple transformations like this is called **model transformation** (or **modeling transformation**), and the matrix that performs model transformation is called the **model matrix**.

As a refresher, let's just look at the multiplication of matrices, which is defined as follows:

$$A = \begin{bmatrix} a_{00} & a_{01} & a_{02} \\ a_{10} & a_{11} & a_{12} \\ a_{20} & a_{21} & a_{22} \end{bmatrix}, B = \begin{bmatrix} b_{00} & b_{01} & b_{02} \\ b_{10} & b_{11} & b_{12} \\ b_{20} & b_{21} & b_{22} \end{bmatrix}$$

Assuming two 3×3 matrices, A and B as shown, the product of A and B is defined as follows:

Equation 4.4

$$\begin{bmatrix} a_{00} \times b_{00} + a_{01} \times b_{10} + a_{02} \times b_{20} & a_{00} \times b_{01} + a_{01} \times b_{11} + a_{02} \times b_{21} & a_{00} \times b_{02} + a_{01} \times b_{12} + a_{02} \times b_{22} \\ a_{10} \times b_{00} + a_{11} \times b_{10} + a_{12} \times b_{20} & a_{10} \times b_{01} + a_{11} \times b_{11} + a_{12} \times b_{21} & a_{10} \times b_{02} + a_{11} \times b_{12} + a_{12} \times b_{22} \\ a_{20} \times b_{00} + a_{21} \times b_{10} + a_{22} \times b_{20} & a_{20} \times b_{01} + a_{21} \times b_{11} + a_{22} \times b_{21} & a_{20} \times b_{02} + a_{21} \times b_{12} + a_{22} \times b_{22} \end{bmatrix}$$

We use 3×3 matrices in the example, but the approach scales to the more usual 4×4 matrices. However, note that the multiplication order of matrices is important. The result of A * B is not equal to that of B * A.

As you would expect, `cuon-matrix.js` supports a method to carry out matrix multiplication on `Matrix4` objects. Let's look at how to use that method to combine two matrices to support a translation followed by a rotation.

Sample Program (RotatedTranslatedTriangle.js)

Listing 4.2 shows `RotatedTranslatedTriangle.js`. The vertex shader and fragment shader are the same as in `RotatedTriangle_Matrix4.js` in the previous section except that the name of the uniform variable is changed from `u_xformMatrix` to `u_ModelMatrix`.

Listing 4.2 RotatedTranslatedTriangle.js

```
 1  // RotatedTranslatedTriangle.js
 2  // Vertex shader program
 3  var VSHADER_SOURCE =
 4    'attribute vec4 a_Position;\n' +
 5    'uniform mat4  u_ModelMatrix;\n' +
 6    'void main() {\n' +
 7    '  gl_Position = u_ModelMatrix * a_Position;\n' +
 8    '}\n';
 9  // Fragment shader program
   ...
16  function main() {
     ...
33    // Set the positions of vertices
34    var n = initVertexBuffers(gl);
     ...
40    // Create Matrix4 object for model transformation
41    var modelMatrix = new Matrix4();
42
43    // Calculate a model matrix
44    var ANGLE = 60.0; // Rotation angle
45    varTx = 0.5; // Translation distance
46    modelMatrix.setRotate(ANGLE, 0, 0, 1); // Set rotation matrix
47    modelMatrix.translate(Tx, 0, 0); // Multiply modelMatrix by the calculated
                                                     ➥translation matrix
48
49    // Pass the model matrix to the vertex shader
50    var u_ModelMatrix = gl.getUniformLocation(gl.program, ' u_ModelMatrix');
     ...
56    gl.uniformMatrix4fv(u_ModelMatrix, false, modelMatrix.elements);
     ...
63    // Draw a triangle
64    gl.drawArrays(gl.TRIANGLES, 0, n);
65  }
66
67  function initVertexBuffers(gl) {
68    var vertices = new Float32Array([
69      0.0, 0.3,   -0.3, -0.3,   0.3, -0.3
70    ]);
71    var n = 3; // The number of vertices
     ...
99    return n;
100 }
```

The key lines in this listing are lines 46 and 47, which calculate
< *rotation matrix* > × < *translation matrix* > :

```
46     modelMatrix.setRotate(ANGLE, 0, 0, 1);  // Set rotation matrix
47     modelMatrix.translate(Tx, 0, 0);  // Multiply modelMatrix by the calculated
                                          ➥translation matrix
```

Because line 46 uses a method with `set` (`setRotate()`), the rotation matrix that is calculated using the parameters is written to the variable `modelMatrix`. The next line, 47, uses a method without `set` (`translate()`), which, as explained earlier, calculates the translation matrix using the parameters and then multiplies the matrix in `modelMatrix` by the newly calculated translation matrix and writes the result back into `modelMatrix`. So, if `modelMatrix` already contains a rotation matrix, this method calculates ⟨*rotation matrix*⟩ × ⟨*translation matrix*⟩ and stores the result back into `modelMatrix`.

You may have noticed that the order of "translate first and then rotate" is the opposite of the order of the matrices in the calculation ⟨*rotation matrix*⟩ × ⟨*translation matrix*⟩ . As shown in Equation 4.3, this is because the transformation matrix is multiplied by the original vertex coordinates of the triangle.

The result of this calculation is passed to `u_ModelMatrix` in the vertex shader at line 56, and then the drawing operation (line 64) is the same as usual. If you now load this program into your browser, you can see a red triangle, which has been translated and then rotated.

Experimenting with the Sample Program

Let's rewrite the sample program to first rotate the triangle and then translate it. This simply requires you to exchange the order of the rotation and translation. In this case, you should note that the translation is performed first by using the `set` method, `setTranslate()`:

```
46   modelMatrix.setTranslate(Tx, 0, 0);
47   modelMatrix.rotate(ANGLE, 0, 0, 1);
```

Figure 4.4 shows this sample program.

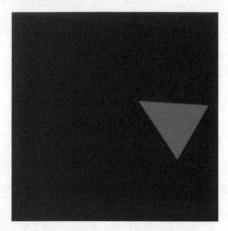

Figure 4.4 A triangle "rotated first and then translated"

As you can see, by changing the order of a rotation and translation, you get a different result. This becomes obvious when you examine Figure 4.5.

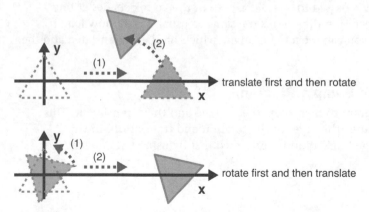

Figure 4.5 The order of transformations will show different results

That concludes the initial explanation of the use of methods defined in `cuon-matrix.js` to create transformation matrices. You'll be using them throughout the rest of this book, so you'll have plenty of chance to study them further.

Animation

So far, this chapter has explained how to transform shapes and use the matrix library to carry out transformation operations. You now have enough knowledge of WebGL to start on the next step of applying this knowledge to animate shapes.

Let's start by constructing a sample program, `RotatingTriangle`, which continually rotates a triangle at a constant rotation speed (45 degrees/second). Figure 4.6 shows multiple overlaid screenshots of `RotatingTriangle` so that you can see the rotation.

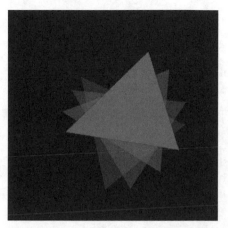

Figure 4.6 Multiple overlaid screenshots of RotatingTriangle

The Basics of Animation

To animate a rotating triangle, you simply need to redraw the triangle at a slightly different angle each time it draws.

Figure 4.7 shows individual triangles that are drawn at times t0, t1, t2, t3, and t4. Each triangle is a still image, but you can see that each has a slightly different rotation angle. When you see a series of these triangles sequentially, your mind interpolates the changes between them and then puts them together as a smooth flow of animation, just like a flip book. Of course, you need to clear the previous triangle before drawing a new one. (This is why you must call `gl.clear()` before drawing something.) You can apply this animation method to both 2D shapes and 3D objects.

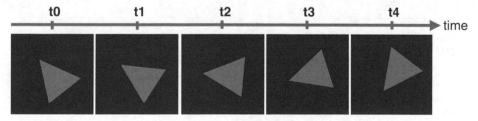

Figure 4.7 Draw a slightly different triangle for each drawing

Achieving animation in this way requires two key mechanisms:

Mechanism 1: Repeatedly calls a function to draw a triangle at times t0, t1, t2, t3, and so on.

Mechanism 2: Clears the previous triangle and then draws a new one with the specified angle each time the function is called.

The second mechanism is just a simple application of the knowledge you've learned so far. However, the first mechanism is new, so let's take it step by step by examining the sample program.

Sample Program (RotatingTriangle.js)

Listing 4.3 shows `RotatingTriangle.js`. The vertex shader and fragment shader are the same as in the previous sample program. However, the vertex shader is listed to show the multiplication of a matrix and vertex coordinates.

The following three points differ from the previous sample program:

- Because the program needs to draw a triangle repeatedly, it's been modified to specify the clear color at line 44, not just before the drawing operation. Remember, the color stays in the WebGL system until it's overwritten.

- The actual mechanism [Mechanism 1] to repeatedly call a drawing function has been added (lines 59 to 64).

- [Mechanism 2] The operations to clear and draw a triangle were defined as a function (`draw()` at line 102).

These differences are highlighted in Listing 4.3 (lines 1 to 3). Let's look at them in more detail.

Listing 4.3 RotatingTriangle.js

```
1   // RotatingTriangle.js
2   // Vertex shader program
3   var VSHADER_SOURCE =
4     'attribute vec4 a_Position;\n' +
5     'uniform mat4  u_ModelMatrix;\n' +
6     'void main() {\n' +
7     '  gl_Position =  u_ModelMatrix * a_Position;\n' +
8     '}\n';
9   // Fragment shader program
    ...
16  // Rotation angle (degrees/second)
17  var ANGLE_STEP = 45.0;
18
```

```
19   function main() {
       ...
36     // Set the positions of vertices
37     var n = initVertexBuffers(gl);
       ...
43     // Set the color for clearing <canvas>                            <- (1)
44     gl.clearColor(0.0, 0.0, 0.0, 1.0);
45
46     // Get the storage location of u_ModelMatrix variable
47     var u_ModelMatrix = gl.getUniformLocation(gl.program, ' u_ModelMatrix');
       ...
53     // Current rotation angle of a triangle
54     varcurrentAngle = 0.0;
55     // Matrix4 object for model transformation
56     var modelMatrix = new Matrix4();
57
58     // Start to draw a triangle                                       <- (2)
59     var tick = function() {
60       currentAngle = animate(currentAngle);// Update the rotation angle
61       draw(gl, n, currentAngle, modelMatrix, u_ModelMatrix);
62       requestAnimationFrame(tick);// Request that the browser calls tick
63     };
64     tick();
65   }
66
67   function initVertexBuffers(gl) {
68     var vertices = new Float32Array ([
69       0.0, 0.5,   -0.5, -0.5,   0.5, -0.5
70     ]);
71     var n = 3;   // The number of vertices
       ...
96     return n;
97   }
98
99   function draw(gl,n, currentAngle, modelMatrix, u_ModelMatrix){      <-(3)
100    // Set up rotation matrix
101    modelMatrix.setRotate(currentAngle, 0, 0, 1);
102
103    // Pass the rotation matrix to the vertex shader
104    gl.uniformMatrix4fv( u_ModelMatrix, false, modelMatrix.elements);
105
106    // Clear <canvas>
107    gl.clear(gl.COLOR_BUFFER_BIT);
108
109    // Draw a triangle
```

```
110     gl.drawArrays(gl.TRIANGLES, 0, n);
111  }
112
113  // Last time when this function was called
114  var g_last = Date.now();
115  function animate(angle) {
116     // Calculate the elapsed time
117     var now = Date.now();
118     var elapsed = now - g_last; // milliseconds
119     g_last = now;
120     // Update the current rotation angle (adjusted by the elapsed time)
121     var newAngle = angle + (ANGLE_STEP * elapsed) / 1000.0;
122     return newAngle %= 360;
126  }
```

Line 7 in the vertex shader is just a multiplication of a matrix and the vertex coordinates in the same way as RotatedTranslatedTriangle.js). u_ModelMatrix is a uniform variable, and the rotation matrix is passed to the variable from a JavaScript program:

```
7    '   gl_Position =  u_ModelMatrix * a_Position;\n' +
```

The variable ANGLE_STEP at line 17 defines the rotation angles per second and is set to 45 degrees/second:

```
17   var ANGLE_STEP = 45.0;
```

The main() function starts from line 19, but because the code from lines 19 to 37, which specifies the vertex coordinates, is the same as before, it is omitted.

The first of the three differences is that you specify the clear color once only: at line 44. Line 47 then retrieves the storage location of u_ModelMatrix in the vertex shader. Because this location never changes, it's more efficient to do only this once:

```
47     var u_ModelMatrix = gl.getUniformLocation(gl.program, 'u_ModelMatrix');
```

The variable u_ModelMatrix is then used in the draw() function (line 99) that draws the triangle.

The value of the variable currentAngle starts at 0 degrees and stores how many degrees the triangle should be rotated from its original position each time it is drawn. As in the simple rotation examples earlier, it calculates the rotation matrix needed for the transformation. The variable modelMatrix defined at line 56 is a Matrix4 object used to hold the rotation matrix in draw(). This matrix could be created within draw(); however, that would require a new Matrix4 object to be created each time draw() is called, which would be inefficient. For this reason, the object is created at line 56 and then passed to draw() at line 61.

Lines 59 to 64 implement Mechanism 1 as the function `tick`, which is repeatedly called to draw the triangle. Before you look at how the overall "tick" mechanism actually works, let's look at what happens each time it is called:

```
53    // Current rotation angle of a triangle
54    varcurrentAngle = 0.0;
55    // Matix4 object for model transformation
56    var modelMatrix = new Matrix4();
57
58    // Start to draw a triangle                              <- (2)
59    var tick = function() {
60      currentAngle = animate(currentAngle); // Update the rotation angle
61      draw(gl, n, currentAngle, modelMatrix,  u_ModelMatrix);
62      requestAnimationFrame(tick);// Request that the browser callstick
63    };
64    tick();
```

Within `tick`, the call to the function `animate()` at line 60 updates the current rotation angle of the triangle, and then the call to `draw()` at line 61 draws a triangle using `gl.drawArrays()`.

`draw()` is passed the rotation matrix, which rotates the triangle to `currentAngle` degrees. In turn, it passes the matrix to the `u_ModelMatrix` variable in the vertex shader before calling `gl.drawArrays()` (lines 104 to 110). This code appears quite complex, so let's examine each part in turn.

Repeatedly Call the Drawing Function (tick())

As described earlier, to animate the triangle, you need to perform the following two steps repeatedly: (1) update the current rotation angle of a triangle (`currentAngle`), and then (2) call the drawing function with the angle to draw the triangle. Lines 59 to 64 implement these processing steps.

In this sample program, these tasks are defined by the three operations of line 60, 61, and 62. These operations are grouped in a single anonymous function using `function()`, and the function is assigned to the variable `tick` (see Figure 4.8). You use an anonymous function if you want to pass the local variables defined in `main()` (`gl`, `n`, `currentAngle`, `modelMatrix`, and `u_ModelMatrix`) to `draw()` as arguments when `draw()` is called at line 61. If you need a refresher on anonymous functions, refer to Chapter 2, "Your First Step with WebGL," where you used one to register an event handler.

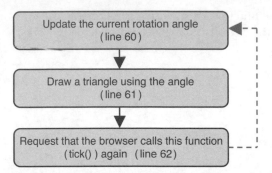

Figure 4.8 The operations assigned to "tick"

You can use this basic approach for all types of animation. It is a key technique in 3D graphics.

When you call `requestAnimationFrame()` at line 62, you are requesting the browser to call the function specified as the first parameter at some future time when the three operations assigned to `tick` will be executed again. You'll look at `requestAnimationFrame()` in a moment. For now, let's finish examining the operations executed in `tick()`.

Draw a Triangle with the Specified Rotation Angle (draw())

The `draw()` function takes the following five parameters:

- *gl:* The context in which to draw the triangle

- *n:* The number of vertices

- *currentAngle:* The current rotation angle

- *modelMatrix:* A Matrix4 object to store the rotation matrix calculated using `currentAngle`

- *u_ModelMatrix:* The location of the uniform variable to which the `modelMatrix` is passed

The actual function code is found in lines 99 to 111:

```
99  function draw(gl, n, currentAngle, modelMatrix,  u_ModelMatrix) {
100     // Set the rotation matrix
101     modelMatrix.setRotate(currentAngle, 0, 0, 1);
102
103     // Pass the rotation matrix to the vertex shader
104     gl.uniformMatrix4fv( u_ModelMatrix, false, modelMatrix.elements);
105
106     // Clear <canvas>
107     gl.clear(gl.COLOR_BUFFER_BIT);
```

```
108
109    // Draw the triangle
110    gl.drawArrays(gl.TRIANGLES, 0, n);
111  }
```

First, line 101 calculates the rotation matrix using the `setRotate()` method provided by `cuon-matrix.js`, writing the resulting matrix to `modelMatrix`:

101 modelMatrix.setRotate(currentAngle, 0, 0, 1);

Next, line 104 passes the matrix to the vertex shader by using `gl.uniformMatrix4fv()`:

104 gl.uniformMatrix4fv(u_ModelMatrix, false, modelMatrix.elements);

After that, line 107 clears the `<canvas>` and then calls `gl.drawArrays()` at line 110 to execute the vertex shader to actually draw the triangle. Those steps are the same as used before.

Now let's return to the third operation, `requestAnimationFrame()`, which requests the browser to call the function `tick()` at some future time.

Request to Be Called Again (requestAnimationFrame())

Traditionally, if you wanted to repeatedly execute specific tasks (functions) in JavaScript, you used the method `setInterval()`.

setInterval(func, delay)		
Call the function specified by *func* multiple times with intervals specified by *delay*.		
Parameters	func	Specifies the function to be called multiple times.
	delay	Specifies the intervals (in milliseconds).
Return value	Timer id	

However, because this JavaScript method was designed before browsers started to support multiple tabs, it executes regardless of which tab is active. This can lead to performance problems, so a new method, `requestAnimationFrame()`, was recently introduced. The function scheduled using this method is only called when the tab in which it was defined is active. Because `requestAnimationFrame()` is a new method and not yet standardized, it is defined in the library supplied by Google, `webgl-utils.js`, which handles the differences among different browsers.

`requestAnimationFrame`(func)

Requests the function specified by *func* to be called on redraw (see Figure 4.9). This request needs to be remade after each callback.

Parameters	func	Specifies the function to be called later. The function takes a "time" parameter, indicating the timestamp of the callback.
Return value	Request id	

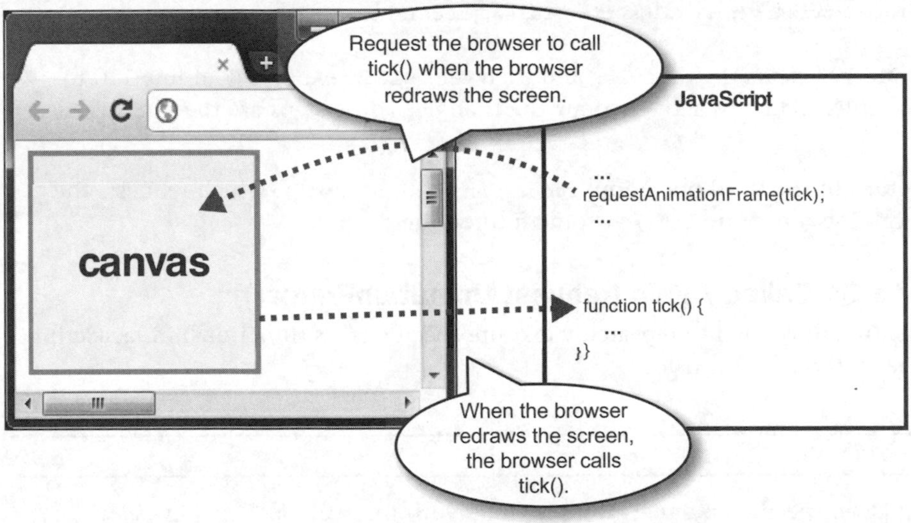

Figure 4.9 The requestAnimationFrame () mechanism

By using this method, you avoid animation in inactive tabs and do not increase the load on the browser. Note, you cannot specify an interval before the function is called; rather, *func* (the first parameter) will be called when the browser wants the web page containing the *element* (the second parameter) to be painted. In addition, after calling the function, you need to request the callback again because the previous request is automatically removed once it's fulfilled. Line 62 makes that request again once `tick` is called and makes it possible to call `tick()` repeatedly:

```
62      requestAnimationFrame(tick); // Request the browser to call tick
```

If you want to cancel the request to call the function, you need to use `cancelAnimationFrame()`.

Update the Rotation Angle (animate())

Finally, let's see how to update the current rotation angle. The program maintains the current rotation angle of the triangle (that is, how many degrees the triangle has been rotated from its original position) in the variable currentAngle (defined at line 54). It calculates the next rotation angle based on this current value.

The update of currentAngle is carried out in the function animate(), which is called at line 60. This function, defined at line 115, takes one parameter, angle, which represents the current rotation angle and returns the new rotation angle:

```
60      currentAngle = animate(currentAngle);// Update the rotation angle
61      draw(gl, n, currentAngle, modelMatrix,  u_ModelMatrix);
            . . .
113  // Last time this function was called
114  var g_last = Date.getTime();
115  function animate(angle) {
116    // Calculate the elapsed time
117    var now = Date.getTime();
118    var elapsed = now - g_last;
119    g_last = now;
120    // Update the current rotation angle (adjusted by the elapsed time)
121    var newAngle = angle + (ANGLE_STEP * elapsed) / 1000.0;
122    return newAngle %= 360;
123  }
```

The process for updating the current rotation angle is slightly complicated. Let's look at the reason for that by using Figure 4.10.

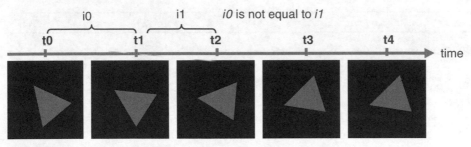

Figure 4.10 The interval times between each tick() vary

Figure 4.10 illustrates the following:

- tick() is called at t0. It calls draw() to draw the triangle and then reregisters tick().

- tick() is called at t1. It calls draw() to draw the triangle and then reregisters tick().

- tick() is called at t2. It calls draw() to draw the triangle and then reregisters tick().

The problem here is that the interval times between t0 and t1, t1 and t2, and t2 and t3 may be different because of the load on the browser at that time. That is, t1 - t0 could be different from t2 - t1.

If the interval time is not constant, then simply adding a fixed amount of angle (degree/ second) to the current rotation angle each time tick() is called will result in an apparent acceleration or deceleration of the rotation speed.

For this reason, the function animate() needs to be a little more sophisticated and must determine the new rotation angle based on how long it has been since the function was last called. To do that, you need to store the time that the function was last called into the variable g_last and store the current time into the variable now. Then you can calculate how long it has been since the function was last called by subtraction and store the result in the variable elapsed (line 118). The amount of rotation is then calculated at line 121 using elapsed as follows.

```
121 varnewAngle = angle + (ANGLE_STEP * elapsed) / 1000.0;
```

The variables g_last and now contain the return value from the method now() of a Date object whose units are a millisecond (1/1000 second). Therefore, if you want to rotate the triangle by ANGLE_STEP (degree/second), you just need to multiply ANGLE_STEP by elapsed/1000 to calculate the rotation angle. At line 121, you actually multiply ANGLE_STEP by elapsed and then divide the result by 1000 because this is slightly more accurate, but both have the same meaning.

Finally, line 122 ensures the value of newAngle is less than 360 (degrees) and returns the result.

If you now load `RotatedTriangle.html` into your browser, you can check that the triangle rotates at a constant speed. We will reuse this approach for animation in the following chapters, so it's worthwhile making sure you have mastered the details.

Experimenting with the Sample Program

In this section, let's create an animation that consists of multiple transformations. `RotatingTranslatedTriangle` translates a triangle 0.35 units in the positive direction of the x-axis first and then rotates the triangle by 45 degrees/second.

This is easy to achieve if you remember that multiple transformations can be realized by multiplying each transformation matrix together (refer to Chapter 3).

To do this, you just need to insert the translation at line 102. Because the variable `model-Matrix` already contains the rotation matrix, you can use `translate()`, rather than `setTranslate()`, to multiply `modelMatrix` by the translation matrix:

```
 99   function draw(gl, n, currentAngle, modelMatrix,  u_ModelMatrix) {
100     // Set a rotation matrix
101     modelMatrix.setRotate(currentAngle, 0, 0, 1);
102     modelMatrix.translate(0.35, 0, 0);
103     // Pass the rotation matrix to the vertex shader
104     gl.uniformMatrix4fv( u_ModelMatrix, false, modelMatrix.elements);
```

If you load the example, you will see the animation shown in Figure 4.11.

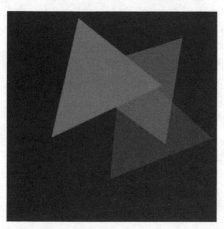

Figure 4.11 Multiple overlaid screenshots of RotatingTranslatedTriangle

Finally, for those of you wanting a little control, on the companion site for this book is a sample program, named `RotatingTriangle_withButtons`, that allows dynamic control of the rotation speed using buttons (see Figure 4.12). You can see the buttons below the `<canvas>`.

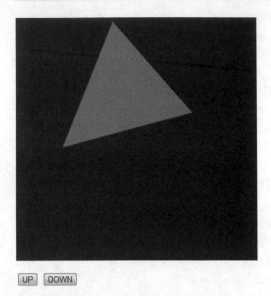

UP   DOWN

Figure 4.12   RotatingTriangle_withButtons

Summary

This chapter explored the process of transforming shapes using the transformation matrix library, combining multiple basic transformations to create a complex transformation, and animating shapes using the library. There are two key lessons in this chapter: (1) Complex transformations can be realized by multiplying a series of basic transformation matrices; (2) You can animate shapes by repeating the transformation and drawing steps.

Chapter 5, "Using Colors and Texture Images," is the last chapter that covers basic techniques. It explores colors and textures. Once you master those, you will have enough knowledge to create your own basic WebGL programs and will be ready to begin exploring some of the more advanced capabilities of WebGL.

Using Colors and Texture Images

The previous chapters explained the key concepts underlying the foundations of WebGL through the use of examples based on 2D shapes. This approach has given you a good understanding of how to deal with single color geometric shapes in WebGL. Building on these basics, you now delve a little further into WebGL by exploring the following three subjects:

- Passing other data such as color information to the vertex shader

- The conversion from a shape to fragments that takes place between the vertex shader and the fragment shader, which is known as the **rasterization process**

- Mapping images (or textures) onto the surfaces of a shape or object

This is the final chapter that focuses on the key functionalities of WebGL. After reading this chapter, you will understand the techniques and mechanism for using colors and textures in WebGL and will have mastered enough WebGL to allow you to create sophisticated 3D scenes.

Passing Other Types of Information to Vertex Shaders

In the previous sample programs, a single buffer object was created first, the vertex coordinates were stored in it, and then it was passed to the vertex shader. However, beside coordinates, vertices involved in 3D graphics often need other types of information such as color information or point size. For example, let us take a look at a program you used in Chapter 3, "Drawing and Transforming Triangles," which draws three points: `MultiPoint.js`. In the shader, in addition to the vertex coordinates, you provided the point size as extra information. However, the point size was a fixed value and set in the shader rather than passed from outside:

```
3 var VSHADER_SOURCE =
4   'attribute vec4 a_Position;\n' +
5   'void main() {\n' +
6   '  gl_Position = a_Position;\n' +
7   '  gl_PointSize = 10.0;\n' +
8   '}\n'
```

Line 6 assigns the vertex coordinates to gl_Position, and line 7 assigns a fixed point size of 10.0 to gl_PointSize. If you now wanted to modify the size of that point from your JavaScript program, you would need a way to pass the point size with the vertex coordinates.

Let's look at an example, MultiAttributeSize, whose goal is to draw three points of different sizes: 10.0, 20.0, and 30.0, respectively (see Figure 5.1).

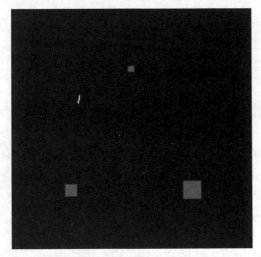

Figure 5.1   MultiAttributeSize

In the previous chapter, you carried out the following steps to pass the vertex coordinates:

1. Create a buffer object.

2. Bind the buffer object to the target.

3. Write the coordinate data into the buffer object.

4. Assign the buffer object to the attribute variable.

5. Enable the assignment.

If you now wanted to pass several items of vertex information to the vertex shader through buffer objects, you could just apply the same steps to all the items of information associated with a vertex. Let's look at a sample program that uses multiple buffers to do just that.

Sample Program (MultiAttributeSize.js)

MultiAttributeSize.js is shown in Listing 5.1. The fragment shader is basically the same as in MultiPoint.js, so let's omit it this time. The vertex shader is also similar, apart from the fact that you add a new attribute variable that specifies the point size. The numbers 1 through 5 on the right of the listing note the five steps previously outlined.

Listing 5.1   MultiAttributeSize.js

```
 1 // MultiAttributeSize.js
 2 // Vertex shader program
 3 var VSHADER_SOURCE =
 4   'attribute vec4 a_Position;\n' +
 5   'attribute float a_PointSize;\n' +
 6   'void main() {\n' +
 7   '  gl_Position = a_Position;\n' +
 8   '  gl_PointSize = a_PointSize;\n' +
 9   '}\n';
     ...
17 function main() {
     ...
34   // Set the vertex information
35   var n = initVertexBuffers(gl);
     ...
47   // Draw three points
48   gl.drawArrays(gl.POINTS, 0, n);
49 }
50
51 function initVertexBuffers(gl) {
52   var vertices = new Float32Array([
53     0.0, 0.5,   -0.5, -0.5,   0.5, -0.5
54   ]);
55   var n = 3;
56
57   var sizes = new Float32Array([
58     10.0, 20.0, 30.0  // Point sizes
59 ]);
60
61   // Create a buffer object
62   var vertexBuffer = gl.createBuffer();                          <-(1)
63   var sizeBuffer = gl.createBuffer();                            <-(1')
     ...
69   // Write vertex coordinates to the buffer object and enable it
70   gl.bindBuffer(gl.ARRAY_BUFFER, vertexBuffer);                  <-(2)
71   gl.bufferData(gl.ARRAY_BUFFER, vertices, gl.STATIC_DRAW);      <-(3)
72   var a_Position = gl.getAttribLocation(gl.program, 'a_Position');
```

```
   ...
77  gl.vertexAttribPointer(a_Position, 2, gl.FLOAT, false, 0, 0);    <-(4)
78  gl.enableVertexAttribArray(a_Position);                          <-(5)
79
80  // Write point sizes to the buffer object and enable it
81  gl.bindBuffer(gl.ARRAY_BUFFER, sizeBuffer);                      <-(2')
82  gl.bufferData(gl.ARRAY_BUFFER, sizes, gl.STATIC_DRAW);           <-(3')
83  var a_PointSize = gl.getAttribLocation(gl.program, 'a_PointSize');
   ...
88  gl.vertexAttribPointer(a_PointSize, 1, gl.FLOAT, false, 0, 0);   <-(4')
89  gl.enableVertexAttribArray(a_PointSize);                         <-(5')
   ...
94  return n;
95  }
```

First of all, let us examine the vertex shader in Listing 5.1. As you can see, the attribute variable a_PointSize, which receives the point size from the JavaScript program, has been added. This variable, declared at line 5 as a float, is then assigned to gl_PointSize at line 8. No other changes are necessary for the vertex shader, but you will need a slight modification to the process in initVertexBuffers() so it can handle several buffer objects. Let us take a more detailed look at it.

Create Multiple Buffer Objects

The function initVertexBuffers() starts at line 51, and the vertex coordinates are defined from lines 52 to 54. The point sizes are then specified at line 57 using the array sizes:

```
57  var sizes = new Float32Array([
58    10.0, 20.0, 30.0  // Point sizes
59  ]);
```

A buffer object is created at line 62 for the vertex data, and at line 63 another buffer object (sizeBuffer) is created for storing the array of "point sizes."

From lines 70 to 78, the program binds the buffer object for the vertex coordinates, writes the data, and finally assigns and enables the attribute variables associated with the buffer object. These tasks are the same as those described in the previous sample programs.

Lines 80 to 89 are new additions for handling the different point sizes. However, the steps are the same as for a vertex buffer. Bind the buffer object for the point sizes (sizeBuffer) to the target (line 81), write the data (line 82), assign the buffer object to the attribute variable a_PointSize (line 88), and enable it.

Once these steps in initVertexBuffers() are completed, the internal state of the WebGL system looks like Figure 5.2. You can see that the two separate buffer objects are created and then assigned to the two separate attribute variables.

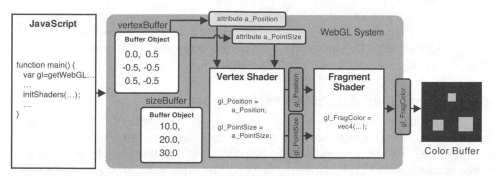

Figure 5.2 Using two buffer objects to pass data to a vertex shader

In this situation, when `gl.drawArrays()` at line 48 is executed, all the data stored inside the buffer objects is sequentially passed to each attribute variable in the order it was stored inside the buffer objects. By assigning this data to `gl_Position` at line 7 and `gl_PointSize` at line 8, respectively (the vertex shader's program in Figure 5.2), you are now able to draw different size objects located at different positions.

By creating a buffer object for each type of data in this way and then allocating it to the attribute variables, you can pass several pieces of information about each vertex to the vertex shader. Other types of information that can be passed include color, texture coordinates (described in this chapter), and normals (see Chapter 7), as well as point size.

The gl.vertexAttribPointer() Stride and Offset Parameters

Although multiple buffer objects are a great way to handle small amounts of data, in a complicated 3D object with many thousands of vertices, you can imagine that managing all the associated vertex data is an extremely difficult task. For example, imagine needing to manually check each of these arrays when the total count of `MultiAttributeSize.js`'s vertices and sizes reaches 1000.[1] However, WebGL allows the vertex coordinates and the size to be bundled into a single component and provides mechanisms to access the different data types. For example, you can group the vertex and size data in the following way (refer to Listing 5.2), often referred to as **interleaving**.

Listing 5.2 An Array Containing Multiple Items of Vertex Information

```
var verticesSizes = new Float32Array([
  // Vertex coordinates and size of a point
    0.0,   0.5, 10.0,   // The 1st point
   -0.5,  -0.5, 20.0,   // The 2nd point
    0.5,  -0.5, 30.0    // The 3rd point
]);
```

---

[1] In practice, because modeling tools that create 3D models actually generate this data, there is no necessity to either manually input them or visually check their consistency. The use of modeling tools and the data they generate will be discussed in Chapter 10.

As just described, once you have stored several types of information pertaining to the vertex in a single buffer object, you need a mechanism to access these different data elements. You can use the fifth (*stride*) and sixth (*offset*) arguments of gl.vertexAttrib-Pointer() to do this, as shown in the example that follows.

Sample Program (MultiAttributeSize_Interleaved.js)

Let's construct a sample program, MultiAttributeSize_Interleaved, which passes multiple data to the vertex shader, just like MultiAttributeSize.js (refer to Listing 5.1), except that it bundles the data into a single array or buffer. Listing 5.3 shows the program in which the vertex shader and the fragment shader are the same as in MultiAttributeSize.js.

Listing 5.3   MultiAttributeSize_Interleaved.js

```
 1 // MultiAttributeSize_Interleaved.js
 2 // Vertex shader program
 3 var VSHADER_SOURCE =
 4   'attribute vec4 a_Position;\n' +
 5   'attribute float a_PointSize;\n' +
 6   'void main() {\n' +
 7   '  gl_Position = a_Position;\n' +
 8   '  gl_PointSize = a_PointSize;\n' +
 9   '}\n';
   ...
17 function main() {
   ...
34   // Set vertex coordinates and point sizes
35   var n = initVertexBuffers(gl);
   ...
48   gl.drawArrays(gl.POINTS, 0, n);
49 }
50
51 function initVertexBuffers(gl) {
52   var verticesSizes = new Float32Array([
53     // Vertex coordinates and size of a point
54      0.0,  0.5,  10.0,  // The 1st vertex
55     -0.5, -0.5,  20.0,  // The 2nd vertex
56      0.5, -0.5,  30.0   // The 3rd vertex
57   ]);
58   var n = 3;
59
60   // Create a buffer object
61   var vertexSizeBuffer = gl.createBuffer();
   ...
```

```
67    // Write vertex coords and point sizes to the buffer and enable it
68    gl.bindBuffer(gl.ARRAY_BUFFER, vertexSizeBuffer);
69    gl.bufferData(gl.ARRAY_BUFFER, verticesSizes, gl.STATIC_DRAW);
70
71    var FSIZE = verticesSizes.BYTES_PER_ELEMENT;
72    // Get the storage location of a_Position, allocate buffer, & enable
73    var a_Position = gl.getAttribLocation(gl.program, 'a_Position');
      . . .
78    gl.vertexAttribPointer(a_Position, 2, gl.FLOAT, false, FSIZE * 3, 0);
79    gl.enableVertexAttribArray(a_Position);  // Enable allocation
80
81    // Get the storage location of a_PointSize, allocate buffer, & enable
82    var a_PointSize = gl.getAttribLocation(gl.program, 'a_PointSize');
      . . .
87    gl.vertexAttribPointer(a_PointSize, 1, gl.FLOAT, false, FSIZE * 3, FSIZE * 2);
88    gl.enableVertexAttribArray(a_PointSize);  // Enable buffer allocation
      . . .
93    return n;
94  }
```

The processing flow of the main() function in JavaScript is the same as MultiAttributeSize.js, and only the initVertexBuffers() process is modified this time, so let's take a look at its content.

First, a typed array is defined at lines 52 to 57, as previously described in Listing 5.2. Following the usual processing steps, from line 61 to 69, a buffer object is created (line 61), the object is bound (line 68), and the data is written to the object (line 69). Next, at line 71, the size (number of bytes) of the element in the verticeSizes array is stored in the variable FSIZE, which will be needed later on. The size (number of bytes) of each element of a typed array can be obtained through the property BYTES_PER_ELEMENT.

From line 73 onward, you assign the buffer object to the attribute variable. Retrieving the storage location of the attribute variable a_Position at line 73 is similar to the previous example, but the usage of the arguments of gl.vertexAttribPointer() at line 78 is different because the buffer now holds two types of data: vertex and point size.

You've already looked at the specification of gl.vertexAttribPointer() in Chapter 3, but let's take another look and focus on two parameters: *stride* and *offset*.

gl.vertexAttribPointer(location, size, type, normalized, stride, offset)

Assign the buffer object bound to gl.ARRAY_BUFFER to the attribute variable specified by *location*. The type and format of the data written in the buffer is also specified.

Parameters	location	Specifies the storage location of the attribute variable.
	size	Specifies the number of components per vertex in the buffer object (valid values are 1 to 4).
	type	Specifies the data format (in this case, gl.FLOAT)
	normalized	true or false. Used to indicate whether non-float data should be normalized to [0, 1] or [–1, 1].
	stride	Specifies the stride length (in bytes) to get vertex data; that is, the number of bytes between each vertex element
	offset	Specifies the offset (in bytes) in a buffer object to indicate where the vertex data is stored from. If the data is stored from the beginning. then offset is 0.

The *stride* specifies the number of bytes used by a group of related vertex data (in this example, vertex coordinates and point size) inside the buffer object.

In previous examples, where you had only one type of information in the buffer—vertices—you set the *stride* to 0. However, in this example, both vertices and point sizes are laid out in the buffer, as shown in Figure 5.3.

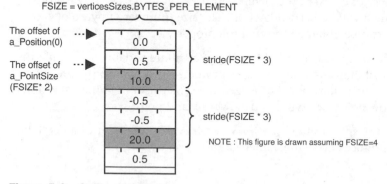

Figure 5.3 Stride and offset

As illustrated in Figure 5.3, there are three components inside each group of vertex data (two coordinates, one size), so you need to set the *stride* equal to three times the size of each component in the group (that is, three times FSIZE [the number of bytes per element of the Floats32Array]).

The *offset* parameter indicates the distance to the first element that is being used for this call. Because you are using the vertex coordinates that are positioned at the head of the verticesSizes array, the *offset* is 0. So, at line 78, you specify them as the fifth (*stride*) and sixth (*offset*) arguments of gl.vertexAttribPointer():

```
78    gl.vertexAttribPointer(a_Position, 2, gl.FLOAT, false, FSIZE * 3, 0);
79    gl.enableVertexAttribArray(a_Position);   // Enable allocation
```

Finally, once the specification of the vertex coordinates has been set up, the assignment to a_Position is enabled at line 79.

Next, from line 82, you need to do the same for the point size data, so assign a buffer object to a_PointSize. However, in this case, you are using the same buffer that you used for vertex data, but you want different data from the buffer. You can make use of the sixth argument *offset* to achieve this by setting the *offset* to the location at which the data (in this case the point size) to be passed to a_PointSize is positioned in the buffer. The first two elements of the array are vertex coordinates, so the *offset* will accordingly be set to FSIZE * 2 (refer to Figure 5.3). Line 87 shows both *stride* and *offset* set up correctly:

```
87    gl.vertexAttribPointer(a_PointSize, 1, gl.FLOAT, false, FSIZE * 3, FSIZE * 2);
88    gl.enableVertexAttribArray(a_PointSize);   // Enable buffer allocation
```

The assignment to a_PointSize is enabled at line 88, and the only remaining task to perform is the draw operation using gl.drawArrays().

Each time a vertex shader is invoked, WebGL will extract data from the buffer object using the values specified in *stride* and *offset* and subsequently pass them to the attribute variables to be used for drawing (see Figure 5.4).

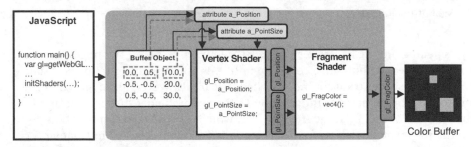

Figure 5.4 Internal behavior when stride and offset are used

Modifying the Color (Varying Variable)

Now that you have seen how to pass several pieces of information to the vertex shader, let's use the technique to modify the color of each point. You can achieve this using the procedure explained previously, substituting color information for point size in the buffer. After storing the vertex coordinates and the color in the buffer object, you will assign the color to the attribute variable, which handles the color.

Let's construct a sample program, MultiAttributeColor, that draws red, blue, and green points. A screenshot is shown in Figure 5.5. (Because this book is black and white, it might be difficult to appreciate the difference between the colors, so load and run the code in your browser.)

Figure 5.5 MultiAttributeColor

As you may remember from Chapter 2, "Your First Step with WebGL," the fragment shader actually handles attributes like color. Up until this point, you've set up color statically in the fragment shader code and not touched it again. However, although you have learned how to pass the point color information to the vertex shader through the attribute variable, the use of the gl_FragColor variable, which sets the color information, is restricted to the fragment shader. (Refer to the section "Fragment Shader" in Chapter 2.) Therefore, you need to find a way to communicate to the fragment shader the color information previously passed to the vertex shader (Figure 5.6).

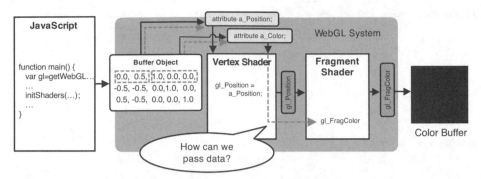

Figure 5.6 Passing data from a vertex shader to a fragment shader

In ColoredPoints (Chapter 2), a uniform variable was used to pass the color information to the fragment shader; however, because it is a "uniform" variable (not varying), it cannot be used to pass different colors for each vertex. This is where a new method to pass data to the fragment shader through the **varying variable** is needed and relies on a mechanism that sends data from the vertex shader to the fragment shader: by using the varying variable. Let's look at a concrete sample program.

Sample Program (MultiAttributeColor.js)

Listing 5.4 shows the program, which looks similar to the program introduced in the previous section, MultiAttributeSize_Stride.js, but the part related to the vertex and fragment shaders is actually slightly different.

Listing 5.4   MultiAttributeColor.js

```
1 // MultiAttributeColor.js
2 // Vertex shader program
3 var VSHADER_SOURCE =
4    'attribute vec4 a_Position;\n' +
5    'attribute vec4 a_Color;\n' +
6 'varying vec4 v_Color;\n' + // varying variable
7    'void main() {\n' +
8    ' gl_Position = a_Position;\n' +
9    ' gl_PointSize = 10.0;\n' +
10 ' v_Color = a_Color;\n' + // Pass the data to the fragment shader
11    '}\n';
12
13 // Fragment shader program
14 var FSHADER_SOURCE =
      ...
18 'varying vec4 v_Color;\n' +
19    'void main() {\n' +
```

```
20  '  gl_FragColor = v_Color;\n' + // Receive the data from the vertex shader
21  '}\n';
22
23 function main() {
   ...
40   // Set vertex coordinates and color
41   var n = initVertexBuffers(gl);
   ...
54   gl.drawArrays(gl.POINTS, 0, n);
55 }
56
57 function initVertexBuffers(gl) {
58   var verticesColors = new Float32Array([
59     // Vertex coordinates and color
60      0.0,  0.5,  1.0,  0.0,  0.0,
61     -0.5, -0.5,  0.0,  1.0,  0.0,
62      0.5, -0.5,  0.0,  0.0,  1.0,
63   ]);
64   var n = 3; // The number of vertices
65
66   // Create a buffer object
67   var vertexColorBuffer = gl.createBuffer();
   ...
73   // Write the vertex coordinates and colors to the buffer object
74   gl.bindBuffer(gl.ARRAY_BUFFER, vertexColorBuffer);
75   gl.bufferData(gl.ARRAY_BUFFER, verticesColors, gl.STATIC_DRAW);
76
77   var FSIZE = verticesColors.BYTES_PER_ELEMENT;
78   // Get the storage location of a_Position, allocate buffer, & enable
79   var a_Position = gl.getAttribLocation(gl.program, 'a_Position');
   ...
84   gl.vertexAttribPointer(a_Position, 2, gl.FLOAT, false, FSIZE * 5, 0);
85   gl.enableVertexAttribArray(a_Position);  // Enable buffer assignment
86
87   // Get the storage location of a_Color, assign buffer, and enable
88   var a_Color = gl.getAttribLocation(gl.program, 'a_Color');
   ...
93   gl.vertexAttribPointer(a_Color, 3, gl.FLOAT, false, FSIZE*5, FSIZE*2);
94  gl.enableVertexAttribArray(a_Color);  // Enable buffer allocation
   ...
96   return n;
97 }
```

At line 5 of the vertex shader, an attribute variable a_Color is declared in order to receive the color data. Next, at line 6, a new varying variable v_Color is declared that will be used to pass its value to the fragment shader. Please note that you can only use float types (and related types vec2, vec3, vec4, mat2, mat3, and mat4) for varying variables:

```
5    'attribute vec4 a_Color;\n' +
6    'varying vec4 v_Color;\n' +
```

At line 10, the value of a_Color is assigned to the variable v_Color declared at line 6:

```
10   '  v_Color = a_Color;\n' +
```

So how can the fragment shader receive the assigned data? The answer is straightforward. All that is required is declaring a variable in the fragment shader with the same name and types as that in the vertex shader:

```
18   'varying vec4 v_Color;\n' +
```

In WebGL, when varying variables declared inside the fragment shader have identical names and types to the ones declared in the vertex shader, the assigned values in the vertex shader are automatically passed to the fragment shader (see Figure 5.7).

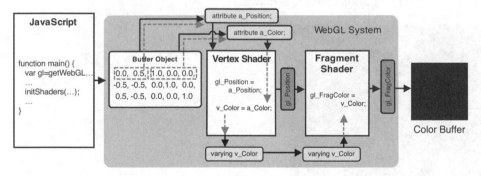

Figure 5.7 The behavior of a varying variable

So, the fragment shader can receive the values assigned to the vertex shader at line 10 simply by assigning the varying variable v_Color to gl_FragColor at line 20. As gl_FragColor sets the fragment color, the color of each point will be modified:

```
20   '  gl_FragColor = v_Color;\n' +
```

The remaining code is similar to MultiAttributeSize.js. The only differences are that the name of the typed array for vertex information defined at line 58 is modified to verticesColors, and the color information such as (1.0, 0.0, 0.0) is added to the data definition at line 60.

As previously explained in Chapter 2, the color information is specified using the 0.0–1.0 range for each component of the RGBA model. Just like `MultiAttributeSize_Stride.js`, you store several different types of data within a single array. The fifth (*stride*) and sixth (*offset*) arguments of `gl.vertexAttribPointer()` are modified at lines 84 and 93, respectively, based on the content of the `verticesColors` array which, because you have introduced some color information in addition to the vertex coordinates, means the *stride* changes to `FSIZE * 5`.

Finally, the draw command at line 54 results in red, blue, and green points being displayed in the browser.

Experimenting with the Sample Program

Let's modify the first argument of `gl.drawArrays()` at line 54 to `gl.TRIANGLES` and see what happens upon execution. Alternatively, you can load the `ColoredTriangle` sample program from the book's website:

```
54    gl.drawArrays(gl.TRIANGLES, 0, n);
```

The execution output is shown in Figure 5.8. It might be difficult to grasp the difference when seen in black and white, but on your screen, notice that a nice smooth-shaded triangle with red, green, and blue corners is drawn.

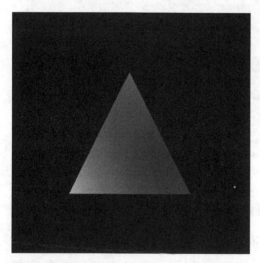

Figure 5.8 ColoredTriangle

This significant change from three colored points to a smoothly shaded triangle occurred just by changing one parameter value. Let's look at how that came about.

Color Triangle (ColoredTriangle.js)

You already explored the subject of coloring triangles using a single color in Chapter 3. This section explains how to specify a different color for each of the triangle's vertices and the process within WebGL that results in a smooth color transition between the different vertices.

To fully comprehend the phenomenon, you need to understand in detail the process carried out between the vertex and the fragment shaders, as well as the functionality of the varying variable.

Geometric Shape Assembly and Rasterization

Let's start the explanation using the example program, `HelloTriangle.js`, introduced in Chapter 3, which simply draws a red triangle. The relevant code snippet necessary for the explanation is shown in Listing 5.5.

Listing 5.5   HelloTriangle.js (Code Snippet)

```
 1 // HelloTriangle.js
 2 // Vertex shader program
 3 var VSHADER_SOURCE =
 4   'attribute vec4 a_Position;\n' +
 5   'void main() {\n' +
 6   '  gl_Position = a_Position;\n' +
 7   '}\n';
 8
 9 // Fragment shader program
10 var FSHADER_SOURCE =
11   'void main() {\n' +
12   '  gl_FragColor = vec4(1.0, 0.0, 0.0, 1.0);\n' +
13   '}\n';
14
15 function main() {
   ...
32   // Set vertex coordinates
33   var n = initVertexBuffers(gl);
...
45   // Draw a triangle
46   gl.drawArrays(gl.TRIANGLES, 0, n);
47 }
48
49 function initVertexBuffers(gl) {
```

```
50    var vertices = new Float32Array([
51      0.0, 0.5,    -0.5, -0.5,    0.5, -0.5
52    ]);
53    var n = 3; // The number of vertices
      ...
74    gl.vertexAttribPointer(a_Position, 2, gl.FLOAT, false, 0, 0);
      ...
81    return n;
82  }
```

In this program, after writing the vertex coordinates (lines 50 to 52) into the buffer object in the function `initVertexBuffers()`, the buffer object is assigned to the attribute variable `a_Position` at line 74. Following that, when `gl.drawArrays()` invokes the vertex shader at line 46, the three vertex coordinates inside the buffer object are passed to `a_Position` at line 4 and assigned to `gl_Position` at line 6, thus making them available to the fragment shader. In the fragment shader, the RGBA value (1.0, 0.0, 0.0, 1.0) associated with the red color is assigned to `gl_FragColor`, so a red triangle is displayed.

Up until now, you haven't actually explored how this works, so let's examine how exactly a fragment shader performs per-fragment operations when you only give it the triangle's three vertex coordinates in `gl_Position`.

In Figure 5.9, you can see the problem. The program gives three vertices, but who identifies that the vertex coordinates assigned to `gl_Position` are the vertices of a triangle? In addition, to make the triangle look like it is filled with a single color, who decides which fragments have to be colored? Finally, who is responsible for invoking the fragment shader and how it handles processing for each of the fragments?

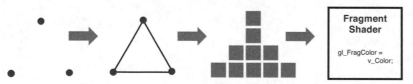

Figure 5.9 Vertex coordinate, identification of a triangle from the vertex coordinates, rasterization, and execution of a fragment shader

Up until now, we have glossed over these details, but there are actually two processes taking place between the vertex and the fragment shaders, which are shown in Figure 5.10.

- **The geometric shape assembly process:** In this stage, the geometric shape is assembled from the specified vertex coordinates. The first argument of `gl.drawArray()` specifies which type of shape should be assembled.

- **The rasterization process:** In this stage, the geometric shape assembled in the geometric assembly process is converted into fragments.

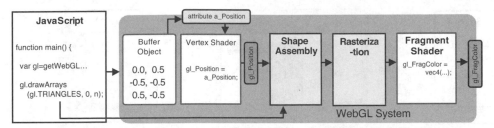

Figure 5.10 Assembly and rasterization between a vertex shader and a fragment shader

As you will have realized from Figure 5.10, `gl_Position` actually acts as the input to the **geometric shape assembly** stage. Note that the geometric shape assembly process is also called the **primitive assembly process** because the basic shapes previously shown in Chapter 2 are also called **primitives**.

Figure 5.11 shows the processes between the vertex and fragment shaders, which are actually performed in assembly and rasterization for `HelloTriangle.js`.

From Listing 5.5, the third argument n of `gl.drawArrays()` (line 46) is set to 3, meaning that the vertex shader is actually invoked three times.

Step 1. The vertex shader is invoked, and then the first coordinate (0.0, 0.5) inside the buffer object is passed to the attribute variable `a_Position`. Once this is assigned to `gl_Position`, this coordinate is communicated to the geometric shape assembly stage and held there. As you will remember, because only the x and y coordinates are passed to `a_Position`, the z and w values are supplied, so actually (0.0, 0.5, 0.0, 1.0) is held.

Step 2. The vertex shader is once again invoked, and in a similar way the second coordinate (–0.5, –0.5) is passed to the geometric shape assembly stage and held there.

Step 3. The vertex shader is invoked a third time, passing the third coordinate (0.5, –0.5) to the geometric shape assembly stage and holding it there.

Now the vertex shader processing is complete, and the three coordinates are readily available for the geometric shape assembly stage.

Step 4. The geometric shape assembly processing starts. Using the three vertices passed and the information (`gl.TRIANGLES`) contained in the first argument of `gl.drawArrays()`, this stage decides how primitives should be assembled. In this case, a triangle is assembled using the three vertices.

Step 5. Because what is displayed on the screen is a triangle consisting of fragments (pixels), the geometric shape is converted to fragments. This process is called **rasterization**. Here, the fragments that make up the triangle will be generated. You can see the example of the generated fragments in the box of the rasterization stage in Figure 5.11.

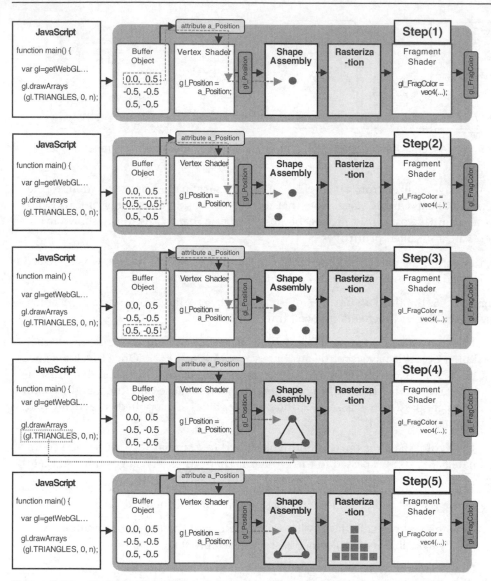

Figure 5.11 The processing flow of geometric shape assembly and rasterization

In this figure, although we show only 10 fragments, the actual number of fragments is determined according to the area where the triangle is finally displayed on the screen.

If you specify a different geometric shape in the first argument of gl.drawArrays(), the geometric shape assembled in Step 4 is modified accordingly, as are the number of fragments and their position in Step 5. For example, if you specify gl.LINES, a line will be assembled out of the first two coordinates, and the remaining one will be discarded. If you set it to gl.LINE_LOOP, a connected group of line segments will be generated, and only a transparent (no fill color) triangle will be drawn.

Fragment Shader Invocations

Once the rasterization stage is completed, the fragment shader is invoked to process each of the generated fragments. So in this example, the fragment shader is invoked 10 times, as illustrated in Figure 5.12. To avoid cluttering the figure, we skip the intermediate steps. All of the fragments are fed one by one to the fragment shader, and for each fragment, the fragment shader sets the color and writes its output to the color buffer. When the last fragment shader process is completed at Step 15, the final output is displayed in the browser.

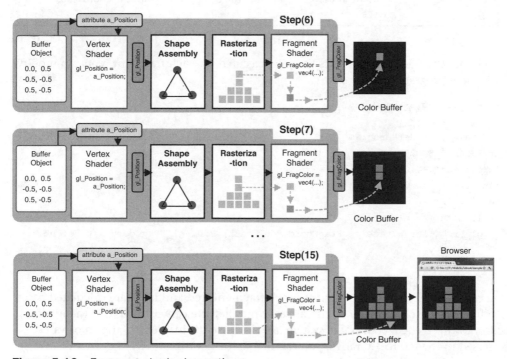

Figure 5.12 Fragment shader invocations

The following fragment shader in HelloTriangle.js colors each fragment in red. As a result, a red filled triangle is written to the color buffer and displayed in the browser.

```
 9 // Fragment shader program
10 var FSHADER_SOURCE =
11   'void main() {\n' +
12   '  gl_FragColor = vec4(1.0, 0.0, 0.0, 1.0);\n' +
13   '}\n';
```

Experimenting with the Sample Program

As an experiment, let's confirm that the fragment shader is called for each fragment by trying to set the color of each fragment based on its location. Each fragment generated by the rasterization stage has its coordinates passed to the fragment shader upon invocation. These coordinates can be accessed through the built-in variables provided inside the fragment shader (Table 5.1).

Table 5.1   Built-In Variables in a Fragment Shade (Input)

Type and Variable Name	Description
vec4 gl_FragCoord	The first and second component are the coordinates of the fragment in the `<canvas>` coordinate system (window coordinate system)

To check that the fragment shader is actually executed for each fragment, you can modify line 12 in the program, as follows:

```
 1 // HelloTriangle_FragCoord.js
   ...
 9 // Fragment shader program
10 var FSHADER_SOURCE =
11   'precision mediump float;\n' +
12   'uniform float u_Width;\n' +
13   'uniform float u_Height;\n' +
14   'void main() {\n' +
15   '  gl_FragColor = vec4(gl_FragCoord.x/u_Width, 0.0, gl_FragCoord.y/u_Height,
                                                                  ➥1.0);\n' +
16   '}\n';
```

As you can see, the color components of each fragment, red and blue, are calculated based on the fragment's coordinates on the canvas. Note that the canvas's y-axis is the inverse direction to the WebGL coordinate system, and because it's in WebGL, the color value is expressed in the 0.0 to 1.0 range, you can divide the coordinates by the size of the `<canvas>` element (that is, 400 pixels) to get the appropriate color value. As you can see, the width and height are passed into the shader using the uniform variables u_Width and u_Height and determined from gl.drawingBufferWidth and gl.drawingBufferHeight. You can see the execution result in Figure 5.13, which is a triangle whose fragments are colored as a function of their position. Running this sample program HelloTriangle_FragCoord, you will see the transition from the left top to the right bottom.

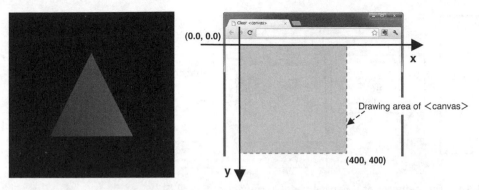

(0.0, 0.0)

x

Drawing area of <canvas>

(400, 400)

y

Figure 5.13 Modifying the color per fragment (the figure on the right side shows the <canvas> coordinate system)

Because you modify the color of each fragment with respect to its coordinates, you will notice that the color progressively changes according to the coordinates. Again, if this is not clear from the black-and-white image in Figure 5.13, run the example from the book's website.

Functionality of Varying Variables and the Interpolation Process

At this stage, you have a better understanding of the process flow taking place between the vertex and the fragment shaders (that is, the geometric shape assembly process and the subsequent rasterization process), as well as the invocation of the fragment shader for each of the generated fragments.

Returning to Figure 5.8, the first ColoredTriangle, let's use what you've learned to understand better why you get such a nicely shaded triangle when you specify a different color for each the triangle's vertex. Previously, you saw that the value assigned to the varying variable inside the vertex shader is passed as a varying variable with identical attributes (same name, same type) to the fragment shader (see Figure 5.14). However, to be more precise, the value assigned to the varying variable in the vertex shader is interpolated at the rasterization stage. Consequently, the value passed to the fragment shader actually differs for each fragment based on that interpolation (see Figure 5.15). This is the reason the varying variable has the name "varying."

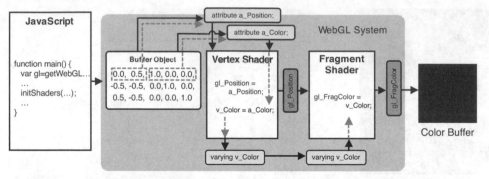

Figure 5.14 The behavior of a varying variable (reprint of Figure 5.7)

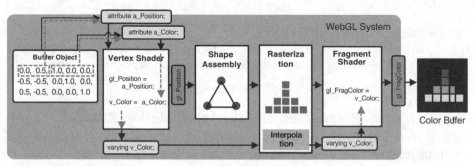

Figure 5.15 Interpolation of a varying variable

More specifically, in `ColoredTriangle`, because we only assign a different value to the varying variable for each of the three vertices, each fragment located between vertices must have its own color interpolated by the WebGL system.

For example, let's consider the case in which the two end points of a line are specified with different colors. One of the vertices is red (1.0, 0.0 0.0), whereas the other one is blue (0.0, 0.0, 1.0). After the colors (red and blue) are assigned to the vertex shader's `v_Color`, the RGB values for each of the fragments located between those two vertices are calculated and passed to the fragment shader's `v_Color` (see Figure 5.16).

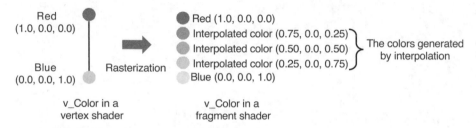

Figure 5.16 Interpolation of color values

In this case, R decreases from 1.0 to 0.0, B increases from 0.0 to 1.0, and all the RGB values between the two vertices are calculated appropriately—this is called the **interpolation process**. Once the new color for each of the fragments located between the two vertices is calculated in this way, it is passed to the fragment shader's `v_Color`.

We follow an identical procedure in the case of the colored triangle, which is reproduced in Listing 5.6. After the three vertices' colors are assigned to the varying variable `v_Color` (line 9), the interpolated color for each fragment is passed to the fragment shader's `v_Color`. Once this is assigned to the `gl_FragColor` at line 19, a colored triangle is drawn, as shown in Figure 5.8. This interpolation process is carried out for each of the varying variables. If you want to understand more about this process, a good source of information is the book **Computer Graphics**.

Listing 5.6 ColoredTriangle.js

```
 1 // ColoredTriangle.js
 2 // Vertex shader program
 3 var VSHADER_SOURCE = '\
   ...
 6 varying vec4 v_Color;\
 7 void main() {\
 8   gl_Position = a_Position;\
 9   v_Color = a_Color;\   <- The color at line 59 is assigned to v_Color
10 }';
11
12 // Fragment shader program
13 var FSHADER_SOURCE =
   ...
17  varying vec4 v_Color;\   <- The interpolated color is passed to v_Color
18  void main() {\
19    gl_FragColor = v_Color;\   <- The color is assigned to gl_FragColor
20  }';
21
22 function main() {
   ...
53   gl.drawArrays(gl.TRIANGLES, 0, n);
54 }
55
56 function initVertexBuffers(gl) {
57   var verticesColors = new Float32Array([
58     // Vertex coordinates and color
59      0.0,  0.5,  1.0,  0.0,  0.0,
60     -0.5, -0.5,  0.0,  1.0,  0.0,
61      0.5, -0.5,  0.0,  0.0,  1.0,
62   ]);
   ...
99 }
```

In summary, this section has highlighted the critical rasterization process that takes place between the vertex and fragment shaders. Rasterization is a key component of 3D graphics and is responsible for taking geometric shapes and building up the fragments that will draw those shapes. After converting the specified geometric shape into fragments (rasterization), it's possible to set a different color for each of the fragments inside the fragment shader. This color can be interpolated or set directly by the programmer.

Pasting an Image onto a Rectangle

In the previous section, you explored how to use color when drawing shapes and how interpolation creates smooth color transitions. Although powerful, this approach is limited when it comes to reproducing complex visual representations. For example, a problem arises if you want to create a wall that has the look and feel of the one shown in Figure 5.17, you would need many triangles, and determining the color and coordinates for each triangle would prove to be daunting.

Figure 5.17 An example of a complex wall surface

As you'd imagine, in 3D graphics, one of the most important processes is actually solving this problem. The problem is resolved using a technique called **texture mapping**, which can re-create the look of real-world materials. The process is actually straightforward and consists of pasting an image (like a decal) on the surface of a geometrical shape. By pasting an image from a real-world photograph on a rectangle made up of two triangles, you can give the rectangle surface an appearance similar to that of a picture. The image is called a **texture image** or a **texture**.

The role of the texture mapping process is to assign the texture image's pixel colors to the fragments generated by the rasterization process introduced in the previous section. The pixels that make up the texture image are called **texels** (texture elements), and each texel codes its color information in the RGB or RGBA format (see Figure 5.18).

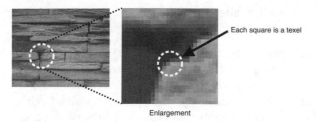

Each square is a texel

Enlargement

Figure 5.18 Texels

Texture mapping involves the following four steps in WebGL:

1. Prepare the image to be mapped on the geometric shape.

2. Specify the image mapping method for the geometric shape.

3. Load the texture image and configure it for use in WebGL.

4. Extract the texels from the image in the fragment shader, and accordingly set the corresponding fragment.

To understand the mechanisms involved in texture mapping, let's examine the sample program `TextureQuad`, which "pastes" an image onto a rectangle. If you run it from the book's website, you'll see the result as shown in Figure 5.19 (left).

Note When you want to run the sample programs that use texture images in Chrome from your local disk, you should add the option `--allow-file-access-from-files` to Chrome. This is for security reasons. Chrome, by default, does not allow access to local files such as `../resources/sky.jpg`. For Firefox, the equivalent parameter, set via `about:config`, is `security.fileuri.strict_origin_policy`, which should be set to `false`. Remember to set it back when you're finished because you open a security loophole if local file access is enabled.

Texture image

sky.jpg

Figure 5.19 TextureQuad (left) and the texture image used (right)

Looking in a little more detail at steps (1) to (4) in the following sections, the image prepared in (1) can be any format that can be displayed in a browser. For now, you can use any pictures you might have taken yourself or alternatively you can use the images located in the `resource` folder of the companion website provided with this book.

The mapping method specified in (2) consists of designating "which part of the texture image" should be pasted to "which part of the geometric shape". The part of the geometric shape meant to be covered with the texture is specified using the coordinates of the vertices that compose a surface. The part of the texture image to be used is specified using **texture coordinates**. These are a new form of coordinates so let's look at how they work.

Texture Coordinates

The texture coordinate system used in WebGL is two-dimensional, as shown in Figure 5.20. To differentiate the texture coordinates from the widely used x and y axis, WebGL changes the denomination to the s and t coordinates (st coordinates system).[2]

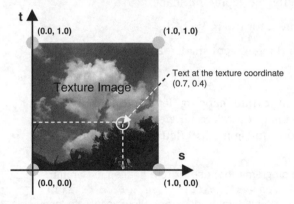

Figure 5.20   WebGL's Texture coordinate system

As you can see from Figure 5.20, the coordinates of the four corners are defined as left bottom corner (0.0, 0.0), right bottom corner (1.0, 0.0), right top corner (1.0, 1.0), and left top corner (0.0, 1.0). Because these values are not related to the image size, this allows a common approach to image handling; for example, whether the texture image's size is 128×128 or 128×256, the right top corner coordinates will always be (1.0, 1.0).

Pasting Texture Images onto the Geometric Shape

As previously mentioned, in WebGL, by defining the correspondence between the texture coordinates and the vertex coordinates of the geometric shape, you can specify how the texture image will be pasted (see Figure 5.21).

---

[2] The `uv` coordinates are often used. However, we are using `st` coordinates because GLSL ES uses the component names to access the texture image.

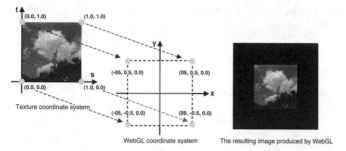

Figure 5.21 Texture coordinates and mapping them to vertices

Here, the texture coordinates (0.0, 1.0) are mapped onto the vertex coordinates (−0.5, 0.5, 0.0), and the texture coordinates (1.0, 1.0) are mapped onto the vertex coordinates (0.5, 0.5, 0.0). By establishing the correspondence for each of the four corners of the texture image, you obtain the result shown in the right part of Figure 5.21.

Now, given your understanding of how images can be mapped to shapes, let's look at the sample program.

Sample Program (TexturedQuad.js)

In `TexturedQuad.js` (see Listing 5.7), the texture mapping affects both the vertex and the fragment shaders. This is because it sets the texture coordinates for each vertex and then applies the corresponding pixel color extracted from the texture image to each fragment. There are five main parts to the example, each identified by the numbers to the right of the code.

Listing 5.7 TexturedQuad.js

```
 1 // TexturedQuad.js
 2 // Vertex shader program                              <- (Part1)
 3 var VSHADER_SOURCE =
 4   'attribute vec4 a_Position;\n' +
 5   'attribute vec2 a_TexCoord;\n' +
 6   'varying vec2 v_TexCoord;\n' +
 7   'void main() {\n' +
 8   '  gl_Position = a_Position;\n' +
 9   '  v_TexCoord = a_TexCoord;\n' +
10   '}\n';
11
12 // Fragment shader program                            <- (Part2)
13 var FSHADER_SOURCE =
   ...
17   'uniform sampler2D u_Sampler;\n' +
18   'varying vec2 v_TexCoord;\n' +
19   'void main() {\n' +
```

```
20    '  gl_FragColor = texture2D(u_Sampler, v_TexCoord);\n' +
21    '}\n';
22
23 function main() {
   ...
40    // Set the vertices information                    <- (Part3)
41    var n = initVertexBuffers(gl);
   ...
50    // Setting the textures
51    if (!initTextures(gl, n)) {
   ...
54    }
55 }
56
57 function initVertexBuffers(gl) {
58   var verticesTexCoords = new Float32Array([
59     // Vertices coordinates, textures coordinates
60     -0.5,   0.5,   0.0, 1.0,
61     -0.5,  -0.5,   0.0, 0.0,
62      0.5,   0.5,   1.0, 1.0,
63      0.5,  -0.5,   1.0, 0.0,
64   ]);
65   var n = 4; // The number of vertices
66
67   // Create the buffer object
68   var vertexTexCoordBuffer = gl.createBuffer();
   ...
74   // Write the vertex coords and textures coords to the object buffer
75   gl.bindBuffer(gl.ARRAY_BUFFER, vertexTexCoordBuffer);
76   gl.bufferData(gl.ARRAY_BUFFER, verticesTexCoords, gl.STATIC_DRAW);
77
78   var FSIZE = verticesTexCoords.BYTES_PER_ELEMENT;
   ...
85   gl.vertexAttribPointer(a_Position, 2, gl.FLOAT, false, FSIZE * 4, 0);
86   gl.enableVertexAttribArray(a_Position);    // Enable buffer allocation
87
88   // Allocate the texture coordinates to a_TexCoord, and enable it.
89   var a_TexCoord = gl.getAttribLocation(gl.program, 'a_TexCoord');
   ...
94   gl.vertexAttribPointer(a_TexCoord, 2, gl.FLOAT, false, FSIZE * 4, FSIZE * 2);
95   gl.enableVertexAttribArray(a_TexCoord);  // Enable buffer allocation
   ...
97   return n;
98 }
99
```

```
100 function initTextures(gl, n)                              <- (Part4)
101   var texture = gl.createTexture();   // Create a texture object
   ...
107   // Get the storage location of the u_Sampler
108   var u_Sampler = gl.getUniformLocation(gl.program, 'u_Sampler');
   ...
114   var image = new Image();  // Create an image object
   ...
119   // Register the event handler to be called on loading an image
120   image.onload = function(){ loadTexture(gl, n, texture, u_Sampler, image); };
121   // Tell the browser to load an image
122   image.src = '../resources/sky.jpg';
123
124   return true;
125 }
126
127 function loadTexture(gl, n, texture, u_Sampler, image){   <- (Part5)
128   gl.pixelStorei(gl.UNPACK_FLIP_Y_WEBGL, 1); // Flip the image's y axis
129   // Enable the texture unit 0
130   gl.activeTexture(gl.TEXTURE0);
131   // Bind the texture object to the target
132   gl.bindTexture(gl.TEXTURE_2D, texture);
133
134   // Set the texture parameters
135   gl.texParameteri(gl.TEXTURE_2D, gl.TEXTURE_MIN_FILTER, gl.LINEAR);
136   // Set the texture image
137   gl.texImage2D(gl.TEXTURE_2D, 0, gl.RGB, gl.RGB, gl.UNSIGNED_BYTE, image);
138
139   // Set the texture unit 0 to the sampler
140   gl.uniform1i(u_Sampler, 0);
   ...
144   gl.drawArrays(gl.TRIANGLE_STRIP, 0, n); // Draw a rectangle
145 }
```

This program is structured into five main parts:

Part 1: Receive the texture coordinates in the vertex shader and then pass them to the fragment shader.

Part 2: Paste the texture image onto the geometric shape inside the fragment shader.

Part 3: Set the texture coordinates (`initVertexBuffers()`).

Part 4: Prepare the texture image for loading, and request the browser to read it. (`initTextures()`).

Part 5: Configure the loaded texture so that it can be used in WebGL (`loadTexture()`).

Let's look at the sequence starting from Part 3: the process to set the texture coordinates using `initVertexBuffers()`. The shaders are executed after loading the image, so we will explain them at the end.

Using Texture Coordinates (initVertexBuffers())

You pass texture coordinates to the vertex shader using the same approach you've been using to pass other vertex data to the vertex shader, by combining vertex coordinates and vertex data into a single buffer. Line 58 defines an array `verticesTexCoords` containing pairs of vertex coordinates and their associated texture coordinates:

```
58   var verticesTexCoords = new Float32Array([
59     // Vertex coordinates and texture coordinates
60     -0.5,   0.5,   0.0,   1.0,
61     -0.5,  -0.5,   0.0,   0.0,
62      0.5,   0.5,   1.0,   1.0,
63      0.5,  -0.5,   1.0,   0.0,
64   ]);
```

As you can see, the first vertex (–0.5, 0.5) is mapped to the texture coordinate (0.0, 1.0), the second vertex (–0.5, –0.5) is mapped to the texture coordinate (0.0, 0.0), the third vertex (0.5, 0.5) is mapped to the texture coordinate (1.0, 10), and the fourth vertex (0.5, –0.5) is mapped to the texture coordinate (1.0, 0.0). Figure 5.21 illustrates these mappings.

Lines 75 to 86 then write vertex coordinates and texture coordinates to the buffer object, assign it to a_Position, and enable the assignment. After that, lines 89 to 94 retrieve the storage location of the attribute variable a_TexCoord and then assign the buffer object containing the texture coordinates to the variable. Finally, line 95 enables the assignment of the buffer object to a_TexCoord:

```
88   // Assign the texture coordinates to a_TexCoord, and enable it.
89   var a_TexCoord = gl.getAttribLocation(gl.program, 'a_TexCoord');
     ...
94   gl.vertexAttribPointer(a_TexCoord, 2, gl.FLOAT, false, FSIZE * 4,
                                                       ➥FSIZE * 2);
95   gl.enableVertexAttribArray(a_TexCoord);
```

Setting Up and Loading Images (initTextures())

This process is performed from lines 101 to 122 in `initTextures()`. Line 101 creates a texture object (`gl.createTexture()`) for managing the texture image in the WebGL system, and line 108 gets the storage location of a uniform variable (`gl.getUniformLocation()`) to pass the texture image to the fragment shader():

```
101  var texture = gl.createTexture(); // Create a texture object
     ...
108   var u_Sampler = gl.getUniformLocation(gl.program, 'u_Sampler');
```

A texture object is created using `gl.createTexture()`.

gl.createTexture()
Create a texture object to hold a texture image.

Parameters	None	
Return value	non-null	The newly created texture object.
	null	Failed to create a texture object.
Errors	None	

This call creates the texture object in the WebGL system, as shown in Figure 5.22. `gl.TEXTURE0` to `gl.TEXTURE7` are texture units for managing a texture image, and each has an associated `gl.TEXTURE_2D`, which is the texture target for specifying the type of texture. This will be explained in detail later.

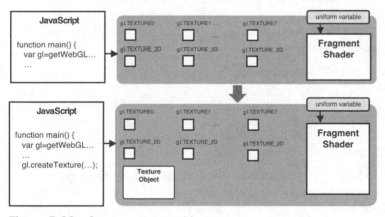

Figure 5.22 Create a texture object

The texture object can be deleted using `gl.deleteTexture()`. Note, if this method is called with a texture object that has already been deleted, the call has no effect.

gl.deleteTexture(texture)
Delete the texture object specified by *texture*.

Parameter	texture	Specifies the texture object to be deleted.
Return value	None	
Errors	None	

In the next step, it's necessary to request that the browser load the image that will be mapped to the rectangle. You need to use an `Image` object for this purpose:

```
114    var image = new Image();   // Create an Image object
    ...
119    // Register an event handler to be called when image loading completes
120    image.onload = function(){ loadTexture(gl, n, texture, u_Sampler, image); };
121    // Tell the browser to load an image
122    image.src = '../resources/sky.jpg';
```

This code snippet creates an `Image` object, registers the event handler (`loadTexture()`) to be called on loading the image, and tells the browser to load the image.

You need to create an `Image` object (a special JavaScript object that handles images) using the `new` operator, just as you would do for an `Array` object or `Date` object. This is done at line 114.

```
114    var image = new Image();   // Create an Image object
```

Because loading of images is performed asynchronously (see the boxed article that follows), when the browser signals completion of loading, it needs to pass the image to the WebGL system. Line 120 handles this, telling the browser that, after loading the image, the anonymous function `loadTexture()` should be called.

```
120    image.onload = function(){ loadTexture(gl, n, texture, u_Sampler, image); };
```

`loadTexture()` takes five parameters, with the newly loaded image being passed via the variable (`Image` object) as the last argument `image`. `gl` is the rendering context for WebGL, `n` is the number of vertices, `texture` is the texture object created at line 101, and `u_Sampler` is the storage location of a uniform variable.

Just like the `<img>` tag in HTML, we can tell the browser to load the texture image by setting the image filename to the property `src` of the `Image` object (line 122). Note that WebGL, because of the usual browser security restrictions, is not allowed to use images located in other domains for texture images:

```
122    image.src = '../resources/sky.jpg';
```

After executing line 122, the browser starts to load the image asynchronously, so the program continues on to the `return` statement at line 124 and then exits. When the browser finishes loading the image and wants to pass the image to the WebGL system, the event handler `loadTexture()` is called.

Asynchronous Loading Texture Images

Usually, OpenGL applications written in C or C++ load the texture image files straight from the hard disk where they are stored. However, because WebGL programs are running inside the browser, it is impossible to load images directly. Instead, it is necessary to read images indirectly by requesting the browser to do it. (Typically, the browser sends a request to the web server to obtain the image.) The advantage is that you can use any kind of image a browser can display, but it also makes the process more complex because you now have to handle two processes (the browser loading request, and the actual WebGL loading) that behave "asynchronously" (they run in the background) and thus do not block execution of the program.

Figure 5.23 shows the substeps between [1] tell the browser to load an image and [7] call the function `loadTexture()` after completing loading the texture image.

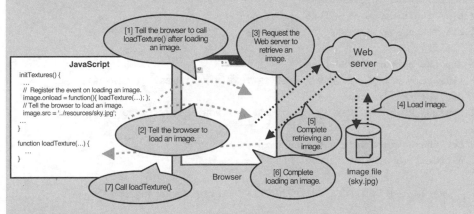

Figure 5.23 Asynchronous loading texture images

In Figure 5.23, [1] and [2] are executed sequentially, but [2] and [7] are not. After requesting the browser to load an image in [2], the JavaScript program doesn't wait for the image to be loaded, but proceeds to the next stage. (This behavior will be explained in detail in a moment.) While the JavaScript program is continuing, the browser sends a request to the web server for the image [3]. When the image loading process is completed [4] and [5], the browser tells the JavaScript program that the image loading has completed [6]. This kind of behavior is referred to as **asynchronous**.

The image loading process is analogous to the way a web page written in HTML displays images. In HTML, an image is displayed by specifying the file URL to the `src` attribute of the `<img>` tag (below) causing the browser to load the image from the specified URL. This part corresponds to [2] shown in Figure 5.23.

```
<img src="../resources/redflower.jpg">
```

The asynchronous nature of the image loading process can be easily understood by considering how a web page that includes numerous images is displayed. Typically, the page text and layout are displayed rapidly, and then images appear slowly as they are loaded. This is because the image loading and display processes are executed asynchronously, allowing you to view and interact with the web page without having to wait for all images to load.

Make the Texture Ready to Use in the WebGL System (loadTexture())

The function `loadTexture()` is defined as follows:

```
127 function loadTexture(gl, n, texture, u_Sampler, image) {   <- (Part5)
128    gl.pixelStorei(gl.UNPACK_FLIP_Y_WEBGL, 1); // Flip the image's y axis
129    // Enable the texture unit 0
130    gl.activeTexture(gl.TEXTURE0);
131    // Bind the texture object to the target
132    gl.bindTexture(gl.TEXTURE_2D, texture);
133
134    // Set the texture parameters
135    gl.texParameteri(gl.TEXTURE_2D, gl.TEXTURE_MIN_FILTER, gl.LINEAR);
136    // Set the texture image
137    gl.texImage2D(gl.TEXTURE_2D, 0, gl.RGB, gl.RGB, gl.UNSIGNED_BYTE, image);
138
139    // Set the texture unit 0 to the sampler
140    gl.uniform1i(u_Sampler, 0);
    ...
144    gl.drawArrays(gl.TRIANGLE_STRIP, 0, n); // Draw a rectangle
145 }
```

Its main purpose is to prepare the image for use by the WebGL system, which it does using a **texture object** that is prepared and used in a similar manner to a buffer object. The following sections explain the code in more detail.

Flip an Image's Y-Axis

Before using the loaded images as a texture, you need to flip the y-axis:

```
128    gl.pixelStorei(gl.UNPACK_FLIP_Y_WEBGL, 1);// Flip the image's y-axis
```

This method flips an image's Y-axis when it's loaded. As shown in Figure 5.24, the t-axis direction of the WebGL texture coordinate system is the inverse of the y-axis direction of the coordinate system used by PNG, BMP, JPG, and so on. For this reason, if you flip the image's Y-axis, you can map the image to the shape correctly. (You could also flip the t coordinates by hand instead of flipping the image.)

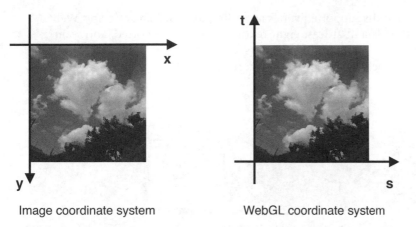

Image coordinate system   WebGL coordinate system

Figure 5.24   The image coordinate system and WebGL texture coordinate system

The following explains `gl.pixelStorei()`.

`gl.pixelStorei(pname, param)`

Perform the process defined by *pname* and *param* after loading an image.

Parameters	pname	Specifies any of the following:
	`gl.UNPACK_FLIP_Y_WEBGL`	Flips an image's Y-axis after loading the image. The default value is `false`.
	`gl.UNPACK_PREMULTIPLY_ALPHA_WEBGL`	Multiplies each component of RGB in an image by *A* in the image. The default value is `false`.
	param	Specifies none-zero (means `true`) or zero (means `false`). It must be specified in the integer.
Return value	None	
Errors	INVALID_ENUM	*pname* is none of these values.

Making a Texture Unit Active (gl.activeTexture())

WebGL supports multiple texture images (multitexturing) using a mechanism called a *texture unit*. A texture unit manages texture images by using a unit number for each texture. Because of this, even if you only want to use a single texture image, you must specify and use a texture unit.

The number of texture units supported varies according to your hardware and WebGL implementation, but by default at least eight texture units are supported, and some systems will support more. The built-in constants, gl.TEXTURE0, gl.TEXTURE1, ..., and gl.TEXTURE7, represent each texture unit (see Figure 5.25).

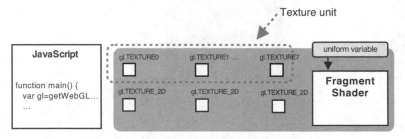

Figure 5.25 Multiple texture units managed by WebGL

Before using a texture unit, it must be made active using a call to gl.activeTexture() (see Figure 5.26):

```
132    // Make the texture unit 0 active
133    gl.activeTexture(gl.TEXTURE0);
```

---

gl.activeTexture(texUnit)

Make the texture unit specified by *texUnit* active.

Parameters	texUnit	Specifies the texture unit to be made active: gl.TEXTURE0, gl.TEXTURE1, ..., or gl.TEXTURE7. The tailing number indicates the texture unit number.
Return value	None	
Errors	INVALID_ENUM:	*texUnit* is none of these values

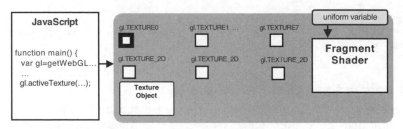

Figure 5.26 Activate texture unit (gl.TEXTURE0)

Binding a Texture Object to a Target (gl.bindTexture())

Next, you need to tell the WebGL system what types of texture image is used in the texture object. You do this by binding the texture object to the target in a similar way to that of the buffer objects explained in the previous chapter. WebGL supports two types of textures, as shown in Table 5.2.

Table 5.2 Types of Textures

Type of Texture	Description
gl.TEXTURE_2D	Two-dimensional texture
gl.TEXTURE_CUBE_MAP	Cube map texture

The sample program uses a two-dimensional image as a texture and specifies gl. TEXTURE_2D at line 132. The cube map texture is beyond the scope of this book. If you are interested in more information, please refer to the book *OpenGL ES 2.0 Programming Guide*:

```
131   // Bind the texture object to the target
132   gl.bindTexture(gl.TEXTURE_2D, texture);
```

---

gl.bindTexture(target, texture)

Enable the texture object specified by *texture* and bind it to the *target*. In addition, if a texture unit was made active by gl.activeTexture(), the texture object is also bound to the texture unit.

Parameters	target	Specifies gl.TEXTURE_2D or gl.TEXTURE_CUBE_MAP.
	texture	Specifies the texture object to be bound.
Return value	None	
Errors	INVALID_ENUM	*target* is none of these values.

Note that this method performs two tasks: enabling the texture object and binding it to target, and binding it to the texture unit. In this case, because the texture unit 0 (gl.TEXTURE0) is active, after executing line 136, the internal state of the WebGL system is changed, as shown in Figure 5.27.

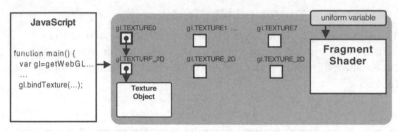

Figure 5.27 Bind a texture object to the target

At this stage, the program has specified the type of texture that is used in the texture object (gl.TEXTURE_2D) and that will be used to deal with the texture object in the future. This is important, because in WebGL, you cannot manipulate the texture object directly. You need to do that through the binding.

Set the Texture Parameters of a Texture Object (gl.texParameteri())

In the next step, you need to set the parameters (texture parameter) that specify how the texture image will be processed when the texture image is mapped to shapes. The generic function gl.texParameteri() can be used to set texture parameters.

---

gl.texParameteri(target, pname, param)

Set the value specified by *param* to the texture parameter specified by *pname* in the texture object bound to *target*.

Parameters	target	Specifies gl.TEXTURE_2D or gl.TEXTURE_CUBE_MAP.
	pname	Specifies the name of the texture parameter (Table 5.3).
	param	Specifies the value set to the texture parameter *pname* (Table 5.4, Table 5.5).
Return value	None	
Errors	INVALID_ENUM	*target* is none of the preceding values
	INVALID_OPERATION	no texture object is bound to *target*

There are four texture parameters available, illustrated in Figure 5.28, which you can specify to *pname*:

- **Magnification method** (gl.TEXTURE_MAG_FILTER): The method to magnify a texture image when you map the texture to a shape whose drawing area is larger than the size of the texture. For example, when you map a 16×16 pixel image to a 32×32 pixel shape, the texture should be doubled in size. WebGL needs to fill the gap between texels due to the magnification, and this parameter specifies the method used to fill the gap.

- **Minification method** (gl.TEXTURE_MIN_FILTER): The method of minifying a texture image when you map the texture to a shape whose drawing area is smaller than the size of the texture. For example, when you map a 32×32 pixel image to a 16×16 pixel shape, the texture should be reduced in size. To do that, the system needs to cull texels to fit the target size. This parameter specifies the method used to cull texels.

- **Wrapping method on the left and right side** (gl.TEXTURE_WRAP_S): How to fill the remaining regions on the left side and the right side of a subregion when you map a texture image to the subregion of a shape.

- **Wrapping method on top and bottom** (gl.TEXTURE_WRAP_T): Similar to (3), the method used to fill the remaining regions in the top and bottom of a subregion.

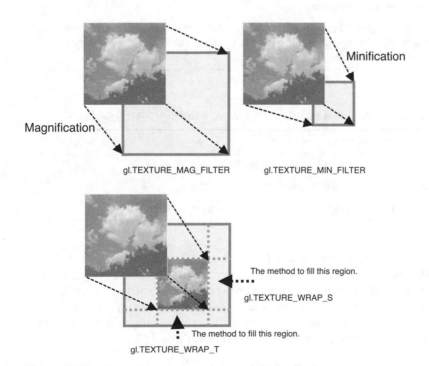

Figure 5.28 Four texture parameters and their effects

Table 5.3 shows each texture parameter and its default value.

Table 5.3 Texture Parameters and Their Default Values

Texture Parameter	Description	Default Value
gl.TEXTURE_MAG_FILTER	Texture magnification	gl.LINEAR
gl.TEXTURE_MIN_FILTER	Texture minification	gl.NEAREST_MIPMAP_LINEAR
gl.TEXTURE_WRAP_S	Texture wrapping in s-axis	gl.REPEAT
gl.TEXTURE_WRAP_T	Texture wrapping in t-axis	gl.REPEAT

We also show the constant values that can be specified to gl.TEXTURE_MAG_FILTER and gl.TEXTURE_MIN_FILTER in Table 5.4 and gl.TEXTURE_WRAP_S and gl.TEXTURE_WRAP_T in Table 5.5.

Table 5.4 Non-Mipmapped Values, Which Can be Specified to gl.TEXTURE_MAG_FILTER and gl.TEXTURE_MIN_FILTER[3]

Value	Description
gl.NEAREST	Uses the value of the texel that is nearest (in Manhattan distance) the center of the pixel being textured.
gl.LINEAR	Uses the weighted average of the four texels that are nearest the center of the pixel being textured. (The quality of the result is clearer than that of gl.NEAREST, but it takes more time.)

Table 5.5 Values that Can be Specified to gl.TEXTURE_WRAP_S and gl.TEXTURE_WRAP_T

Value	Description
gl.REPEAT	Use a texture image repeatedly
gl.MIRRORED_REPEAT	Use a texture image mirrored-repeatedly
gl.CLAMP_TO_EDGE	Use the edge color of a texture image

As shown in Table 5.3, each parameter has a default value, and you can generally use the default value as is. However, the default value of gl.TEXTURE_MIN_FILTER is for a special texture format called *MIPMAP*. A MIPMAP is a sequence of textures, each of which is a progressively lower resolution representation of the same image. Because a MIPMAP texture is not often used, we don't cover it in this book. For this reason, you set the value gl.LINEAR to the texture parameter gl.TEXTURE_MIN_FILTER at line 135:

---

[3] Although omitted in this table, other values can be specified for a MIPMAP texture: gl.NEAREST_MIPMAP_NEAREST, gl.LINEAR_MIPMAP_NEAREST, gl.NEAREST_MIPMAP_LINEAR, and gl.LINEAR_MIPMAP_LINEAR. See the book *OpenGL Programming Guide* for these values.

```
134   // Set the texture parameters
135   gl.texParameteri(gl.TEXTURE_2D, gl.TEXTURE_MIN_FILTER, gl.LINEAR);
```

After executing line 139, the value is set to the texture object, and then the internal state of the WebGL system is modified as shown in Figure 5.29.

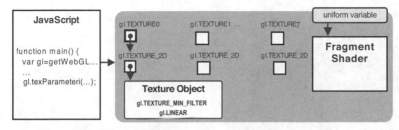

Figure 5.29   Set texture parameter

The next step is to assign a texture image to the texture object.

Assigning a Texture Image to a Texture Object (gl.texImage2D())

To assign an image to a texture object, you use the method gl.texImage2D(). In addition to assigning a texture, this method allows you to tell the WebGL system about the image characteristics.

gl.texImage2D(target, level, internalformat, format, type, image)		
Set the image specified by *image* to the texture object bound to *target*.		
Parameters	target	Specifies gl.TEXTURE_2D or gl.TEXTURE_CUBE_MAP.
	level	Specified as 0. (Actually, this parameter is used for a MIPMAP texture, which is not covered in this book.)
	internalformat	Specifies the internal format of the image (Table 5.6).
	format	Specifies the format of the texel data. This must be specified using the same value as *internalformat*.
	type	Specifies the data type of the texel data (Table 5.7).
	image	Specifies an Image object containing an image to be used as a texture.
Return value	None	
Errors	INVALID_ENUM	*target* is none of the above values.
	INVALID_OPERATION	No texture object is bound to *target*

This method is used at line 136 in the sample program:

```
137 gl.texImage2D(gl.TEXTURE_2D, 0, gl.RGBA, gl.RGBA, gl.UNSIGNED_BYTE, image);
```

After executing line 144, the texture image loaded into the Image object `image` in JavaScript is passed to the WebGL system (see Figure 5.30).

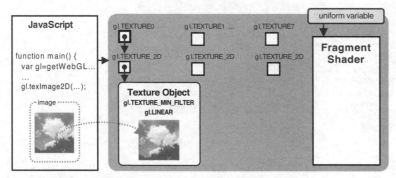

Figure 5.30 Assign an image to the texture object

Let's take a quick look at each parameter of this method. You must specify 0 to *level* because you aren't using a MIPMAP texture. The *format* specifies the format of the texel data, with available formats shown in Table 5.6. You need to select an appropriate format for the image used as a texture. The sample program uses `gl.RGB` format because it uses a JPG image in which each pixel is composed of RGB components. For other formats, such as PNG, images are usually specified as `gl.RGBA`, and BMP images are usually specified as `gl.RGB`. `gl.LUMINANCE` and `gl.LUMINANCE_ALPHA` are used for a grayscale image and so on.

Table 5.6 The Format of the Texel Data

Format	Components in a Texel
gl.RGB	Red, green, blue
gl.RGBA	Red, green, blue, alpha
gl.ALPHA	(0.0, 0.0, 0.0, alpha)
gl.LUMINANCE	L, L, L, 1 L: Luminance
gl.LUMINANCE_ALPHA	L, L. L. alpha

Here, luminance is the perceived brightness of a surface. It is often calculated as a weighted average of red, green, and blue color values that gives the perceived brightness of the surface.

As shown in Figure 5.30, this method stores the image in the texture object in the WebGL system. Once stored, you must tell the system about the type of format the image uses using the *internalformat* parameter. As mentioned, in WebGL, *internalformat* must specify the same value as *format*.

The *type* specifies the data type of the texel data (see Table 5.7). Usually, we specify gl. UNSIGNED_BYTE as the data type. Other data types are also available, such as gl.UNSIGNED_ SHORT_5_6_5 (which packs RGB components into 16 bits). These types are used for passing compressed images to the WebGL system to reduce loading time.

Table 5.7 The Data Type of Texel Data

Type	Description
gl.UNSIGNED_BYTE	Unsigned byte format. Each color component has 1 byte.
gl.UNSIGNED_SHORT_5_6_5	RGB: Each component has 5, 6, and 5 bits, respectively.
gl.UNSIGNED_SHORT_4_4_4_4	RGBA: Each component has 4, 4, 4, and 4 bits, respectively.
gl.UNSIGNED_SHORT_5_5_5_1	RGBA: Each RGB component has 5 bits, and A has 1 bit.

Pass the Texture Unit to the Fragment Shader (gl.uniform1i())

Once the texture image has been passed to the WebGL system, it must be passed to the fragment shader to map it to the surface of the shape. As explained before, a uniform variable is used for this purpose because the texture image does not change for each fragment:

```
13 var FSHADER_SOURCE =
   . . .
17   'uniform sampler2D u_Sampler;\n' +
18   'varying vec2 v_TexCoord;\n' +
19   'void main() {\n' +
20   '  gl_FragColor = texture2D(u_Sampler, v_TexCoord);\n' +
21   '}\n';
```

This uniform variable must be declared using the special data type for textures shown in Table 5.8. The sample program uses a two-dimensional texture (gl.TEXTURE_2D), so the data type is set to sampler2D.

Table 5.8 Special Data Types for Accessing a Texture

Type	Description
sampler2D	Data type for accessing the texture bound to gl.TEXTURE_2D
samplerCube	Data type for accessing the texture bound to gl.TEXTURE_CUBE_MAP

The call to initTextures() (line 100) gets the storage location of this uniform variable u_Sampler at line 108 and then passes it to loadTexture() as an argument. The uniform

variable u_Sampler is set at line 139 by specifying the **texture unit number** ("n" in
gl.TEXTUREn) of the texture unit that manages this texture object. In this sample program,
you specify 0 because you are using the texture object bound to gl.TEXTURE0 in the call to
gl.uniformi():

```
138   // Set the texture unit 0 to the sampler
139   gl.uniform1i(u_Sampler, 0);
```

After executing line 139, the WebGL system is modified as shown in Figure 5.31, thereby
allowing access to the image in the texture object from the fragment shader.

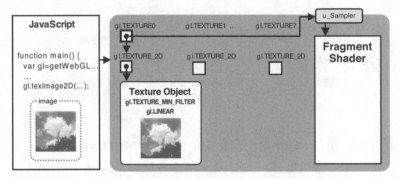

Figure 5.31   Set texture unit to uniform variable

Passing Texture Coordinates from the Vertex Shader to the Fragment Shader

Because the texture coordinates for each vertex are passed to the attribute variable
a_TexCoord, it's possible to pass the data to the fragment shader through the varying
variable v_TexCoord. Remember that varying variables of the same name and type are
automatically copied between the vertex shader and the fragment shader. The texture
coordinates are interpolated between vertices, so you can use the interpolated texture
coordinates in a fragment shader to specify each texture coordinate for each fragment:

```
2 // Vertex shader program
3 var VSHADER_SOURCE =
4   'attribute vec4 a_Position;\n' +
5   'attribute vec2 a_TexCoord;\n' +
6   'varying vec2 v_TexCoord;\n' +
7   'void main() {\n' +
8   '  gl_Position = a_Position;\n' +
9   '  v_TexCoord = a_TexCoord;\n' +
10  '}\n';
```

At this stage, you have completed the preparations for using the texture image in the
WebGL system.

All that's left is to read the color of the texel located at the corresponding texture coordinates from the texture image and then use it to set the color of the fragment.

Retrieve the Texel Color in a Fragment Shader (texture2D())

Retrieving a color of a texel from the texture image is done at line 20 in the fragment shader:

```
20   '  gl_FragColor = texture2D(u_Sampler, v_TexCoord);\n' +
```

It uses the GLSL ES built-in function `texture2D()` to read out the texel color from the shader. `texture2D()` is an easy-to-use function that can retrieve the texel color at a texture coordinate by specifying the texture unit number in the first parameter and the texture coordinates in the second parameter. However, because this function is a built-in function of GLSL ES, note the data type of the parameters and the return value of the function.

---

vec4 texture2D(sampler2D sampler, vec2 coord)

Retrieve a texel color at the texture coordinates specified by *coord* from the texture image specified by *sampler*.

Parameters	sampler	Specifies the texture unit number.
	coord	Specifies the texture coordinates.
Return value		The texel color (vec4) for the coordinates. The color format changes according to the *internalformat* specified by `gl.texImage2D()`. Table 5.9 shows the differences. If the texture image is not available for some reason, this function returns (0.0, 0.0, 0.0, 1.0).

Table 5.9   Return Value of texture2D()

Internalformat	Return Value	
gl.RGB	(R, G, B, 1.0)	
gl.RGBA	(R, G, B, A)	
gl.ALPHA	(0.0, 0.0, 0.0, A)	
gl.LUMINANCE	(L, L, L, 1.0)	L indicates luminance
gl.LUMINANCE_ALPHA	(L, L, L, A)	

The texture magnification and minification parameters determine the return value in cases where WebGL interpolates the texel. Once this function executes, by assigning the return value to `gl_FragColor`, the fragment is displayed using the color. As a result of this operation, the texture image is mapped to the shape to be drawn (in this case, a rectangle).

This is the final step in the process needed for texture mapping. At this stage, your texture image has been loaded, set up in the WebGL system and mapped to the shape you are drawing.

As you have seen, texture mapping in WebGL seems a complex process partly because it must deal with an image and request the browser to load it, and partly because you are required to use the texture unit even if you use only a single texture. However, once you master the basic steps, they are the same each time you want to map a texture.

The next section explores the use of textures and will familiarize you with the whole process.

Experimenting with the Sample Program

To familiarize you with texture mapping, let's modify the sample program by changing the texture coordinates. For example, modify the texture coordinates in TexturedQuad as follows:

```
var verticesTexCoords = new Float32Array([
  // Vertex coordinates and texture coordinates
  -0.5,  0.5,   -0.3, 1.7,
  -0.5, -0.5,   -0.3, -0.2,
   0.5,  0.5,    1.7, 1.7,
   0.5, -0.5,    1.7, -0.2
]);
```

If you load the modified program TexturedQuad_Repeat, you'll see an effect like the screenshot of Figure 5.32 (left side). To understand what's happening here, take a look at the figure on the right side, which shows each texture coordinate in the texture coordinate system.

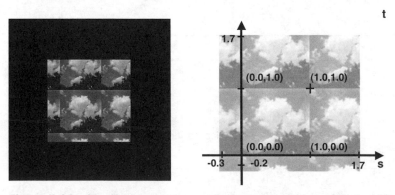

Figure 5.32　Modify the texture coordinate (a screenshot of TexturedQuad_Repeat)

The image isn't sufficient to cover the larger shape, so as you can see, the texture image is being repeated. This is driven by the value of gl.TEXTURE_WRAP_S and gl.TEXTURE_WRAP_T, which are set to `gl.REPEAT` in the sample program, telling the WebGL system to repeat the texture image to fill the area.

Now let's modify the texture parameters as follows to see what other effects we can achieve. The modified program is saved as `TexturedQuad_Clamp_Mirror`, and Figure 5.33 shows the result when run in your browser:

```
// Set texture parameters
gl.texParameteri(gl.TEXTURE_2D, gl.TEXTURE_MIN_FILTER, gl.LINEAR);
gl.texParameteri(gl.TEXTURE_2D, gl.TEXTURE_WRAP_S, gl.CLAMP_TO_EDGE);
gl.texParameteri(gl.TEXTURE_2D, gl.TEXTURE_WRAP_T, gl.MIRRORED_REPEAT);
```

You can see that the edge color of the texture is repeated in the s-axis (horizontal axis), and the texture image itself is mirrored-repeated in the t-axis (vertical axis).

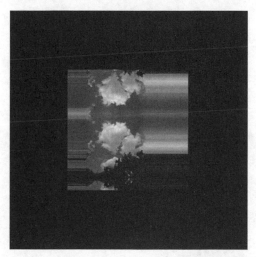

Figure 5.33 TexturedQuad_Clamp_Mirror

That concludes the explanation of the basic texture mapping technique available in WebGL. The next section builds on this basic technique and explores texture mapping using multiple texture images.

Pasting Multiple Textures to a Shape

Earlier in the chapter, you learned that WebGL can deal with multiple texture images, which was the reason for the multiple texture units. The examples so far have used only one texture, and thus one element of the unit. This section will construct a sample program, `MultiTexture`, which pastes two texture images to a rectangle, allowing a better examination of the texture unit mechanism. Figure 5.34 shows a screenshot of `MultiTexture`. As you can see, the two texture images are "blended" to create the composite in the figure.

Figure 5.34 MultiTexture

Figure 5.35 shows the two separate texture images used in this sample program. To highlight WebGL's ability to deal with various image formats, the sample program intentionally uses different image formats for each file.

Figure 5.35 Texture images (sky.jpg on left; circle.gif on right) used in MultiTexture

Essentially, you can map multiple texture images to a shape by repeating the process of mapping a single texture image to a shape described in the previous section. Let's examine the sample program to see how that is done.

Sample Program (MultiTexture.js)

Listing 5.8 shows the basic processing flow of `MultiTexture.js`, which is similar to `TexturedQuad.js` with three key differences: (1) the fragment shader accesses two textures, (2) the final fragment color is calculated from the two texels from both textures, and (3) `initTextures()` creates two texture objects.

Listing 5.8 MultiTexture.js

```
 1 // TexturedQuad.js
   ...
13 var FSHADER_SOURCE =
   ...
17   'uniform sampler2D u_Sampler0;\n' +
18   'uniform sampler2D u_Sampler1;\n' +
19   'varying vec2 v_TexCoord;\n' +
20   'void main() {\n' +
21   '  vec4 color0 = texture2D(u_Sampler0, v_TexCoord);\n' +       <-(1)
22   '  vec4 color1 = texture2D(u_Sampler1, v_TexCoord);\n' +
23   '  gl_FragColor = color0 * color1;\n' +                        <-(2)
24   '}\n';
25
26 function main() {
   ...
53   // Set textures
54   if (!initTextures(gl, n)) {
   ...
58 }
59
60 function initVertexBuffers(gl) {
61   var verticesTexCoords = new Float32Array([
62     // Vertex coordinates and texture coordinates
63     -0.5,  -0.5,   0.0, 1.0,
64     -0.5,  -0.5,   0.0, 0.0,
65      0.5,  -0.5,   1.0, 1.0,
66      0.5,  -0.5,   1.0, 0.0,
67   ]);
68   var n = 4; // The number of vertices
   ...
100   return n;
101 }
102
103 function initTextures(gl, n) {
104   // Create a texture object
105   var texture0 = gl.createTexture();                             <-(3)
106   var texture1 = gl.createTexture();
   ...
112   // Get the storage locations of u_Sampler1 and u_Sampler2
113   var u_Sampler0 = gl.getUniformLocation(gl.program, 'u_Sampler0');
114   var u_Sampler1 = gl.getUniformLocation(gl.program, 'u_Sampler1');
   ...
120   // Create Image objects
```

```
121   var image0 = new Image();
122   var image1 = new Image();
      ...
127   // Register the event handler to be called when image loading is completed
128   image0.onload = function(){ loadTexture(gl, n, texture0, u_Sampler0,
                                                          ➥image0, 0); };
129   image1.onload = function(){ loadTexture(gl, n, texture1, u_Sampler1,
                                                          ➥image1, 1); };
130   // Tell the browser to load an Image
131   image0.src = '../resources/redflower.jpg';
132   image1.src = '../resources/circle.gif';
133
134   return true;
135 }
136 // Specify whether the texture unit is ready to use
137 var g_texUnit0 = false, g_texUnit1 = false;
138 function loadTexture(gl, n, texture, u_Sampler, image, texUnit) {
139   gl.pixelStorei(gl.UNPACK_FLIP_Y_WEBGL, 1);// Flip the image's y-axis
140   // Make the texture unit active
141   if (texUnit == 0) {
142     gl.activeTexture(gl.TEXTURE0);
143     g_texUnit0 = true;
144   } else {
145     gl.activeTexture(gl.TEXTURE1);
146     g_texUnit1 = true;
147   }
148   // Bind the texture object to the target
149   gl.bindTexture(gl.TEXTURE_2D, texture);
150
151   // Set texture parameters
152   gl.texParameteri(gl.TEXTURE_2D, gl.TEXTURE_MIN_FILTER, gl.LINEAR);
153   // Set the texture image
154   gl.texImage2D(gl.TEXTURE_2D, 0, gl.RGBA, gl.RGBA, gl.UNSIGNED_BYTE, image);
155   // Set the texture unit number to the sampler
156   gl.uniform1i(u_Sampler, texUnit);
      ...
161   if (g_texUnit0 && g_texUnit1) {
162     gl.drawArrays(gl.TRIANGLE_STRIP, 0, n); // Draw a rectangle
163   }
164 }
```

First, let's examine the fragment shader. In TexturedQuad.js, because the fragment shader used only one texture image, it prepared a single uniform variable, u_Sampler. However, this sample program uses two texture images and needs to define two sampler variables as follows:

```
17   'uniform sampler2D u_Sampler0;\n' +
18   'uniform sampler2D u_Sampler1;\n' +
```

`main()` in the fragment shader fetches the texel value from each texture image at lines 21 and 22, storing them to the variables `color0` and `color1`, respectively:

```
21   '  vec4 color0 = texture2D(u_Sampler0, v_TexCoord);\n' +
22   '  vec4 color1 = texture2D(u_Sampler1, v_TexCoord);\n' +
23   '  gl_FragColor = color0 * color1;\n' +
```

There are many possible ways to calculate the final fragment color (`gl_FragColor`) using the texels. This sample program uses a component-wise multiplication of both texel colors because the result is easy to understand. GLSL ES offers a simple way to write this multiplication in a single line as a multiplication of two vec4 variables at line 23 (see Figure 5.36).

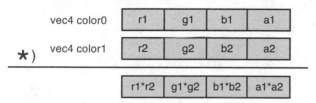

Figure 5.36   Multiplication of two vec4 variables

Although this sample program uses two texture images, `initVertexBuffers()` from line 60 is the same as in `TexturedQuad.js` because it uses the same texture coordinates for both texture images.

In this sample, `initTextures()` at line 103 has been modified to repeat the process of dealing with a texture image twice because now it deals with two images rather than the single image of the previous example.

Lines 105 and 106 create the two texture objects, one for each texture image. The last character of each variable name ("0" in `texture0` and "1" in `texture1`) indicates which texture unit (texture unit 0 or texture unit 1) is used. This naming convention of using the unit number also applies to the variable names for the storage location of uniform variables (line 113 and 114) and image objects (lines 120 and 121).

Registration of the event handler (`loadTexture()`) is the same as in `TexturedQuad.js`, with the last argument set to indicate the different texture units:

```
128   image0.onload = function() { loadTexture(gl, n, texture0, u_Sampler0,
                                                    ➥image0, 0); };
129   image1.onload = function() { loadTexture(gl, n, texture1,u_Sampler1,
                                                    ➥image1, 1); };
```

The request to load the texture images is in lines 131 and 132:

```
131   image0.src = '../resources/redflower.jpg';
132   image1.src = '../resources/circle.gif';
```

In this sample program, the function loadTexture() has to be modified to deal with two textures. The function is defined from line 138 with its core part as follows:

```
137 var g_texUnit0 = false, g_texUnit1 = false;
138 function loadTexture(gl, n, texture, u_Sampler, image, texUnit) {
139   gl.pixelStorei(gl.UNPACK_FLIP_Y_WEBGL, 1);// Flip the image's y-axis
140   // Make the texture unit active
141   if (texUnit == 0) {
142     gl.activeTexture(gl.TEXTURE0);
143     g_texUnit0 = true;
144   } else {
145     gl.activeTexture(gl.TEXTURE1);
146     g_texUnit1 = true;
147   }
148
149   gl.bindTexture(gl.TEXTURE_2D, texture); // Bind the texture object
150
151   // Set texture parameters
152   gl.texParameteri(gl.TEXTURE_2D, gl.TEXTURE_MIN_FILTER, gl.LINEAR);
153   // Set the texture image
154   gl.texImage2D(gl.TEXTURE_2D, 0, gl.RGBA, gl.RGBA, gl.UNSIGNED_BYTE, image);
155   // Set the texture unit number to the sampler
156   gl.uniform1i(u_Sampler, texUnit);
    ...
164   if (g_texUnit0 && g_texUnit1) {
165     gl.drawArrays(gl.TRIANGLE_STRIP, 0, n); // Draw a rectangle
166   }
167 }
```

The important difference in loadTexture() is that you cannot predict which texture image is loaded first because the browser loads them asynchronously. The sample program handles this by starting to draw only after loading both textures. To do this, it uses two global variables (g_texUnit0 and g_texUnit1) at line 137 indicating which textures have been loaded.

These variables are initialized to false at line 137 and changed to true in the if statement at line 141. This if statement checks the variable texUnit passed as the last parameter in loadTexture(). If it is 0, the texture unit 0 is made active and g_texUnit0 is set to true; if it is 1, the texture unit 1 is made active and then g_texUnit1 is set to true.

Line 156 sets the texture unit number to the uniform variable. Note that the parameter texUnit of loadTexture() is passed to gl.uniform1i(). After loading two texture images, the internal state of the system is changed, as shown in Figure 5.37.

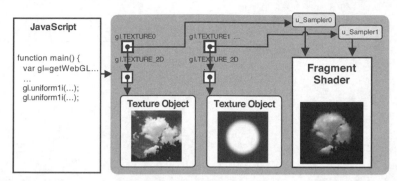

Figure 5.37 Internal state of WebGL when handling two texture images

Finally, the program invokes the vertex shader after checking whether both texture images are available at line 165 using `g_texUnit0` and `g_texUnit1`. The images are then combined as they are mapped to the shape, resulting in the screenshot in Figure 5.34.

Summary

In this chapter, you ventured deep into the WebGL world. At this stage you have acquired all the basic skills needed to use WebGL to deal with 2D geometric shapes and are ready for the next step: 3D objects. Fortunately, when you deal with 3D objects instead of 2D shapes, the way you use shaders is surprisingly similar, so you can quickly apply all the knowledge you've learned so far.

The rest of this book focuses mainly on covering the techniques necessary for managing 3D objects. However, before introducing you to the 3D world, the next chapter will take a brief tour of the OpenGL ES shading language (GLSL ES), covering some features and functionality that have been only touched on in the chapters so far.

Chapter 6

The OpenGL ES Shading Language (GLSL ES)

This chapter takes a break from examining WebGL sample programs and explains the essential features of the OpenGL ES Shading Language (GLSL ES) in detail.

As you have seen, shaders are the core mechanism within WebGL for constructing 3DCG programs, and GLSL ES is the dedicated programming language for writing those shader programs. This chapter covers:

- Data, variables, and variable types

- Vector, matrix, structure, array, and sampler types

- Operators, control flow, and functions

- Attributes, uniform, and varying variables

- Precision qualifiers

- Preprocessor and directives

By the end of this chapter, you will have a good understanding of GLSL ES and how to use it to write a variety of shaders. This knowledge will help you tackle the more complex 3D manipulations introduced in Chapters 7 through 9. Note that language specifications can be quite dry, and for some of you, this may be more detail than you need. If so, it's safe to skip this chapter and use it as a reference when you look at the examples in the rest of the book.

Recap of Basic Shader Programs

As you can see from Listings 6.1 and 6.2, you can construct shader programs in a similar manner to constructing programs using the C programming language.

Listing 6.1 Example of a Simple Vertex Shader

```
// Vertex shader
attribute vec4 a_Position;
attribute vec4 a_Color;
uniform mat4 u_MvpMatrix;
varying vec4 v_Color;
void main() {
  gl_Position = u_MvpMatrix * a_Position;
  v_Color = a_Color;
}
```

Variables are declared at the beginning of the code, and then the `main()` routine defines the entry point for the program.

Listing 6.2 Example of a Simple Fragment Shader

```
// Fragment shader
#ifdef GLSL_ES
precision mediump float;
#endif
varying vec4 v_Color;
void main() {
  gl_FragColor = v_Color;
}
```

The version of GLSL ES dealt with in this chapter is 1.00. However, you should note that WebGL does not support all features defined in GLSL ES 1.00[1]; rather, it supports a subset of 1.00 with core features needed for WebGL.

Overview of GLSL ES

The **GLSL ES** programming language was developed from the OpenGL Shading Language (GLSL) by reducing or simplifying functionality, assuming that the target platforms were consumer electronics or embedded devices such as smart phones and game consoles. A prime goal was to allow hardware manufacturers to simplify the hardware needed to execute GLSL ES programs. This had two key benefits: reducing power consumption by devices and, perhaps more importantly, reducing manufacturing costs.

GLSL ES supports a limited (and partially extended) version of the C language syntax. Therefore, if you are familiar with the C language, you'll find it easy to understand GLSL ES. Additionally, the shading language is beginning to be used for general-purpose processing such as image processing and numerical computation (so called GPGPU), meaning that GLSL ES has an increasingly wide application domain, thus increasing the benefits of studying the language.

---

[1] http://www.khronos.org/registry/gles/specs/2.0/GLSL_ES_Specification_1.0.17.pdf

Hello Shader!

By tradition, most programming books begin with a "Hello World!" example, or in our case the corresponding shader program. However, because you have already seen several shader programs in previous chapters, let's skip that and take a look at the basics of GLSL ES, using Listing 6.1 and Listing 6.2 shown earlier.

Basics

Like many programming languages, you need to pay attention to the following two items when you write shader programs using GLSL ES:

- The programs are case-sensitive (`marina` and `Marina` are different).

- A semicolon (;) must be specified at the end of each command.

Order of Execution

Once a JavaScript program is loaded, program lines are executed in the order in which they were written—sequentially starting from the first program line. However, like C, shader programs are executed from the function `main()` and therefore must have one (and only one) `main()` function that cannot have any parameters. Looking back, you can see that each shader program shown in Listing 6.1 and Listing 6.2 defines a single `main()`.

You must prepend the keyword `void` to `main()`, which indicates that the function has no return value. (See the section "Functions" later in this chapter.) This is different from JavaScript, where you can define a function using the keyword `function`, and you don't have to worry whether the function returns a value. In GLSL ES, if the function returns a value, you must specify its data type in front of the function name, or if it doesn't return a value, specify `void` so that the system doesn't expect a return value.

Comments

As with JavaScript, you can write comments in your shader program, and in fact use the same syntax as JavaScript. So, the following two types of comment are supported:

- // characters followed by any sequence of characters up to the end of line:

  ```
  int kp = 496; // kp is a Kaprekar number
  ```

- /* characters, followed by any sequence of characters (including new lines), followed by the */ characters:

  ```
  /* I have a day off today.
     I want to take a day off tomorrow.
   */
  ```

Data (Numerical and Boolean Values)

GLSL ES supports only two data types:

- **Numerical value:** GLSL ES supports integer numbers (for example, 0, 1, 2) and floating point numbers (for example, 3.14, 29.98, 0.23571). Numbers without a decimal point (.) are treated as integer numbers, and those with a decimal point are treated as floating point numbers.

- **Boolean value:** GLSL ES supports `true` and `false` as boolean constants.

GLSL ES does not support character strings, which may initially seem strange but makes sense for a 3D graphics language.

Variables

As you have seen in the previous chapters, you can use any variable names you want as long as the name follows the basic naming rules:

- The character set for variables names contains only the letters a–z, A–Z, the underscore (_), and the numbers 0–9.

- Numbers are not allowed to be used as the first character of variable names.

- The keywords shown in Table 6.1 and the reserved keywords shown in Table 6.2 are not allowed to be used as variable names. However, you can use them as part of the variable name, so the variable name `if` will result in error, but `iffy` will not.

- Variable names starting with `gl_`, `webgl_`, or `_webgl_` are reserved for use by OpenGL ES. No user-defined variable names may begin with them.

Table 6.1 Keywords Used in GLSL ES

attribute	bool	break	bvec2	bvec3	bvec4
const	continue	discard	do	else	false
float	for	highp	if	in	inout
Int	invariant	ivec2	ivec3	ivec4	lowp
mat2	mat3	mat4	medium	out	precision
return	sampler2D	samplerCube	struct	true	uniform
varying	vec2	vec3	vec4	void	while

Table 6.2 Reserved Keywords for Future Version of GLSL ES

asm	cast	class	default
double	dvec2	dvec3	dvec4
enum	extern	external	fixed
flat	fvec2	fvec3	fvec4
goto	half	hvec2	hvec3
hvec4	inline	input	interface
long	namespace	noinline	output
packed	public	sampler1D	sampler1DShadow
sampler2DRect	sampler2DRectShadow	sampler2DShadow	sampler3D
sampler3DRect	short	sizeof	static
superp	switch	template	this
typedef	union	unsigned	using
volatile			

GLSL ES Is a Type Sensitive Language

GLSL ES does not require the use of `var` to declare variables, but it does require you to specify the type of data a variable will contain. As you have seen in the sample programs, you declare variables using the form

```
<data type> <variable name>
```

such as `vec4 a_Position`.

As discussed, when you define a function like `main()`, you must also specify the data type of the return value of the function. Equally, the type of data on the left side of the assignment operation (=) and that of data on the right side must have the same type; otherwise, it will result in an error.

For these reasons, GLSL ES is called a **type sensitive language**, meaning that it belongs to a class of languages that require you to specify and pay attention to types.

Basic Types

GLSL ES supports the basic data types shown in Table 6.3.

Table 6.3 GLSL Basic Types

Type	Description
float	The data type for a single floating point number. It indicates the variable will contain a single floating point number.
int	The data type for a single integer number. It indicates the variable will contain a single integer number.
bool	The data type for a boolean value. It indicates the variable will contain a boolean value.

Specifying the data type for variables allows the WebGL system to check errors in advance and process the program efficiently. The following are examples of variable declarations using basic types.

```
float klimt;   // The variable will contain a single floating number
int utrillo;   // The variable will contain a single integer number
bool doga;     // The variable will contain a single boolean value
```

Assignment and Type Conversion

Assignments of values to variables are performed using the assignment operator (=). As mentioned, because GLSL ES is a type-sensitive language, if the data type of the left-side variable is not equal to that of the assigned data (or variable), it will result in an error:

```
int i = 8;       // OK
float f1 = 8;    // Error
float f2 = 8.0;  // OK
float f3 = 8.0f; // Error: Expressions like 8.0f used in C are not allowed.
```

Semantically, 8 and 8.0 are the same values. However, when you assign 8 to a floating point variable f1, it will result in an error. In this case, you would see the following error message:

```
failed to compile shader: ERROR: 0:11: '=' : cannot convert from 'const mediump int'
to 'float'.
```

If you want to assign an integer number to a floating point variable, you need to convert the integer number to a floating point number. This conversion is called **type conversion**. To convert an integer into a floating point number, you can use the built-in function float(), as follows:

```
int i = 8;
float f1 = float(i); // 8 is converted to 8.0 and assigned to f1
float f2 = float(8); // equivalent to the above operation
```

GLSL ES supports a number of other built-in functions for type conversion, which are shown in Table 6.4.

Table 6.4 The Built-In Functions for Type Conversion

Conversion	Function	Description
To an integer number	`int(float)`	The fractional part of the floating-point value is dropped (for example, 3.14 → 3).
	`int(bool)`	`true` is converted to 1, or `false` is converted to 0.
To a floating point number	`float(int)`	The integer number is converted to a floating point number (for example, 8 → 8.0).
	`float(bool)`	`true` is converted to 1.0, or `false` is converted to 0.0.
To a boolean value	`bool(int)`	0 is converted to `false`, or non-zero values are converted to `true`.
	`bool(float)`	0.0 is converted to `false`, or non-zero values are converted to `true`.

Operations

The operators applicable to the basic types are similar to those in JavaScript and are shown in Table 6.5.

Table 6.5 The Operators Available for the Basic Types

Operator	Operation	Applicable Data Type
-	Negation (for example, for specifying a negative number)	`int` or `float`.
*	Multiplication	`int` or `float`. The data type of the result of the operation is the same as operands.
/	Division	
+	Addition	
-	Subtraction	
++	Increment (postfix and prefix)	`int` or `float`. The data type of the result of the operation is the same as operands.
--	Decrement (postfix and prefix)	
=	Assignment	`int`, `float`, or `bool`
+= -= *= /=	Arithmetic assignment	`int` or `float`.

Operator	Operation	Applicable Data Type
`< > <= >=`	Comparison	`int` or `float`.
`== !=`	Comparison (equality)	`int`, `float`, or `bool`.
`!`	Not	`bool` or an expression that results in `bool` [1].
`&&`	Logical and	
`||`	Logical inclusive or	
`^^`	Logical exclusive or [2]	
`condition?` `expression1:expression2`	Ternary selection	*condition* is `bool` or an expression that results in `bool`. Data types other than array can be used in *expression1* and *expression2*.

[1] The second operand in a logical and (`&&`) operation is evaluated if and only if the first operand evaluates to `true`. The second operand in a logical or (`\|\|`) operation is evaluated if and only if the first operand evaluates to `false`.

[2] If either the left-side condition or the right-side one is `true`, the result is `true`. If both sides are `true`, the result is `false`.

The followings are examples of basic operations:

```
int i1 = 954, i2 = 459;
int kp = i1 - i2; // 495 is assigned to kp.
float f = float(kp) + 5.5; // 500.5 is assigned to f.
```

Vector Types and Matrix Types

GLSL ES supports vector and matrix data types which, as you have seen, are useful when dealing with computer graphics. Both these types contain multiple data elements. A vector type, which arranges data in a list, is useful for representing vertex coordinates or color data. A matrix arranges data in an array and is useful for representing transformation matrices. Figure 6.1 shows an example of both types.

$$(3 \quad 7 \quad 1) \quad \begin{bmatrix} 3 & 7 & 1 \\ 1 & 5 & 3 \\ 4 & 0 & 7 \end{bmatrix}$$

Figure 6.1 A vector and a matrix

GLSL ES supports a variety of vector or matrix types, as shown in Table 6.6.

Table 6.6 Vector Types and Matrix Types

Category	Types in GLSL ES	Description
Vector	vec2, vec3, vec4	The data types for 2, 3, and 4 component vectors of floating point numbers
	ivec2, ivec3, ivec4	The data types for 2, 3, and 4 component vectors of integer numbers
	bvec2, bvec3, bvec4	The data types for 2, 3, and 4 component vectors of boolean values
Matrix	mat2, mat3, mat4	The data type for 2×2, 3×3, and 4×4 matrix of floating point numbers (with 4, 9, and 16 elements, respectively)

The following examples show the use of the vector and matrix types:

```
vec3 position;  // variable for 3-component vector of float
                // For example: (10.0, 20.0, 30.0)
ivec2 offset;   // variable for 2-component vector of integer
                // For example: (10, 20)
mat4 mvpMatrix; // the variable for 4×4 matrix of float
```

Assignments and Constructors

Assignment of data to variables of the type vector or matrix is performed using the = operator. Remember that the type of data on the left side of the assignment operation and that of the data/variable on the right side must be the same. In addition, the number of elements on the left side of the assignment operation must be equal to that of the data/ variable on the right side. To illustrate that, the following example will result in an error:

```
vec4 position = 1.0; // vec4 variable requires four floating point numbers
```

In this case, because a vec4 variable requires four floating point numbers, you need to pass four floating numbers in some way. A solution is to use the built-in functions with the same name of the data type so; for example, in the case of vec4, you can use the constructor vec4(). (See Chapter 2, "Your First Step with WebGL.") For example, to assign 1.0, 2.0, 3.0, and 4.0 to a variable of type vec4, you can use vec4() to bundle them into a single data element as follows:

```
vec4 position = vec4(1.0, 2.0, 3.0, 4.0);
```

Functions for making a value of the specified data type are called **constructor functions**, and the name of the constructor is always identical to that of the data type.

Vector Constructors

Vectors are critical in GLSL ES so, as you'd imagine, there are multiple ways to specify arguments to a vector constructor. For example:

```
vec3 v3 = vec3(1.0, 0.0, 0.5);  // sets v3 to(1.0, 0.0, 0.5)
vec2 v2 = vec2(v3);  // sets v2 to (1.0, 0.0) using the 1st and 2nd elements of v3
vec4 v4 = vec4(1.0); // sets v4 to (1.0, 1.0, 1.0, 1.0)
```

In the second example, the constructor ignores the third element of v3, and only the first and second elements of v3 are used to create the new vector. Similarly, in the third example, if a single value is specified to a vector constructor, the value is used to initialize all components of the constructed vector. However, if more than one value is specified to a vector constructor but the number of the values is less than the number of elements required by the constructor, it will result in an error.

Finally, a vector can be constructed from multiple vectors:

```
vec4 v4b = vec4(v2, v4);    // sets (1.0, 0.0, 1.0, 1.0) to v4b
```

The rule here is that the vector is filled with values from the first vector (v2), and then any missing values are supplied by the second vector (v4).

Matrix Constructors

Constructors are also available for matrices and operate in a similar manner to vector constructors. However, you should make sure the order of elements stored in a matrix is in a column major order. (See Figure 3.27 for more details of "column-major order.") The following examples show different ways of using the matrix constructor:

- If multiple values are specified to a matrix constructor, a matrix is constructed using them in column major order:

```
mat4 m4 = mat4 (    1.0,   2.0,    3.0,     4.0,
                    5.0,   6.0,    7.0,     8.0,
                    9.0,  10.0,   11.0,    12.0,
                   13.0,  14.0,   15.0,    16.0 );
```

$$\begin{bmatrix} 1.0 & 5.0 & 9.0 & 13.0 \\ 2.0 & 6.0 & 10.0 & 14.0 \\ 3.0 & 7.0 & 11.0 & 15.0 \\ 4.0 & 8.0 & 12.0 & 16.0 \end{bmatrix}$$

- If multiple vectors are specified to a matrix constructor, a matrix is constructed using the elements of each vector in column major order:

```
// two vec2 are used to construct a mat2
vec2 v2_1 = vec2(1.0, 3.0);
vec2 v2_2 = vec2(2.0, 4.0);
mat2 m2_1 = mat2(v2_1, v2_2); // 1.0 2.0
                              // 3.0 4.0
// vec4 is used to construct mat2
vec4 v4 = vec4(1.0, 3.0, 2.0, 4.0);
```

```
mat2 m2_2 = mat2(v4);  // 1.0 2.0
                       // 3.4 4.0
```

- If multiple values and multiple vectors are specified to a matrix constructor, a matrix is constructed using them in column major order:

```
// Two floating point numbers and vec2 are used to construct a mat2
mat2 m2 = mat2(1.0, 3.0, v2_2); // 1.0 2.0
                                // 3.0 4.0
```

- If a single value is specified to a matrix constructor, a matrix is constructed using the value as its diagonal elements:

```
mat4 m4 = mat4(1.0);  // 1.0 0.0 0.0 0.0
                      // 0.0 1.0 0.0 0.0
                      // 0.0 0.0 1.0 0.0
                      // 0.0 0.0 0.0 1.0
```

Similar to a vector constructor, if an insufficient number of values is specified to the constructor (but more than one), it will result in an error.

```
mat4 m4 = mat4(1.0, 2.0, 3.0); // Error. mat4 requires 16 elements.
```

Access to Components

To access the components in a vector or matrix, you can use the operators . and [], as shown in the following subsections.

The . Operator

An individual component in a vector can be accessed by the variable name followed by period (.) and then the component name, as shown in Table 6.7.

Table 6.7 Component Names

Category	Description
x, y, z, w	Useful for accessing vertex coordinates.
r, g, b, a	Useful for accessing colors.
s, t, p, q	Useful for accessing texture coordinates. (Note that this book uses only s and t. p is used instead of r because r is used for colors.)

Because vectors are used for storing various types of data such as vertex coordinates, colors, and texture coordinates, three types of component names are supported to increase the readability of programs. However, any of the component names x, r, or s accesses the first component; any of y, g, or t accesses the second one; and so on, so you can use them interchangeably if you prefer. For example:

```
vec3 v3 = vec3(1.0, 2.0, 3.0);  // sets v3 to(1.0, 2.0, 3.0)
float f;


f = v3.x; // sets f to 1.0
f = v3.y; // sets f to 2.0
f = v3.z; // sets f to 3.0

f = v3.r; // sets f to 1.0
f = v3.s; // sets f to 1.0
```

As you can see from the comments of these examples, x, r, and s have different names but always access the first component. Attempting to access a component beyond the number of components in the vector will result in an error:

```
f = v3.w; // w requires access to the fourth element, which doesn't exist.
```

Multiple components can be selected by appending their names (from the same name set) after the period (.). This is known as **swizzling**. In the following example, x, y, z, and w will be used, but other sets of component names have the same effect:

```
vec2 v2;
v2 = v3.xy; // sets v2 to (1.0, 2.0)
v2 = v3.yz; // sets v2 to (2.0, 3.0). Any component can be omitted
v2 = v3.xz; // sets v2 to (1.0, 3.0). You can skip any component.
v2 = v3.yx; // sets v2 to (2.0, 1.0). You can reverse the order.
v2 = v3.xx; // sets v2 to (1.0, 1.0). You can repeat any component.


vec3 v3a;
v3a = v3.zyx; // sets v3a to (3.0, 2.0, 1.0). You can use all names.
```

The component name can also be used in the left-side expression of an assignment operator (=):

```
vec4 position = vec4(1.0, 2.0, 3.0, 4.0);
position.xw = vec2(5.0, 6.0); // position = (5.0, 2.0, 3.0, 6.0)
```

Remember, the component names must come from the same set so, for example, v3.was is not allowed.

The [ ] Operator

In addition to the . operator, the components of a vector or a matrix can be accessed using the array indexing operator [ ]. Note that the elements in a matrix are also read out in column major order. Just like JavaScript, the index starts from 0, so applying [0] to a matrix selects the first column in the matrix, [1] selects the second one, [2] selects the third one, and so on. The following shows an example:

```
mat4 m4 = mat4 ( 1.0,  2.0,  3.0,  4.0,
                 5.0,  6.0,  7.0,  8.0,
                 9.0, 10.0, 11.0, 12.0,
                13.0, 14.0, 15.0, 16.0);
vec4 v4 = m4[0]; // Retrieve the 1st column from m4: (1.0, 2.0, 3.0, 4.0)
```

In addition, two [ ] operators can be used to select a column and then a row of a matrix:

```
float m23 = m4[1][2]; // sets m23 to the third component of the second
                      // column of m4 (7.0).
```

A component name can be used to select a component in conjunction with the [ ] operator, as follows:

```
float m32 = m4[2].y; // sets m32 to the second component of the third
                     // column of m4 (10.0).
```

One restriction is that only a **constant index** can be specified as the index number in the [ ] operator. The constant index is defined as

- A integral literal value (for example, 0 or 1)
- A global or local variable qualified as const, excluding function parameters (see the section "const Variables")
- Loop indices (see the section "Conditional Control Flow and Iteration")
- Expressions composed from any of the preceding

The following examples use the type int constant index:

```
const int index = 0;  // "const" keyword specifies the variable is a
                      // read-only variable.
vec4 v4a = m4[index]; // is the same as m4[0]
```

The following example uses an expression composed of constant indices as an index.

```
vec4 v4b = m4[index + 1]; // is the same as m4[1]
```

Remember, you cannot use an `int` variable without the `const` qualifier as an index because it is not a constant index (unless it is a loop index):

```
int index2 = 0;
vec4 v4c = m4[index2]; // Error: because index2 is not a constant index.
```

Operations

You can apply the operators shown in Table 6.8 to a vector or a matrix. These operators are similar to the operators for basic types. Note that the only comparative operators available for a vector and matrix are `==` and `!=`. The `<`, `>`, `<=`, and `>=` operators cannot be used for comparisons of vectors or matrices. In such cases, you can use built-in functions such as `lessThan()`. (See Appendix B, "Built-In Functions of GLSL ES 1.0.")

Table 6.8 The Operators Available for a Vector and a Matrix

Operators	Operation	Applicable Data Types
*	Multiplication	`vec[234]` and `mat[234]`. The operations on `vec[234]` and `mat[234]` will be explained below.
/	Division	
+	Addition	The data type of the result of operation is the same as the operands.
-	Subtraction	
++	Increment (postfix and prefix)	`vec[234]` and `mat[234]`. The data type of the result of this operation is the same as the operands.
--	Decrement (postfix and prefix)	
=	Assignment	`vec[234]` and `mat[234]`.
+=, -=, *=, /=	Arithmetic assignment	`vec[234]` and `mat[234]`.
==, !=	Comparison	`vec[234]` and `mat[234]`. With `==`, if all components of the operands are equal, the result is `true`. For `!=`, if any of components of the operands are not equal, then the result is `true` [1].

[1] If you want component-wise equality, you can use the built-in function `equal()` or `notEqual()`. (See Appendix B.)

Note that when an arithmetic operator operates on a vector or a matrix, it is operating independently on each component of the vector or matrix in component-wise order.

Examples

The following examples show frequently used cases. In the examples, we assume that the types of variables are defined as follows:

```
vec3 v3a, v3b, v3c;
mat3 m3a, m3b, m3c;
float f;
```

Operations on a Vector and Floating Point Number

An example showing the use of the + operator:

```
// The following example uses the + operator, but the -, *, and /
// operators also have the same effect.
v3b = v3a + f;    // v3b.x = v3a.x + f;
                  // v3b.y = v3a.y + f;
                  // v3b.z = v3a.z + f;
```

For example, v3a = vec3(1.0, 2.0, 3.0) and f = 1.0 will result in v3b=(2.0, 3.0, 4.0).

Operations on Vectors

These operators operate on each component of a vector:

```
// The following example uses the + operator, but the -, *, and /
// operators also have the same effect.
v3c = v3a + v3b;  // v3a.x + v3b.x;
                  // v3a.y + v3b.y;
                  // v3a.z + v3b.z;
```

For example, v3a = vec3(1.0, 2.0, 3.0) and v3b = vec3(4.0, 5.0, 6.0) will result in v3c=(5.0, 7.0, 9.0).

Operations on a Matrix and a Floating Point Number

These operators operate on each component of the matrix:

```
// The following example uses the + operator, but the -, *, and /
// operators also have the. same effect.
m3b = m3a * f;    // m3b[0].x = m3a[0].x * f; m3b[0].y = m3a[0].y * f;
                  // m3b[0].z = m3a[0].z * f;
                  // m3b[1].x = m3a[1].x * f; m3b[1].y = m3a[1].y * f;
                  // m3b[1].z = m3a[1].z * f;
                  // m3b[2].x = m3a[2].x * f; m3b[2].y = m3a[2].y * f;
                  // m3b[2].z = m3a[2].z * f;
```

Multiplication of a Matrix and a Vector

For multiplication, the result is the sum of products of each element in a matrix and vector. This result is the same as Equation 3.5 that you saw back in Chapter 3, "Drawing and Transforming Triangles":

```
v3b = m3a * v3a;   // v3b.x = m3a[0].x * v3a.x + m3a[1].x * v3a.y
                   //                         + m3a[2].x * v3a.z;
                   // v3b.y = m3a[0].y * v3a.x + m3a[1].y * v3a.y
                   //                         + m3a[2].y * v3a.z;
                   // v3b.z = m3a[0].z * v3a.x + m3a[1].z * v3a.y
                   //                         + m3a[2].z * v3a.z;
```

Multiplication of a Vector and a Matrix

Multiplication of a vector and a matrix is possible, as you can see from the following expressions. Note that this result is different from that when multiplying a matrix by a vector:

```
v3b = v3a * m3a; // v3b.x = v3a.x * m3a[0].x + v3a.y * m3a[0].y
                 //                          + v3a.z * m3a[0].z;
                 // v3b.y = v3a.x * m3a[1].x + v3a.y * m3a[1].y
                 //                          + v3a.z * m3a[1].z;
                 // v3b.z = v3a.x * m3a[2].x + v3a.y * m3a[2].y
                 //                          + v3a.z * m3a[2].z;
```

Multiplication of Matrices

This is the same as Equation 4.4 in Chapter 4, "More Transformations and Basic Animation":

```
m3c = m3a * m3b; // m3c[0].x = m3a[0].x * m3b[0].x + m3a[1].x * m3b[0].y
                 //                               + m3a[2].x * m3b[0].z;
                 // m3c[1].x = m3a[0].x * m3b[1].x + m3a[1].x * m3b[1].y
                 //                               + m3a[2].x * m3b[1].z;
                 // m3c[2].x = m3a[0].x * m3b[2].x + m3a[1].x * m3b[2].y
                 //                               + m3a[2].x * m3b[2].z;

                 // m3c[0].y = m3a[0].y * m3b[0].x + m3a[1].y * m3b[0].y
                 //                               + m3a[2].y * m3b[0].z;
                 // m3c[1].y = m3a[0].y * m3b[1].x + m3a[1].y * m3b[1].y
                 //                               + m3a[2].y * m3b[1].z;
                 // m3c[2].y = m3a[0].y * m3b[2].x + m3a[1].y * m3b[2].y
                 //                               + m3a[2].y * m3b[2].z;

                 // m3c[0].z = m3a[0].z * m3b[0].x + m3a[1].z * m3b[0].y
                 //                               + m3a[2].z * m3b[0].z;
                 // m3c[1].z = m3a[0].z * m3b[1].x + m3a[1].z * m3b[1].y
                 //                               + m3a[2].z * m3b[1].z;
                 // m3c[2].z = m3a[0].z * m3b[2].x + m3a[1].z * m3b[2].y
                 //                               + m3a[2].z * m3b[2].z;
```

Structures

GLSL ES also supports user-defined types, called **structures**, which aggregate other already defined types using the keyword `struct`. For example:

```
struct light {   // defines the structure "light"
  vec4 color;
  vec3 position;
}
light l1, l2;    // declares variable "l1" and "l2" of the type "light"
```

This example defines the new structure type `light` that consists of two members: the variable `color` and `position`. Then two variables `l1` and `l2` of type `light` are declared after the definition. Unlike C, the `typedef` keyword is not necessary because, by default, the name of the structure becomes the name of the type.

In addition, as a convenience, variables of the new type can be declared with the definition of the structure, as follows:

```
struct light {   // declares structure and its variable all together
  vec4 color;    // color of a light
  vec3 position; // position of a light
} l1;            // variable "l1" of the structure
```

Assignments and Constructors

Structures support the standard constructor, which has the same name as the structure. The arguments to the constructor must be in the same order and of the same type as they were declared in the structure. Figure 6.2 shows an example.

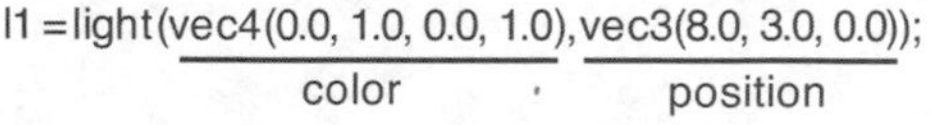

l1 = light(vec4(0.0, 1.0, 0.0, 1.0), vec3(8.0, 3.0, 0.0));
              color   ·   position

Figure 6.2 A constructor of structure

Access to Members

Each member of a structure can be accessed by appending the variable name with a period (.) and then the member name. For example:

```
vec4 color = l1.color;
vec3 position = l1.position;
```

Operations

For each member in the structure, you can use any operators allowed for that member's type. However, the operators allowed for the structure itself are only the assignment (=) and comparative operators (== and !=); see Table 6.9.

Table 6.9 The Operators Available for a Structure

Operator	Operation	Description
=	Assignment	The assignment and comparison operators are not allowed for the structures that contain arrays or sampler types
==, !=	Comparison	

When using the == operator, the result is `true` if, and only if, all the members are component-wise equal. When using the !=, the result is `false` if one of the members is not component-wise equal.

Arrays

GLSL ES arrays have a similar form to the array in JavaScript, with only one-dimensional arrays being supported. Unlike arrays in JavaScript, the `new` operator is not necessary to create arrays, and methods such as `push()` and `pop()` are not supported. The arrays can be declared by a name followed by brackets ([]) enclosing their sizes. For example:

```
float floatArray[4]; // declares an array consisting of four floats
vec4 vec4Array[2];   // declares an array consisting of two vec4s
```

The array size must be specified as an **integral constant expression** greater than zero where the integral constant expression is defined as follows:

- A numerical value (for example, 0 or 1)

- A global or local variable qualified as `const`, excluding function parameters (see the section "const Variables")

- Expressions composed of both of the above

Therefore, the following will result in an error:

```
int size = 4;
vec4 vec4Array[size]; // Error. If you declare "const int size = 4;"
                      // it will not result in an error
```

Note that arrays cannot be qualified as `const`.

Array elements can be accessed using the array indexing operator ([]). Note that, like C, the index starts from 0. For example, the third element of the float Array defined earlier can be accessed as follows:

```
float f = floatArray[2];
```

Only an integral constant expression or uniform variable (see the section "Uniform Variables") can be used as an index of an array. In addition, unlike JavaScript or C, an array cannot be initialized at declaration time. So each element of the array must be initialized explicitly as follows:

```
vec4Array[0] = vec4(4.0, 3.0, 6.0, 1.0);
vec4Array[1] = vec4(3.0, 2.0, 0.0, 1.0);
```

Arrays support only [] operators. However, elements in an array do support the standard operators available for their type. For example, the following operator can be applied to the elements of floatArray or vec4Array:

```
// multiplies the second element of floatArray by 3.14
float f = floatArray[1] * 3.14;
// multiplies the first element of vec4Array by vec4(1.0, 2.0, 3.0, 4.0);
vec4 v4 = vec4Array[0] * vec4(1.0, 2.0, 3.0, 4.0);
```

Samplers

GLSL ES supports a dedicated type called sampler for accessing textures. (See Chapter 5, "Using Colors and Texture Images.") Two types of samplers are available: sampler2D and samplerCube. Variables of the sampler type can be used only as a uniform variable (see the section "Uniform Variables") or an argument of the functions that can access textures such as texture2D(). (See Appendix B.) For example:

```
uniform sampler2D u_Sampler;
```

In addition, the only value that can be assigned to the variable is a texture unit number, and you must use the WebGL method gl.uniform1i() to set the value. For example, TexturedQuad.js in Chapter 5 uses gl.uniform1i(u_Sampler, 0) to pass the texture unit 0 to the shader.

Variables of type sampler are not allowed to be operands in any expressions other than =, ==, and !=.

Unlike other types explained in the previous sections, the number of sampler type variables is limited depending on the shader type (see Table 6.10). In the table, the keyword mediump is a precision qualifier. (This qualifier is explained in detail in the section "Precision Qualifiers," toward the end of this chapter.)

Table 6.10 Minimum Number of Variables of the Sampler Type

Shaders that Use the Variable	Built-In Constants Representing the Maximum Number	Minimum Number
Vertex shader	`const mediump int gl_MaxVertexTextureImageUnits`	0
Fragment shader	`const mediump int gl_MaxTextureImageUnits`	8

Precedence of Operators

Operator precedence is shown in Table 6.11. Note the table contains several operators that are not explained in this book but are included for reference.

Table 6.11 The Precedence of Operators

Precedence	Operators
1	parenthetical grouping (())
2	function calls, constructors (()), array indexing ([]), period (.)
3	increment/decrement (++, –), negate (-), **inverse(~)**, not(!)
4	multiplication (*), division (/), **remainder (%)**
5	addition (+), subtraction (-)
6	**bit-wise shift (<<, >>)**
7	comparative operators (<, <=, >=, >)
8	equality (==, !=)
9	**bit-wise and (&)**
10	**bit-wise exclusive or (^)**
11	**bit-wise or (|)**
12	and (&&)
13	exclusive or (^^)
14	or (||)
15	ternary selection (? :)
16	assignment (=), arithmetic assignments (+=, -=, *=, /=, **%=, <<=, >>=, &=, ^=, |=**)
17	sequence(,)

Bold font indicates operators reserved for future versions of GLSL.

Conditional Control Flow and Iteration

Conditional control flow and iteration in the shading language are almost the same as in JavaScript or C.

if Statement and if-else Statement

A conditional control flow can use either `if` or `if-else`. An `if-else` statement follows the pattern shown here:

```
if (conditional-expression1) {
  commands here are executed if conditional-expression1 is true.
} else if (conditional-expression2) {
  commands here are executed if conditional-expression1 is false but conditional-
  expression2 is true.
} else {
  commands here are executed if conditional-expression1 is false and conditional-
  expression2 is false.
}
```

The following shows a code example using the `if-else` statement:

```
if(distance < 0.5) {
  gl_FragColor = vec4(1.0, 0.0, 0.0, 1.0); // red
} else {
  gl_FragColor = vec4(0.0, 1.0, 0.0, 1.0); // green
}
```

As shown in this example, the conditional expression in the `if` or `if-else` statement must be either a boolean value or an expression that becomes a boolean value. Boolean vector types, such as `bvec2`, are not allowed in the conditional expression.

`switch` statement are not allowed, and you should note that usage of the `if` or `if-else` statement will slow down the shaders.

for Statement

The `for` statement can be used as follows:

```
for (for-init-statement; conditional-expression; loop-index-expression) {
  the commands which you want to execute repeatedly.
}
```

For example:

```
for (int i = 0; i < 3; i++) {
  sum += i;
}
```

Note that the loop index (i in the preceding example) of the for statement can be declared only in the *for-init-statement*. The *conditional-expression* can be omitted, and an empty condition becomes true. The for statement has the following restrictions:

- Only a single loop index is allowed. The loop index must have the type int or float.

- *loop-index-expression* must have one of the following forms (supposing that i is a loop index):

  i++, i--, i+=*constant-expression*, i-=*constant-expression*

- *conditional-expression* is a comparison between a loop index and an integral constant expression. (See the section "Array.")

- Within the body of the loop, the loop index cannot be assigned.

These limitations are in place so that the compiler can perform inline expansion of for statements.

continue, break, discard Statements

Just like JavaScript or C, continue and break statements are allowed only within a for statement and are generally used within if statements:

continue skips the remainder of the body of the innermost loop containing the continue, increases/decreases the loop index, and then moves to the next loop.

break exits the innermost loop containing the break. No further execution of the loop is done.

The following show examples of the continue statement:

```
for (int i = 0; i < 10; i++) {
  if (i == 8) {
     continue; // skips the remainder of the body of the innermost loop
  }
  // When i == 8, this line is not executed
}
```

The following shows an example of the break statement:

```
for (int i = 0; i < 10; i++) {
  if (i == 8) {
    break; // exits "for" loop
  }
  // When i >= 8, this line is not executed.
}
// When i == 8, this line is executed.
```

The discard statement is only allowed in fragment shaders and discards the current fragment, abandoning the operation on the current fragment and skipping to the next fragment. The use of discard will be explained in more detail in the section "Make a Rounded Point" in Chapter 10, "Advanced Techniques."

Functions

In contrast to the way functions are defined in JavaScript, the functions in GLSL ES are defined in the same manner as in C. For example:

```
returnType functionName(type0 arg0, type1 arg1, ..., typen argn) {
   do some computation
   return returnValue;
}
```

Argument types must use one of the data types explained in this chapter, and like main(), functions with no arguments are allowed. When the function returns no value, the return statement does not need to be included. In this case, returnType must be void. You can also specify a structure as the returnValue, but the structure returned cannot contain an array.

The following example shows a function to convert an RGBA value into a luminance value:

```
float luma (vec4 color) {
   float r = color.r;
   float g = color.g;
   float b = color.b;
   return 0.2126 * r + 0.7162 * g + 0.0722 * b;
   // The preceding four lines could be rewritten as follows:
   // return 0.2126 * color.r + 0.7162 * color.g + 0.0722 * color.b;
}
```

You can call the function declared above in the same manner as in JavaScript or C by using its name followed by a list of arguments in parentheses:

```
attribute vec4 a_Color; // (r, g, b, a) is passed
void main() {
   ...
   float brightness = luma(a_Color);
   ...
}
```

Note that an error will result if, when called, argument types do not match the declared parameter types. For example, the following will result in an error because the type of the parameter is float, but the caller passes an integer:

```
float square(float value) {
  return value * value;
}
void main() {
  ...
  float x2 = square(10); // Error: Because 10 is integer. 10.0 is OK.
  ...
}
```

As you can see from the previous examples, functions work just like those in JavaScript or C except that you cannot call the function itself from inside the body of the function (that is, a recursive call of the function isn't allowed). For the more technically minded, this is because the compilers can in-line function calls.

Prototype Declarations

When a function is called before it is defined, it must be declared with a prototype. The prototype declaration tells WebGL in advance about the types of parameters and the return value of the function. Note that this is different from JavaScript, which doesn't require a prototype. The following is an example of a prototype declaration for luma(), which you saw in the previous section:

```
float luma(vec4); // a prototype declaration
main() {
...
float brightness = luma(color); // luma() is called before it is defined.
...
}

float luma (vec4 color) {
  return 0.2126 * color.r + 0.7162 * color.g + 0.0722 * color.b;
}
```

Parameter Qualifiers

GLSL ES supports qualifiers for parameters that control the roles of parameters within a function. They can define that a parameter (1) is to be passed into a function, (2) is to be passed back out of a function, and (3) is to be passed both into and out of a function. (2) and (3) can be used just like a pointer in C. These are shown in Table 6.12.

Table 6.12 Parameter Qualifiers

Qualifiers	Roles	Description
in	Passes a value into the function	The parameter is passed by value. Its value can be referred to and modified in the function. The caller cannot refer to the modification.
const in	Passes a value into the function	The parameter is passed by constant value. Its value can be referred to but cannot be modified.
out	Passes a value out of the function	The parameter is passed by reference. If its value is modified, the caller can refer to the modification.
inout	Passes a value both into/out of the function	The parameter is passed by reference, and its value is copied in the function. Its value can be referred to and modified in the function. The caller can also refer to the modification.
<none: default>	Passes a value into the function	Same as in.

For example, `luma()` can return the result of its calculation using a parameter qualified by out instead of a return value, as follows:

```
void luma2 (in vec3 color, out float brightness) {
  brightness = 0.2126 * color.r + 0.7162 * color.g + 0.0722 * color.b;
}
```

Because the function itself no longer returns a value, the return type of this function is changed from float to void. Additionally, the qualifier in, in front of the first parameter, can be omitted because in is a default parameter qualifier.

This function can be used as follows:

```
luma2(color, brightness); // the result is stored into "brightness"
                          // same as brightness = luma(color)
```

Built-In Functions

In addition to user-defined functions, GLSL ES supports a number of built-in functions that perform operations frequently used in computer graphics. Table 6.13 gives an overview of the built-in functions in GLSL ES, and you can look at Appendix B for the detailed definition of each function.

Table 6.13 Built-In Functions in GLSL ES

Category	Built-In Functions
Angle functions	`radians` (converts degrees to radians), `degrees` (converts radians to degrees)
Trigonometry functions	`sin` (sine function), `cos` (cosine function), `tan` (tangent function), `asin` (arc sine function), `acos` (arc cosine function), and `atan` (arc tangent function)
Exponential functions	`pow` (x^y), `exp` (natural exponentiation), `log` (natural logarithm), `exp2` (2^x), `log2` (base 2 logarithm), `sqrt` (square root), and `inversesqrt` (inverse of `sqrt`)
Common functions	`abs` (absolute value), `min` (minimum value), `max` (maximum value), `mod` (remainder), `sign` (sign of a value), `floor` (floor function), `ceil` (ceil function), `clamp` (clamping of a value), `mix` (linear interpolation), `step` (step function), `smoothstep` (Hermite interpolation), and `fract` (fractional part of the argument)
Geometric functions	`length` (length of a vector), `distance` (distance between two points), `dot` (inner product), `cross` (outer product), `normalize` (vector with length of 1), `reflect` (reflection vector), and `faceforward` (converting normal when needed to "faceforward")
Matrix functions	`matrixCompMult` (component-wise multiplication)
Vector relational functions	`lessThan` (component-wise "<"), `lessThanEqual` (component-wise "<="), `greaterThan` (component-wise ">"), `greaterThanEqual` (component-wise ">="), `equal` (component-wise "=="), `notEqual` (component-wise "!="), `any` (true if any component is true), `all` (true if all components are true), and `not` (component-wise logical complement)
Texture lookup functions	`texture2D` (texture lookup in the 2D texture), `textureCube` (texture lookup in the cube map texture), `texture2DProj` (projective version of `texture2D()`), `texture2DLod` (level of detail version of `texture2D()`), `textureCubeLod` (lod version of `textureCube()`), and `texture2DProjLod` (projective version of `texture2DLod()`)

Global Variables and Local Variables

Just like JavaScript or C, GLSL ES supports both global variables and local variables. Global variables can be accessed from anywhere in the program, and local variables can be accessed only from within a limited portion of the program.

In GLSL ES, in a similar manner to JavaScript or C, variables declared "outside" a function become global variables, and variables declared "inside" a function become local variables. The local variables can be accessed only from within the function containing them. For this reason, the attribute, uniform, and varying variables described in the next section must be declared as global variables because they are accessed from outside the function.

Storage Qualifiers

As explained in the previous chapters, GLSL ES supports storage qualifiers for attribute, uniform, and varying variables (see Figure 6.3). In addition, a `const` qualifier is supported to specify a constant variable to be used in a shader program.

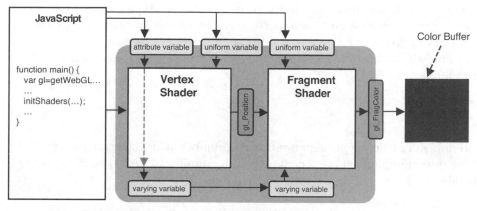

Figure 6.3 Attribute, uniform, and varying variables

const Variables

Unlike JavaScript, GLSL ES supports the `const` qualifier to specify a constant variable, or one whose value cannot be modified.

The `const` qualifier is specified in front of the variable type, just like an attribute variable. Variables qualified by `const` must be initialized at their declaration time; otherwise, they are unusable because no data can be assigned to them after their declaration. Some examples include:

```
const int lightspeed = 299792458;          // light speed (m/s)
const vec4 red = vec4(1.0, 0.0, 0.0, 1.0); // red
const mat4 identity = mat4(1.0);           // identity matrix
```

Assigning data to the variable qualified by `const` will result in an error. For example:

```
const int lightspeed;
lightspeed = 299792458;
```

will result in the following error message:

```
failed to compile shader: ERROR: 0:11: 'lightspeed' : variables
with qualifier 'const' must be initialized
ERROR: 0:12: 'assign': l-value required (can't modify a const variable)
```

Attribute Variables

As you have seen in previous chapters, attribute variables are available only in vertex shaders. They must be declared as a global variable and are used to pass per-vertex data to the vertex shader. You should note that it is "per-vertex." For example, if there are two vertices, (4.0, 3.0, 6.0) and (8.0, 3.0, 0.0), data for each vertex can be passed to an attribute variable. However, data for other coordinates, such as (6.0, 3.0, 3.0), which is a halfway point between the two vertices and not a specified vertex, cannot be passed to the variable. If you want to do that, you need to add the coordinates as a new vertex. Attribute variables can only be used with the data types float, vec2, vec3, vec4, mat2, mat3, and mat4. For example:

```
attribute vec4 a_Color;
attribute float a_PointSize;
```

There is an implementation-dependent limit on the number of attribute variables available, but the minimum number is 8. The limits on the number of each type of variable are shown in Table 6.14.

Table 6.14 The Limitation on the Number of Attribute, Uniform, and Varying Variables

Types of Variables		The Built-In Constants for the Maximum Number	Minimum Number
attribute variables		const mediump int gl_MaxVertexAttribs	8
uniform variables	Vertex shader	const mediump int gl_MaxVertexUniformVectors	128
	Fragment shader	const mediump int gl_MaxFragmentUniformVectors	16
varying variables		const mediump int gl_MaxVaryingVectors	8

Uniform Variables

Uniform variables are allowed to be used in both vertex and fragment shaders and must be declared as global variables. Uniform variables are read-only and can be declared as any data types other than array and structure. If a uniform variable of the same name and data type is declared in both a vertex shader and a fragment shader, it is shared between them. Uniform variables contain "uniform" (common) data, so your JavaScript program must only use them to pass such data. For example, because transformation matrices contain the uniform values for all vertices, they can be passed to uniform variables:

```
uniform mat4 u_ViewMatrix;
uniform vec3 u_LightPosition;
```

There is an implementation-dependent limit on the number of uniform variables that can be used (Table 6.14). Note that the limit in a vertex shader is different from that in a fragment shader.

Varying Variables

The last type of qualifier is `varying`. Varying variables also must be declared as global variables and are used to pass data from a vertex shader to a fragment shader by declaring a variable with the same type and name in both shaders. (See `v_Color` in Listing 6.1 and Listing 6.2.) The following are examples of varying variable declarations:

```
varying vec2 v_TexCoord;
varying vec4 v_Color;
```

Just like attribute variables, the varying variables can be declared only with the following data types: `float`, `vec2`, `vec3`, `vec4`, `mat2`, `mat3`, and `mat4`. As explained in Chapter 5, the value of a varying variable written by a vertex shader is not passed to a fragment shader as is. Rather, the rasterization process between the vertex and fragment shaders interpolates the value according to the shape to be drawn, and then the interpolated value is passed per fragment. This interpolation process is the reason for the limitations on the data types that can be used with a varying variable.

The number of varying variables also has an implementation dependent limit. The minimum number is 8 (see Table 6.14).

Precision Qualifiers

Precision qualifiers were newly introduced in GLSL ES to make it possible to execute shader programs more efficiently and to reduce their memory size. As the name suggests, it is a simple mechanism to specify how much precision (the number of bits) each data type should have. Simply put, specifying higher precision data requires more memory and computation time, and specifying lower precision requires less. By using these qualifiers, you can exercise fine-grained control over aspects of performance and size. However, precision qualifiers are optional, and a reasonable default compromise can be specified using the following lines:

```
#ifdef GL_ES
precision mediump float;
#endif
```

Because WebGL is based on OpenGL ES 2.0, which was designed for consumer electronics and embedded systems, WebGL programs may end up executing on a range of hardware platforms. In some cases, the computation time and memory efficiency could be improved by using lower precision data types when performing calculations and operations. Perhaps more importantly, this also enables reduced power consumption and thus extended battery life on mobile devices.

You should note, however, that just specifying lower precision may lead to incorrect results within WebGL, so it's important to balance efficiency and correctness.

As shown in Table 6.15, WebGL supports three types of precision qualifiers: highp (high precision), mediump (medium precision), and lowp (lower precision).

Table 6.15 Precision Qualifiers

Precision Qualifiers	Descriptions	Default Range and Precision	
		Float	int
highp	High precision. The minimum precision required for a vertex shader.	$(-2^{62}, 2^{62})$ Precision: 2^{-16}	$(-2^{16}, 2^{16})$
mediump	Medium precision. The minimum precision required for a fragment shader. More than lowp, and less than highp.	$(-2^{14}, 2^{14})$ Precision: 2^{-10}	$(-2^{10}, 2^{10})$
lowp	Low precision. Less than mediump, but all colors can be represented.	$(-2, 2)$ Precision: 2^{-8}	$(-2^{8}, 2^{8})$

There are a couple of things to note. First, fragment shaders may not support highp in some WebGL implementations; a way to check this is shown later in this section. Second, the actual range and precision are implementation dependent, which you can check by using gl.getShaderPrecisionFormat().

The following are examples of the declaration of variables using the precision qualifiers:

```
mediump float size;    // float of medium precision
highp vec4 position;   // vec4 composed of floats of high precision
lowp vec4 color;       // vec4 composed of floats of lower precision
```

Because specifying a precision for all variables is time consuming, a default for each data type can be set using the keyword precision, which must be specified at the top of a vertex shader or fragment shader using the following syntax:

```
precision precision-qualifier name-of-type;
```

This sets the precision of the data type specified by *name-of-type* to the precision specified by *precision-qualifier*. In this case, variables declared without a precision qualifier have this default precision automatically set. For example:

```
precision mediump float; // All floats have medium precision
precision highp int;     // All ints have high precision
```

This specifies all data types related to float, such as `vec2` and `mat3`, to have medium precision, and all integers to have high precision. For example, because `vec4` consists of four float types, each float of the vector is set to medium precision.

You may have noticed that in the examples in previous chapters, you didn't specify precision qualifiers to the data types other than `float` in fragment shaders. This is because most data types have a default precision value; however, there is no default precision for `float` in a fragment shader. See Table 6.16 for details.

Table 6.16   Default Precision of Type

Type of Shader	Data Type	Default Precision
Vertex shader	int	highp
	float	highp
	sampler2D	lowp
	samplerCube	lowp
Fragment shader	int	medium
	float	**None**
	sampler2D	lowp
	samplerCube	lowp

The fact that there is no default precision for float requires programmers to carefully use floats in their fragment shaders. So, for example, using a float without specifying the precision will result in the following error:

```
failed to compile shader: ERROR: 0:1 : No precision specified for (float).
```

As mentioned, whether a WebGL implementation supports `highp` in a fragment shader is implementation dependent. If it is supported, the built-in macro `GL_FRAGMENT_PRECISION_HIGH` is defined (see the next section).

Preprocessor Directives

GLSL ES supports preprocessor directives, which are commands (directives) for the preprocessor stage before actual compilation. They are always preceded by a hash mark (#). The following example was used in `ColoredPoints.js`:

```
#ifdef GL_ES
precision mediump float;
#endif
```

These lines check to see if the macro GL_ES is defined, and if so the lines between #ifdef and #endif are executed. They are similar to an if statement in JavaScript or C.

The following three preprocessor directives are available in GLSL ES:

```
#if constant-expression
If the constant-expression is true, this part is executed.
#endif

#ifdef macro
If the macro is defined, this part is executed.
#endif

#ifndef macro
If the macro is not defined, this part is executed.
#endif
```

The #define is used to define macros. Unlike C, macros in GLSL ES cannot have macro parameters:

```
#define macro-name string
```

You can use #undef to undefine the macro:

```
#undef macro-name
```

You can use #else directives just like an if statement in JavaScript or C. For example:

```
#define NUM 100
#if NUM == 100
If NUM == 100 then this part is executed.
#else
If NUM != 100 then this part is executed.
#endif
```

Macros can use any name except for the predefined macros names shown in Table 6.17.

Table 6.17 Predefined Macros

Macro	Description
GL_ES	Defined and set to 1 in OpenGL ES 2.0
GL_FRAGMENT_PRECISION_HIGH	highp is supported in a fragment shader

So you can use the macro with preprocessor directives as follows:

```
#ifdef GL_ES
#ifdef GL_FRAGMENT_PRECISION_HIGH
precision highp float; // highp is supported. floats have high precision
#else
precision mediump float; // highp is not supported. floats have medium precision
#endif
#endif
```

You can specify which version of GLSL ES is used in the shader by using the `#version` directive:

```
#version number
```

Accepted versions include 100 (for GLSL ES 1.00) and 101 (for GLSL ES 1.01). By default, shaders that do not include a `#version` directive will be treated as written in GLSL ES version 1.00. The following example specifies version 1.01:

```
#version 101
```

The `#version` directive must be specified at the top of the shader program and can only be preceded by comments and white space.

Summary

This chapter explained the core features of the OpenGL ES Shading Language (GLSL ES) in some detail.

You have seen that the GLSL ES shading language has many similarities to C but has been specialized for computer graphics and has had unnecessary C features removed. The specialized computer graphics features include support for vector and matrix data types, special component names for accessing the components of a vector or matrix, and operators for a vector or matrix. In addition, GLSL ES supports many built-in functions for operations frequently used in computer graphics, all designed to allow you to create efficient shader programs.

Now that you have a better understanding of GLSL ES, the next chapter will return to WebGL and explore more sophisticated examples using this new knowledge.

Chapter 7

Toward the 3D World

In the previous chapters, we used examples based on 2D geometrical shapes to explain how the WebGL system works and how it supports the behavior of shaders, transformations such as translation and rotation, animation, and texture mapping. However, the techniques you've learned so far can be applied not only to 2D shapes but also to 3D objects. In this chapter you'll take the first step into the 3D world and explore the implications of moving from 2D to 3D. In particular, you will explore:

- Representing the user's view into the 3D world

- Controlling the volume of 3D space that is viewed

- Clipping

- Handling foreground and background objects

- Drawing a 3D object (a cube)

All these issues have a significant impact on how the 3D scene is drawn and presented to viewers, and a mastery of them is critical to building compelling 3D scenes. As usual, we'll take you step by step so you will quickly master the basics and be able to move on to the more complex issues of lighting and performance in the final chapters.

What's Good for Triangles Is Good for Cubes

So far, you've used the humble triangle in many of the explorations and programs. As previously discussed, you've seen how 3D objects are composed of 2D shapes—in particular the triangle. Figure 7.1 shows a cube that has been built up from 12 triangles.

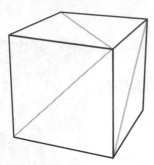

Figure 7.1 A cube composed of triangles

So when you deal with 3D objects, you just need to apply the techniques you have learned to each triangle that makes up the objects. The only difference from past examples, and it's a significant one, is that you now need to consider the **depth information** of the triangles in addition to the x and y coordinates. Let's begin by exploring how you specify and control the viewing direction—that is, the view into the 3D scene the user has—and then look at the visible range that controls how much of the scene the user sees. The explanations focus on the basic triangle because it simplifies things; however, what's true for triangles is true for 3D objects.

Specifying the Viewing Direction

The critical factor when considering 3D objects is that they have depth in a 3D space. This means you need to take care of several issues that you didn't have to consider when using 2D shapes. First, because of the nature of 3D space, you can look at the object from anywhere in the space; that is, your viewpoint can be anywhere. When describing the way you view objects, two important points need consideration:

- The viewing direction (where you are looking from, and at which part of the scene are you looking?)

- The visible range (given the viewing direction, where can you actually see?)

In this first section let's explore viewing direction and the techniques that allow you to place the eye point anywhere in 3D space and then look at objects from various directions. You'll take a look at the second item and see how to specify the visible range in the next section.

As introduced in Chapter 2, "Your First Step with WebGL" (refer to Figure 2.16), let's assume that, by default, the eye point is placed at the origin (0, 0, 0), and the line of sight extends along the z-axis in the negative direction (inward toward your computer screen). In this section, you will move the eye point from the default location to other locations and then view a triangle from there.

Let's construct a sample program, LookAtTriangles, that locates the eye point at (0.20, 0.25, 0.25) and then views three triangles from there toward the origin (0, 0, 0). Using three triangles makes it easy to understand the depth information in the 3D scene. Figure 7.2 shows a screen shot of LookAtTriangles and the color and z coordinate of each triangle.

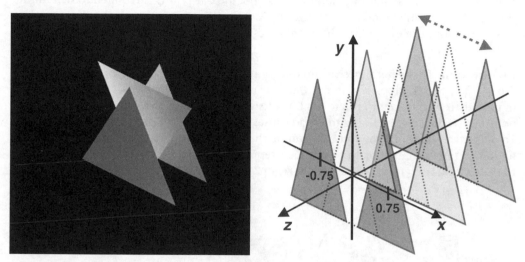

Figure 7.2 LookAtTriangles (left), and the color and z coordinate of each triangle (right)

The program uses softer colors because they are easier on the eyes.

Eye Point, Look-At Point, and Up Direction

To specify where you are looking from and which part of the scene you are looking at in the 3D space, you need two items of position information: the eye point (where you are looking from) and the look-at point (which part of the scene you are looking at). In addition, in 3DCG, you need to specify which direction is up in the scene. As such, a total of three items of information are required to specify the viewing direction (see Figure 7.3).

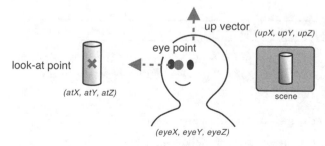

Figure 7.3 Eye point, look-at point, and up direction

Eye point: This is the starting point from which the 3D space is viewed. In the following sections, the coordinates of this position are referred to as (eyeX, eyeY, eyeZ).

Look-at point: This is the point at which you are looking and which determines the direction of the line of sight from the eye point. As the name suggests, the eye point is a point, not a vector, so another point (such as the look-at point) is required to determine the direction in which you are looking. The look-at point is a point on the line of sight extending from the eye point. The coordinates of the look-at point are referred to as (atX, atY, atZ).

Up direction: This determines the up direction in the scene that is being viewed from the eye point to the look-at point. If only the eye point and the look-at point are determined, there is freedom to rotate the line of sight from the eye point to the look-at point. (In Figure 7.4, inclining the head causes the top and bottom of the scene to shift.) To define the rotation, you must determine the up direction along the line of sight. The up direction is specified by three numbers representing the direction. The coordinates for this direction are referred to as (upX, upY, upZ).

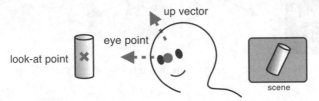

Figure 7.4 Eye point, look-at point, and up direction

In WebGL, you can specify the position and direction the eye point faces by converting these three items of information in a matrix and passing the matrix to a vertex shader. This matrix is called a view transformation matrix or **view matrix**, because it changes the view of the scene. In cuon-matrix.js, the method Matrix4.setLookAt() is defined to calculate the view matrix from the three items of information: eye point, look-at point and up direction.

Matrix4.setLookAt(eyeX, eyeY, eyeZ, atX, atY, atZ, upX, upY, upZ)

Calculate the view matrix derived from the eye point (*eyeX, eyeY, eyeZ*), the look-at point (*atX, atY, atZ*), and the up direction (*upX, upY, upZ*). This view matrix is set up in the Matrix4 object. The look-at point is mapped to the center of the <canvas>.

Parameters	eyeX, eyeY, eyeZ	Specify the position of the eye point.
	atX, atY, atZ	Specify the position of the look-at point.

In WebGL, the default settings when using `Matrix4.setLookAt()` are defined as follows:

- The eye point is placed at (0, 0, 0) (that is, the origin of the coordinate system).

- The look-at point is along the negative z-axis, so a good value is (0, 0, –1).[1] The up direction is specified along the positive y-axis, so a good value is (0, 1, 0).

So, for example, if the up direction is specified as (1, 0, 0), the positive x-axis becomes the up direction; in this case, you will see the scene tilted by 90 degrees.

A view matrix representing the default settings in WebGL can be simply produced as follows (see Figure 7.5).

```
var initialViewMatrix = new Matrix4();
initialViewMatrix.setLookAt(0, 0, 0, 0, 0, -1, 0, 1, 0);
```

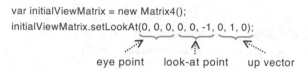

eye point　　look-at point　　up vector

Figure 7.5 An example of setLookAt()

Now you understand how to use the method `setLookAt()`, so let's take a look at its use in an actual sample program.

Sample Program (LookAtTriangles.js)

`LookAtTriangles.js`, shown in Listing 7.1, is a program that changes the position of the eye point and then draws the three triangles shown in Figure 7.2. Although it is difficult to see on paper, the three triangles are, in order of proximity, blue, yellow, and green, respectively, all fading to red in the bottom-right corner.

Listing 7.1 LookAtTriangles.js

```
1 // LookAtTriangles.js
2 // Vertex shader program
3 var VSHADER_SOURCE =
4   'attribute vec4 a_Position;\n' +
5   'attribute vec4 a_Color;\n' +
6   'uniform mat4 u_ViewMatrix;\n' +
```

---

[1] The z component could be any negative value. The value -1 is an example but we could have chosen any other negative value.

```
7    'varying vec4 v_Color;\n' +
8    'void main() {\n' +
9    ' gl_Position = u_ViewMatrix * a_Position;\n' +
10   ' v_Color = a_Color;\n' +
11   '}\n';
12
13 // Fragment shader program
14 var FSHADER_SOURCE =
   ...
18   'varying vec4 v_Color;\n' +
19   'void main() {\n' +
20   ' gl_FragColor = v_Color;\n' +
21   '}\n';
22
23 function main() {
   ...
40   // Set the vertex coordinates and color (blue triangle is in front)
41   var n = initVertexBuffers(gl);
   ...
50   // Get the storage location of u_ViewMatrix variable
51   var u_ViewMatrix = gl.getUniformLocation(gl.program,'u_ViewMatrix');
   ...
57   // Set the eye point, look-at point, and up direction
58   var viewMatrix = new Matrix4();
59   viewMatrix.setLookAt(0.20, 0.25, 0.25, 0, 0, 0, 0, 1, 0);
60
61   // Pass the view matrix to u_ViewMatrix variable
62   gl.uniformMatrix4fv(u_ViewMatrix, false, viewMatrix.elements);
   ...
67   // Draw a triangle
68   gl.drawArrays(gl.TRIANGLES, 0, n);
69 }
70
71 function initVertexBuffers(gl) {
72   var verticesColors = new Float32Array([
73     // vertex coordinates and color
74     0.0,  0.5,  -0.4,  0.4 1.0,  0.4, // The back green triangle
75    -0.5, -0.5,  -0.4,  0.4 1.0,  0.4,
76     0.5, -0.5,  -0.4,  1.0,  0.4 0.4,
77
78     0.5,  0.4,  -0.2,  1.0,  0.4 0.4, // The middle yellow triangle
79    -0.5,  0.4,  -0.2,  1.0,  1.0,  0.4,
80     0.0, -0.6,  -0.2,  1.0,  1.0,  0.4,
81
82     0.0,  0.5,   0.0,  0.4 0.4  1.0,  // The front blue triangle
```

```
83    -0.5, -0.5,   0.0,  0.4  0.4  1.0,
84   0.5, -0.5,   0.0,  1.0,  0.4  0.4
85   ]);
86   var n = 9;
87
88   // Create a buffer object
89   var vertexColorbuffer = gl.createBuffer();
     ...
96   gl.bindBuffer(gl.ARRAY_BUFFER, vertexColorbuffer);
97   gl.bufferData(gl.ARRAY_BUFFER, verticesColors, gl.STATIC_DRAW);
     ...
121   return n;
122 }
```

This program is based on `ColoredTriangle.js` in Chapter 5, "Using Colors and Texture Images." The fragment shader, the method of passing the vertex information, and so on, is the same as in `ColoredTriangle.js`. The three main differences follow:

- The view matrix is passed to the vertex shader (line 6) and then multiplied by the vertex coordinates (line 9).

- The vertex coordinates and color values of the three triangles (line 72 to 85) are set up in `initVertexBuffers()`, which is called from line 41 of `main()` in JavaScript.

- The view matrix is calculated at lines 58 and 59 in `main()` and passed to the uniform variable `u_ViewMatrix` in the vertex shader at line 62. You should note that the position of the eye point is (0.2, 0.25, 0.25); the position of the look-at point is (0, 0, 0); the up direction is (0, 1, 0).

Let's start by looking at the second difference and the function `initVertexBuffers()` (line 71). The difference between this program and the original program, `ColoredTriangle.js`, is that `verticesColors` at line 72 (which is the array of vertex coordinates and colors for a single triangle) is modified for the three triangles, and the z coordinates are added in the array. These coordinates and colors are stored together in the buffer object `vertexColorBuffer` (lines 96 and 97) created at line 89. Because you are now dealing with three triangles (each with three vertices), you need to specify 9 as the third argument of `gl.drawArrays()` at line 68.

To specify the view matrix (that is, where you are looking and which part of the scene you are looking at [item 3]), you need to set up and pass the view matrix to the vertex shader. To do this, a `Matrix4` object `viewMatrix` is created at line 58, and you use `setLookAt()` to calculate and store the view matrix to `viewMatrix` at line 59. This view matrix is passed to `u_ViewMatrix` at line 62, which is the uniform variable used in the vertex shader:

```
57   // Set the eye point, look-at point, and up direction
58   var viewMatrix = new Matrix4();
59   viewMatrix.setLookAt(0.20, 0.25, 0.25, 0, 0, 0, 0, 1, 0);
60
```

```
61    // Pass the view matrix to the u_ViewMatrix variable
62    gl.uniformMatrix4fv(u_ViewMatrix, false, viewMatrix.elements);
```

Those are all the changes needed in the JavaScript program. Now let's examine what is happening in the vertex shader:

```
 2 // Vertex shader program
 3 var VSHADER_SOURCE =
 4   'attribute vec4 a_Position;\n' +
 5   'attribute vec4 a_Color;\n' +
 6   'uniform mat4 u_ViewMatrix;\n' +
 7   'varying vec4 v_Color;\n' +
 8   'void main() {\n' +
 9   '  gl_Position = u_ViewMatrix * a_Position;\n' +
10   '  v_Color = a_Color;\n' +
11   '}\n';
```

The vertex shader starts from line 4. The only two lines that differ from ColoredTriangle.js are indicated by boldface: Line 6 defines the uniform variable u_ViewMatrix, and line 9 multiplies the matrix by the vertex coordinates. These modifications seem quite trivial, so how do they change the position of the eye point?

Comparing LookAtTriangles.js with RotatedTriangle_Matrix4.js

Looking at the vertex shader in this sample program, you may notice a similarity with that in RotatedTriangle_Matrix4.js, which was explained in Chapter 4, "More Transformations and Basic Animation." That vertex shader created a rotation matrix using a Matrix4 object and then used the matrix to rotate a triangle. Let's take a look at that shader again:

```
1 // RotatedTriangle_Matrix4.js
2 // Vertex shader program
3 var VSHADER_SOURCE =
4   'attribute vec4 a_Position;\n' +
5   'uniform mat4 u_rotMatrix;\n' +
6   'void main() {\n' +
7   '  gl_Position = u_rotMatrix * a_Position;\n' +
8   '}\n';
```

The vertex shader in this section (LookAtTriangles.js) is listed as follows:

```
1 // LookAtTriangles.js
2 // Vertex shader program
3 var VSHADER_SOURCE =
4   'attribute vec4 a_Position;\n' +
5   'attribute vec4 a_Color;\n' +
6   'uniform mat4 u_ViewMatrix;\n' +
```

```
7     'varying vec4 v_Color;\n' +
8     'void main() {\n' +
9     '   gl_Position = u_ViewMatrix * a_Position;\n' +
10    '   v_Color = a_Color;\n' +
11    '}\n';
```

As you can see, the attribute variable for color values (a_Color) and the varying variable that passes the values to the fragment shader (v_Color) were added, and the name of the uniform variable was changed from u_rotMatrix to u_ViewMatrix. Despite these differences, the calculation of the value assigned to gl_Position is the same as that in the vertex shader of RotatedTriangle_Matrix4.js: multiplying a mat4 matrix by a_Position. (Compare line 7 in RotatedTriangle_Matrix4.js with line 9 in LookAtTriangles.js.)

This tells you that the operation performing "where you are looking and which part of the scene you are looking at" is actually equivalent to transformations such as translating or rotating a triangle.

Let's use an example to explain this. Assume that you are looking at a triangle from the origin (0, 0, 0) along the negative direction of the z-axis, and then the eye point moves to the position (0, 0, 1) (the left-side figure of Figure 7.6). In this case, the distance between the eye point and the triangle has increased by 1.0 unit of the z-axis. To achieve the same effect, you could leave the eye point alone and instead move the triangle 1.0 unit away (the right-side figure of Figure 7.6).

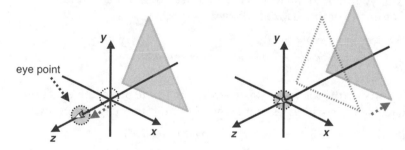

Figure 7.6   Movement of the eye point is identical to that of objects in the scene

This is exactly what happens in our sample program. The setLookAt() method of the Matrix4 object just calculates the matrix to carry out this transformation using the information about the position of the eye point, look-at point, and up direction. So, by then multiplying the matrix by the vertex coordinates of the objects in the scene, you obtain the same effect as moving the eye point. Essentially, instead of moving the eye point in one direction, the objects viewed (that is, the world itself) are moved in the opposite direction. You can use the same approach to handle rotation of the eye point.

Because moving the eye point is the same type of transformation as rotating or translating a triangle, you can represent both of them as a transformation matrix. Let's look at how you calculate the matrix when you want to rotate a triangle *and* move the position of the eye point.

Looking at Rotated Triangles from a Specified Position

`RotatedTriangle_Matrix4` in Chapter 4 displayed the triangle rotated around the z-axis. In this section, you modify `LookAtTriangles` to display the triangles viewed from a specified eye point along the line of sight. In this case, two matrices are required: a rotation matrix to rotate the triangles and a view matrix to specify the view of the scene. The first issue to consider is in which order you should multiply them.

So far, you know that multiplying a matrix by a vertex coordinate will apply the transformation defined by the matrix to the coordinates. That is to say, multiplying a rotation matrix by a vertex coordinate causes it to be rotated.

Multiplying a view matrix by a vertex coordinate causes the vertex to be transformed to the correct position as viewed from the eye position. In this sample program, we want to view the rotated triangles from a specified position, so we need to rotate the triangles and then look at them from the specified eye position. In other words, we need to rotate the three vertex coordinates comprising the triangle. Then we need to transform the rotated vertex coordinates (the rotated triangle) as we look at them from the specified position. We can achieve this by carrying out a matrix multiplication in the order described in the previous sentence. Let's check the equations.

As explained previously, if you want to rotate a shape, you need to multiply a rotation matrix by the vertex coordinates of the shape as follows:

$$\langle \text{"rotated" vertex coordinates} \rangle = $$
$$\langle \text{rotation matrix} \rangle \times \langle \text{original vertex coordinates} \rangle$$

By multiplying a view matrix by the rotated vertex coordinates in the preceding equation, you can obtain the rotated vertex coordinates that are viewed from the specified position.

$$\langle \text{"rotated" vertex coordinates "viewed from specified position"} \rangle = $$
$$\langle \text{view matrix} \rangle \times \langle \text{"rotated" vertex coordinates} \rangle$$

If you substitute the first expression into the second one, you obtain the following:

$$\langle \text{"rotated" vertex coordinates "viewed from specified position"} \rangle = $$
$$\langle \text{view matrix} \rangle \times \langle \text{rotation matrix} \rangle \times \langle \text{original vertex coordinates} \rangle$$

In this expression, you use a rotation matrix, but you can also apply a translation matrix, a scaling matrix, or a combination of them. Such a matrix is generally called a **model matrix**. Using that term, you can rewrite the expression shown in Equation 7.1.

Equation 7.1

$$\langle \text{view matrix} \rangle \times \langle \text{model matrix} \rangle \times \langle \text{vertex coordinates} \rangle$$

Now you need to implement this expression in a shader program, but because it is quite a simple expression, you can implement it as-is in a vertex shader. The sample program `LookAtRotatedTriangles` implements the transformation, and a screen shot is shown in Figure 7.7. Note, in this figure, that the white dashed line shows the triangle before rotation so that you can easily see the rotation.

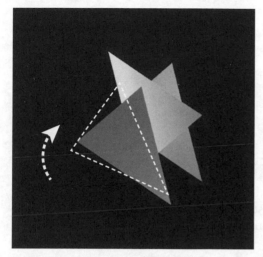

Figure 7.7   LookAtRotatedTriangles

Sample Program (LookAtRotatedTriangles.js)

`LookAtRotatedTriangles.js` is programmed by slightly modifying `LookAtTriangles.js`. You just need to add the uniform variable `u_ModelMatrix` to pass the model matrix to the shader and then add some processing in JavaScript's `main()` function to pass the matrix to the variable. The relevant code is shown in Listing 7.2.

Listing 7.2   LookAtRotatedTriangles.js

```
 1 // LookAtRotatedTriangles.js
 2 // Vertex shader program
 3 var VSHADER_SOURCE =
 4   'attribute vec4 a_Position;\n' +
 5   'attribute vec4 a_Color;\n' +
 6   'uniform mat4 u_ViewMatrix;\n' +
 7   'uniform mat4 u_ModelMatrix;\n' +
 8   'varying vec4 v_Color;\n' +
 9   'void main() {\n' +
10   '  gl_Position = u_ViewMatrix * u_ModelMatrix * a_Position;\n' +
11   '  v_Color = a_Color;\n' +
12   '}\n';
     ...
```

```
24 function main() {
   ...
51    // Get the storage locations of u_ViewMatrix and u_ModelMatrix
52    varu_ViewMatrix = gl.getUniformLocation(gl.program,'u_ViewMatrix');
53    var u_ModelMatrix = gl.getUniformLocation(gl.program, 'u_ModelMatrix');
   ...
59    // Specify the eye point and line of sight
60    var viewMatrix = new Matrix4();
61    viewMatrix.setLookAt(0.20, 0.25, 0.25, 0, 0, 0, 0, 1, 0);
62
63    // Calculate the rotation matrix
64    var modelMatrix = new Matrix4();
65    modelMatrix.setRotate(-10, 0, 0, 1);   // Rotate around z-axis
66
67    // Pass each matrix to each uniform variable
68    gl.uniformMatrix4fv(u_ViewMatrix, false, viewMatrix.elements);
69    gl.uniformMatrix4fv(u_ModelMatrix, false, modelMatrix.elements);
```

First, let's examine the vertex shader. You can see that line 10 simply implements Equation 7.1 as-is by using u_ModelMatrix at line 7, which receives data from the JavaScript program:

```
10  '  gl_Position = u_ViewMatrix * u_ModelMatrix * a_Position;\n' +
```

In the main() function in JavaScript, you already have the code for calculating a view matrix, so you just need to add the code for calculating the rotation matrix performing a –10 degree rotation around the z-axis. Line 53 gets the storage location of the u_ModelMatrix variable, and line 64 creates modelMatrix for the rotation matrix. Then line 65 calculates the matrix using Matrix4.setRotate(), and line 69 passes it to u_ModelMatrix.

When you run this sample program, you will see the triangles shown in Figure 7.6 illustrating that the matrices multiplied by the vertex coordinates (a_Position) have the desired effect. That is, the vertex coordinates were rotated by u_ModelMatrix, and then the resulting coordinates were transformed by u_ViewMatrix to the correct position as if viewed from the specified position.

Experimenting with the Sample Program

In LookAtRotatedTriangles.js, you implemented Equation 7.1 as- is. However, because the multiplication of the view matrix and model matrix is performed per vertex in the vertex shader, this implementation is inefficient when processing many vertices. The result of the matrix multiplication in Equation 7.1 is identical for each vertex, so you can calculate it in advance and pass the result to the vertex shader. The matrix obtained by multiplying a view matrix by a model matrix is called a **model view matrix**. That is,

$$\langle model\ view\ matrix\ \rangle = \langle view\ matrix \rangle \times \langle model\ matrix \rangle$$

Then, you can rewrite the expression in Equation 7.1 as shown in Equation 7.2.

Equation 7.2

$$\langle model\ view\ matrix \rangle \times \langle vertex\ coordinates \rangle$$

If you use Equation 7.2, you can rewrite the sample program shown in Listing 7.3. This sample program is `LookAtRotatedTriangles_mvMatrix`.

Listing 7.3 LookAtRotatedTriangles_mvMatrix.js

```
 1  // LookAtRotatedTriangles_mvMatrix.js
 2  // Vertex shader program
 3  var VSHADER_SOURCE =
    ...
 6    'uniform mat4 u_ModelViewMatrix;\n' +
 7    'varying vec4 v_Color;\n' +
 8    'void main() {\n' +
 9    '  gl_Position = u_ModelViewMatrix * a_Position;\n' +
10    '  v_Color = a_Color;\n' +
11    '}\n';
    ...
23  function main() {
    ...
50    // Get the storage locations of u_ModelViewMatrix and u_ModelMatrix
51    var u_ModelViewMatrix = gl.getUniformLocation(gl.program, 'u_ModelViewMatrix');
    ...
59    viewMatrix.setLookAt(0.20, 0.25, 0.25, 0, 0, 0, 0, 1, 0);
    ...
63    modelMatrix.setRotate(-10, 0, 0, 1); // Calculate rotation matrix
64
65    // Multiply both matrices
66    var modelViewMatrix = viewMatrix.multiply(modelMatrix);
67
68    // Pass the model viewmatrix to u_ModelViewMatrix
69    gl.uniformMatrix4fv(u_ModelViewMatrix, false, modelViewMatrix.elements);
```

In the vertex shader, the name of the uniform variable was modified to u_ModelViewMatrix and calculated in line 9. However, the processing steps in the vertex shader are identical to the original `LookAtTriangles.js`.

Within the JavaScript program, the method of calculating `viewMatrix` and `modelMatrix` from lines 59 to 63 is identical to that in `LookAtRotatedTriangles.js` and, when multiplied, result in `modelViewMatrix` (line 66). The `multiply()` method is used to multiply

`Matrix4` objects. It multiplies the matrix on the right side (`viewMatrix`) by the matrix specified by the argument (`modelMatrix`) of the method. So this code actually performs `modelViewMatrix= viewMatrix * modelMatrix`. Unlike with GLSL ES, you need to use a method to perform matrix multiplication instead of the `*` operator.

Having obtained `modelViewMatrix`, you just need to pass it to the `u_ModelViewMatrix` variable at line 69. Once you run the program, you can see the same result as shown in Figure 7.6.

As a final point, in this sample program, each matrix was calculated piece by piece at lines 59, 63, and 66 to better show the flow of the calculation. However, this could be rewritten in one line for efficiency:

```
var modelViewMatrix = new Matrix4();
modelViewMatrix.setLookAt(0.20, 0.25, 0.25, 0, 0, 0, 0, 1, 0).rotate(-10, 0, 0, 1);
// Pass the model view matrix to the uniform variable
gl.uniformMatrix4fv(u_ModelViewMatrix, false, modelViewMatrix.elements);
```

Changing the Eye Point Using the Keyboard

Let's modify `LookAtTriangles` to change the position of the eye point when the arrow keys are pressed. `LookAtTrianglesWithKeys` uses the right arrow key to increase the x coordinate of the eye point by 0.01 and the left arrow key to decrease the coordinate by 0.01. Figure 7.8 shows a screen shot of the sample program when run. If you hold down the left arrow key, the scene changes to that seen on the right side of Figure 7.8.

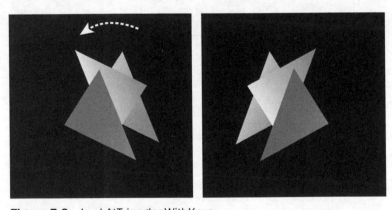

Figure 7.8   LookAtTrianglesWithKeys

Sample Program (LookAtTrianglesWithKeys.js)

Listing 7.4 shows the sample code. The vertex shader and the fragment shader are the same as those in `LookAtTriangles.js`. The basic processing flow of `main()` in JavaScript is also the same. The code for registering the event handler called on a key press is added to the sample program, and the code for drawing the triangles has been moved into the function `draw()`.

Listing 7.4 LookAtTrianglesWithKeys.js

```
1  // LookAtTrianglesWithKeys.js
2  // Vertex shader program
3  var VSHADER_SOURCE =
4    'attribute vec4 a_Position;\n' +
5    'attribute vec4 a_Color;\n' +
6    'uniform mat4 u_ViewMatrix;\n' +
7    'varying vec4 v_Color;\n' +
8    'void main() {\n' +
9    '  gl_Position = u_ViewMatrix * a_Position;\n' +
10   '  v_Color = a_Color;\n' +
11   '}\n';
     ...
23 function main() {
     ...
50   // Get the storage location of the u_ViewMatrix variable
51   varu_ViewMatrix = gl.getUniformLocation(gl.program,'u_ViewMatrix');
     ...
57   // Create Matrix4 object for a view matrix
58   var viewMatrix = new Matrix4();
59   // Register the event handler to be called on key press
60   document.onkeydown = function(ev){ keydown(ev, gl, n, u_ViewMatrix,
                                                  ➥viewMatrix); };
61
62   draw(gl, n, u_ViewMatrix, viewMatrix);  // Draw a triangle
63 }
     ...
117 var g_eyeX = 0.20, g_eyeY = 0.25, g_eyeZ = 0.25; // The eye point
118 function keydown(ev, gl, n, u_ViewMatrix, viewMatrix) {
119    if(ev.keyCode == 39) { // The right arrow key was pressed
120      g_eyeX += 0.01;
121    } else
122    if (ev.keyCode == 37) { // The left arrow key was pressed
123      g_eyeX -= 0.01;
124    } else { return; } // Prevent unnecessary drawing
125    draw(gl, n, u_ViewMatrix, viewMatrix);
126 }
127
128 function draw(gl, n, u_ViewMatrix, viewMatrix) {
129   // Set the eye point and line of sight
130   viewMatrix.setLookAt(g_eyeX, g_eyeY, g_eyeZ, 0, 0, 0, 0, 1, 0);
```

```
131
132   // Pass the view matrix to the u_ViewMatrix variable
133   gl.uniformMatrix4fv(u_ViewMatrix, false, viewMatrix.elements);
134
135   gl.clear(gl.COLOR_BUFFER_BIT); // Clear <canvas>
136
137   gl.drawArrays(gl.TRIANGLES, 0, n); // Draw a triangle
138 }
```

In this sample, you are using the event handler to change the position of the eye point when the right arrow key or the left arrow key is pressed. Before explaining the event handler, let's look at the function draw() that is called from the event handler.

The process performed in draw() is straightforward. Line 130 calculates the view matrix using the global variables g_eyeX, g_eyeY, and g_eyeZ defined at line 117, which contain 0.2, 0.25, and 0.25, respectively. Then the matrix is passed to the uniform variable u_ViewMatrix in the vertex shader at line 133. Back in main(), the storage location of u_ViewMatrix is retrieved at line 51, and a Matrix4 object (viewMatrix) is created at line 58. These two operations are carried out in advance because it is redundant if you perform them for each draw operation, particularly retrieving the storage. After that, line 135 clears <canvas>, and line 137 draws the triangles.

The variables g_eyeX, g_eyeY, and g_eyeZ specify the eye position and are recalculated in the event handler whenever a key is pressed. To call the event handler on key press, you need to register it to the onkeydown property of the document object. In this event handler, because you need to call draw() to draw the triangles, you must pass all arguments that draw() requires. This is why an anonymous function registers the handler as follows:

```
59   // Register the event handler to be called on key press
60   document.onkeydown = function(ev){ keydown(ev, gl, n, u_ViewMatrix,
                                              ➥viewMatrix); };
```

This sets up the event handler keydown() to be called when the key is pressed. Let's examine how keydown() is implemented.

```
118 function keydown(ev, gl, n, u_ViewMatrix, viewMatrix) {
119   if(ev.keyCode == 39) {  // The right arrow key was pressed
120     g_eyeX += 0.01;
121   } else
122   if (ev.keyCode == 37) { // The left arrow key was pressed
123     g_eyeX -= 0.01;
124   } else { return ; }      // Prevent unnecessary drawing
125     draw(gl, n, u_ViewMatrix, viewMatrix);   // Draw a triangle
126 }
```

What `keydown()` is doing is also straightforward. When a key is pressed, `keydown()` is called with the information about the event stored in the first parameter, ev, of `keydown()`. Then you just need to check which key was pressed by examining the value of ev.keyCode, modify g_eyeX, and draw the triangles. When the right arrow key is pressed, the code increases g_eyeX by 0.01, and when the left arrow key is pressed, it decreases g_eyeX by 0.01.

If you run the sample program, you can see the triangles shift every time you press the arrow key.

Missing Parts

As you play with the sample program, you may notice that as you shift the eye position to the extreme right or left, part of the triangle disappears (see Figure 7.9).

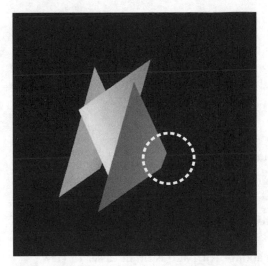

Figure 7.9 Part of the triangle disappears

This is because you haven't specified the **visible range** (the boundaries of what you can actually see) correctly. As mentioned in the first section of this chapter, WebGL does not display objects outside the visible range. In the case of Figure 7.9, part of the triangle went out of the visible range while pressing the arrow keys.

Specifying the Visible Range (Box Type)

Although WebGL allows you to place 3D objects anywhere in 3D space, it only displays those that are in the visible range. In WebGL, this is primarily a performance issue; there's no point in drawing 3D objects if they are not visible to the viewer. In a way, this mimics the way human sight works (see Figure 7.10); we see objects within the visible range based on our line of sight, which is approximately 200 degrees in the horizontal field of view. WebGL also has a similar limited range and does not display 3D objects outside of that range.

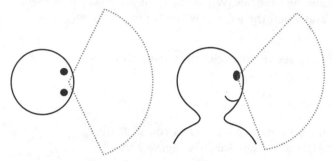

Figure 7.10 Human visual field

In addition to the up/down, left/right range along the line of sight, WebGL has a depth range that indicates how far you can see. These ranges are called the **viewing volume**. In Figure 7.9, because the depth range was not sufficient, part of the triangle disappears as it moves out of the viewing volume.

Specify the Viewing Volume

There are two ways of specifying a viewing volume:

- Using a rectangular parallelepiped, or more informally, a box (**orthographic projection**)

- Using a quadrangular pyramid (**perspective projection**)

Perspective projection gives more information about depth and is often easier to view because you use perspective views in real life. You should use this projection to show the 3D scene in perspective, such as a character or a battlefield in a 3D shooting game. Orthographic projection makes it much easier to compare two objects, such as two parts of a molecule model, because there is no question about how the viewpoint may affect the perception of distance. You should use the projection to show 3D objects in an orthographic view like those in technical drawing.

First, we will explain how the viewing volume works based on the box-shaped viewing volume.

The box-shaped viewing volume is shaped as shown in Figure 7.11. This viewing volume is set from the eye point toward the line of sight and occupies the space delimited by the two planes: the **near clipping plane** and the **far clipping plane**. The near clipping plane is defined by (*right, top, -near*), (*-left, top, -near*), (*-left, -bottom, -near*), and (*right, -bottom, -near*). The far clipping plane is defined by (*right, top, -far*), (*-left, top, -far*), (*-left, -bottom, -far*), and (*right, -bottom, -far*).

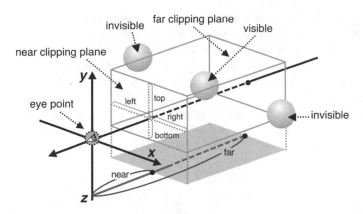

Figure 7.11 Box-shaped viewing volume

The scene viewed from the near clipping plane toward the line of sight is displayed on the <canvas>. If the aspect ratio of the near clipping plane is different from that of <canvas>, the scene is scaled according to the ratio, and the aspect ratio of the geometric shapes or objects in the scene are distorted. (You will explore this behavior in the last part of this section.) The range from the near clipping plane to the far clipping plane defines the viewing volume. Only objects inside this volume are displayed. If the objects lie partially inside the volume, only the part inside the volume is displayed.

Defining a Box-Shaped Viewing Volume

To set the box-shaped viewing volume, you use the method setOrtho() supported by the Matrix4 object defined in cuon-matrix.js.

Matrix4.setOrtho(left, right, bottom, top, near, far)

Calculate the matrix (orthographic projection matrix) that defines the viewing volume specified by its arguments, and store it in Matrix4. However, *left* must not be equal to *right*, *bottom* not equal to *top*, and *near* not equal to *far*.

Parameters	left, right	Specify the distances to the left side and right side of the near clipping plane.
	bottom, top	Specify the distances to the bottom and top of the near clipping plane.
	near, far	Specify the distances to the near and far clipping planes along the line of sight.
Return value	None	

Here, you are using a matrix again, which in this case is referred to as the **ortho-graphic projection matrix**. The sample program OrthoView will use this type of projection matrix to set the box-shaped viewing volume and then draw three trian-gles—as used in LookAtRotatedTriangles—to test the effect of the viewing volume. In LookAtRotatedTriangles, you placed the eye point at a different location from that of the origin. However, in this sample program, you'll use the origin (0, 0, 0) and set the line of sight along the negative z-axis to make it easy to check the effect of the viewing volume. The viewing volume is specified as shown in Figure 7.12, which uses *near*=0.0, *far*=0.5, *left*=–1.0, *right*=1.0, *bottom*=–1.0, and *top*=1.0 because the triangles lie between 0.0 and –0.4 along the z-axis (refer to Figure 7.2).

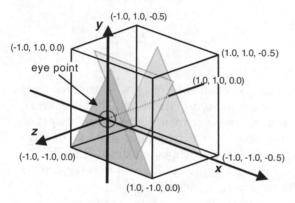

Figure 7.12 The box-shaped viewing volume used in OrthoView

In addition, we add key-press event handlers to change the values of *near* and *far* to check the effect of changing the size of the viewing volume. The following are the active keys and their mappings.

Arrow Key	Action
Right	Increases *near* by 0.01
Left	Decreases *near* by 0.01
Up	Increases *far* by 0.01
Down	Decreases *far* by 0.01

So that you can see the current values of near and far, they are displayed below the canvas, as shown in Figure 7.13.

near: 0, far: 0.5

Figure 7.13   OrthoView

Let's examine the sample program.

Sample Program (OrthoView.html)

Because this sample program shows the *near* and *far* value on the web page and not in the <canvas>, you need to add something to the HTML file listing as shown in Listing 7.5 (OrthoView.html).

Listing 7.5   OrthoView.html

```
1  <!DOCTYPE html>
2  <html>
3    <head lang="ja">
4      <meta charset="utf-8" />
5      <title>Set Box-shaped Viewing Volume</title>
6    </head>
7
8    <body onload="main()">
9      <canvas id="webgl" width="400" height="400">
10     Please use a browser that supports <canvas>
11     </canvas>
12     <p id="nearFar">The near and far values are displayed here.</p>
13
14     <script src="../lib/webgl-utils.js"></script>
   ...
18     <script src="OrthoView.js"></script>
```

```
19    </body>
20 </html>
```

As you can see, line 12 was added. This line shows "The near and far values are displayed here" and uses JavaScript to rewrite the contents of nearFar to show the current near and far values.

Sample Program (OrthoView.js)

Listing 7.6 shows OrthoView.js. This program is almost the same as LookAtTrianglesWithKeys.js, which changes the position of the eye point by using the arrow keys.

Listing 7.6   OrthoView.js

```
 1 // OrthoView.js
 2 // Vertex shader program
 3 var VSHADER_SOURCE =
 4   'attribute vec4 a_Position;\n' +
 5   'attribute vec4 a_Color;\n' +
 6   'uniform mat4 u_ProjMatrix;\n' +
 7   'varying vec4 v_Color;\n' +
 8   'void main() {\n' +
 9   '  gl_Position = u_ProjMatrix * a_Position;\n' +
10   '  v_Color = a_Color;\n' +
11   '}\n';
   ...
23 function main() {
24   // Retrieve<canvas> element
25   var canvas = document.getElementById('webgl');
26   // Retrieve the nearFar element
27   var nf = document.getElementById('nearFar');
   ...
52   // Get the storage location of u_ProjMatrix variable
53   var u_ProjMatrix = gl.getUniformLocation(gl.program,'u_ProjMatrix');
   ...
59   // Create the matrix to set the eye point and line of sight
60   var projMatrix = new Matrix4();
61   // Register the event handler to be called on key press
62   document.onkeydown = function(ev) { keydown(ev, gl, n, u_ProjMatrix,
                                         ➥projMatrix, nf); };
63
64   draw(gl, n, u_ProjMatrix, projMatrix, nf);  // Draw triangles
65 }
   ...
116 // The distances to the near and far clipping plane
```

```
117 var g_near = 0.0, g_far = 0.5;
118 function keydown(ev, gl, n, u_ProjMatrix, projMatrix, nf) {
119   switch(ev.keyCode) {
120     case 39: g_near += 0.01; break; // The right arrow key was pressed
121     case 37: g_near -= 0.01; break; // The left arrow key was pressed
122     case 38: g_far += 0.01;  break; // The up arrow key was pressed
123     case 40: g_far -= 0.01;  break; // The down arrow key was pressed
124     default: return; // Prevent the unnecessary drawing
125   }
126
127   draw(gl, n, u_ProjMatrix, projMatrix, nf);
128 }
129
130 function draw(gl, n, u_ProjMatrix, projMatrix, nf) {
131   // Set the viewing volume using a matrix
132   projMatrix.setOrtho(-1, 1, -1, 1, g_near, g_far);
133
134   // Set the projection matrix to u_ProjMatrix variable
135   gl.uniformMatrix4fv(u_ProjMatrix, false, projMatrix.elements);
136
137   gl.clear(gl.COLOR_BUFFER_BIT);  // Clear <canvas>
138
139   // Display the current near and far values
140   nf.innerHTML = 'near: ' + Math.round(g_near * 100)/100 + ', far: ' +
                                       ➥Math.round(g_far*100)/100;
141
142   gl.drawArrays(gl.TRIANGLES, 0, n);  // Draw the triangles
143 }
```

In a similar way to LookAtTrianglesWithKeys, keydown(), defined at line 118, is called on key press, and draw() is called at the end of keydown() (line 127). The draw() function defined at line 130 sets the viewing volume, rewrites the near and far value on the web page, and then draws the three triangles. The key point in this program is the draw() function; however, before explaining the function, let's quickly show how to rewrite HTML elements using JavaScript.

Modifying an HTML Element Using JavaScript

The method of modifying an HTML element using JavaScript is similar to that of drawing in a <canvas> with WebGL. That is, after retrieving the HTML element by using getElementById() and the id of the element, you write a message to the element in JavaScript.

In this sample program, you modify the following <p> element to show the message such as "near: 0.0, far: 0.5":

```
12    <p id="nearFar">The near and far values are displayed here.</p>
```

This element is retrieved at line 27 in `OrthoView.js` using `getElementById()` as before. Once you've retrieved the element, you need to specify the string (`'nearFar'`) that was bound to `id` at line 12 in the HTML file, as follows:

```
26  // Retrieve nearFar element
27  var nf = document.getElementById('nearFar');
```

Once you retrieve the `<p>` element into the variable `nf` (actually, `nf` is a JavaScript object), you just need to change the content of this element. This is straightforward and uses the `innerHTML` property of the object. For example, if you write:

```
nf.innerHTML = 'Good Morning, Marisuke-san!';
```

You will see the message "Good Morning, Marisuke-san!" on the web page. You can also insert HTML tags in the message. For example, 'Good Morning, Marisuke-san!' will highlight "Marisuke."

In `OrthoView.js`, you use the following equation to display the current *near* and *far* values. These values are stored in the global variables `g_near` and `g_far` declared at line 117. When printing them, they are formatted using `Math.round()` as follows:

```
139  // Display the current near and far values
140  nf.innerHTML = 'near: ' + Math.round(g_near*100)/100 + ', far: ' +
                                            ↪Math.round(g_far*100)/100;
```

The Processing Flow of the Vertex Shader

As you can see with the following code, the processing flow in the vertex shader is almost the same as that in `LookAtRotatedTriangles.js` except that the uniform variable name (`u_ProjMatrix`) at line 6 was changed. This variable holds the matrix used to set the viewing volume. So you just need to multiply the matrix (`u_ProjMatrix`) by the vertex coordinates to set the viewing volume at line 9:

```
2  // Vertex shader program
3  var VSHADER_SOURCE =
   ...
6    'uniform mat4 u_ProjMatrix;\n' +
7    'varying vec4 v_Color;\n' +
8    'void main() {\n' +
9    '  gl_Position = u_ProjMatrix * a_Position;\n' +
10   '  v_Color = a_Color;\n' +
11   '}\n';
```

Line 62 registers the event handler for the arrow key press. Note that `nf` is passed as the last argument to the handler to allow it to access the `<p>` element. The event handler use the key press to determine the contents of the element in `draw()`, which is called in the handler:

```
61    // Register the event handler to be called on key press
62    document.onkeydown = function(ev) { keydown(ev, gl, n, u_ProjMatrix,
                                           ➥projMatrix, nf); };
```

The `keydown()` at line 121 identifies which arrow key is pressed and then modifies the value of `g_near` and `g_far` before calling `draw()` at line 127. Line 117 defines `g_near` and `g_far`, which are used by the `setOrtho()` method. These are defined as global variables because they are used in both `keydown()` and `draw()`:

```
116 // The distances to the near and far clipping plane
117 var g_near = 0.0, g_far = 0.5;
118 function keydown(ev, gl, n, u_ProjMatrix, projMatrix, nf) {
119   switch(ev.keyCode) {
120     case 39: g_near += 0.01; break; // The right arrow key was pressed
    ...
123     case 40: g_far -= 0.01;  break;  // The down arrow key was pressed
124     default: return; // Prevent the unnecessary drawing
125   }
126
127   draw(gl, n, u_ProjMatrix, projMatrix, nf);
128 }
```

Let's examine the function `draw()`. The processing flow of `draw()`, defined at line 130, is the same as in `LookAtTrianglesWithKeys.js` except for changing the message on the web page at line 140:

```
130 function draw(gl, n, u_ProjMatrix, projMatrix, nf) {
131   // Set the viewing volume
132   projMatrix.setOrtho(-1.0, 1.0, -1.0, 1.0, g_near, g_far);
133
134   // Set the projection matrix to u_ProjMatrix variable
135   gl.uniformMatrix4fv(u_ProjMatrix, false, projMatrix.elements);
    ...
139   // Display the current near and far values
140   nf.innerHTML = 'near: ' + Math.round(g_near * 100)/100 + ', far: ' +
                                           ➥Math.round(g_far*100)/100;
141
142   gl.drawArrays(gl.TRIANGLES, 0, n); // Draw the triangles
143 }
```

Line 132 calculates the matrix for the viewing volume (`projMatrix`) and passes it to `u_ProjMatrix` at line 135. Line 140 displays the current *near* and *far* value on the web page. Finally, at line 142, the triangles are drawn.

Changing Near or Far

When you run this program and increase the near value (right-arrow key), the display will change, as shown in Figure 7.14.

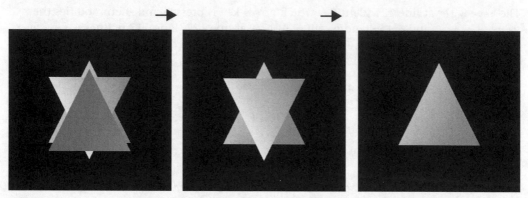

Figure 7.14 Increase the near value using the right arrow key

By default, *near* is 0.0, so all three triangles are displayed. Next, when you increase *near* using the right arrow key, the blue triangle (the front triangle) disappears because the viewing volume moves past it, as shown in Figure 7.15. This result is shown as the middle figure in Figure 7.14.

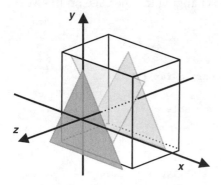

Figure 7.15 The blue triangle went outside the viewing volume

Again, if you continue to increase *near* by pressing the right arrow key, when *near* becomes larger than 0.2, the near plane moves past the yellow triangle, so it is outside the viewing volume and disappears. This leaves only the green triangle (the right figure in Figure 7.14). At this point, if you use the left arrow key to decrease *near* so it becomes less than 0.2, the yellow triangle becomes visible again. Alternatively, if you keep on increasing *near*, the green triangle will also disappear, leaving the black canvas.

As you can imagine, the behavior when you alter the *far* value is similar. As shown in Figure 7.16, when *far* becomes less than 0.4, the back triangle (the green one) will disappear. Again, if you keep decreasing *far*, only the blue triangle will remain.

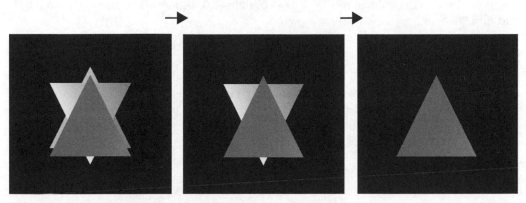

Figure 7.16 Decrease the far value using the down arrow key

This example should clarify the role of the viewing volume. Essentially, for any object you want to display, you need to place it inside the viewing volume.

Restoring the Clipped Parts of the Triangles (LookAtTrianglesWithKeys_ViewVolume.js)

In LookAtTrianglesWithKeys, when you kept pressing the arrow keys, part of the triangle is clipped, as shown in Figure 7.17. From the previous discussion, it's clear this is because some part went outside the viewing volume. In this section, you will modify the sample program to display the triangle correctly by setting the appropriate viewing volume.

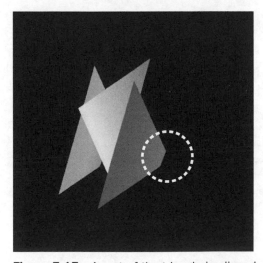

Figure 7.17 A part of the triangle is clipped.

As you can see from the figure, the far corner of the triangle from the eye point is clipped. Obviously, the far clipping plane is too close to the eye point, so you need to move the far clipping plane farther out than the current one. To achieve this, you can modify the arguments of the viewing volume so that *left*=–1.0, *right*=1.0, *bottom*=–1.0, *top*=1.0, *near*=0.0, and *far*=2.0.

You will use two matrices in this program: the matrix that sets the viewing volume (the orthographic projection matrix), and the matrix that sets the eye point and the line of sight (view matrix). Because `setOrtho()` sets the viewing volume from the eye point, you need to set the position of the eye point and then set the viewing volume. Consequently, you will multiply the view matrix by the vertex coordinates to get the vertex coordinates, which are "viewed from the eye position" first, and then multiply the orthographic projection matrix by the coordinates. You can calculate them as shown in Equation 7.3.

Equation 7.3

$$\langle orthographic\ projection\ matrix \rangle \times \langle view\ matrix \rangle \times \langle vertex\ coordinates \rangle$$

This can be implemented in the vertex shader, as shown in Listing 7.7.

Listing 7.7 LookAtTrianglesWithKeys_ViewVolume.js

```
1  // LookAtTrianglesWithKeys_ViewVolume.js
2  // Vertex shader program
3  var VSHADER_SOURCE =
4    'attribute vec4 a_Position;\n' +
5    'attribute vec4 a_Color;\n' +
6    'uniform mat4 u_ViewMatrix;\n' +
7    'uniform mat4 u_ProjMatrix;\n' +
8    'varying vec4 v_Color;\n' +
9    'void main() {\n' +
10   '  gl_Position = u_ProjMatrix * u_ViewMatrix * a_Position;\n' +
11   '  v_Color = a_Color;\n' +
12   '}\n';
   ...
24 function main() {
   ...
51   // Get the storage locations of u_ViewMatrix and u_ProjMatrix
52   varu_ViewMatrix = gl.getUniformLocation(gl.program,'u_ViewMatrix');
53   var u_ProjMatrix = gl.getUniformLocation(gl.program,'u_ProjMatrix');
   ...
59   // Create the matrix to specify the view matrix
60   var viewMatrix = new Matrix4();
61   // Register the event handler to be called on key press
62   document.onkeydown = function(ev) { keydown(ev, gl, n, u_ViewMatrix,
                                          ➥viewMatrix); };
```

```
63
64    // Create the matrix to specify the viewing volume and pass it to u_ProjMatrix
65    var projMatrix = new Matrix4();
66    projMatrix.setOrtho(-1.0, 1.0, -1.0, 1.0, 0.0, 2.0);
67    gl.uniformMatrix4fv(u_ProjMatrix, false, projMatrix.elements);
68
69    draw(gl, n, u_ViewMatrix, viewMatrix); // Draw the triangles
70  }
```

Line 66 calculates the orthographic projection matrix (projMatrix) by modifying *far* from 1.0 to 2.0. The result matrix is passed to u_ProjMatrix in the vertex shader at line 67. A uniform variable is used because the elements in the matrix are uniform for all vertex coordinates. If you run this sample program and move the eye point as before, you can see that the triangle no longer gets clipped (see Figure 7.18).

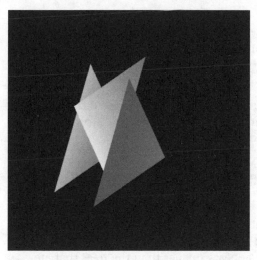

Figure 7.18   LookAtTrianglesWithKeys_ViewVolume

Experimenting with the Sample Program

As we explained in the section "Specify the Viewing Volume," if the aspect ratio of `<canvas>` is different from that of the near clipping plane, distorted objects are displayed. Let's explore this. First, in OrthoView_halfSize (based on Listing 7.7), you reduce the current size of the near clipping plane to half while keeping its aspect ratio:

```
projMatrix.setOrtho(-0.5, 0.5, -0.5, 0.5, 0, 0.5);
```

The result is shown on the left of Figure 7.19. As you can see, the triangles appear twice as large as those of the previous sample because the size of `<canvas>` is the same as before. Note that the parts of the triangles outside the near clipping plane are clipped.

Figure 7.19 Modify the size of the near clipping plane

In `OrthoView_halfWidth`, you reduce only the width of the near clipping plane by changing the first two arguments in `setOrtho()` as follows:

```
projMatrix.setOrtho(-0.3, 0.3, -1.0, 1.0, 0.0, 0.5);
```

You can see the results on the right side of Figure 7.19. This is because the near clipping plane is horizontally reduced and then horizontally extended (and thus distorted) to fit the square-shaped `<canvas>` when the plane is displayed.

Specifying the Visible Range Using a Quadrangular Pyramid

Figure 7.20 shows a tree-lined road scene. In this picture, all the trees on the left and right sides are approximately of the same height, but the farther back they are, the smaller they look. Equally, the building in the distance appears smaller than the trees that are closer to the viewer, even though the building is actually taller than the trees. This effect of distant objects looking smaller gives the feeling of depth. Although our eyes perceive reality in this way, it's interesting to notice that children's drawings rarely show this kind of perspective.

Figure 7.20 Tree-lined road

In the case of the box-shaped viewing volume explained in the previous section, identically sized triangles are drawn the same size, regardless of their distance from the eye point. To overcome this constraint, you can use the quadrangular pyramid viewing volume, which allows you to give this sense of depth, as seen in Figure 7.20.

Here you construct the sample program PerspectiveView, which sets a quadrangular pyramid viewing volume that points along the negative z-axis from the eye point set at (0, 0, 5). Figure 7.21 shows a screen shot of PerspectiveView and the location of each triangle.

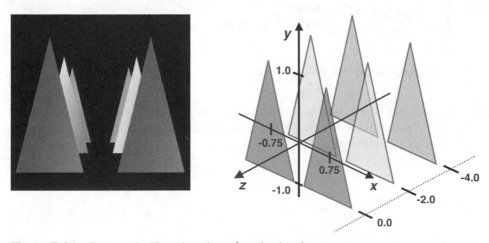

Figure 7.21 PerspectiveView; location of each triangle

As can be seen from the figure on the right, three identically sized triangles are positioned on the right and left sides along the coordinate's axes, in a way similar to the tree-lined road. By using a quadrangular pyramid viewing volume, WebGL can automatically display remote objects as if they are smaller, thus achieving the sense of depth. This is shown in the left side of the figure.

To really notice the change in size, as in the real world, the objects need to be located at a substantial distance. For example, when looking at the box, to actually make the background area looks smaller than the foreground area, this box needs to have considerable depth. So this time, you will use a slightly more distant position (0, 0, 0.5) than the default value (0, 0, 0) for the eye point.

Setting the Quadrangular Pyramid Viewing Volume

The quadrangular pyramid viewing volume is shaped as shown in Figure 7.22. Just like the box-shaped configuration, the viewing volume is set at the eye point along the line of sight, and objects located between the far and near clipping planes are displayed. Objects positioned outside the viewing volume are not shown, while those straddling the boundary will only have parts located inside the viewing volume visible.

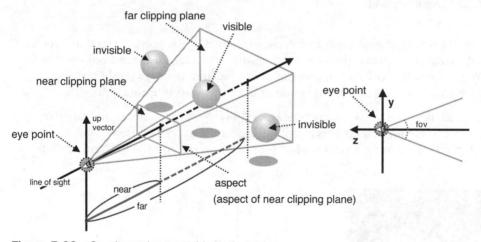

Figure 7.22 Quadrangular pyramid viewing volume

Regardless of whether it is a quadrangular pyramid or a box, you set the viewing volume using matrices, but the arguments differ. The Matrix4's method setPerspective() is used to configure the quadrangular pyramid viewing volume.

Matrix4.setPerspective(fov, aspect, near, far)

Calculate the matrix (the perspective projection matrix) that defines the viewing volume specified by its arguments, and store it in Matrix4. However, the *near value must be less than the far value.*

Parameters	fov	Specifies field of view, angle formed by the top and bottom planes. It must be greater than 0.
	aspect	Specifies the aspect ratio of the near plane (width/height).
	near, far	Specify the distances to the near and far clipping planes along the line of sight (*near* > 0 and *far* > 0).
Return value	None	

The matrix that sets the quadrangular pyramid viewing volume is called the **perspective projection matrix**.

Note that the specification for the near plane is different from that of the box type with the second argument, *aspect,* representing the near plane aspect ratio. For example, if we set the height to 100 and the width to 200, the aspect ratio is 0.5.

The positioning of the triangles with regard to the viewing volume we are using is illustrated in Figure 7.23. It is specified by *near*=1.0, *far*=100, *aspect*=1.0 (the same aspect ratio as the canvas), and *fov*=30.0.

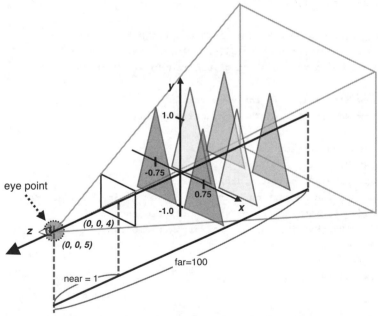

Figure 7.23 The positions of the triangles with respect to the quadrangular pyramid viewing volume

The basic processing flow is similar to that of LookAtTrianglesWithKeys_ViewVolume.js in the previous section. So let's take a look at the sample program.

Sample Program (PerspectiveView.js)

The sample program is detailed in Listing 7.8.

Listing 7.8 PerspectiveView.js

```
 1 // PerspectiveView.js
 2 // Vertex shader program
 3 var VSHADER_SOURCE =
 4   'attribute vec4 a_Position;\n' +
 5   'attribute vec4 a_Color;\n' +
 6   'uniform mat4 u_ViewMatrix;\n' +
 7   'uniform mat4 u_ProjMatrix;\n' +
 8   'varying vec4 v_Color;\n' +
 9   'void main() {\n' +
10   '  gl_Position = u_ProjMatrix * u_ViewMatrix * a_Position;\n' +
11   '  v_Color = a_Color;\n' +
12   '}\n';
   ...
24 function main() {
   ...
41   // Set the vertex coordinates and color (blue triangle is in front)
42   var n = initVertexBuffers(gl);
   ...
51   // Get the storage locations of u_ViewMatrix and u_ProjMatrix
52   varu_ViewMatrix = gl.getUniformLocation(gl.program,'u_ViewMatrix');
53   var u_ProjMatrix = gl.getUniformLocation(gl.program,'u_ProjMatrix');
   ...
59   var viewMatrix = new Matrix4();  // The view matrix
60   var projMatrix = new Matrix4();  // The projection matrix
61
62   // Calculate the view and projection matrix
63   viewMatrix.setLookAt(0, 0, 5, 0, 0, -100, 0, 1, 0);
64   projMatrix.setPerspective(30, canvas.width/canvas.height, 1, 100);
65   // Pass The view matrix and projection matrix to u_ViewMatrix and u_ProjMatrix
66   gl.uniformMatrix4fv(u_ViewMatrix, false, viewMatrix.elements);
67   gl.uniformMatrix4fv(u_ProjMatrix, false, projMatrix.elements);
   ...
72   // Draw the rectangles
73   gl.drawArrays(gl.TRIANGLES, 0, n);
74 }
75
```

```
76 function initVertexBuffers(gl) {
77    var verticesColors = new Float32Array([
78      // Three triangles on the right side
79      0.75,  1.0, -4.0, 0.4,  1.0, 0.4, // The green triangle in back
80      0.25, -1.0, -4.0, 0.4,  1.0, 0.4,
81      1.25, -1.0, -4.0, 1.0,  0.4, 0.4,
82
83      0.75,  1.0, -2.0, 1.0,  1.0, 0.4, // The yellow triangle in middle
84      0.25, -1.0, -2.0, 1.0,  1.0, 0.4,
85      1.25, -1.0, -2.0, 1.0,  0.4, 0.4,
86
87      0.75,  1.0,  0.0, 0.4,  0.4, 1.0, // The blue triangle in front
88      0.25, -1.0,  0.0, 0.4,  0.4, 1.0,
89      1.25, -1.0,  0.0, 1.0,  0.4, 0.4,
90
91      // Three triangles on the left side
92     -0.75,  1.0, -4.0, 0.4,  1.0, 0.4, // The green triangle in back
93     -1.25, -1.0, -4.0, 0.4,  1.0, 0.4,
94     -0.25, -1.0, -4.0, 1.0,  0.4, 0.4,
95
96     -0.75,  1.0, -2.0, 1.0,  1.0, 0.4, // The yellow triangle in middle
97     -1.25, -1.0, -2.0, 1.0,  1.0, 0.4,
98     -0.25, -1.0, -2.0, 1.0,  0.4, 0.4,
99
100    -0.75,  1.0,  0.0, 0.4,  0.4, 1.0, // The blue triangle in front
101    -1.25, -1.0,  0.0, 0.4,  0.4, 1.0,
102    -0.25, -1.0,  0.0, 1.0,  0.4, 0.4,
103   ]);
104   var n = 18; // Three vertices per triangle * 6
      ...
138   return n;
139 }
```

The vertex and fragment shaders are completely identical (including the names of the variables) to the ones used in LookAtTriangles_ViewVolume.js.

The processing flow of main() in JavaScript is also similar. Calling initVertexBuffers() at line 42 writes the vertex coordinates and colors of the six triangles to be displayed into the buffer object. In initVertexBuffers(), the vertex coordinates and colors for the six triangles are specified: three triangles positioned on the right side from line 79 and three triangles positioned on the left side from line 92. As a result, the number of vertices to be drawn at line 104 is changed to 18 (3×6=18, to handle six triangles).

At lines 52 and 53 in main(), the locations of the uniform variables that store the view matrix and perspective projection matrix are retrieved. Then at line 59 and 60, the variables used to hold the matrices are created.

At line 63, the view matrix is calculated, with the eye point set at (0, 0, 5), the line of sight set along the z-axis in the negative direction, and the up direction set along the y-axis in the positive direction. Finally at line 64, the projection matrix is set up using a quadrangular pyramid viewing volume:

```
64   projMatrix.setPerspective(30, canvas.width/canvas.height, 1, 100);
```

The second argument *aspect* (the horizontal to vertical ratio of the near plane) is derived from the `<canvas>` width and height (`width` and `height` property), so any modification of the `<canvas>` aspect ratio doesn't lead to distortion of the objects displayed.

Next, as the view and perspective projection matrices are available, you pass them to the appropriate uniform variables at lines 66 and 67. Finally, you draw the triangles at line 73, and upon execution you get a result including perspective similar to that shown in Figure 7.20.

Finally, one aspect touched on earlier but not fully explained is why matrices are used to set the viewing volume. Without using mathematics, let's explore that a little.

The Role of the Projection Matrix

Let's start by examining the perspective projection matrix. Looking at the screen shot of `PerspectiveView` in Figure 7.24, you can see that, after applying the projection matrix, the objects in the distance are altered in two ways.

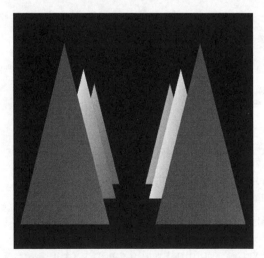

Figure 7.24   PerspectiveView

First, the farther away the triangles are, the smaller they appear. Second, the triangles are parallel shifted so they look as if they are positioned inward toward the line of sight. In comparison to the identically sized triangles that are laid out as shown on the left side of Figure 7.25, the following two transformations have been applied: (1) triangles farther from the viewer are scaled down (transformed) in proportion to the distance from the viewer, and (2) the triangles are then transformed to be shifted toward the line of sight, as illustrated on the right side of Figure 7.25. These two transformations, shown on the right side of Figure 7.25, enable the effect you see in the photograph scene shown in Figure 7.20.

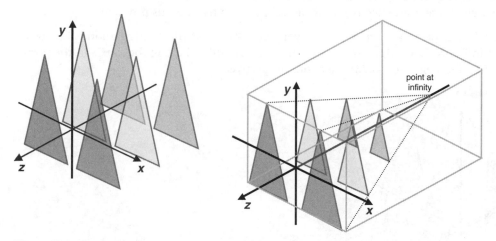

Figure 7.25 Conceptual rendering of the perspective projection transformation

This means that the specification of the viewing volume can be represented as a combination of transformations, such as the scaling or translation of geometric shapes and objects, in accordance with the shape of the viewing volume. The `Matrix4` object's method `setPerspective()` automatically calculates this transformation matrix from the arguments of the specified viewing volume. The elements of the matrix are discussed in Appendix C, "Projection Matrices." If you are interested in the mathematical explanation of the coordinate transform related to the viewing volume, please refer to the book *Computer Graphics*.

To put it another way, the transformation associated with the perspective projection transforms the quadrangular pyramid viewing volume into a box-shaped viewing volume (right part of Figure 7.25).

Note that the orthographic projection matrix does not perform all the work needed for this transformation to generate the required optical effect. Rather, it performs the preliminary preparation that is required by the post vertex shader processing—where the actual processing is done. If you are interested in this, please refer to Appendix D, "WebGL/OpenGL: Left or Right Handed?"

The projection matrix, combined with the model matrix and the view matrix, is able to handle all the necessary geometric transformations (translation, rotation, scaling) for achieving the different optical effects. The following section will explore how to combine these matrices to do that using a simple example.

Using All the Matrices (Model Matrix, View Matrix, and Projection Matrix)

One of the issues with `PerspectiveView.js` is the amount of code needed to set up the vertex coordinates and the color data. Because we only have to deal with six triangles in this case, it's still manageable, but it could get messy if the number of triangles increased. Fortunately, there is an effective drawing technique to handle this problem.

If you take a close look at the triangles, you will notice that the configuration is identical to that in Figure 7.26, where the dashed triangles are shifted along the x-axis in the positive (0.75) and negative (–0.75) directions, respectively.

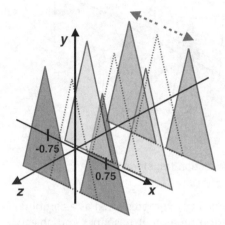

Figure 7.26 Drawing after translation

Taking advantage of this, it is possible to draw the triangles in `PerspectiveView` in the following way:

1. Prepare the vertex coordinates data of the three triangles that are laid out centered along the z-axis.

2. Translate the original triangles by 0.75 units along the x-axis, and draw them.

3. Translate the original triangles by –0.75 units along the x-axis, and draw them.

Now let's try to use this approach in some sample code (`PerspectiveView_mvp`).

In the original `PerspectiveView` program the projection and view matrices were used to specify the viewer's viewpoint and viewing volume and `PerspectiveView_mvp`, the model matrix, was used to perform the translation of the triangles.

At this point, it's worthwhile to review the actions these matrices perform. To do that, let's refer to `LookAtTriangles`, which you wrote earlier to allow the viewer to look at a rotated triangle from a specific location. At that time, you used this expression, which is identical to Equation 7.1:

$$\langle view\ matrix \rangle \times \langle model\ matrix \rangle \times \langle vertex\ coordinates \rangle$$

Building on that, in `LookAtTriangles_ViewVolume`, which correctly displays the clipped triangle, you used the following expression, which, when you use projection matrix to include either orthographic projection or perspective projection, is identical to Equation 7.3:

$$\langle projection\ matrix \rangle \times \langle view\ matrix \rangle \times \langle vertex\ coordinates \rangle$$

You can infer the following from these two expressions:

Equation 7.4

$$\langle projection\ matrix \rangle \times \langle view\ matrix \rangle \times \langle model\ matrix \rangle \times \langle vertex\ coordinates \rangle$$

This expression shows that, in WebGL, you can calculate the final vertex coordinates by using three types of matrices: the model matrix, the view matrix, and the projection matrix.

This can be understood by considering that Equation 7.1 is identical to Equation 7.4, in which the projection matrix becomes the identity matrix, and Equation 7.3 is identical to Equation 7.4, whose model matrix is turned into the identity matrix. As explained in Chapter 4, the identity matrix behaves for matrix multiplication like the scalar 1 does with scalar multiplication. Multiplying by the identity matrix has no effect on the other matrix.

So let's construct the sample program using Equation 7.4.

Sample Program (PerspectiveView_mvp.js)

`PerspectiveView_mvp.js` is shown in Listing 7.9. The basic processing flow is similar to that of `PerspectiveView.js`. The only difference is the modification of the calculation in the vertex shader (line 11) to implement Equation 7.4, and the passing of the additional matrix (`u_ModelMatrix`) used for the calculation.

Listing 7.9 PerspectiveView_mvp.js

```
1 // PerspectiveView_mvp.js
2 // Vertex shader program
3 var VSHADER_SOURCE =
4   'attribute vec4 a_Position;\n' +
5   'attribute vec4 a_Color;\n' +
6   'uniform mat4 u_ModelMatrix;\n' +
7   'uniform mat4 u_ViewMatrix;\n' +
8   'uniform mat4 u_ProjMatrix;\n' +
9   'varying vec4 v_Color;\n' +
10  'void main() {\n' +
11  '  gl_Position = u_ProjMatrix * u_ViewMatrix * u_ModelMatrix * a_Position;\n' +
12  '  v_Color = a_Color;\n' +
```

```
13   '}\n';
     ...
25 function main() {
     ...
42   // Set the vertex coordinates and color (blue triangle is in front)
43   var n = initVertexBuffers(gl);
     ...
52   // Get the storage locations of u_ModelMatrix, u_ViewMatrix, and u_ProjMatrix.
53   var u_ModelMatrix = gl.getUniformLocation(gl.program, 'u_ModelMatrix');
54   var u_ViewMatrix = gl.getUniformLocation(gl.program,'u_ViewMatrix');
55   var u_ProjMatrix = gl.getUniformLocation(gl.program,'u_ProjMatrix');
     ...
61   var modelMatrix = new Matrix4(); // Model matrix
62   var viewMatrix = new Matrix4();  // View matrix
63   var projMatrix = new Matrix4();  // Projection matrix
64
65   // Calculate the model matrix, view matrix, and projection matrix
66   modelMatrix.setTranslate(0.75, 0, 0); // Translate 0.75 units
67   viewMatrix.setLookAt(0, 0, 5, 0, 0, -100, 0, 1, 0);
68   projMatrix.setPerspective(30, canvas.width/canvas.height, 1, 100);
69   // Pass the model, view, and projection matrix to uniform variables.
70   gl.uniformMatrix4fv(u_ModelMatrix, false, modelMatrix.elements);
71   gl.uniformMatrix4fv(u_ViewMatrix, false, viewMatrix.elements);
72   gl.uniformMatrix4fv(u_ProjMatrix, false, projMatrix.elements);
73
74   gl.clear(gl.COLOR_BUFFER_BIT);// clear <canvas>
75
76   gl.drawArrays(gl.TRIANGLES, 0, n);  // Draw triangles on right
77
78   // Prepare the model matrix for another pair of triangles
79   modelMatrix.setTranslate(-0.75, 0, 0); // Translate -0.75
80   // Modify only the model matrix
81   gl.uniformMatrix4fv(u_ModelMatrix, false, modelMatrix.elements);
82
83   gl.drawArrays(gl.TRIANGLES, 0, n);// Draw triangles on left
84 }
85
86 function initVertexBuffers(gl) {
87   var verticesColors = new Float32Array([
88     // Vertex coordinates and color
89      0.0,  1.0,  -4.0, 0.4,  1.0, 0.4, // The back green triangle
90     -0.5, -1.0,  -4.0, 0.4,  1.0, 0.4,
91      0.5, -1.0,  -4.0, 1.0,  0.4, 0.4,
92
93      0.0,  1.0,  -2.0, 1.0,  1.0, 0.4, // The middle yellow triangle
```

```
94      -0.5, -1.0,  -2.0, 1.0,   1.0, 0.4,
95       0.5, -1.0,  -2.0, 1.0,   0.4, 0.4,
96
97       0.0,  1.0,   0.0, 0.4,   0.4, 1.0,   // The front blue triangle
98      -0.5, -1.0,   0.0, 0.4,   0.4, 1.0,
99       0.5, -1.0,   0.0, 1.0,   0.4, 0.4,
100    ]);

       ...

135    return n;
136  }
```

This time, you need to pass the model matrix to the vertex shader, so u_ModelMatrix is added at line 6. The matrix is used at line 11, which implements Equation 7.5:

```
11   '  gl_Position = u_ProjMatrix * u_ViewMatrix * u_ModelMatrix * a_Position;\n' +
```

Next, main() in JavaScript calls initVertexBuffers() at line 43. In this function, the vertex coordinates of the triangles to be passed to the buffer object are defined (line 87). This time, you are handling the vertex coordinates of three triangles centered along the z-axis instead of the six triangles used in PerspectiveView.js. As mentioned before, this is because you will use the three triangles in conjunction with a translation.

At line 53, the storage location of u_ModelMatrix in the vertex shader is obtained. At line 61, the arguments for the matrix (modelMatrix) passed to the uniform variable are prepared, and at line 66, the matrix is calculated. First, this matrix will translate the triangles by 0.75 units along the x-axis:

```
65   // Calculate the view matrix and the projection matrix
66   modelMatrix.setTranslate(0.75, 0, 0);  // Translate 0.75
...
70   gl.uniformMatrix4fv(u_ModelMatrix, false, modelMatrix.elements);
...
76   gl.drawArrays(gl.TRIANGLES, 0, n);  // Draw a triangle
```

The matrix calculations, apart from the model matrix at line 66, are the same as in PerspectiveView.js. The model matrix is passed to u_ModelMatrix at line 70 and used to draw the right side row of triangles (line 76).

In a similar manner, the row of triangles for the left side is translated by –0.75 units along the x-axis, and then the model matrix is calculated again at line 79. Because the view matrix and projection matrix make use of this model matrix, you only need to assign the model matrix to the uniform variable once (line 81). Once the matrix is set up, you perform the draw operation at line 83 with gl.drawArrays():

```
78   // Prepare the model matrix for another pair of triangles
79   modelMatrix.setTranslate(-0.75, 0, 0); // Translate -0.75
80   // Modify only the model matrix
```

```
81    gl.uniformMatrix4fv(u_ModelMatrix, false, modelMatrix.elements);
82
83    gl.drawArrays(gl.TRIANGLES, 0, n);  // Draw triangles on left
```

As you have seen, this approach allows you to draw two sets of triangles from a single set of triangle data, which reduces the number of vertices needed but increases the number of calls to gl.drawArrays(). The choice of which approach to use for better performance depends on the application and the WebGL implementation.

Experimenting with the Sample Program

In PerspectiveView_mvp, you calculated $\langle projection\ matrix \rangle \times \langle view\ matrix \rangle \times \langle model\ matrix \rangle$ directly inside the vertex shader. This calculation of is the same for all the vertices, so there is no need to recalculate it inside the shader for each vertex. It can be computed in advance inside the JavaScript code, as it was in LookAtRotatedTriangles_mvMatrix earlier in the chapter, allowing a single matrix to be passed to the vertex shader. This matrix is called the **model view projection matrix**, and the name of the variable that passes it is u_MvpMatrix. The sample program used to show this is ProjectiveView_mvpMatrix, in which the vertex shader is modified as shown next and, as you can see, is significantly simpler:

```
1  // PerspectiveView_mvpMatrix.js
2  // Vertex shader program
3  var VSHADER_SOURCE =
4    'attribute vec4 a_Position;\n' +
5    'attribute vec4 a_Color;\n' +
6    'uniform mat4 u_MvpMatrix;\n' +
7    'varying vec4 v_Color;\n' +
8    'void main() {\n' +
9    '  gl_Position = u_MvpMatrix * a_Position;\n' +
10   '  v_Color = a_Color;\n' +
11   '}\n';
```

In JavaScript, main(), the storage location of u_ModelMatrix is retrieved at line 51, and then the matrix to be stored in the uniform variable is calculated at line 57:

```
50    // Get the storage location of u_MvpMatrix
51    var u_MvpMatrix = gl.getUniformLocation(gl.program, 'u_MvpMatrix');
      ...
57    var modelMatrix = new Matrix4(); // The model matrix
58    var viewMatrix = new Matrix4();  // The view matrix
```

```
59   var projMatrix = new Matrix4();   // The projection matrix
60   var mvpMatrix = new Matrix4();     // The model view projection matrix
61
62   // Calculate the model, view, and projection matrices
63   modelMatrix.setTranslate(0.75, 0, 0);
64   viewMatrix.setLookAt(0, 0, 5, 0, 0, -100, 0, 1, 0);
65   projMatrix.setPerspective(30, canvas.width/canvas.height, 1, 100);
66   // Calculate the model view projection matrix
67   mvpMatrix.set(projMatrix).multiply(viewMatrix).multiply(modelMatrxi);
68   // Pass the model view projection matrix to u_MvpMatrix
69   gl.uniformMatrix4fv(u_MvpMatrix, false, mvpMatrix.elements);
     ...
73   gl.drawArrays(gl.TRIANGLES, 0, n); // Draw a rectangle
74
75   // Prepare the model matrix for another pair of triangles
76   modelMatrix.setTranslate(-0.75, 0, 0);
77   // Calculate the model view projection matrix
78   mvpMatrix.set(projMatrix).multiply(viewMatrix).multiply(modelMatrxi);
79   // Pass the model view projection matrix to u_MvpMatrix
80   gl.uniformMatrix4fv(u_MvpMatrix, false, mvpMatrix.elements);
81
82   gl.drawArrays(gl.TRIANGLES, 0, n); // Draw a rectangle
83 }
```

The critical calculation is carried out at line 67. The projection matrix (projMatrix) is assigned to mvpMatrix. Then the view matrix (viewMatrix) is multiplied by the model matrix (modelMatrix), and the result is written back to mvpMatrix, using the set version of the method. This is in turn assigned to u_MvpMatrix at line 69, and the triangles on the right side are drawn at line 73. Similarly, the calculation of the model view projection matrix for the triangles on the left side is performed at line 78. It is then passed to u_MvpMatrix at line 80, and the triangles are drawn at line 82.

With this information, you are now able to write code that moves the eye point, sets the viewing volume, and allows you to view three-dimensional objects from various angles. Additionally, you have learned how to deal with clipping that resulted in partially missing objects. However, one potential problem remains. As you move the eye point to a different location, it's possible for objects in the foreground to be hidden by objects in the background. Let's look at how this problem comes about.

Correctly Handling Foreground and Background Objects

In the real world, if you place two boxes on a desk as shown in Figure 7.27, the foreground box partially hides the background one.

Figure 7.27 The front object partially hides the back object

Looking at the sample programs constructed so far, such as the screen shot of PerspectiveView (refer to Figure 7.21), the green triangle located at the back is partially hidden by the yellow and blue triangles. It looks as if WebGL, being designed for displaying 3D objects, has naturally figured out the correct order.

However, that is unfortunately not the case. By default, WebGL, to accelerate the drawing process, draws objects in the order of the vertices specified inside the buffer object. Up until now, you have always arranged the order of the vertices so that the objects located in the background are drawn first, thus resulting in a natural rendering.

For example, in PerspectiveView_mvpMatrix.js, you specified the coordinates and color of the triangles in the following order. Note the z coordinates (bold font):

```
var verticesColors = new Float32Array([
  // vertex coordinates and color
  0.0, 1.0, -4.0, 0.4, 1.0, 0.4, // The green one at the back
 -0.5, -1.0, -4.0, 0.4, 1.0, 0.4,
  0.5, -1.0, -4.0, 1.0, 0.4, 0.4,
  0.0, 1.0, -2.0, 1.0, 1.0, 0.4, // The yellow one in the middle
 -0.5, -1.0, -2.0, 1.0, 1.0, 0.4,
  0.5, -1.0, -2.0, 1.0, 0.4, 0.4,
  0.0, 1.0, 0.0, 0.4, 0.4, 1.0,  // The blue one in the front
 -0.5, -1.0, 0.0, 0.4, 0.4, 1.0,
  0.5, -1.0, 0.0, 1.0, 0.4, 0.4,
]);
```

WebGL draws the triangles in the order z in which you specified the vertices (that is, the green triangle [back], then the yellow triangle [middle], and finally the blue triangle [front]). This ensures that objects closer to the eye point cover those farther away, as seen in Figure 7.13.

To verify this, let's modify the order in which the triangles are specified by first drawing the blue triangle in the front, then the yellow triangle in the middle, and finally the green triangle at the back:

```
var verticesColors = new Float32Array([
  // vertex coordinates and color
   0.0,  1.0,   0.0,  0.4,  0.4,  1.0, // The blue one in the front
  -0.5, -1.0,   0.0,  0.4,  0.4,  1.0,
   0.5, -1.0,   0.0,  1.0,  0.4,  0.4

   0.0,  1.0,  -2.0,  1.0,  1.0,  0.4, // The yellow one in the middle
  -0.5, -1.0,  -2.0,  1.0,  1.0,  0.4,
   0.5, -1.0,  -2.0,  1.0,  0.4,  0.4,

   0.0,  1.0,  -4.0,  0.4,  1.0,  0.4, // The green one at the back
  -0.5, -1.0,  -4.0,  0.4,  1.0,  0.4,
   0.5, -1.0,  -4.0,  1.0,  0.4,  0.4,
]);
```

When you run this, you'll see the green triangle, which is supposed to be located at the back, has been drawn at the front (see Figure 7.28).

Figure 7.28   The green triangle in the back is displayed at the front

Drawing objects in the specified order, the default behavior in WebGL, can be quite efficient when the sequence can be determined beforehand and the scene doesn't subsequently change. However, when you examine the object from various directions by moving the eye point, it is impossible to decide the drawing order in advance.

Hidden Surface Removal

To cope with this problem, WebGL provides a **hidden surface removal** function. This function eliminates surfaces hidden behind foreground objects, allowing you to draw the scene so that the objects in the back are properly hidden by those in front, regardless of the specified vertex order. This function is already embedded in WebGL and simply needs to be enabled.

Enabling hidden surface removal and preparing WebGL to use it requires the following two steps:

1. Enabling the hidden surface removal function

   ```
   gl.enable(gl.DEPTH_TEST);
   ```

2. Clearing the depth buffer used for the hidden surface removal before drawing

   ```
   gl.clear(gl.DEPTH_BUFFER_BIT);
   ```

The function `gl.enable()`, used in step 1, actually enables various functions in WebGL.

`gl.enable(cap)`		
Enable the function specified by *cap* (capability).		
Parameters	cap	Specifies the function to be enabled.
	`gl.DEPTH_TEST`[2]	Hidden surface removal
	`gl.BLEND`	Blending (see Chapter 9, "Hierarchical Objects")
	`gl.POLYGON_OFFSET_FILL`	Polygon offset (see the next section), and so on[3]
Return value	None	
Errors:	INVALID_ENUM	None of the acceptable values is specified in *cap*

---

[2] A "DEPTH_TEST" in the hidden surface removal function might sound strange, but actually its name comes from the fact that it decides which objects to draw in the foreground by verifying (TEST) the depth (DEPTH) of each object.

[3] Although not covered in this book, you can also specify `gl.CULL_FACE`, `gl.DITHER`, `gl.SAMPLE_ALPHA_TO_COVERAGE`, `gl.SAMPLE_COVERAGE`, `gl.SCISSOR_TEST`, and `gl.STENCIL_TEST`. See the book *OpenGL Programming Guide* for more information on these.

The **depth buffer** cleared in the `gl.clear()` statement (step 2) is a buffer used internally to remove hidden surfaces. While WebGL draws objects and geometric shapes in the color buffer displayed on the `<canvas>`, hidden surface removal requires the depth (from the eye point) for each geometrical shape and object. The depth buffer holds this information (see Figure 7.29). The depth direction is the same as the z-axis direction, so it is sometimes called the z-buffer.

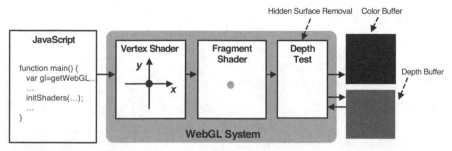

Figure 7.29 Depth buffer used in hidden surface removal

Because the depth buffer is used whenever a drawing command is issued, it must be cleared before any drawing operation; otherwise, you will see incorrect results. You specify the depth buffer using `gl.DEPTH_BUFFER_BIT` and proceed as follows to clear it:

```
gl.clear(gl.DEPTH_BUFFER_BIT);
```

Up until now, you only cleared the color buffer. Because you now need to also clear the depth buffer, you can clear both buffers simultaneously by taking the bitwise or (|) of `gl.COLOR_BUFFER_BIT` (which represents the color buffer) and `gl.DEPTH_BUFFER_BIT` (which represents the depth buffer) and specifying it as an argument to `gl.clear()`:

```
gl.clear(gl.COLOR_BUFFER_BIT | gl.DEPTH_BUFFER_BIT);
```

You can use the bitwise `or` operation this way whenever you need to clear both buffers at the same time.

To disable the function you enabled with `gl.enable()`, you use `gl.disable()`.

`gl.disable(cap)`

Disable the function specified by *cap* (capability).

Parameters	cap	Same as `gl.enable()`.
Return value	None	
Errors	INVALID_ENUM	None of the acceptable values is specified in *cap*

Sample Program (DepthBuffer.js)

Let's add the hidden surface removal methods from (1) and (2) to `PerspectiveView_mvpMatrix.js` and change the name to `DepthBuffer.js`. Note that the order of the vertex coordinates specified inside the buffer object is not changed, so you will draw from front to back the blue, yellow, and green triangles. The result is identical to that of the `PerspectiveView_mvpMatrix`. We detail the program in Listing 7.10.

Listing 7.10 DepthBuffer.js

```
 1 // DepthBuffer.js
   ...
23 function main() {
   ...
41   var n = initVertexBuffers(gl);
   ...
47   // Specify the color for clearing <canvas>
48   gl.clearColor(0, 0, 0, 1);
49   // Enable the hidden surface removal function
50   gl.enable(gl.DEPTH_TEST);

73   // Clear the color and depth buffer
74   gl.clear(gl.COLOR_BUFFER_BIT | gl.DEPTH_BUFFER_BIT);
75
76   gl.drawArrays(gl.TRIANGLES, 0, n);  // Draw triangles
   ...
85   gl.drawArrays(gl.TRIANGLES, 0, n);  // Draw triangles
86 }
87
88 function initVertexBuffers(gl) {
89   var verticesColors = new Float32Array([
90     //  Vertex coordinates and color
91      0.0,  1.0,   0.0, 0.4,  0.4, 1.0,  // The blue triangle in front
92     -0.5, -1.0,   0.0, 0.4,  0.4, 1.0,
93      0.5, -1.0,   0.0, 1.0,  0.4, 0.4,
94
95      0.0,  1.0,  -2.0, 1.0,  1.0, 0.4, // The yellow triangle in middle
96     -0.5, -1.0,  -2.0, 1.0,  1.0, 0.4,
97      0.5, -1.0,  -2.0, 1.0,  0.4, 0.4,
98
99      0.0,  1.0,  -4.0, 0.4,  1.0, 0.4, // The green triangle in back
100    -0.5, -1.0,  -4.0, 0.4,  1.0, 0.4,
101     0.5, -1.0,  -4.0, 1.0,  0.4, 0.4,
102   ]);
103   var n = 9;
   ...
```

```
137    return n;
138 }
```

If you run `DepthBuffer`, you can see that hidden face removal is performed and that objects placed at the back are hidden by objects located at the front. This demonstrates that the hidden surface removal function can eliminate the hidden surfaces regardless of the position of the eye point. Equally, this also shows that in anything but a trivial 3D scene, you will always need to enable hidden surface removal and systematically clear the depth buffer before any drawing operation.

You should note that hidden surface removal requires you to correctly set up the viewing volume. If you fail to do this (use WebGL in its default configuration), you are likely to see incorrect results. You can specify either a box or a quadrangular pyramid for the viewing volume.

Z Fighting

Hidden surface removal is a sophisticated and powerful feature of WebGL that correctly handles most of the cases where surfaces need to be removed. However, it fails when two geometrical shapes or objects are located at extremely close positions and results in the display looking a little unnatural. This phenomenon is known as **Z fighting** and is illustrated in Figure 7.30. Here, we draw two triangles sharing the same z coordinate.

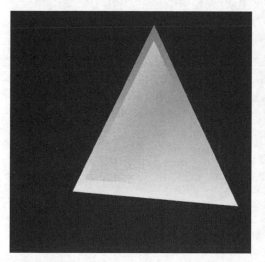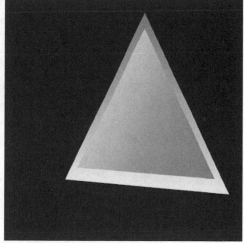

Figure 7.30   Visual artifact generated by Z fighting (the left side)

The Z fighting occurs because of the limited precision of the depth buffer and means the system is unable to asses which object is in front and which is behind. Technically, when handling 3D models, you could avoid this by paying thorough attention to the z coordinates' values at the model creation stage; however, implementing this workaround would prove to be unrealistic when dealing with the animation of several objects.

To help resolve this problem, WebGL provides a feature known as the **polygon offset**. This works by automatically adding an offset to the z coordinate, whose value is a function of each object's inclination with respect to the viewer's line of sight. You only need to add two lines of code to enable this function.

1. Enabling the polygon offset function:

```
gl.enable(gl.POLYGON_OFFSET_FILL);
```

2. Specifying the parameter used to calculate the offset (before drawing):

```
gl.polygonOffset(1.0, 1.0);
```

The same method that enabled the hidden surface removal function is used, but with a different parameter. The details for `gl.polygonOffset()` are shown here.

---

gl.polygonOffset(factor, units)

Specify the offset to be added to the z coordinate of each vertex drawn afterward. The offset is calculated with the formula m * *factor* + r * *units*, where m represents the inclination of the triangle with respect to the line of sight, and where r is the smallest difference between two z coordinates values the hardware can distinguish.

Return value   None

Errors   None

Let's look at the program Zfighting, which uses the polygon offset to reduce z fighting (see Listing 7.11).

Listing 7.11 Zfighting.js

```
 1 // Zfighting.js
   ...
23 function main() {
   ...
69   // Enable the polygon offset function
70   gl.enable(gl.POLYGON_OFFSET_FILL);
71   // Draw a rectangle
72   gl.drawArrays(gl.TRIANGLES, 0, n/2);    // The green triangle
73   gl.polygonOffset(1.0, 1.0);       // Set the polygon offset
74   gl.drawArrays(gl.TRIANGLES, n/2, n/2); // The yellow triangle
75 }
76
77 function initVertexBuffers(gl) {
```

```
78    var verticesColors = new Float32Array([
79      // Vertex coordinates and color
80        0.0,  2.5,  -5.0,  0.0,  1.0,  0.0, // The green triangle
81       -2.5, -2.5,  -5.0,  0.0,  1.0,  0.0,
82        2.5, -2.5,  -5.0,  1.0,  0.0,  0.0,
83
84        0.0,  3.0,  -5.0,  1.0,  0.0,  0.0, // The yellow triangle
85       -3.0, -3.0,  -5.0,  1.0,  1.0,  0.0,
86        3.0, -3.0,  -5.0,  1.0,  1.0,  0.0,
87    ]);
88    var n = 6;
```

If you look at the program from line 80, you can see that the z coordinate for each vertex is set to –5.0, so z fighting should occur.

Within the rest of the code, the polygon offset function is enabled at line 70. After that, the green and yellow triangles are drawn at lines 72 and 74. For ease of reading, the program uses only one buffer object, so `gl.drawArrays()` requires the second and third arguments to be correctly set. The second argument represents the number of the vertex to start from, while the third argument gives the number of vertices to be drawn. Once the green triangle has been drawn, the polygon offset parameter is set using `gl.polygonOffset()`. Subsequently, all the vertices drawn will have their z coordinate offset. If you load this program, you will see the two triangles drawn correctly with no z fighting effects, as in Figure 7.28 (right side). If you now comment out line 73 and reload the program, you will notice that z fighting occurs and looks similar to the left side of Figure 7.28.

Hello Cube

So far, the explanation of various WebGL features has been illustrated using simple triangles. You now have enough understanding of the basics to draw 3D objects. Let's start by drawing the cube shown in Figure 7.31. (The coordinates for each vertex are shown on the right side.) The program used is called HelloCube, in which the eight vertices that define the cube are specified using the following colors: white, magenta (bright reddish-violet), red, yellow, green, cyan (bright blue), blue, and black. As was explained in Chapter 5, "Using Colors and Texture Images," because colors between the vertices are interpolated, the resulting cube is shaded with an attractive color gradient (actually a "color solid," an analog of the two-dimensional "color wheel").

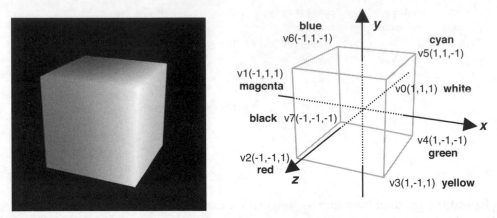

Figure 7.31 HelloCube and its vertex coordinates

Let's consider the case where you would like to draw the cube like this with the command you've been relying upon until now: gl.drawArrays(). In this case, you need to draw using one of the following modes: gl.TRIANGLES, gl.TRIANGLE_STRIP, or gl.TRIANGLE_FAN. The most simple and straightforward method would consist of drawing each face with two triangles. In other words, you can draw a face defined by four vertices (v0, v1, v2, v3), using two triangles defined by the two sets of three vertices (v0, v1, v2) and (v0, v2, v3), respectively, and repeat the same process for all the other faces. In this case, the vertices coordinates specified inside the buffer object would be these:

```
var vertices = new Float32Array([
    1.0, 1.0, 1.0,  -1.0,  1.0, 1.0, -1.0, -1.0,  1.0, // v0, v1, v2
    1.0, 1.0, 1.0,  -1.0, -1.0, 1.0,  1.0, -1.0,  1.0, // v0, v2, v3
    1.0, 1.0, 1.0,   1.0, -1.0, 1.0,  1.0, -1.0, -1.0, // v0, v3, v4
    ...
]);
```

Because one face is made up of two triangles, you need to know the coordinates of six vertices to define it. There are six faces, so a total of 6×6 = 36 vertices are necessary. After having specified the coordinates of each of the 36 vertices, write them in the buffer object and then call gl.drawArrays(gl.TRIANGLES, 0, 36), which draws the cube. This approach requires that you specify and handle 36 vertices, although the cube actually only requires 8 unique vertices because several triangles share common vertices.

You could, however, take a more frugal approach by drawing a single face with gl.TRIANGLE_FAN. Because gl.TRIANGLE_FAN allows you to draw a face defined by the 4-vertex set (v0, v1, v2, v3), you end up only having to deal with a total of 4×6=24 vertices[4]. However, you now need to call gl.drawArrays() separately for each face (six faces). So, each of these two approaches has both advantages and drawbacks, but neither seems ideal.

---

[4] You can cut down on the number of vertices using this kind of representation. It decreases the number of necessary vertices to 14, which can be drawn with gl.TRIANGLE_STRIP.

As you would expect, WebGL has a solution: `gl.drawElements()`. It's an alternative way to directly draw a three-dimensional object in WebGL, with a minimum of vertices. To use this method, you will need the vertex coordinates of the entire object, which you will use to explicitly describe how you want WebGL to draw the shape (the cube).

If we break our cube (see the right side of Figure 7.31) into vertices that constitute triangles, we get the structure shown in Figure 7.32. Looking at the left side of the figure, you can see that Cube points to a Faces list, which, as the name implies, shows that the cube is split into six faces: front, right, left, top, bottom, and back. In turn, each face is composed of two triangles picked up from the Triangles list. The numbers in the Triangles list represent the indices assigned to the Coordinate list. The vertex coordinates' indices are numbered in order starting from zero.

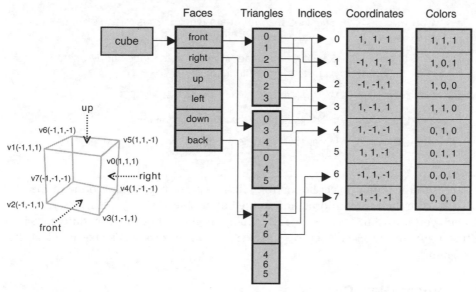

Figure 7.32 The associations of the faces that make up the cube, triangles, vertex coordinates, and colors

This approach results in a data structure that describes the way the object (a cube) can be built from its vertex and color data.

Drawing the Object with Indices and Vertices Coordinates

So far, you have been using `gl.drawArrays()` to draw vertices. However, WebGL supports an alternative approach, `gl.drawElements()`, that looks similar to that of `gl.drawArrays()`. However, it has some advantages that we'll explain later. First, let's look at how to use `gl.drawElements()`. You need to specify the indices based, not on `gl.ARRAY_BUFFER`, but on `gl.ELEMENT_ARRAY_BUFFER` (introduced in the explanation of the buffer object in Chapter 4). The key difference is that `gl.ELEMENT_ARRAY_BUFFER` handles data structured by the indices.

gl.drawElements(mode, count, type, offset)

Executes the shader and draws the geometric shape in the specified *mode* using the indices specified in the buffer object bound to gl.ELEMENT_ARRAY_BUFFER.

Parameters	mode	Specifies the type of shape to be drawn (refer to Figure 3.17).
		The following symbolic constants are accepted:
		gl.POINTS, gl.LINE_STRIP, gl.LINE_LOOP, gl.LINES, gl.TRIANGLE_STRIP, gl.TRIANGLE_FAN, or gl.TRIANGLES
	count	Number of indices to be drawn (integer).
	type	Specifies the index data type: gl.UNSIGNED_BYTE or gl.UNSIGNED_SHORT[5]
	offset	Specifies the offset in bytes in the index array where you want to start rendering.
Return value	None	
Errors	INVALID_ENUM	*mode* is none of the preceding values.
	INVALID_VALUE	A negative value is specified for *count* or *offset*

Writing indices to the buffer object bound to gl.ELEMENT_ARRAY_BUFFER is done in the same way you write the vertex information to the buffer object with gl.drawArrays(). That is to say, you use gl.bindBuffer() and gl.bufferData(), but the only difference is that the first argument, target, is set to gl.ELEMENT_ARRAY_BUFFER. Let's take a look at the sample program.

Sample Program (HelloCube.js)

The sample program is shown in Listing 7.12. The vertex and fragment shaders set a quadrangular pyramid viewing volume and perform a perspective projection transformation like ProjectiveView_mvpMatrix.js. It's important to understand that gl.drawElements() doesn't do anything special. The vertex shader simply transforms the vertex coordinates, and the fragment shader sets the color passed by the varying variable to gl_FragColor. The key difference from the previous programs comes down to the processing of the buffer object in initVertexBuffers().

---

[5] Even if *type* doesn't correspond to the type (Uint8Array or Uint16Array) of the data array specified in gl.ELEMENT_ARRAY_BUFFER, no error is returned. However, if, for example, you specify the index with a Uint16Array type, and set type to gl.UNSIGNED_BYTE, in some cases, the object might not be completely displayed.

Listing 7.12   HelloCube.js

```
1 // HelloCube.js
2 // Vertex shader program
3 var VSHADER_SOURCE =
  ...
8   'void main() {\n' +
9   '  gl_Position = u_MvpMatrix * a_Position;\n' +
10  '  v_Color = a_Color;\n' +
11  '}\n';
12
13 // Fragment shader program
14 var FSHADER_SOURCE =
  ...
19  'void main() {\n' +
20  '  gl_FragColor = v_Color;\n' +
21  '}\n';
22
23 function main() {
  ...
40   // Set the vertex coordinates and color
41   var n = initVertexBuffers(gl);
  ...
47   // Set the clear color and enable the hidden surface removal
48   gl.clearColor(0.0, 0.0, 0.0, 1.0);
49   gl.enable(gl.DEPTH_TEST);
  ...
58   // Set the eye point and the viewing volume
59   var mvpMatrix = new Matrix4();
60   mvpMatrix.setPerspective(30, 1, 1, 100);
61   mvpMatrix.lookAt(3, 3, 7, 0, 0, 0, 0, 1, 0);
62
63   // Pass the model view projection matrix to u_MvpMatrix
64   gl.uniformMatrix4fv(u_MvpMatrix, false, mvpMatrix.elements);
65
66   // Clear the color and depth buffer
67   gl.clear(gl.COLOR_BUFFER_BIT | gl.DEPTH_BUFFER_BIT);
68
69   // Draw the cube
70   gl.drawElements(gl.TRIANGLES, n, gl.UNSIGNED_BYTE, 0);
71 }
72
73 function initVertexBuffers(gl) {
  ...
82   var verticesColors = new Float32Array([
```

```
83    // Vertex coordinates and color
84     1.0,  1.0,  1.0,     1.0,  1.0,  1.0,  // v0 White
85    -1.0,  1.0,  1.0,     1.0,  0.0,  1.0,  // v1 Magenta
86    -1.0, -1.0,  1.0,     1.0,  0.0,  0.0,  // v2 Red
   ...
91    -1.0, -1.0, -1.0,     0.0,  0.0,  0.0   // v7 Black
92  ]);
93
94   // Indices of the vertices
95   var indices = new Uint8Array([
96     0, 1, 2,   0, 2, 3,    // front
97     0, 3, 4,   0, 4, 5,    // right
98     0, 5, 6,   0, 6, 1,    // up
99     1, 6, 7,   1, 7, 2,    // left
100    7, 4, 3,   7, 3, 2,    // down
101    4, 7, 6,   4, 6, 5     // back
102  ]);
103
104  // Create a buffer object
105  var vertexColorBuffer = gl.createBuffer();
106  var indexBuffer = gl.createBuffer();
   ...
111  // Write the vertex coordinates and color to the buffer object
112  gl.bindBuffer(gl.ARRAY_BUFFER, vertexColorBuffer);
113  gl.bufferData(gl.ARRAY_BUFFER, verticesColors, gl.STATIC_DRAW);
114
115  var FSIZE = verticesColors.BYTES_PER_ELEMENT;
116  // Assign the buffer object to a_Position and enable it
117  var a_Position = gl.getAttribLocation(gl.program, 'a_Position');
   ...
122  gl.vertexAttribPointer(a_Position, 3, gl.FLOAT, false, FSIZE * 6, 0);
123  gl.enableVertexAttribArray(a_Position);
124  // Assign the buffer object to a_Position  and enable it
125  var a_Color = gl.getAttribLocation(gl.program, 'a_Color');
   ...
130  gl.vertexAttribPointer(a_Color, 3, gl.FLOAT, false, FSIZE * 6, FSIZE * 3);
131  gl.enableVertexAttribArray(a_Color);
132
133  // Write the indices to the buffer object
134  gl.bindBuffer(gl.ELEMENT_ARRAY_BUFFER, indexBuffer);
135  gl.bufferData(gl.ELEMENT_ARRAY_BUFFER, indices, gl.STATIC_DRAW);
136
137  return indices.length;
138 }
```

The processing flow in the JavaScript `main()` is the same as in `ProjectiveView_mvpMatrix.js`, but let's quickly review it. After having written the vertex data in the buffer object through a call to `initVertexBuffers()` at line 41, you enable the hidden surface removal function at line 49. This is necessary to allow WebGL to correctly draw the cube, taking into consideration the relationship between the front and the back faces.

You set the eye point and the viewing volume from line 59 to line 61 and pass the model view projection matrix to the vertex shader's uniform variable `u_MvpMatrix`.

At line 67, you clear the color and depth buffers and then draw the cube using `gl.drawElements()` at line 70. The use of `gl.drawElements()` in this program is the main difference to `ProjectiveView_mvpMatrix.js`, so let's take a look at that.

Writing Vertex Coordinates, Colors, and Indices to the Buffer Object

The method to assign the vertex coordinates and the color information to the attribute variable using the buffer object in `initVertexBuffers()` is unchanged. This time, because you won't necessarily use the vertex information in the order specified in the object buffer, you need to additionally specify in which order you will use it. For that you will use the vertex order specified in `verticesColors` as indices. In short, the vertex information specified first in the buffer object will be set to index 0, the vertex information specified in second place in the buffer object will be set to index 1, and so on. Here, we show the part of the program that specifies the indices in `initVertexBuffers()`:

```
 73 function initVertexBuffers(gl) {
     ...
 82   var verticesColors = new Float32Array([
 83     // Vertex coordinates and color
 84      1.0,  1.0,  1.0,     1.0,  1.0,  1.0,  // v0 White
 85     -1.0,  1.0,  1.0,     1.0,  0.0,  1.0,  // v1 Magenta
     ...
 91     -1.0, -1.0, -1.0,     0.0,  0.0,  0.0   // v7 Black
 92   ]);
 93
 94   // Indices of the vertex coordinates
 95   var indices = new Uint8Array([
 96      0, 1, 2,   0, 2, 3,    // front
 97      0, 3, 4,   0, 4, 5,    // right
 98      0, 5, 6,   0, 6, 1,    // up
 99      1, 6, 7,   1, 7, 2,    // left
100      7, 4, 3,   7, 3, 2,    // down
101      4, 7, 6,   4, 6, 5     // back
102   ]);
103
104   // Create a buffer object
105   var vertexColorBuffer = gl.createBuffer();
```

```
106    var indexBuffer = gl.createBuffer();
       ...
136    // Write the indices to the buffer object
137    gl.bindBuffer(gl.ELEMENT_ARRAY_BUFFER, indexBuffer);
138    gl.bufferData(gl.ELEMENT_ARRAY_BUFFER, indices, gl.STATIC_DRAW);
139
140    return indices.length;
141  }
```

As you may have noticed, at line 106, you create the buffer object (indexBuffer) in which to write the indices. These indices are stored in the array indices at line 95. Because the indices are integers (0, 1, 2, ...), you use an integer typed array Uint8Array (unsigned 8-bit encoded integer). If there are more than 256 indices, use Uint16Array instead. The content of this array is the triangles list of Figure 7.33, where each grouping of three indices points to the three vertex coordinates for that triangle. Generally, this index doesn't need to be manually created because 3D modeling tools, introduced in the next chapter, usually generate it along with the vertices information.

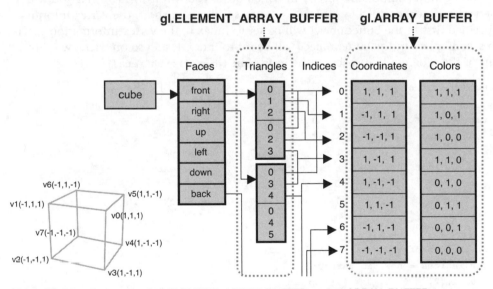

Figure 7.33 Contents of gl.ELEMENT_ARRAY_BUFFER and gl.ARRAY_BUFFER

The setup for the specified indices is performed at lines 134 and 135. This is similar to the way buffer objects have been written previously, with the difference that the first argument is modified to gl.ELEMENT_ARRAY_BUFFER. This is to let the WebGL system know that the contents of the buffer are indices.

Once executed, the internal state of the WebGL system is as detailed in Figure 7.34.

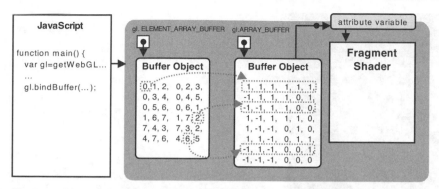

Figure 7.34 gl.ELEMENT_ARRAY_BUFFER and gl.ARRAY_BUFFER

Once set up, the call to gl.drawElements() at line 70 draws the cube:

```
69    // Draw the cube
70    gl.drawElements(gl.TRIANGLES, n, gl.UNSIGNED_BYTE, 0);
```

You should note that the second argument of gl.drawElements(), the number of indices, represents the number of vertex coordinates involved in the drawing, but it is not identical to the number of vertices coordinates written to gl.ARRAY_BUFFER.

When you call gl.drawElements(), the indices are extracted from the buffer object (indexBuffer) bound to gl.ELEMENT_ARRAY_BUFFER, while the associated vertex information is retrieved from the buffer object (vertexColorBuffer) bound to gl.ARRAY_BUFFER. All these pieces of information are then passed to the attribute variable. The process is repeated for each index, and then the whole cube gets drawn by a single call to gl.drawElements(). With this approach, because you refer to the vertex information through indices, you can recycle the vertex information. Although gl.drawElements() allows you to curb memory usage by sharing the vertex information, the cost is a process to convert the indices to vertex information (that is, a level of indirection). This means that the choice between gl.drawElements() and gl.drawArrays(), because they both have pros and cons, will eventually depend on the system implementation.

At this stage, although it's clear that gl.drawElements() is an efficient way to draw 3D shapes, one key feature is missing. There is no way to control color, so it is helpful to draw a cube using a single solid color, as shown in Figure 7.31.

For example, let's consider the case where you would like to modify the color of each face of the cube, as shown in Figure 7.35, or map textures to the faces. You need to know the color or texture information for each face, yet you cannot implement this with the combination of indices, triangle list, and vertex coordinates shown in Figure 7.33.

Figure 7.35 Cube with differently colored faces

In the following section, we will examine how to address this problem and specify the color information for each face.

Adding Color to Each Face of a Cube

As discussed before, you can only pass per-vertex information to the vertex shader. This implies that you need to pass the face's color and the vertices of the triangles as vertex information to the vertex shader. For instance, to draw the "front" face in blue, made up of v0, v1, v2, and v3 (Figure 7.33), you need to specify the same blue color for each of the vertices.

However, as you may have noticed, v0 is also shared by the "right" and "top" faces as well as the "front" face. Therefore, if you specify the color blue for the vertices that form the "front" face, you are then unable to choose a different color for those vertices that also belong to another face. To cope with this problem, although this might not seem as efficient, you must create duplicate entries for the shared vertices in the vertices coordinates listing, as illustrated in Figure 7.36. Doing so, you will have to handle common vertices with identical coordinates in the face's triangle list as separate entities.[6]

---

[6] If you break down all the faces into triangles and draw using `gl.drawArrays()`, you have to process 6 vertices * 6 faces = 36 vertices, so the difference between `gl.drawArrays()` and `gl.drawElements()` in memory usage is negligible. This is because a cube or a cuboid is a special 3D object whose faces are connected vertically; therefore, each vertex needs to have three colors. However, in the case of complex 3D models, specifying several colors to a single vertex would be rare.

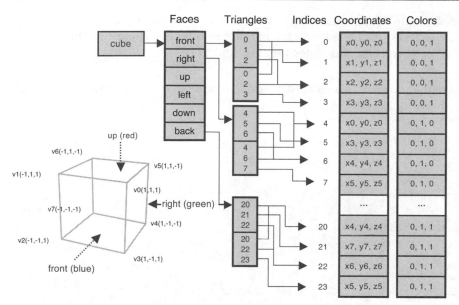

Figure 7.36 The faces that constitute the cube, the triangles, and the relationship between vertices coordinates (configured so that you can choose a different color for each face)

When opting for such a configuration, the contents of the index list, which consists of the face's triangle list, will differ from face to face, thus allowing you to modify the color for each face. This approach can also be used if you want to map a texture to each face. You would need to specify the texture coordinates for each vertex, but you can actually deal with this by rewriting the color list (Figure 7.36) as texture coordinates. The sample program in the section "Rotate Object" in Chapter 10 covers this approach in more detail.

Let's take a look at the sample program ColoredCube, which displays a cube with each face painted a different color. The screen shot of ColoredCube is identical to Figure 7.35.

Sample Program (ColoredCube.js)

The sample program is shown in Listing 7.13. Because the only difference from HelloCube.js is the method of storing vertex information into the buffer object, let's look in more detail at the code related to the initVertexBuffers(). The main differences to HelloCube.js are

- In HelloCube.js, the vertex coordinates and color are stored in a single buffer object, but because this make the array unwieldy, the program has been modified so that they are now stored in separate buffer objects.

- The respective contents of the vertex array (which stores the vertex coordinates), the color array (which stores the color information), and the index array (which stores the indices) are modified in accordance with the configuration described in Figure 7.36 (lines 83, 92, and 101).

- To keep the sample program as compact as possible, the function
  `initArrayBuffer()` is defined, which bundles the buffer object creation, binding,
  writing of data, and enabling (lines 116, 119, and 129).

As you examine the program, take note of how the second bullet is implemented to match
the structure shown in Figure 7.36.

Listing 7.13 ColoredCube.js

```
 1 // ColoredCube.js
   ...
23 function main() {
   ...
40   // Set the vertex information
41   var n = initVertexBuffers(gl);
   ...
69   // Draw the cube
70   gl.drawElements(gl.TRIANGLES, n, gl.UNSIGNED_BYTE, 0);
71 }
72
73 function initVertexBuffers(gl) {
   ...
83   var vertices = new Float32Array([   // Vertex coordinates
84      1.0, 1.0, 1.0,  -1.0, 1.0, 1.0,  -1.0,-1.0, 1.0,   1.0,-1.0, 1.0,
85      1.0, 1.0, 1.0,   1.0,-1.0, 1.0,   1.0,-1.0,-1.0,   1.0, 1.0,-1.0,
86      1.0, 1.0, 1.0,   1.0, 1.0,-1.0,  -1.0, 1.0,-1.0,  -1.0, 1.0, 1.0,
   ...
89      1.0,-1.0,-1.0,  -1.0,-1.0,-1.0,  -1.0, 1.0,-1.0,   1.0, 1.0,-1.0
90   ]);
91
92   var colors = new Float32Array([   // Colors
93     0.4, 0.4, 1.0,   0.4, 0.4, 1.0,   0.4, 0.4, 1.0,   0.4, 0.4, 1.0,
94     0.4, 1.0, 0.4,   0.4, 1.0, 0.4,   0.4, 1.0, 0.4,   0.4, 1.0, 0.4,
95     1.0, 0.4, 0.4,   1.0, 0.4, 0.4,   1.0, 0.4, 0.4,   1.0, 0.4, 0.4,
   ...
98     0.4, 1.0, 1.0,   0.4, 1.0, 1.0,   0.4, 1.0, 1.0,   0.4, 1.0, 1.0
99   ]);
100
101  var indices = new Uint8Array([        // Indices of the vertices
102     0, 1, 2,   0, 2, 3,    // front
103     4, 5, 6,   4, 6, 7,    // right
104     8, 9,10,   8,10,11,    // up
   ...
107    20,21,22,  20,22,23     // back
108  ]);
```

```
109
110  // Create a buffer object
111  var indexBuffer = gl.createBuffer();
     ...
115  // Write the vertex coordinates and color to the buffer object
116  if (!initArrayBuffer(gl, vertices, 3, gl.FLOAT, 'a_Position'))
117    return -1;
118
119  if (!initArrayBuffer(gl, colors, 3, gl.FLOAT, 'a_Color'))
120    return -1;
     ...
122  // Write the indices to the buffer object
123  gl.bindBuffer(gl.ELEMENT_ARRAY_BUFFER, indexBuffer);
124  gl.bufferData(gl.ELEMENT_ARRAY_BUFFER, indices, gl.STATIC_DRAW);
125
126  return indices.length;
127 }
128
129 function initArrayBuffer(gl, data, num, type, attribute) {
130  var buffer = gl.createBuffer();    // Create a buffer object
     ...
135  // Write date into the buffer object
136  gl.bindBuffer(gl.ARRAY_BUFFER, buffer);
137  gl.bufferData(gl.ARRAY_BUFFER, data, gl.STATIC_DRAW);
138  // Assign the buffer object to the attribute variable
139  var a_attribute = gl.getAttribLocation(gl.program, attribute);
     ...
144  gl.vertexAttribPointer(a_attribute, num, type, false, 0, 0);
145  // Enable the assignment of the buffer object to the attribute variable
146  gl.enableVertexAttribArray(a_attribute);
147
148  return true;
149 }
```

Experimenting with the Sample Program

In ColoredCube, you specify a different color for each face. So what happens when you choose an identical color for all the faces? For example, let's try to set the color information in ColoredCube.js's colors array to "white," as shown next. We will call this program ColoredCube_singleColor.js:

```
 1  // ColoredCube_singleColor.js
    ...
92  var colors = new Float32Array([
93    1.0, 1.0, 1.0,  1.0, 1.0, 1.0,  1.0, 1.0, 1.0,  1.0, 1.0, 1.0,
```

```
94    1.0, 1.0, 1.0,  1.0, 1.0, 1.0,  1.0, 1.0, 1.0,  1.0, 1.0, 1.0,
   ...
98    1.0, 1.0, 1.0,  1.0, 1.0, 1.0,  1.0, 1.0, 1.0,  1.0, 1.0, 1
99  ]);
```

When you execute the program, you see an output like the screenshot shown in Figure 7.37. One result of using a single color is that it becomes difficult to actually recognize the cube. Up until now you could differentiate each face because they were differently colored; therefore, you could recognize the whole shape as a solid. However, when you switch to a unique color, you lose this three-dimensional impression.

Figure 7.37 Cube with its faces being identically colored

In contrast, in the real world, when you put a white box on a table, you can identify it as a solid (see Figure 7.38). This is because each face, although the same white color, presents a slightly different appearance because each is lit slightly differently. In ColoredCube_ singleColor, such an effect is not programmed, so the cube is hard to recognize. We will explore how to correctly light 3D scenes in the next chapter.

Figure 7.38 White box in the real world

Summary

In this chapter, through the introduction of the depth information, you have examined setting the viewer's eye point and viewing volume, looked at how to draw real 3D objects, and briefly examined the local and world coordinate system. Many of the examples were similar to those previously explained for the two-dimensional world, except for the introduction of the z-axis to handle depth information.

The next chapter explains how to light 3D scenes and how to draw and manipulate three-dimensional shapes with complex structures. We will also return to the function `initShaders()`, which has hidden a number of complex issues that you now have enough understanding to explore.

Chapter 8

Lighting Objects

This chapter focuses on lighting objects, looking at different light sources and their effects on the 3D scene. Lighting is essential if you want to create realistic 3D scenes because it helps to give the scene a sense of depth.

The following key points are discussed in this chapter:

- Shading, shadows, and different types of light sources including point, directional, and ambient

- Reflection of light in the 3D scene and the two main types: diffuse and ambient

- The details of shading and how to implement the effect of light to make objects, such as the pure white cube in the previous chapter, look three-dimensional

By the end of this chapter, you will have all the knowledge you need to create lighted 3D scenes populated with both simple and complex 3D objects.

Lighting 3D Objects

When light hits an object in the real world, part of the light is reflected by the surface of the object. Only after this reflected light enters your eyes can you see the object and distinguish its color. For example, a white box reflects white light which, when it enters your eyes, allows you to tell that the box is white.

In the real world, two important phenomena occur when light hits an object (see Figure 8.1):

- Depending on the light source and direction, surface color is shaded.

- Depending on the light source and direction, objects "cast" shadows on the ground or the floor.

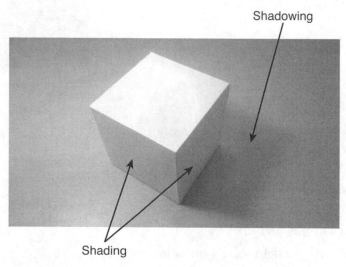

Shadowing

Shading

Figure 8.1 Shading and shadowing

In the real world, you usually notice shadows, but you quite often don't notice shading, which gives 3D objects their feeling of depth. Shading is subtle but always present. As shown in Figure 8.1, even surfaces of a pure white cube are distinguishable because each surface is shaded differently by light. As you can see, the surfaces hit by more light are brighter, and the surfaces hit by less light are darker, or more shaded. These differences allow you to distinguish each surface and ensure that the cube looks cubic.

In 3D graphics, the term **shading**[1] is used to describe the process that re-creates this phenomenon where the colors differ from surface to surface due to light. The other phenomenon, that the shadow of an object falls on the floor or ground, is re-created using a process called **shadowing**. This section discusses shading. Shadowing is discussed in Chapter 10, which focuses on a set of useful techniques that build on your basic knowledge of WebGL.

---

[1] Shading is so critical to 3D graphics that the core language, GLSL ES, is a shader language, the OpenGL ES Shading Language. The original purpose of shaders was to re-create the phenomena of shading.

When discussing shading, you need to consider two things:

- The type of light source that is emitting light

- How the light is reflected from surfaces of an object and enters the eye

Before we begin to program, let's look at different types of light sources and how light is reflected from different surfaces.

Types of Light Source

When light illuminates an object, a light source emits the light. In the real world, light sources are divided into two main categories: **directional light**, which is something like the sun that emits light naturally, and **point light**, which is something like a light bulb that emits light artificially. In addition, there is **ambient light** that represents indirect light (that is, light emitted from all light sources and reflected by walls or other objects (see Figure 8.2). In 3D graphics, there are additional types of light sources. For example, there is a spot light representing flashlights, headlamps, and so on. However, in this book, we don't address these more specialized light sources. Refer to the book *OpenGL ES 2.0 Programming Guide* for further information on these specialized light sources.

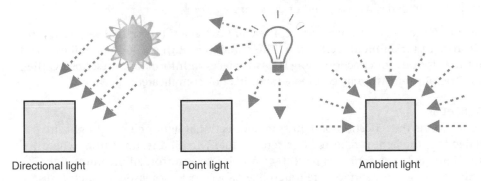

Directional light   Point light   Ambient light

Figure 8.2 Directional light, point light, and ambient light

Focusing on the three main types of light source covered in this book:

Directional light: A directional light represents a light source whose light rays are parallel. It is a model of light whose source is considered to be at an infinite distance, such as the sun. Because of the distance travelled, the rays are effectively parallel by the time they reach the earth. This light source is considered the simplest, and because its rays are parallel can be specified using only direction and color.

Point light: A point light represents a light source that emits light in all directions from one single point. It is a model of light that can be used to represent light bulbs, lamps, flames, and so on. This light source is specified by its position and color.[2] However, the light direction is determined from the position of the light source and the position at which the light strikes a surface. As such, its direction can change considerably within the scene.

Ambient light: Ambient light (indirect light) is a model of light that is emitted from the other light source (directional or point), reflected by other objects such as walls, and reaches objects indirectly. It represents light that illuminates an object from all directions and has the same intensity.[3] For example, if you open the refrigerator door at night, the entire kitchen becomes slightly lighter. This is the effect of the ambient light. Ambient light does not have position and direction and is specified only by its color.

Now that you know the types of light sources that illuminate objects, let's discuss how light is reflected by the surface of an object and then enters the eye.

Types of Reflected Light

How light is reflected by the surface of an object and thus what color the surface will become is determined by two things: the type of the light and the type of surface of the object. Information about the type of light includes its color and direction. Information about the surface includes its color and orientation.

When calculating reflection from a surface, there are two main types: **diffuse reflection** and **environment** (or **ambient**) **reflection**. The remainder of this section describes how to calculate the color due to reflection using the two pieces of information described earlier. There is a little bit of math to be considered, but it's not complicated.

Diffuse Reflection

Diffuse reflection is the reflection of light from a directional light or a point light. In diffuse reflection, the light is reflected (scattered) equally in all directions from where it hits (see Figure 8.3). If a surface is perfectly smooth like a mirror, all incoming light is reflected; however, most surfaces are rough like paper, rock, or plastic. In such cases, the light is scattered in random directions from the rough surface. Diffuse reflection is a model of this phenomenon.

---

[2] This type of light actually attenuates; that is, it is strong near the source and becomes weaker farther from the source. For the sake of simplicity of the description and sample programs, light is treated as nonattenuating in this book. For attenuation, please refer to the book *OpenGL ES 2.0 Programming Guide*.

[3] In fact, ambient light is the combination of light emitted from light sources and reflected by various surfaces. It is approximated in this way because it would otherwise need complicated calculations to take into account all the many light sources and how and where they are reflected.

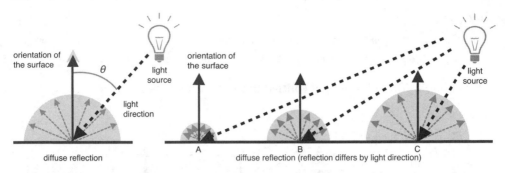

Figure 8.3 Diffuse reflection

In diffuse reflection, the color of the surface is determined by the color and the direction of light and the base color and orientation of the surface. The angle between the light direction and the orientation of the surface is defined by the angle formed by the light direction and the direction "perpendicular" to the surface. Calling this angle θ, the surface color by diffuse reflection is calculated using the following formula.

Equation 8.1

$$\langle surface\ color\ by\ diffuse\ reflection \rangle = \langle light\ color \rangle \times \langle base\ color\ of\ surface \rangle \times \cos\theta$$

where <*light color*> is the color of light emitted from a directional light or a point light. Multiplication with the <*base color of the surface*> is performed for each RGB component of the color. Because light by diffuse reflection is scattered equally in all directions from where it hits, the intensity of the reflected light at a certain position is the same from any angle (see Figure 8.4).

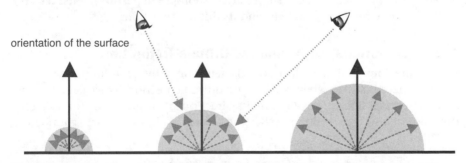

Figure 8.4 The intensity of light at a given position is the same from any angle

Ambient Reflection

Ambient reflection is the reflection of light from another light source. In ambient reflection, the light is reflected at the same angle as its incoming angle. Because an ambient light illuminates an object equally from all directions with the same intensity, its brightness is the same at any position (see Figure 8.5). It can be approximated as follows.

Equation 8.2

$$\langle surface\ color\ by\ ambient\ reflection \rangle =$$
$$\langle light\ color \rangle \times \langle base\ color\ of\ surface \rangle$$

where *<light color>* is the color of light emitted from other light source.

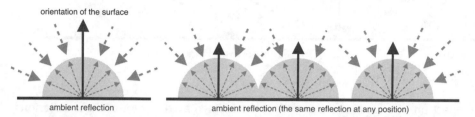

Figure 8.5 Ambient reflection

When both diffuse reflection and ambient reflection are present, the color of the surface is calculated by adding, as follows.

Equation 8.3

$$\langle surface\ color\ by\ diffuse\ and\ ambient\ reflection \rangle =$$
$$\langle surface\ color\ by\ diffuse\ reflection \rangle + \langle surface\ color\ by\ ambient\ reflection \rangle$$

Note that it is not required to always use both light sources, or use the formulas exactly as mentioned here. You are free to modify each formula to achieve the effect you require when showing the object.

Now let's construct some sample programs that perform shading (shading and coloring the surfaces of an object by placing a light source at an appropriate position). First let's try to implement shading due to directional light and its diffuse reflection.

Shading Due to Directional Light and Its Diffuse Reflection

As described in the previous section, surface color is determined by light direction and the orientation of the surface it strikes when considering diffuse reflection. The calculation of the color due to directional light is easy because its direction is constant. The formula for calculating the color of a surface by diffuse reflection (Equation 8.1) is shown again here:

$$\langle surface\ color\ by\ diffuse\ reflection \rangle =$$
$$\langle light\ color \rangle \times \langle base\ color\ of\ surface \rangle \times \cos\theta$$

The following three pieces of information are used:

- The color of the light source (directional light)

- The base color of the surface

- The angle *(θ)* between the light and the surface

The color of a light source may be white, such as sunlight, or other colors, such as the orange of lighting in road tunnels. As you know, it can be represented by RGB. White light such as sunlight has an RGB value of (1.0, 1.0, 1.0). The base color of a surface means the color that the surface was originally defined to have, such as red or blue. To calculate the color of a surface, you need to apply the formula for each of the three RGB components; the calculation is performed three times.

For example, assume that the light emitted from a light source is white (1.0, 1.0, 1.0), and the base color of the surface is red (1.0, 0.0, 0.0). From Equation 8.1, when θ is 0.0 (that is, when the light hits perpendicularly), cos θ becomes 1.0. Because the R component of the light source is 1.0, the R component of the base surface color is 1.0, and the cos θ is 1.0, the R component of the surface color by diffuse reflection is calculated as follows:

R = 1.0 * 1.0 * 1.0 = 1.0

The G and B components are also calculated in the same way, as follows:

G = 1.0 * 0.0 * 1.0 = 0.0

B = 1.0 * 0.0 * 1.0 = 0.0

From these calculations, when white light hits perpendicularly on a red surface, the surface color by diffuse reflection turns out to be (1.0, 0.0, 0.0), or red. This is consistent with real-world experience. Conversely, when the color of the light source is red and the base color of a surface is white, the result is the same.

Let's now consider the case when θ is 90 degrees, or when the light does not hit the surface at all. From your real-world experience, you know that in this case the surface will appear black. Let's validate this. Because cos θ is 0 when θ is 90 degrees, and anything multiplied by zero is zero, the result of the formula is 0 for R, G, and B; that is, the surface color becomes (0.0, 0.0, 0.0), or black, as expected. Equally, when θ is 60 degrees, you'd expect that a small amount of light falling on a red surface would result in a darker red color, and because cos θ is 0.5, the surface color is (0.5, 0.0, 0.0), which is dark red, as expected.

These simple examples have given you a good idea of how to calculate surface color due to diffuse reflection. To allow you to factor in directional light, let's transform the preceding formula to make it easy to handle so you can then explore how to draw a cube lit by directional light.

Calculating Diffuse Reflection Using the Light Direction and the Orientation of a Surface

In the previous examples, an arbitrary value for θ was chosen. However, typically it is complicated to get the angle θ between the light direction and the orientation of a surface. For example, when creating a model, the angle at which light hits each surface cannot be determined in advance. In contrast, the orientation of each surface can be determined regardless of where light hits from. Because the light direction is also determined when its light source is determined, it seems convenient to try to use these two pieces of information.

Fortunately, mathematics tells us that cos θ is derived by calculating the dot product of the light direction and the orientation of a surface. Because the dot product is so often used, GLSL ES provides a function to calculate it.[4] (More details can be found in Appendix B, "Built-In Functions of GLSL ES 1.0.") When representing the dot product by "·", cos θ is defined as follows:

$$\cos\theta = \langle light\ direction \rangle \bullet \langle orientation\ of\ a\ surface \rangle$$

From this, Equation 8.1 can be transformed as following Equation 8.4:

Equation 8.4

$$\langle surface\ color\ by\ diffuse\ reflection \rangle =$$
$$\langle light\ color \rangle \times \langle base\ color\ of\ surface \rangle \times$$
$$(\langle light\ direction \rangle \bullet \langle orientation\ of\ a\ surface \rangle)$$

Here, there are two points to be considered: the length of the vector and the light direction. First, the length of vectors that represent light direction and orientation of the surface, such as (2.0, 2.0, 1.0), must be 1.0,[5] or the color of the surface may become too dark or bright. Adjusting the components of a vector so that its length becomes 1.0 is called **normalization**.[6] GLSL ES provides functions for normalizing vectors that you can use directly.

The second point to consider concerns the light direction for the reflected light. The light direction is the opposite direction from that which the light rays travel (see Figure 8.6).

---

[4] Mathematically, the dot product of two vectors n and l is written as follows:

$n \bullet 1 = |n| \times |1| \times \cos \theta$

where $|\ |$ means the length of the vector. From this equation, you can see that when the lengths of n and l are 1.0, the dot product is equal to cos θ. If n is (n_x, n_y, n_z) and l is (l_x, l_y, l_z), then $n_l = n_x * l_x + n_y * l_y + n_z * l_z$ from the law of cosines.

[5] If the components of the vector n are (n_x, n_y, n_z), its length is as follows:

length of n $= |n| = \sqrt{n_x^2 + n_y^2 + n_z^2}$

[6] Normalized n is $(n_x/m, n_y/m, n_z/m)$, where m is the length of n. $|n|$ = sqrt(9) = 3. The vector (2.0, 2.0, 1.0) above is normalized into (2.0/3.0, 2.0/3.0, 1.0/3.0).

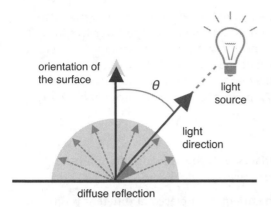

Figure 8.6 The light direction is from the reflecting surface to the light source

Because we aren't using an angle to specify the orientation of the surface, we need another mechanism to do that. The solution is to use normal vectors.

The Orientation of a Surface: What Is the Normal?

The orientation of a surface is specified by the direction perpendicular to the surface and is called a **normal** or a **normal vector**. This direction is represented by a triple number, which is the direction of a line from the origin $(0, 0, 0)$ to (n_x, n_y, n_z) specified as the normal. For example, the direction of the normal $(1, 0, 0)$ is the positive direction of the x-axis, and the direction of the normal $(0, 0, 1)$ is the positive direction of the z-axis. When considering surfaces and their normals, two properties are important for our discussion.

A Surface Has Two Normals

Because a surface has a front face and a back face, each side has its own normal; that is, the surface has two normals. For example, the surface perpendicular to the z-axis has a front face that is facing toward the positive direction of the z-axis and a back face that is facing the negative direction of the z-axis, as shown in Figure 8.7. Their normals are $(0, 0, 1)$ and $(0, 0, -1)$, respectively.

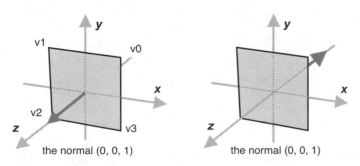

Figure 8.7 Normals

In 3D graphics, these two faces are distinguished by the order in which the vertices are specified when drawing the surface. When you draw a surface specifying vertices in the order[7] v0, v1, v2, and v3, the front face is the one whose vertices are arranged in a clockwise fashion when you look along the direction of the normal of the face (same as the right-handed rule determining the positive direction of rotation in Chapter 3, "Drawing and Transforming Triangles"). So in Figure 8.7, the front face has the normal (0, 0, –1) as in the right side of the figure.

The Same Orientation Has the Same Normal

Because a normal just represents direction, surfaces with the same orientation have the same normal regardless of the position of the surfaces.

If there is more than one surface with the same orientation placed at different positions, the normals of these surfaces are identical. For example, the normals of a surface perpendicular to the z-axis, whose center is placed at (10, 98, 9), are still (0, 0, 1) and (0, 0, –1). They are the same as when it is positioned at the origin (see Figure 8.8).

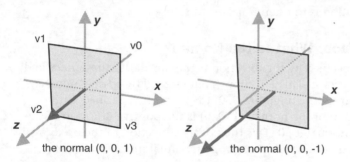

Figure 8.8 If the orientation of the surface is the same, the normal is identical regardless of its position

The left side of Figure 8.9 shows the normals that are used in the sample programs in this section. Normals are labeled using, for example "n(0, 1, 0)" as in this figure.

---

[7] Actually, this surface is composed of two triangles: a triangle drawn in the order v0, v1, and v2, and a triangle drawn in the order v0, v2, and v3.

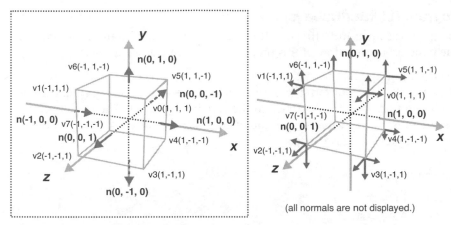

(all normals are not displayed.)

Figure 8.9 Normals of the surfaces of a cube

Once you have calculated the normals for a surface, the next task is to pass that data to the shader programs. In the previous chapter, you passed color data for a surface to the shader as "per-vertex data." You can pass normal data using the same approach: as per-vertex data stored in a buffer object. In this section, as shown in Figure 8.9 (right side), the normal data is specified for each vertex, and in this case there are three normals per vertex, just as there are three color data specified per vertex.[8]

Now let's construct a sample program LightedCube that displays a red cube lit by a white directional light. The result is shown in Figure 8.10.

Figure 8.10 LightedCube

---

[8] Cubes or cuboids are simple but special objects whose three surfaces are connected perpendicularly. They have three different normals per vertex. On the other hand, smooth objects such as game characters have one normal per vertex.

Sample Program (LightedCube.js)

The sample program is shown in Listing 8.1. It is based on ColoredCube from the previous chapter, so the basic processing flow of this program is the same as ColoredCube.

As you can see from Listing 8.1, the vertex shader has been significantly modified so that it calculates Equation 8.4. In addition, the normal data is added in initVertexBuffers() defined at line 89, so that they can be passed to the variable a_Normal. The fragment shader is the same as in ColoredCube, and unmodified. It is reproduced so that you can see that no fragment processing is needed.

Listing 8.1 LightedCube.js

```
 1 // LightedCube.js
 2 // Vertex shader program
 3 var VSHADER_SOURCE =
 4   'attribute vec4 a_Position;\n' +
 5   'attribute vec4 a_Color;\n' +
 6   'attribute vec4 a_Normal;\n' +        // Normal
 7   'uniform mat4 u_MvpMatrix;\n' +
 8   'uniform vec3 u_LightColor;\n' +      // Light color
 9   'uniform vec3 u_LightDirection;\n' + // world coordinate, normalized
10   'varying vec4 v_Color;\n' +
11   'void main() {\n' +
12   ' gl_Position = u_MvpMatrix * a_Position ;\n' +
13   '   // Make the length of the normal 1.0
14   ' vec3 normal = normalize(vec3(a_Normal));\n' +
15   '   // Dot product of light direction and orientation of a surface
16   ' float nDotL = max(dot(u_LightDirection, normal), 0.0);\n' +
17   '   // Calculate the color due to diffuse reflection
18   ' vec3 diffuse = u_LightColor * vec3(a_Color) * nDotL;\n' +
19   ' v_Color = vec4(diffuse, a_Color.a);\n' +
20   '}\n';
21
22 // Fragment shader program
   ...
28   'void main() {\n' +
29   ' gl_FragColor = v_Color;\n' +
30   '}\n';
31
32 function main() {
   ...
49   // Set the vertex coordinates, the color, and the normal
50   var n = initVertexBuffers(gl);
   ...
```

```
61   var u_MvpMatrix = gl.getUniformLocation(gl.program, 'u_MvpMatrix');
62   var u_LightColor = gl.getUniformLocation(gl.program, 'u_LightColor');
63   var u_LightDirection = gl.getUniformLocation(gl.program, 'u_LightDirection');
     ...
69   // Set the light color (white)
70   gl.uniform3f(u_LightColor, 1.0, 1.0, 1.0);
71   // Set the light direction (in the world coordinate)
72   var lightDirection = new Vector3([0.5, 3.0, 4.0]);
73   lightDirection.normalize();        // Normalize
74   gl.uniform3fv(u_LightDirection, lightDirection.elements);
75
76   // Calculate the view projection matrix
77   var mvpMatrix = new Matrix4();     // Model view projection matrix
78   mvpMatrix.setPerspective(30, canvas.width/canvas.height, 1, 100);
79   mvpMatrix.lookAt(3, 3, 7, 0, 0, 0, 0, 1, 0);
80   // Pass the model view projection matrix to the variable u_MvpMatrix
81   gl.uniformMatrix4fv(u_MvpMatrix, false, mvpMatrix.elements);
     ...
86   gl.drawElements(gl.TRIANGLES, n, gl.UNSIGNED_BYTE, 0);// Draw a cube
87 }
88
89 function initVertexBuffers(gl) {
     ...
98   var vertices = new Float32Array([ // Vertices
99      1.0, 1.0, 1.0,  -1.0, 1.0, 1.0,  -1.0,-1.0, 1.0,   1.0,-1.0, 1.0,
100     1.0, 1.0, 1.0,   1.0,-1.0, 1.0,   1.0,-1.0,-1.0,   1.0, 1.0,-1.0,
     ...
104     1.0,-1.0,-1.0,  -1.0,-1.0,-1.0,  -1.0, 1.0,-1.0,   1.0, 1.0,-1.0
105  ]);
     ...
117
118  var normals = new Float32Array([ // Normals
119     0.0, 0.0, 1.0,   0.0, 0.0, 1.0,   0.0, 0.0, 1.0,   0.0, 0.0, 1.0,
120     1.0, 0.0, 0.0,   1.0, 0.0, 0.0,   1.0, 0.0, 0.0,   1.0, 0.0, 0.0,
     ...
124     0.0, 0.0,-1.0,   0.0, 0.0,-1.0,   0.0, 0.0,-1.0,   0.0, 0.0,-1.0
125  ]);
     ...
140  if(!initArrayBuffer(gl,'a_Normal', normals, 3, gl.FLOAT)) return -1;
     ...
154  return indices.length;
155 }
```

As a reminder, here is the calculation that the vertex shader performs (Equation 8.4):

$$\langle surface\ color\ by\ diffuse\ reflection \rangle =$$
$$\langle light\ color \rangle \times \langle base\ color\ of\ surface \rangle \times$$
$$(\langle light\ direction \rangle \bullet \langle orientation\ of\ a\ surface \rangle)$$

You can see that four pieces of information are needed to calculate this equation: (1) light color, (2) a surface base color, (3) light direction, and (4) surface orientation. In addition, *<light direction>* and *<surface orientation>* must be normalized (1.0 in length).

Processing in the Vertex Shader

From the four pieces of information necessary for Equation 8.4, the base color of a surface is passed as a_Color at line 5 in the following code, and the surface orientation is passed as a_Normal at line 6. The light color is passed using u_LightColor at line 8, and the light direction is passed as u_LightDirection at line 9. You should note that only u_LightDirection is passed in the world coordinate[9] system and has been normalized in the JavaScript code for ease of handling. This avoids the overhead of normalizing it every time it's used in the vertex shader:

```
4   'attribute vec4 a_Position;\n' +
5   'attribute vec4 a_Color;\n' +              <-(2) surface base color
6   'attribute vec4 a_Normal;\n' +   // Normal <-(4) surface orientation
7   'uniform mat4 u_MvpMatrix;\n' +
8   'uniform vec3 u_LightColor;\n' +   // Light color              <-(1)
9   'uniform vec3 u_LightDirection;\n' + // world coordinate,normalized <-(3)
10  'varying vec4 v_Color;\n' +
11  'void main() {\n' +
12  '  gl_Position = u_MvpMatrix * a_Position ;\n' +
13     // Make the length of the normal 1.0
14  '  vec3 normal = normalize(vec3(a_Normal));\n' +
15     // Dot product of light direction and orientation of a surface
16  '  float nDotL = max(dot(u_LightDirection, normal), 0.0);\n' +
17     // Calculate the color due to diffuse reflection
18  '  vec3 diffuse = u_LightColor * vec3(a_Color) * nDotL;\n' +
19  '  v_Color = vec4(diffuse, a_Color.a);\n' +
20  '}\n';
```

Once the necessary information is available, you can carry out the calculation. First, the vertex shader normalizes the vector at line 14. Technically, because the normal used in this sample program is 1.0 in length, this process is not necessary. However, it is good practice, so it is performed here:

---

[9] In this book, the light effect with shading is calculated in the world coordinate system (see Appendix G, "World Coordinate System Versus Local Coordinate System") because it is simpler to program and more intuitive with respect to the light direction. It is also safe to calculate it in the view coordinate system but more complex.

```
14   '   vec3 normal = normalize(vec3(a_Normal));\n' +
```

Although a_Normal is of type vec4, a normal represents a direction and uses only the x, y, and z components. So you extract these components with .xyz and then normalize. If you pass the normal using a type vec3, this process is not necessary. However, it is passed as a type vec4 in this code because a vec4 will be needed when we extend the code for the next example. We will explain the details in a later sample program. As you can see, GLSL ES provides normalize(), a built-in function to normalize a vector specified as its argument. In the program, the normalized normal is stored in the variable normal for use later.

Next, you need to calculate the dot product ⟨*light direction*⟩ • ⟨*surface orientation*⟩ from Equation 8.4. The light direction is stored in u_LightDirection. Because it is already normalized, you can use it as is. The orientation of the surface is the normal that was normalized at line 14. The dot product "•" can then be calculated using the built-in function dot(), which again is provided by GLSL ES and returns the dot product of the two vectors specified as its arguments. That is, calling dot(u_LightDirection, normal) performs ⟨*light direction*⟩ • ⟨*surface orientation*⟩ . This calculation is performed at line 16.

```
16   '   float nDotL = max(dot(u_LightDirection, normal), 0.0);\n' +
```

Once the dot product is calculated, if the result is positive, it is assigned to nDotL. If it is negative then 0.0 is assigned. The function max() used here is a GLSL ES built-in function that returns the greater value from its two arguments.

A negative dot product means that θ in cos θ is more than 90 degrees. Because θ is the angle between the light direction and the surface orientation, a value of θ greater than 90 degrees means that light hits the surface on its back face (see Figure 8.11). This is the same as no light hitting the front face, so 0.0 is assigned to nDotL.

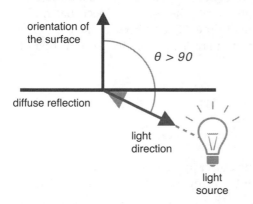

Figure 8.11   A normal and light in case θ is greater than 90 degrees

Now that the preparation is completed, you can calculate Equation 8.4. This is performed at line 18, which is a direct implementation of Equation 8.4. a_Color, which is of type vec4 and holds the RGBA values, is converted to a vec3 (.rgb) because its transparency (alpha value) is not used in lighting.

In fact, transparency of an object's surface has a significant effect on the color of the surface. However, because the calculation of the light passing through an object is complicated, we ignore transparency and don't use the alpha value in this program:

```
18   '  vec3 diffuse = u_LightColor * vec3(a_Color) * nDotL;\n' +
```

Once calculated, the result, `diffuse`, is assigned to the varying variable `v_Color` at line 19. Because `v_Color` is of type `vec4`, `diffuse` is also converted to `vec4` with `1.0`:

```
19   '  v_Color = vec4(diffuse, 1.0);\n' +
```

The result of the processing steps above is that a color, depending on the direction of the vertex's normal, is calculated, passed to the fragment shader, and assigned to `gl_FragColor`. In this case, because you use a directional light, vertices that make up the same surface are the same color, so each surface will be a solid color.

That completes the vertex shader code. Let's now take a look at how the JavaScript program passes the data needed for Equation 8.4 to the vertex shader.

Processing in the JavaScript Program

The light color (`u_LightColor`) and the light direction (`u_LightDirection`) are passed to the vertex shader from the JavaScript program. Because the light color is white (1.0, 1.0, 1.0), it is simply written to `u_LightColor` using `gl.uniform3f()`:

```
69   // set the Light color (white)
70   gl.uniform3f(u_LightColor, 1.0, 1.0, 1.0);
```

The next step is to set up the light direction, which must be passed after normalization, as discussed before. You can normalize it with the `normalize()` function for `Vector3` objects that is provided in `cuon-matrix.js`. Usage is simple: Create the `Vector3` object that specifies the vector you want to normalize as its argument (line 72), and invoke the `normalize()` method on the object. Note that the notation in JavaScript is different from that of GLSL ES:

```
71   // Set the light direction (in the world coordinate)
72   var lightDirection = new Vector3([0.5, 3.0, 4.0]);
73   lightDirection.normalize();       // Normalize
74   gl.uniform3fv(u_LightDirection, lightDirection.elements);
```

The result is stored in the `elements` property of the object in an array of type `Float32Array` and then assigned to `u_LightDirection` using `gl.uniform3fv()` (line 74).

Finally, the normal data is written in `initVertexBuffers()`, defined at line 89. Actual normal data is stored in the array `normals` at line 118 per vertex along with the color data, as in `ColoredCube.js`. Data is assigned to `a_Normal` in the vertex shader by invoking `initArrayBuffer()` at line 140:

```
140 if(!initArrayBuffer(gl, 'a_Normal', normals, 3, gl.FLOAT)) return -1;
```

`initArrayBuffer()`, which was also used in `ColoredCube`, assigns the array specified by the third argument (`normals`) to the attribute variable that has the name specified by the second argument (`a_Normal`).

Add Shading Due to Ambient Light

Although at this stage you have successfully added lighting to the scene, as you can see from Figure 8.9, when you run `LightedCube`, the cube is a little different from the box in the real world. In particular, the surface on the opposite side of the light source appears almost black and not clearly visible. You can see this problem more clearly if you animate the cube. Try the sample program `LightedCube_animation` (see Figure 8.12) to see the problem more clearly.

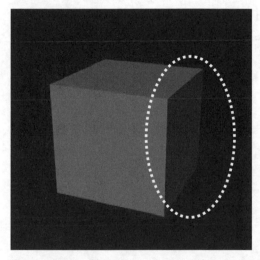

Figure 8.12 The result of LightedCube_animation

Although the scene is correctly lit as the result of Equation 8.4, our real-world experiences tells us that something isn't right. It is unusual to see such a sharp effect because, in the real world, surfaces such as the back face of the cube are also lit by diffuse or reflected light. The ambient light described in the previous section represents this indirect light and can be used to make the scene more lifelike. Let's add that to the scene and see if the effect is more realistic. Because ambient light models the light that hits an object from all directions with constant intensity, the surface color due to the reflection is determined only by the light color and the base color of the surface. The formula that calculates this was shown as Equation 8.2. Let's see it again:

$$\langle surface\ color\ by\ ambient\ reflection \rangle =$$
$$\langle light\ color \rangle \times \langle base\ color\ of\ surface \rangle$$

Let's try to add the color due to ambient light described by this formula to the sample program LightedCube. To do this, use Equation 8.3 shown here:

$$\langle \textit{surface color by diffuse and ambient reflection} \rangle =$$
$$\langle \textit{surface color by diffuse reflection} \rangle + \langle \textit{surface color by ambient reflection} \rangle$$

Ambient light is weak because it is the light reflected by other objects like the walls. For example, if the ambient light color is (0.2, 0.2, 0.2) and the base color of a surface is red, or (1.0, 0.0, 0.0), then, from Equation 8.2, the surface color due to the ambient light is (0.2, 0.0, 0.0). For example, if there is a white box in a blue room—that is, the base color of the surface is (1.0, 1.0, 1.0) and the ambient light is (0.0, 0.0, 0.2)—the color becomes slightly blue (0.0, 0.0, 0.2).

Let's implement the effect of ambient reflection in the sample program LightedCube_ambient, which results in the cube shown in Figure 8.13. You can see that the surface that the light does not directly hit is now also slightly colored and more closely resembles the cube in the real world.

Figure 8.13   LightedCube_ambient

Sample Program (LightedCube_ambient.js)

Listing 8.2 illustrates the sample program. Because it is almost the same as LightedCube, only the modified parts are shown.

Listing 8.2   LightedCube_ambient.js

```
1 // LightedCube_ambient.js
2 // Vertex shader program
 . . .
```

```
 8   'uniform vec3 u_LightColor;\n' +        // Light color
 9   'uniform vec3 u_LightDirection;\n' + // World coordinate, normalized
10   'uniform vec3 u_AmbientLight;\n' +     // Color of an ambient light
11   'varying vec4 v_Color;\n' +
12   'void main() {\n' +
  ...
16       // The dot product of the light direction and the normal
17   '   float nDotL = max(dot(lightDirection, normal), 0.0);\n' +
18       // Calculate the color due to diffuse reflection
19   '   vec3 diffuse = u_LightColor * a_Color.rgb * nDotL;\n' +
20       // Calculate the color due to ambient reflection
21   '   vec3 ambient = u_AmbientLight * a_Color.rgb;\n' +
22       // Add surface colors due to diffuse and ambient reflection
23   '   v_Color = vec4(diffuse + ambient, a_Color.a);\n' +
24   '}\n';
  ...
36 function main() {
  ...
64   // Get the storage locations of uniform variables and so on
  ...
68   var u_AmbientLight = gl.getUniformLocation(gl.program, 'u_AmbientLight');
  ...
80   // Set the ambient light
81   gl.uniform3f(u_AmbientLight, 0.2, 0.2, 0.2);
  ...
95 }
```

u_AmbientLight at line 10 is added to the vertex shader to pass in the color of ambient light. After Equation 8.2 is calculated using it and the base color of the surface (a_Color), the result is stored in the variable ambient (line 21). Now that both diffuse and ambient are determined, the surface color is calculated at line 23 using Equation 8.3. The result is passed to v_Color, just like in LightedCube, and the surface is painted with this color.

As you can see, this program simply adds ambient at line 23, causing the whole cube to become brighter. This implements the effect of the ambient light hitting an object equally from all directions.

The examples so far have been able to handle static objects. However, because objects are likely to move within a scene, or the viewpoint changes, you have to be able to handle such transformations. As you will recall from Chapter 4, "More Transformations and Basic Animation," an object can be translated, scaled, or rotated using coordinate transformations. These transformations may also change the normal direction and require a recalculation of lighting as the scene changes. Let's take a look at how to achieve that.

Lighting the Translated-Rotated Object

The program `LightedTranslatedRotatedCube` uses a directional light source to light a cube that is rotated 90 degrees clockwise around the z-axis and translated 0.9 units in the y-axis direction. A part from a directional light as described in the previous section, the sample, `LightedCube_ambient`, uses diffuse reflection and ambient reflection and rotates and translates the cube. The result is shown in Figure 8.14.

Figure 8.14   LightedTranslatedRotatedCube

You saw in the previous section that the normal direction may change when coordinate transformations are applied. Figure 8.15 shows some examples of that. The leftmost figure in Figure 8.15 shows the cube used in this sample program looking along the negative direction of the z-axis. The only normal (1, 0, 0), which is toward the positive direction of the x-axis, is shown. Let's perform some coordinate transforms on this figure, which are the three figures on the right.

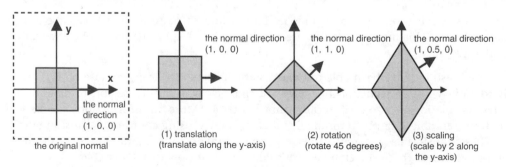

Figure 8.15   The changes of the normal direction due to coordinate transformations

You can see the following from Figure 8.15:

- The normal direction is **not changed** by a translation because the orientation of the object does not change.

- The normal direction is **changed** by a rotation according to the orientation of the object.

- Scaling has a more complicated effect on the normal. As you can see, the object in the rightmost figure is rotated i and then scaled two times only in the y-axis. In this case, the normal direction is **changed** because the orientation of the surface changes. On the other hand, if an object is scaled equally in all axes the normal direction is **not changed**. Finally, **even if** an object is scaled unequally, the normal direction may **not change**. For example, when the leftmost figure (the original normal) is scaled two times only in the y-axis direction, the normal direction does not change.

Obviously, the calculation of the normal under various transformations is complex, particularly when dealing with scaling. However, a mathematical technique can help.

The Magic Matrix: Inverse Transpose Matrix

As described in Chapter 4, the matrix that performs a coordinate transformation on an object is called a model matrix. The normal direction can be calculated by multiplying the normal by the **inverse transpose matrix** of a model matrix. The inverse transpose matrix is the matrix that transposes the inverse of a matrix.

The inverse of the matrix M is the matrix R, where both R*M and M*R become the identity matrix. The term **transpose** means the operation that exchanges rows and columns of a matrix. The details of this are explained in Appendix E, "The Inverse Transpose Matrix." For our purposes, it can be summarized simply using the following rule:

Rule: You can calculate the normal direction if you multiply the normal by the inverse transpose of the model matrix.

The inverse transpose matrix is calculated as follows:

1. Invert the original matrix.

2. Transpose the resulting matrix.

This can be carried out using convenient methods supported by the `Matrix4` object (see Table 8.1).

Table 8.1 Matrix4 Methods for an Inverse Transpose Matrix

Method	Description
`Matrix4.setInverseOf(m)`	Calculates the inverse of the matrix stored in *m* and stores the result in the `Matrix4` object, where *m* is a `Matrix4` object
`Matrix4.transpose()`	Transposes the matrix stored in the `Matrix4` object and writes the result back into the `Matrix4` object

Assuming that a model matrix is stored in `modelMatrix`, which is a `Matrix4` object, the following code snippet will get its inverse transpose matrix. The result is stored in the variable named `normalMatrix`, because it performs the coordinate transformation of a normal:

```
Matrix4 normalMatrix = new Matrix4();
// Calculate the model matrix
...
// Calculate the matrix to transform normal according to the model matrix
normalMatrix.setInverseOf(modelMatrix);
normalMatrix.transpose();
```

Now let's see the program `LightedTranslatedRotatedCube.js` that lights the cube, which is rotated 90 degrees clockwise around the z-axis and translated 0.9 along the y-axis, all using directional light. You'll use the cube that was transformed by the model matrix in `LightedCube_ambient` from the previous section.

Sample Program (LightedTranslatedRotatedCube.js)

Listing 8.3 shows the sample program. The changes from `LightedCube_ambient` are that `u_NormalMatrix` is added (line 8) to pass the matrix for coordinate transformation of the normal to the vertex shader, and the normal is transformed at line 16 using this matrix. `u_NormalMatrix` is calculated within the JavaScript.

Listing 8.3 LightedTranslatedRotatedCube.js

```
1 // LightedTranslatedRotatedCube.js
2 // Vertex shader program
3 var VSHADER_SOURCE =
  ...
6   'attribute vec4 a_Normal;\n' +
7   'uniform mat4 u_MvpMatrix;\n' +
8   'uniform mat4 u_NormalMatrix;\n'+    // Transformation matrix of normal
9   'uniform vec3 u_LightColor;\n' +      // Light color
10  'uniform vec3 u_LightDirection;\n' +  // World coordinate, normalized
11  'uniform vec3 u_AmbientLight;\n' +    // Ambient light color
12  'varying vec4 v_Color;\n' +
```

```
13    'void main() {\n' +
14    '  gl_Position = u_MvpMatrix * a_Position;\n' +
15       // Recalculate normal with normal matrix and make its length 1.0
16    '  vec3 normal = normalize(vec3(u_NormalMatrix * a_Normal));\n' +
17       // The dot product of the light direction and the normal
18    '  float nDotL = max(dot(u_LightDirection, normal), 0.0);\n' +
19       // Calculate the color due to diffuse reflection
20    '  vec3 diffuse = u_LightColor * a_Color.rgb * nDotL;\n' +
21       // Calculate the color due to ambient reflection
22    '  vec3 ambient = u_AmbientLight * a_Color.rgb;\n' +
23       // Add the surface colors due to diffuse and ambient reflection
24    '  v_Color = vec4(diffuse + ambient, a_Color.a);\n' +
25    '}\n';
      ...
37 function main() {
      ...
65    // Get the storage locations of uniform variables and so on
66    var u_MvpMatrix = gl.getUniformLocation(gl.program, 'u_MvpMatrix');
67    var u_NormalMatrix = gl.getUniformLocation(gl.program, 'u_NormalMatrix');
      ...
85    var modelMatrix = new Matrix4();  // Model matrix
86    var mvpMatrix = new Matrix4();     // Model view projection matrix
87    var normalMatrix = new Matrix4(); // Transformation matrix for normal
88
89    // Calculate the model matrix
90    modelMatrix.setTranslate(0, 1, 0); // Translate to y-axis direction
91    modelMatrix.rotate(90, 0, 0, 1);    // Rotate around the z-axis
92    // Calculate the view projection matrix
93    mvpMatrix.setPerspective(30, canvas.width/canvas.height, 1, 100);
94    mvpMatrix.lookAt(-7, 2.5, 6, 0, 0, 0, 0, 1, 0);
95    mvpMatrix.multiply(modelMatrix);
96    // Pass the model view projection matrix to u_MvpMatrix
97    gl.uniformMatrix4fv(u_MvpMatrix, false, mvpMatrix.elements);
98
99    // Calculate matrix to transform normal based on the model matrix
100   normalMatrix.setInverseOf(modelMatrix);
101   normalMatrix.transpose();
102   // Pass the transformation matrix for normal to u_NormalMatrix
103   gl.uniformMatrix4fv(u_NormalMatrix, false, normalMatrix.elements);
      ...
110 }
```

The processing in the vertex shader is almost the same as in `LightedCube_ambient`. The difference, in line with the preceding rule, is that you multiply `a_Normal` by the inverse transpose of the model matrix at line 16 instead of using it as-is:

```
15      // Recalculate normal with normal matrix and make its length 1.0
16    '   vec3 normal = normalize(vec3(u_NormalMatrix * a_Normal));\n' +
```

Because you passed `a_Normal` as type `vec4`, you can multiply it by `u_NormalMatrix`, which is of type `mat4`. You only need the x, y, and z components of the result of the multiplication, so the result is converted into type `vec3` with `vec3()`. It is also possible to use `.xyz` as before, or write `(u_NormalMatrix * a_Normal).xyz`. However, `vec3()` is used here for simplicity. Now that you understand how the shader calculates the normal direction resulting from the rotation and translation of the object, let's move on to the explanation of the JavaScript program. The key point here is the calculation of the matrix that will be passed to `u_NormalMatrix` in the vertex shader.

`u_NormalMatrix` is the inverse transpose of the model matrix, so the model matrix is first calculated at lines 90 and 91. Because this program rotates an object around the z-axis and translates it in the y-axis direction, you can use the `setTranslate()` and `rotate()` methods of a `Matrix4` object as described in Chapter 4. It is at lines 100 and 101 that the inverse transpose matrix is actually calculated. It is passed to `u_NormalMatrix` in the vertex shader at line 103, in the same way as `mvpMatrix` at line 97. The second argument of `gl.uniformMatrix4f()` specifies whether to transpose the matrix (Chapter 3):

```
 99     // Calculate matrix to transform normal based on the model matrix
100     normalMatrix.setInverseOf(modelMatrix);
101     normalMatrix.transpose();
102     // Pass the normal transformation matrix to u_NormalMatrix
103     gl.uniformMatrix4fv(u_NormalMatrix, false, normalMatrix.elements);
```

When run, the output is similar to Figure 8.14. As you can see, the shading is the same as `LightedCube_ambient` with the cube translated in the y-axis direction. That is because (1) the translation doesn't change the normal direction, (2) neither does the rotation by 90 degrees, because the rotation simply switches the surfaces of the cube, (3) the light direction of the directional light does not change regardless of the position of the object, and (4) diffuse reflection reflects the light in all directions with equal intensity.

You now have a good understanding of the basics of how to implement light and shade in 3D graphics. Let's build on this by exploring another type of light source: the point light.

Using a Point Light Object

In contrast to a directional light, the direction of the light from a point light source differs at each position in the 3D scene (see Figure 8.16). So, when calculating shading, you need to calculate the light direction at the specific position on the surface where the light hits.

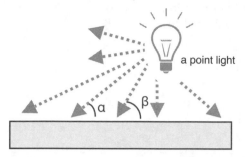

a point light

Figure 8.16 The direction of a point light varies by position

In the previous sample programs, you calculated the color at each vertex by passing the normal and the light direction for each vertex. You will use the same approach here, but because the light direction changes, you need to pass the position of the light source and then calculate the light direction at each vertex position.

Here, you construct the sample program PointLightedCube that displays a red cube lit with white light from a point light source. We again use diffuse reflection and ambient reflection. The result is shown in Figure 8.17, which is a version of LightedCube_ambient from the previous section but now lit with a point light.

Figure 8.17 PointLightedCube

Sample Program (PointLightedCube.js)

Listing 8.4 shows the sample program in which only the vertex shader is changed from LightedCube_ambient. The variable u_ModelMatrix for passing the model matrix and the variable u_LightPosition representing the light position are added. Note that because you use a point light in this program, you will use the light position instead of the light direction. Also, to make the effect easier to see, we have enlarged the cube.

Listing 8.4 PointLightedCube.js

```
1 // PointLightedCube.js
2 // Vertex shader program
3 var VSHADER_SOURCE =
4   'attribute vec4 a_Position;\n' +
  ...
8   'uniform mat4 u_ModelMatrix;\n' +  // Model matrix
9   'uniform mat4 u_NormalMatrix;\n' + // Transformation matrix of normal
10   'uniform vec3 u_LightColor;\n' +   // Light color
11   'uniform vec3 u_LightPosition;\n' +  // Position of the light source (in the
                                         ➥world coordinate system)
12   'uniform vec3 u_AmbientLight;\n' +   // Ambient light color
13   'varying vec4 v_Color;\n' +
14   'void main() {\n' +
15   '  gl_Position = u_MvpMatrix * a_Position;\n' +
16   '  // Recalculate normal with normal matrix and make its length 1.0
17   '  vec3 normal = normalize(vec3(u_NormalMatrix * a_Normal));\n' +
18     // Calculate the world coordinate of the vertex
19   '  vec4 vertexPosition = u_ModelMatrix * a_Position;\n' +
20     // Calculate the light direction and make it 1.0 in length
21   '  vec3 lightDirection = normalize(u_LightPosition - vec3(vertexPosition));\n' +
22     // The dot product of the light direction and the normal
23   '  float nDotL = max(dot( lightDirection, normal), 0.0);\n' +
24     // Calculate the color due to diffuse reflection
25   '  vec3 diffuse = u_LightColor * a_Color.rgb * nDotL;\n' +
26     // Calculate the color due to ambient reflection
27   '  vec3 ambient = u_AmbientLight * a_Color.rgb;\n' +
28     // Add surface colors due to diffuse and ambient reflection
29   '  v_Color = vec4(diffuse + ambient, a_Color.a);\n' +
30   '}\n';
  ...
42 function main() {
  ...
70   // Get the storage locations of uniform variables and so on
71   var u_ModelMatrix = gl.getUniformLocation(gl.program, 'u_ModelMatrix');
  ...
74   var u_LightColor = gl.getUniformLocation(gl.program,'u_LightColor');
75   var u_LightPosition = gl.getUniformLocation(gl.program, 'u_LightPosition');
  ...
82   // Set the light color (white)
```

```
83   gl.uniform3f(u_LightColor, 1.0, 1.0, 1.0);
84   // Set the position of the light source (in the world coordinate)
85   gl.uniform3f(u_LightPosition, 0.0, 3.0, 4.0);
     ...
89   var modelMatrix = new Matrix4();   // Model matrix
90   var mvpMatrix = new Matrix4();      // Model view projection matrix
91   var normalMatrix = new Matrix4();  // Transformation matrix for normal
92
93   // Calculate the model matrix
94   modelMatrix.setRotate(90, 0, 1, 0); // Rotate around the y-axis
95   // Pass the model matrix to u_ModelMatrix
96   gl.uniformMatrix4fv(u_ModelMatrix, false, modelMatrix.elements);
     ...
```

The key differences in the processing within the vertex shader are at line 19 and 21. At line 19, you transform the vertex coordinates into world coordinates in order to calculate the light direction at the vertex coordinates. Because a point light emits light in all directions from its position, the light direction at a vertex is the result of subtracting the vertex position from the light source position. Because the light position is passed to the variable u_LightPosition using world coordinates at line 11, you also have to convert the vertex coordinates into world coordinates to calculate the light direction. The light direction is then calculated at line 21. Note that it is normalized with normalize() so that it will be 1.0 in length. Using the resulting light direction (lightDirection), the dot product is calculated at line 23 and then the surface color at each vertex is calculated based on this light direction.

If you run this program, you will see a more realistic result, as shown in Figure 8.17. Although this result is more realistic, a closer look reveals an artifact: There are unnatural lines of shade on the cube's surface (see Figure 8.18). You can see this more easily if the cube rotates as it does when you load PointLightedCube_animation.

Figure 8.18 The unnatural appearance when processing the point light at each vertex

This comes about because of the interpolation process discussed in Chapter 5, "Using Colors and Texture Images." As you will remember, the WebGL system interpolates the colors between vertices based on the colors you supply at the vertices. However, because the direction of light from a point light source varies by position to shade naturally, you have to calculate the color at every position the light hits instead of just at each vertex. You can see this problem more clearly using a sphere illuminated by a point light, as shown in Figure 8.19.

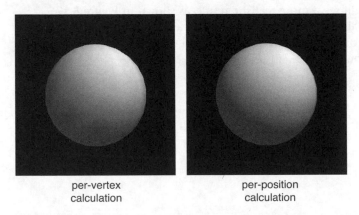

per-vertex   per-position
calculation   calculation

Figure 8.19 The spheres illuminated by a point light

As you can see, the border between the brighter parts and darker parts is unnatural in the left figure. If the effect is hard to see on the page, the left figure is PointLightedSphere, and the right is PointLightedSphere_perFragment. We will describe how to draw them correctly in the next section.

More Realistic Shading: Calculating the Color per Fragment

At first glance, it may seem daunting to have to calculate the color at every position on a cube surface where the light hits. However, essentially it means calculating the color **per fragment**, so the power of the fragment shader can now be used.

This sample program you will use is `PointLightedCube_perFragment`, and its result is shown in Figure 8.20.

Figure 8.20   PointLightedCube_perFragment

Sample Program (PointLightedCube_perFragment.js)

The sample program, which is based on `PointLightedCube.js`, is shown in Listing 8.5. Only the shader code has been modified and, as you can see, there is less processing in the vertex shader and more processing in the fragment shader.

Listing 8.5   PointLightedCube_perFragment.js

```
 1 // PointLightedCube_perFragment.js
 2 // Vertex shader program
 3 var VSHADER_SOURCE =
 4   'attribute vec4 a_Position;\n' +
   ...
 8   'uniform mat4 u_ModelMatrix;\n' +  // Model matrix
 9   'uniform mat4 u_NormalMatrix;\n' + // Transformation matrix of normal
10   'varying vec4 v_Color;\n' +
11   'varying vec3 v_Normal;\n' +
12   'varying vec3 v_Position;\n' +
13   'void main() {\n' +
```

```
14   '  gl_Position = u_MvpMatrix * a_Position;\n' +
15      // Calculate the vertex position in the world coordinate
16   '  v_Position = vec3(u_ModelMatrix * a_Position);\n' +
17   '  v_Normal = normalize(vec3(u_NormalMatrix * a_Normal));\n' +
18   '  v_Color = a_Color;\n' +
19   '}\n';
20
21 // Fragment shader program
22 var FSHADER_SOURCE =
   ...
26   'uniform vec3 u_LightColor;\n' +      // Light color
27   'uniform vec3 u_LightPosition;\n' +   // Position of the light source
28   'uniform vec3 u_AmbientLight;\n' +    // Ambient light color
29   'varying vec3 v_Normal;\n' +
30   'varying vec3 v_Position;\n' +
31   'varying vec4 v_Color;\n' +
32   'void main() {\n' +
33      // Normalize normal because it's interpolated and not 1.0 (length)
34   '  vec3 normal = normalize(v_Normal);\n' +
35      // Calculate the light direction and make it 1.0 in length
36   '  vec3 lightDirection = normalize(u_LightPosition - v_Position);\n' +
37      // The dot product of the light direction and the normal
38   '  float nDotL = max(dot( lightDirection, normal), 0.0);\n' +
39      // Calculate the final color from diffuse and ambient reflection
40   '  vec3 diffuse = u_LightColor * v_Color.rgb * nDotL;\n' +
41   '  vec3 ambient = u_AmbientLight * v_Color.rgb;\n' +
42   '  gl_FragColor = vec4(diffuse + ambient, v_Color.a);\n' +
43   '}\n';
```

To calculate the color per fragment when light hits, you need (1) the position of the fragment in the world coordinate system and (2) the normal direction at the fragment position. You can utilize interpolation (Chapter 5) to obtain these values per fragment by just calculating them per vertex in the vertex shader and passing them via varying variables to the fragment shader.

These calculations are performed at lines 16 and 17, respectively, in the vertex shader. At line 16, the vertex position in world coordinates is calculated by multiplying each vertex coordinate by the model matrix. After assigning the vertex position to the varying variable v_Position, it will be interpolated between vertices and passed to the corresponding variable (v_Position) in the fragment shader as the world coordinate of the fragment. The normal calculation at line 17 is carried out for the same purpose.[10] By assigning the result to v_Normal, it is also interpolated and passed to the corresponding variable (v_Normal) in the fragment shader as the normal of the fragment.

Processing in the fragment shader is the same as that in the vertex shader of `PointLightedCube.js`. First, at line 34, the interpolated normal passed from the vertex shader is normalized. Its length may not be 1.0 anymore because of the interpolation. Next, at line 36, the light direction is calculated and normalized. Using these results, the dot product of the light direction and the normal is calculated at line 38. The colors due to the diffuse reflection and ambient reflection are calculated at lines 40 and 41 and added to get the fragment color, which is assigned to `gl_FragColor` at line 42.

If you have more than one light source, after calculating the color due to diffuse reflection and ambient reflection for each light source, you can obtain the final fragment color by adding all the colors. In other words, you only have to calculate Equation 8.3 as many times as the number of light sources.

Summary

This chapter explored how to light a 3D scene, the different types of light used, and how light is reflected and diffused through the scene. Using this knowledge, you then implemented the effects of different light sources to illuminate a 3D object and examined various shading techniques to improve the realism of the objects. As you have seen, a mastery of lighting is essential to adding realism to 3D scenes, which can appear flat and uninteresting if they're not correctly lit.

---

[10] In this sample program, this normalization is not necessary because all normals are passed to a_Normal with a length of 1.0. However, we normalize them here as good programming practice so the code is more generic.

Chapter 9

Hierarchical Objects

This chapter is the final one that describes the core features and how to program with WebGL. Once you've read it, you will have mastered the basics of WebGL and will have enough knowledge to create realistic and interactive 3D scenes. This chapter focuses on hierarchical objects, which are important because they allow you to progress beyond single objects like cubes or blocks to more complex objects that you can use for game characters, robots, and even humans.

The following key points are discussed in this chapter:

- Modeling complex connected structures such as a robot arm using a hierarchical structure.

- Drawing and manipulating hierarchical objects made up of multiple simpler objects.

- Combining model and rotation matrices to mimic joints such as elbow or wrist joints

- Internally implementing `initShaders()`, which you've used but not examined so far.

By the end of this chapter, you will have all the knowledge you need to create compelling 3D scenes populated by both simple and complex 3D objects.

Drawing and Manipulating Objects Composed of Other Objects

Until now, we have described how to translate and rotate a single object, such as a two-dimensional triangle or a three-dimensional cube. But many of the objects in 3D graphics, game characters, robots, and so on, consist of more than one object (or segment). For a simple example, a robot arm is shown in Figure 9.1. As you can see, this consists of multiple boxes. The program name is `MultiJointModel`. First, let's load the program and experiment by pressing the arrow, x, z, c, and v keys to understand what you will construct in the following sections.

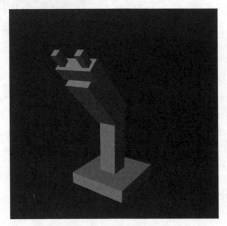

←→: arm1 rotation, ↑ ↓: joint1 rotation, xz: joint2(wrist) rotation, cv: finger rotation

Figure 9.1 A robot arm consisting of multiple objects

One of the key issues when drawing an object consisting of multiple objects (segments) is that you have to program to avoid conflicts when the segments move. This section will explore this issue by describing how to draw and manipulate a robot arm that consists of multiple segments. First, let's consider the structure of the human body from the shoulder to the fingertips to understand how to model our robot arm. An arm consists of multiple segments, such as the upper arm, lower arm, palm, and fingers, each of which is connected by a joint, as shown on the left of Figure 9.2.

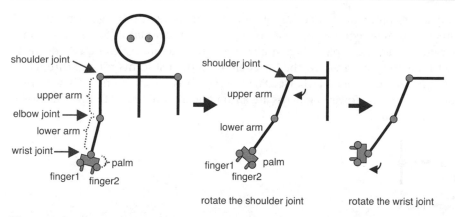

Figure 9.2 The structure and movement from the arm to the fingers

Each segment moves around a joint as follows:

- When you move the upper arm by rotating around the shoulder joint, depending on the upper arm movement, the lower arm, palm, and fingers move (the middle of Figure 9.2) accordingly.

- When you move the lower arm using an elbow joint, the palm and fingers move but the upper arm does not.

- When you move the palm using the wrist joint, both palm and fingers move but the upper and lower arm do not (the right of Figure 9.2).

- When you move fingers, the upper arm, lower arm, and palm do not move.

To summarize, when you move a segment, the segments located below it move, while the segments located above are not affected. In addition, all movement, including twisting, is actually rotation around a joint.

Hierarchical Structure

The typical method used to draw and manipulate the object with such features is to draw each part object (such as a box) in the order of the object's hierarchical structure from upper to lower, applying each model matrix (rotation matrix) at every joint. For example, in Figure 9.2, shoulder, elbow, wrist, and finger joints all have respective rotation matrices.

It is important to note that, unlike humans or robots, segments in 3D graphics are not physically joined. So if you inadvertently rotate the object corresponding to an upper arm at the shoulder joint, the lower parts would be left behind. When you rotate the shoulder joint, you should explicitly make the lower parts follow the movement. To do this, you need to rotate the lower elbow and wrist joints through the same angle that you rotate the shoulder joint.

It is straightforward to program so that the rotation of one segment propagates to the lower segments and simply requires that you use the same model matrix for the rotation of the lower segments. For example, when you rotate a shoulder joint through 30 degrees using one model matrix, you can draw the lower elbow and wrist joints rotated through 30 degrees using the same model matrix (see Figure 9.3). Thus, by changing only the angle of the shoulder rotation, the lower segments are automatically rotated to follow the movement of the shoulder joint.

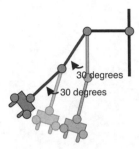

rotate the shoulder joint

Figure 9.3 The lower segments following the rotation of the upper segment

For more complex cases, such as when you want to rotate the elbow joint 10 degrees after rotating the shoulder joint 30 degrees, you can rotate the elbow joint by using the model matrix and rotating 10 degrees more than the shoulder-joint model matrix. This can be calculated by multiplying the shoulder-joint model matrix by a 10-degree rotation matrix, which we refer to as the "elbow-joint model matrix." The parts below the elbow will follow the movement of the elbow when drawn using this elbow-joint model matrix.

By programming in such a way, the upper segments are not affected by rotation of the lower segments. Thus, the upper segments will not move no matter how much the lower segments move.

Now that you have a good understanding of the principles involved when moving multi-segment objects, let's look at a sample program.

Single Joint Model

Let's begin with a simple single joint model. You will construct the program `JointModel` that draws a robot arm consisting of two parts that can be manipulated with the arrow keys. The screen shot and the hierarchy structure are shown on the left and right of Figure 9.4, respectively. This robot arm consists of arm1 and arm2, which are joined by joint1. You should imagine that the arm is raised above the shoulder and that arm1 is the upper part and arm2 the lower part. When you add the hand later, it will become clearer.

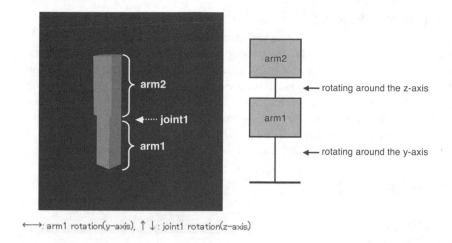

←——→: arm1 rotation(y-axis), ↑ ↓ : joint1 rotation(z-axis)

Figure 9.4   JointModel and the hierarchy structure used in the program

If you run the program, you will see that arm1 is rotated around the y-axis using the right and left arrow keys, and joint1 is rotated around the z-axis with the up and down arrow keys (Figure 9.5). When pressing the down arrow key, joint1 is rotated and arm2 leans forward, as shown on the left of Figure 9.5. Then if you press the right arrow key, arm1 is rotated, as shown on the right of Figure 9.5.

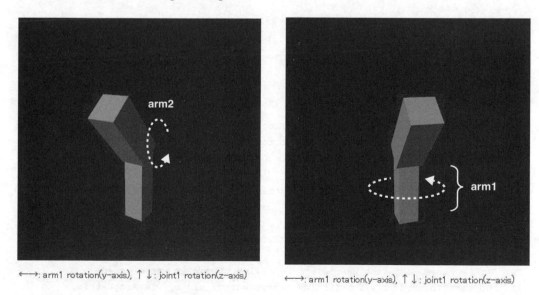

←——→: arm1 rotation(y-axis), ↑ ↓ : joint1 rotation(z-axis)   ←——→: arm1 rotation(y-axis), ↑ ↓ : joint1 rotation(z-axis)

Figure 9.5   The display change when pressing the arrow keys in JointModel

As you can see, the movement of arm2 by rotation of joint1 does not affect arm1. In contrast, arm2 is rotated if you rotate arm1.

Sample Program (JointModel.js)

`JointModel.js` is shown in Listing 9.1. The actual vertex shader is a little complicated because of the shading process and has been removed from the listing here to save space. However, if you are interested in how the lessons learned in the earlier part of the chapter are applied, please look at the full listing available by downloading the examples from the book website. The lighting used is a directional light source and simplified diffuse reflection, which makes the robot arm look more three-dimensional. However, as you can see, there are no special lighting calculations needed for this joint model, and all the code required to draw and manipulate the joint model is in the JavaScript program.

Listing 9.1 JointModel.js

```
 1 // JointModel.js
 2 // Vertex shader program
 3 var VSHADER_SOURCE =
 4   'attribute vec4 a_Position;\n' +
 5   'attribute vec4 a_Normal;\n' +
 6   'uniform mat4 u_MvpMatrix;\n' +
   ...
 9   'void main() {\n' +
10   '  gl_Position = u_MvpMatrix * a_Position;\n' +
11   // Shading calculation to make the arm look three-dimensional
   ...
17   '}\n';
   ...
29 function main() {
   ...
46   // Set the vertex coordinate.
47   var n = initVertexBuffers(gl);
   ...
57   // Get the storage locations of uniform variables
58   var u_MvpMatrix = gl.getUniformLocation(gl.program, 'u_MvpMatrix');
59   var u_NormalMatrix = gl.getUniformLocation(gl.program, 'u_NormalMatrix');
   ...
65   // Calculate the view projection matrix
66   var viewProjMatrix = new Matrix4();
67   viewProjMatrix.setPerspective(50.0, canvas.width / canvas.height, 1.0, 100.0);
68   viewProjMatrix.lookAt(20.0, 10.0, 30.0, 0.0, 0.0, 0.0, 0.0, 1.0, 0.0);
69
70   // Register the event handler to be called when keys are pressed
71   document.onkeydown = function(ev){ keydown(ev, gl, n, viewProjMatrix,
                                       ➥u_MvpMatrix, u_NormalMatrix); };
72   // Draw robot arm
73   draw(gl, n, viewProjMatrix, u_MvpMatrix, u_NormalMatrix);
74 }
```

```
 75
 76 var ANGLE_STEP = 3.0;    // The increments of rotation angle (degrees)
 77 var g_arm1Angle = 90.0;  // The rotation angle of arm1 (degrees)
 78 var g_joint1Angle = 0.0; // The rotation angle of joint1 (degrees)
 79
 80 function keydown(ev, gl, n, viewProjMatrix, u_MvpMatrix, u_NormalMatrix) {
 81   switch (ev.keyCode) {
 82     case 38: // Up arrow key -> positive rotation of joint1 (z-axis)
 83       if (g_joint1Angle < 135.0) g_joint1Angle += ANGLE_STEP;
 84       break;
 85     case 40: // Down arrow key -> negative rotation of joint1 (z-axis)
 86       if (g_joint1Angle > -135.0) g_joint1Angle -= ANGLE_STEP;
 87       break;
     ...
 91     case 37: // Left arrow key -> negative rotation of arm1 (y-axis)
 92       g_arm1Angle = (g_arm1Angle - ANGLE_STEP) % 360;
 93       break;
 94     default: return;
 95   }
 96   // Draw the robot arm
 97   draw(gl, n, viewProjMatrix, u_MvpMatrix, u_NormalMatrix);
 98 }
 99
100 function initVertexBuffers(gl) {
101   // Vertex coordinates
    ...
148 }
    ...
174 // Coordinate transformation matrix
175 var g_modelMatrix = new Matrix4(), g_mvpMatrix = new Matrix4();
176
177 function draw(gl, n, viewProjMatrix, u_MvpMatrix, u_NormalMatrix) {
    ...
181   // Arm1
182   var arm1Length = 10.0; // Length of arm1
183   g_modelMatrix.setTranslate(0.0, -12.0, 0.0);
184   g_modelMatrix.rotate(g_arm1Angle, 0.0, 1.0, 0.0);   // Rotate y-axis
185   drawBox(gl, n, viewProjMatrix, u_MvpMatrix, u_NormalMatrix); // Draw
186
187   // Arm2
188   g_modelMatrix.translate(0.0, arm1Length, 0.0);     // Move to joint1
189   g_modelMatrix.rotate(g_joint1Angle, 0.0, 0.0, 1.0);// Rotate z-axis
190   g_modelMatrix.scale(1.3, 1.0, 1.3); // Make it a little thicker
191   drawBox(gl, n, viewProjMatrix, u_MvpMatrix, u_NormalMatrix); // Draw
192 }
```

```
193
194 var g_normalMatrix = new Matrix4(); // Transformation matrix for normal
195
196 // Draw a cube
197 function drawBox(gl, n, viewProjMatrix, u_MvpMatrix, u_NormalMatrix) {
198   //Calculate the model view project matrix and pass it to u_MvpMatrix
199   g_mvpMatrix.set(viewProjMatrix);
200   g_mvpMatrix.multiply(g_modelMatrix);
201   gl.uniformMatrix4fv(u_MvpMatrix, false, g_mvpMatrix.elements);
202   // Calculate the normal transformation matrix and pass it to u_NormalMatrix
203   g_normalMatrix.setInverseOf(g_modelMatrix);
204   g_normalMatrix.transpose();
205   gl.uniformMatrix4fv(u_NormalMatrix, false, g_normalMatrix.elements);
206   // Draw
207   gl.drawElements(gl.TRIANGLES, n, gl.UNSIGNED_BYTE, 0);
208 }
```

The function `main()` from line 29 follows the same structure as before, with the first major difference being the `initVertexBuffers()` function call at line 47. In `initVertexBuffers()`, the vertex data for arm1 and arm2 are written into the appropriate buffer objects. Until now, you've been using cubes, with each side being 2.0 in length and the origin at the center of the cube. Now, to better model the arm, you will use a cuboid like that shown in the left side of Figure 9.6. The cuboid has its origin at the center of the bottom surface and is 3.0 by 3.0 and 10.0 units in height. By setting the origin at the center of the bottom surface, its rotation around the z-axis is the same as that of joint1 in Figure 9.5, making it convenient to program. Both arm1 and arm2 are drawn using this cuboid.

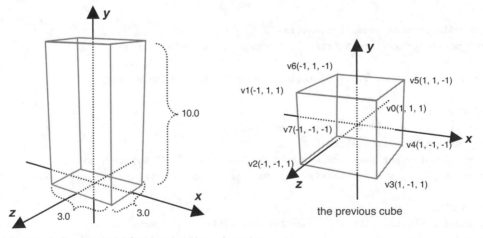

Figure 9.6   A cuboid for drawing the robot arm

From lines 66 to 68, a view projection matrix (`viewProjMatrix`) is calculated with the specified viewing volume, the eye position, and the view direction.

Because the robot arm in this program is moved by using the arrow keys, the event handler `keydown()` is registered at line 71:

```
70   // Register the event handler to be called when keys are pressed
71   document.onkeydown = function(ev){ keydown(ev, gl, n, viewProjMatrix,
                                    ➥u_MvpMatrix, u_NormalMatrix); };
72   // Draw the robot arm
73   draw(gl, n, viewProjMatrix, u_MvpMatrix, u_NormalMatrix);
```

The `keydown()` function itself is defined at line 80. Before that, at lines 76, 77, and 78, the definition of global variables used in `keydown()` is defined:

```
76 var ANGLE_STEP = 3.0;     // The increments of rotation angle (degrees)
77 var g_arm1Angle = -90.0; // The rotation angle of arm1 (degrees)
78 var g_joint1Angle = 0.0; // The rotation angle of joint1 (degrees)
79
80 function keydown(ev, gl, n, u_MvpMatrix, u_NormalMatrix) {
81   switch (ev.keyCode) {
82   case 38: // Up arrow key -> the positive rotation of joint1 (z-axis)
83     if (g_joint1Angle < 135.0) g_joint1Angle += ANGLE_STEP;
84     break;
...
88   case 39: // Right arrow key -> the positive rotation of arm1 (y-axis)
89     g_arm1Angle = (g_arm1Angle + ANGLE_STEP) % 360;
90     break;
...
95   }
96   // Draw the robot arm
97   draw(gl, n, u_MvpMatrix, u_NormalMatrix);
98 }
```

ANGLE_STEP at line 76 is used to control how many degrees arm1 and joint1 are rotated each time the arrow keys are pressed and is set at 3.0 degrees. g_arm1Angle (line 77) and g_joint1Angle (line 78) are variables that store the current rotation angle of arm1 and joint1, respectively (see Figure 9.7).

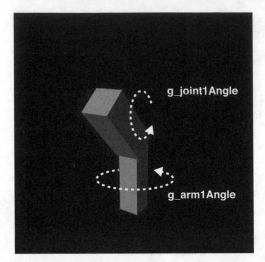

g_joint1Angle

g_arm1Angle

Figure 9.7   g_joint1Angle and g_arm1Angle

The keydown() function, from line 80, increases or decreases the value of the rotation angle of arm1 (g_arm1Angle) or joint1 (g_joint1Angle) by ANGLE_STEP, according to which key is pressed. joint1 can only be rotated through the range from –135 degrees to 135 degrees so that arm2 does not interfere with arm1. Then the whole robot arm is drawn at line 97 using the function draw().

Draw the Hierarchical Structure (draw())

The draw() function draws the robotic arm according to its hierarchical structure and is defined at line 177. Two global variables, g_modelMatrix and g_mvpMatrix, are created at line 175 and will be used in both draw() and drawBox():

```
174 // Coordinate transformation matrix
175 var g_modelMatrix = new Matrix4(), g_mvpMatrix = new Matrix4();
176
177 function draw(gl, n, viewProjMatrix, u_MvpMatrix, u_NormalMatrix) {
    ...
181    // Arm1
182    var arm1Length = 10.0; // Length of arm1
183    g_modelMatrix.setTranslate(0.0, -12.0, 0.0);
184    g_modelMatrix.rotate(g_arm1Angle, 0.0, 1.0, 0.0); // Rotate y-axis
185    drawBox(gl, n, viewProjMatrix, u_MvpMatrix, u_NormalMatrix); // Draw
186
187    // Arm2
188    g_modelMatrix.translate(0.0, arm1Length, 0.0); // Move to joint1
189    g_modelMatrix.rotate(g_joint1Angle, 0.0, 0.0, 1.0); // Rotate z-axis
190    g_modelMatrix.scale(1.3, 1.0, 1.3);       // Make it a little thicker
191    drawBox(gl, n, viewProjMatrix, u_MvpMatrix, u_NormalMatrix); // Draw
192 }
```

As you can see, draw() draws the segments by using drawBox(), starting with the upper part (arm1) followed by the lower part (arm2).

When drawing each part, the same process is repeated: (1) translation (setTranslate(), translate()), (2) rotation (rotate()), and (3) drawing the part (drawBox()).

When drawing a hierarchical model performing a rotation, typically you will process from upper to lower in the order of (1) translation, (2) rotation, and (3) drawing segments.

arm1 is translated to (0.0, –12.0, 0.0) with setTranslate() at line 183 to move to an easily visible position. Because this arm is rotated around the y-axis, its model matrix (g_model-Matrix) is multiplied by the rotation matrix around the y-axis at line 184. g_arm1Angle is used here. Once arm1's coordinate transformation has been completed, you then draw using the drawBox() function.

Because arm2 is connected to the tip of arm1, as shown in Figure 9.7, it has to be drawn from the tip of arm1. This can be achieved by translating it along the y-axis in the positive direction by the length of arm1 (arm1Length) and applying the translation to the model matrix, which is used when drawing arm1 (g_modelMatrix).

This is done as shown in line 188, where the second argument of translate() is arm1Length. Also notice that the method uses translate() rather than setTranslate() because arm2 is drawn at the tip of arm1:

```
187    // Arm2
188    g_modelMatrix.translate(0.0, arm1Length, 0.0); // Move to joint1
189    g_modelMatrix.rotate(g_joint1Angle, 0.0, 0.0, 1.0); // Rotate z-axis
190    g_modelMatrix.scale(1.3, 1.0, 1.3); // Make it a little thicker
191    drawBox(gl, n, viewProjMatrix, u_MvpMatrix, u_NormalMatrix); // Draw
```

Line 189 handles the rotation of arm2 which, as can be seen, uses g_joint1Angle. You make arm2 a little thicker at line 190 by scaling it along the x and z direction. This makes it easier to distinguish between the two arm segments but is not essential to the robotic arm's movement.

Now, by updating g_arm1Angle and g_joint1Angle in keydown() as described in the previous section and then invoking draw(), arm1 is rotated by g_arm1Angle and arm2 is, in addition, rotated by g_joint1Angle.

The drawBox() function is quite simple. It calculates a model view project matrix and passes it to the u_MvpMatrix variable at lines 199 and 200. Then it just calculates the normal transformation matrix for shading from the model matrix, sets it to u_NormalMatrix at lines 203 and 204, and draws the cuboid in Figure 9.6 at line 207.

This basic approach, although used here for only a single joint, can be used for any complex hierarchical models simply by repeating the process steps used earlier.

Obviously, our simple robot arm, although modeled on a human arm, is more like a skeleton than a real arm. A more realistic model of a real arm would require the skin to be modeled, which is beyond the scope of this book. Please refer to the *OpenGL ES 2.0 Programming Guide* for more information about skinning.

A Multijoint Model

Here, you will extend `JointModel` to create `MultiJointModel`, which draws a multijoint robot arm consisting of two arm segments, a palm, and two fingers, all of which you can manipulate using the keyboard. As shown in Figure 9.8, we call the arm extending from the base arm1, the next segment arm2, and the joint between the two arms joint1. There is a palm at the tip of arm2. The joint between arm2 and the palm is called joint2. The two fingers attached at the end of the palm are respectively finger1 and finger2.

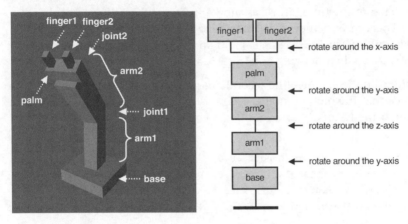

Figure 9.8 The hierarchical structure of MultiJointModel

Manipulation of arm1 and joint1 using the arrow keys is the same as `JointModel`. In addition, you can rotate joint2 (wrist) with the X and Z keys and move (rotate) the two fingers with the C and V keys. The variables controlling the rotation angle of each part are shown in Figure 9.9.

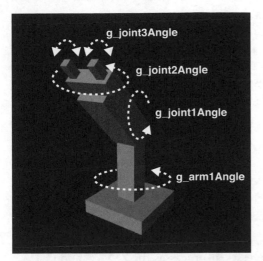

g_joint3Angle

g_joint2Angle

g_joint1Angle

g_arm1Angle

Figure 9.9 The variables controlling the rotation of segments

Sample Program (MultiJointModel.js)

This program is similar to `JointModel`, except for extensions to `keydown()` to handle the additional control keys, and `draw()`, which draws the extended hierarchical structure. First let's look at `keydown()` in Listing 9.2.

Listing 9.2 MultiJointModel.js (Code for Key Processing)

```
 1 // MultiJointModel.js
   ...
76 var ANGLE_STEP = 3.0;     // The increments of rotation angle (degrees)
77 var g_arm1Angle = 90.0;   // The rotation angle of arm1 (degrees)
78 var g_joint1Angle = 45.0; // The rotation angle of joint1 (degrees)
79 var g_joint2Angle = 0.0;  // The rotation angle of joint2 (degrees)
80 var g_joint3Angle = 0.0;  // The rotation angle of joint3 (degrees)
81
82 function keydown(ev, gl, n, viewProjMatrix, u_MvpMatrix, u_NormalMatrix) {
83   switch (ev.keyCode) {
84     case 40: // Up arrow key -> positive rotation of joint1 (z-axis)
   ...
95       break;
96     case 90: // Z key -> the positive rotation of joint2
97       g_joint2Angle = (g_joint2Angle + ANGLE_STEP) % 360;
98       break;
99     case 88: // X key -> the negative rotation of joint2
100       g_joint2Angle = (g_joint2Angle - ANGLE_STEP) % 360;
101       break;
```

```
102     case 86: // V key -> the positive rotation of joint3
103       if (g_joint3Angle < 60.0)  g_joint3Angle = (g_joint3Angle +
                                         ➥ANGLE_STEP) % 360;
104     break;
105     case 67: // C key -> the negative rotation of joint3
106       if (g_joint3Angle > -60.0) g_joint3Angle = (g_joint3Angle -
                                         ➥ANGLE_STEP) % 360;
107     break;
108   default: return;
109   }
110   // Draw the robot arm
111   draw(gl, n, viewProjMatrix, u_MvpMatrix, u_NormalMatrix);
112 }
```

keydown() is basically the same as that of JointAngle, but in addition to changing g_arm1Angle and g_joint1Angle based on key presses, it processes the Z, X, V, and C keys at lines 96, 99, 102, and 105. These key presses change g_joint2Angle, which is the rotation angle of joint2, and g_joint3Angle, which is the rotation angle of joint3, respectively. After changing them, it calls draw() at line 111 to draw the hierarchy structure. Let's take a look at draw() in Listing 9.3.

Although you are using the same cuboid for the base, arm1, arm2, palm, finger1, and finger2, the segments are different in width, height, and depth. To make it easy to draw these segments, let's extend drawBox() with three more arguments than that used in the single-joint model:

```
function drawBox(gl, n, width, height, depth, viewProjMatrix, u_MvpMatrix,
                                         ➥u_NormalMatrix)
```

By specifying the width, height, and depth using the third to fifth argument, this function draws a cuboid of the specified size with its origin at the center of the bottom surface.

Listing 9.3   MultiJointModel.js (Code for Drawing the Hierarchy Structure)

```
188 // Coordinate transformation matrix
189 var g_modelMatrix = new Matrix4(), g_mvpMatrix = new Matrix4();
190
191 function draw(gl, n, viewProjMatrix, u_MvpMatrix, u_NormalMatrix) {
192   // Clear color buffer and depth buffer
193   gl.clear(gl.COLOR_BUFFER_BIT | gl.DEPTH_BUFFER_BIT);
194
195   // Draw a base
196   var baseHeight = 2.0;
197   g_modelMatrix.setTranslate(0.0, -12.0, 0.0);
198   drawBox(gl, n, 10.0, baseHeight, 10.0, viewProjMatrix, u_MvpMatrix,
                                         ➥u_NormalMatrix);
```

```
199
200   // Arm1
201   var arm1Length = 10.0;
202   g_modelMatrix.translate(0.0, baseHeight, 0.0); // Move onto the base
203   g_modelMatrix.rotate(g_arm1Angle, 0.0, 1.0, 0.0);  // Rotation
204   drawBox(gl, n, 3.0, arm1Length, 3.0, viewProjMatrix, u_MvpMatrix,
                                        ↪u_NormalMatrix); // Draw
295
206   // Arm2
      ...
212   // A palm
213   var palmLength = 2.0;

      ...
218   // Move to the center of the tip of the palm
219   g_modelMatrix.translate(0.0, palmLength, 0.0);
220
221   // Draw finger1
222   pushMatrix(g_modelMatrix);
223     g_modelMatrix.translate(0.0, 0.0, 2.0);
224     g_modelMatrix.rotate(g_joint3Angle, 1.0, 0.0, 0.0);  // Rotation
225     drawBox(gl, n, 1.0, 2.0, 1.0, viewProjMatrix, u_MvpMatrix, u_NormalMatrix);
226   g_modelMatrix = popMatrix();
227
228   // Draw finger2
229   g_modelMatrix.translate(0.0, 0.0, -2.0);
230   g_modelMatrix.rotate(-g_joint3Angle, 1.0, 0.0, 0.0);  // Rotation
231   drawBox(gl, n, 1.0, 2.0, 1.0, viewProjMatrix, u_MvpMatrix, u_NormalMatrix);
232 }
233
234 var g_matrixStack = []; // Array for storing a matrix
235 function pushMatrix(m) { // Store the specified matrix to the array
236   var m2 = new Matrix4(m);
237   g_matrixStack.push(m2);
238 }
239
240 function popMatrix() { // Retrieve the matrix from the array
241   return g_matrixStack.pop();
242 }
```

The draw() function operates in the same way as in JointModel; that is, each part
is handled following the order of (1) translation, (2) rotation, and (3) draw (using
drawBox()). First, because the base is not rotated, after moving to the appropriate position at line 197, it draws a base there with drawBox(). The third to fifth arguments of
drawBox() specify a width of 10, height of 2, and depth of 10, which cause a flat stand to
be drawn.

The arm1, arm2, and palm are each drawn following the same order of (1) translation, (2) rotation, and (3) draw and by moving down the object hierarchy toward the lower level in the same manner as JointModel.

The main difference in this sample program is the drawing of finger1 and finger2 from line 222. Because they do not have a parent-child relationship, a little more care is needed. In particular, you have to pay attention to the contents of the model matrix. First, let's look at finger1, whose position is translated 2.0 along the z-axis direction from the center of the tip of the palm and rotated around the x-axis. finger1 can be drawn in the order of (1) translating, (2) rotating, and (3) drawing segments as before. The program is as follows:

```
g_modelMatrix.translate(0.0, 0.0, 2.0);
g_modelMatrix.rotate(g_joint3Angle, 1.0, 0.0, 0.0); // Rotation
drawBox(gl, n, 1.0, 2.0, 1.0, u_MvpMatrix, u_NormalMatrix);
```

Next, looking at finger2, if you follow the same procedure a problem occurs. finger2's intended position is a translation of –2.0 units along the z-axis direction from the center of the tip of the palm and rotated around the x-axis. However, because the model matrix has changed, if you draw finger2, it will be drawn at the tip of finger1.

Clearly, the solution is to restore the model matrix to its state before finger1 was drawn. A simple way to achieve this is to store the model matrix before drawing finger1 and retrieving it after drawing finger1. This is actually done at lines 222 and 226 and uses the functions pushMatrix() and popMatrix() to store the specified matrix and retrieve it. At line 222, you store the model matrix specified as pushMatrix()'s argument (g_modelMatrix). Then, after drawing finger1 at lines 223 to 225, you retrieve the old model matrix at line 226, with popMatrix(), and assign it to g_modelMatrix. Now, because the model matrix has reverted back, you can draw finger2 in the same way as before.

pushMatrix() and popMatrix() are shown next. pushMatrix() stores the matrix specified as its argument in an array named g_matrixStack at line 234. popMatrix() retrieves the matrix stored in g_matrixStack and returns it:

```
234 var g_matrixStack = [];  // Array for storing matrices
235 function pushMatrix(m) { // Store the specified matrix
236   var m2 = new Matrix4(m);
237   g_matrixStack.push(m2);
238 }
239
240 function popMatrix() { // Retrieve a matrix from the array
241   return g_matrixStack.pop();
242 }
```

This approach can be used to draw an arbitrarily long robot arm. It will scale when new segments are added to the hierarchy. You only need to use pushMatrix() and popMatrix() when the hierarchy structure is a sibling relation, not a parent-child relation.

Draw Segments (drawBox())

Finally, let's take a look at drawBox(), which draws the segments of the robot arm using the following arguments:

```
247 function drawBox(gl, n, width, height, depth, viewMatrix, u_MvpMatrix,
                                          ➥u_NormalMatrix) {
```

The third to fifth arguments, *width, height,* and *depth*, specify the width, height, and depth of the cuboid being drawn. As for the remaining argument, *viewMatrix* is a view matrix, and *u_MvpMatrix* and *u_NormalMatrix* are the arguments for setting the coordinate transformation matrices to the corresponding uniform variables in the vertex shader, just like JointModel.js. The model view projection matrix is passed to *u_MvpMatrix*, and the matrix for transforming the coordinates of the normal, described in the previous section, is passed to *u_NormalMatrix*.

The three-dimensional object used here, unlike JointModel, is a cube whose side is 1.0 unit long. Its origin is located at the center of the bottom surface so that you can easily rotate the arms, the palm, and the fingers. The function drawBox() is shown here:

```
244 var g_normalMatrix = new Matrix4();// Transformation matrix for normal
245
246 // Draw a cuboid
247 function drawBox(gl, n, width, height, depth, viewProjMatrix,
                                          ➥u_MvpMatrix, u_NormalMatrix) {
248   pushMatrix(g_modelMatrix);    // Save the model matrix
249     // Scale a cube and draw
250     g_modelMatrix.scale(width, height, depth);
251     // Calculate model view project matrix and pass it to u_MvpMatrix
252     g_mvpMatrix.set(viewProjMatrix);
253     g_mvpMatrix.multiply(g_modelMatrix);
254     gl.uniformMatrix4fv(u_MvpMatrix, false, g_mvpMatrix.elements);
255     // Calculate transformation matrix for normals and pass it to u_NormalMatrix
    . . .
259     // Draw
260     gl.drawElements(gl.TRIANGLES, n, gl.UNSIGNED_BYTE, 0);
261   g_modelMatrix = popMatrix();    // Retrieve the model matrix
262 }
```

As you can see, the model matrix is multiplied by a scaling matrix at line 250 so that the cube will be drawn with the size specified by *width, height,* and *depth*. Note that you store the model matrix at line 248 and retrieve it at line 261 using pushMatrix() and popMatrix(). Otherwise, when you draw arm2 after arm1, the scaling used for arm1 is left in the model matrix and affects the drawing of arm2. By retrieving the model matrix at line 261, which is saved at line 248, the model matrix reverts to the state before scaling was applied at line 250.

As you can see, the use of `pushMatrix()` and `popMatrix()` adds an extra degree of complexity but allows you to specify only one set of vertex coordinates and use scaling to create different cuboids. The alternative approach, using multiple objects specified by different sets of vertices, is also possible. Let's take a look at how you would program that.

Draw Segments (drawSegment())

In this section, we will explain how to draw segments by switching between buffer objects in which the vertex coordinates representing the shape of each segment are stored. Normally, you would need to specify the vertex coordinates, the normal, and the indices for each segment. However, in this example, because all segments are cuboids, you can share the normals and indices and simply specify the vertices for each segment. For each segment (the base, arm1, arm2, palm, and fingers), the vertices are stored in their respective object buffers, which are then switched when drawing the arm parts. Listing 9.4 shows the sample program.

Listing 9.4   MultiJointModel_segment.js

```
  1 // MultiJointModel_segment.js
    ...
 29 function main() {
    ...
 47   var n = initVertexBuffers(gl);
    ...
 57   // Get the storage locations of attribute and uniform variables
 58   var a_Position = gl.getAttribLocation(gl.program, 'a_Position');
    ...
 74   draw(gl, n, viewProjMatrix, a_Position, u_MvpMatrix, u_NormalMatrix);
 75 }
    ...
115 var g_baseBuffer = null;      // Buffer object for a base
116 var g_arm1Buffer = null;      // Buffer object for arm1
117 var g_arm2Buffer = null;      // Buffer object for arm2
118 var g_palmBuffer = null;      // Buffer object for a palm
119 var g_fingerBuffer = null;    // Buffer object for fingers
120
121 function initVertexBuffers(gl){
122   // Vertex coordinate (Coordinates of cuboids for all segments)
123   var vertices_base = new Float32Array([ // Base(10x2x10)
124      5.0, 2.0, 5.0, -5.0, 2.0, 5.0, -5.0, 0.0, 5.0,  5.0, 0.0, 5.0,
125      5.0, 2.0, 5.0,  5.0, 0.0, 5.0,  5.0, 0.0,-5.0,  5.0, 2.0,-5.0,
    ...
129      5.0, 0.0,-5.0, -5.0, 0.0,-5.0, -5.0, 2.0,-5.0,  5.0, 2.0,-5.0
130   ]);
131
```

```
132   var vertices_arm1 = new Float32Array([  // Arm1(3x10x3)
133      1.5, 10.0, 1.5, -1.5, 10.0, 1.5, -1.5,  0.0, 1.5,  1.5,  0.0, 1.5,
134      1.5, 10.0, 1.5,  1.5,  0.0, 1.5,  1.5,  0.0,-1.5,  1.5, 10.0,-1.5,
   ...
138      1.5,  0.0,-1.5, -1.5,  0.0,-1.5, 10.0,-1.5,  1.5, 10.0,-1.5
139   ]);
   ...
159   var vertices_finger = new Float32Array([  // Fingers(1x2x1)
   ...
166   ]);
167
168   // normals
169   var normals = new Float32Array([
   ...
176   ]);
177
178   // Indices of vertices
179   var indices = new Uint8Array([
180      0, 1, 2,   0, 2, 3,    // front
181      4, 5, 6,   4, 6, 7,    // right
   ...
185     20,21,22,  20,22,23     // back
186   ]);
187
188   // Write coords to buffers, but don't assign to attribute variables
189   g_baseBuffer = initArrayBufferForLaterUse(gl, vertices_base, 3, gl.FLOAT);
190   g_arm1Buffer = initArrayBufferForLaterUse(gl, vertices_arm1, 3, gl.FLOAT);
   ...
193   g_fingerBuffer = initArrayBufferForLaterUse(gl, vertices_finger, 3, gl.FLOAT);
   ...
196   // Write normals to a buffer, assign it to a_Normal, and enable it
197   if (!initArrayBuffer(gl, 'a_Normal', normals, 3, gl.FLOAT)) return null;
198
199   // Write indices to a buffer
200   var indexBuffer = gl.createBuffer();
   ...
205   gl.bindBuffer(gl.ELEMENT_ARRAY_BUFFER, indexBuffer);
206   gl.bufferData(gl.ELEMENT_ARRAY_BUFFER, indices, gl.STATIC_DRAW);
207
208   return indices.length;
209 }
   ...
255 function draw(gl, n, viewProjMatrix, a_Position, u_MvpMatrix, u_NormalMatrix) {
   ...
```

```
259   // Draw a base
260   var baseHeight = 2.0;
261   g_modelMatrix.setTranslate(0.0, -12.0, 0.0);
262   drawSegment(gl, n, g_baseBuffer, viewProjMatrix, a_Position,
                                        ↦u_MvpMatrix, u_NormalMatrix);
263
264   // Arm1
265   var arm1Length = 10.0;
266   g_modelMatrix.translate(0.0, baseHeight, 0.0); // Move to the tip of the base
267   g_modelMatrix.rotate(g_arm1Angle, 0.0, 1.0, 0.0);  // Rotate y-axis
268   drawSegment(gl, n, g_arm1Buffer, viewProjMatrix, a_Position,
                                        ↦u_MvpMatrix, u_NormalMatrix);
269
270   // Arm2
      ...
292   // Finger2
      ...
295   drawSegment(gl, n, g_fingerBuffer, viewProjMatrix, a_Position,
                                        ↦u_MvpMatrix, u_NormalMatrix);
296  }
      ...
310 // Draw segments
311 function drawSegment(gl, n, buffer, viewProjMatrix, a_Position,
                                        ↦u_MvpMatrix, u_NormalMatrix) {
312   gl.bindBuffer(gl.ARRAY_BUFFER, buffer);
313   // Assign the buffer object to the attribute variable
314   gl.vertexAttribPointer(a_Position, buffer.num, buffer.type, false, 0, 0);
315   // Enable the assignment
316   gl.enableVertexAttribArray(a_Position);
317
318   // Calculate the model view project matrix and set it to u_MvpMatrix
      ...
322   // Calculate matrix for normal and pass it to u_NormalMatrix
      ...
327   gl.drawElements(gl.TRIANGLES, n, gl.UNSIGNED_BYTE, 0);
328 }
```

The key points in this program are (1) creating the separate buffer objects that contain the vertex coordinates for each segment, (2) before drawing each segment, assigning the corresponding buffer object to the attribute variable a_Position, and (3) enabling the buffer and then drawing the segment.

The main() function from line 29 in the JavaScript code follows the same steps as before. Switching between buffers for the different segments is added to initVertexBuffers(), called at line 47. The stored location of a_Position is retrieved at line 58, and then draw() is called at line 73.

Let's examine initVertex(), defined at line 121. Lines 115 to 119 declare the buffer objects as global variables, used to store the vertex coordinates of each segment. Within the function, one of the main differences from MultiJointModel.js is the definition of the vertex coordinates from line 123. Because you are not using a single cuboid transformed differently for the different segments, you need to define the vertex coordinates for all the parts separately (for example, the base (vertices_base) at line 123, coordinates for arm1 (vertices_arm1), at line 132. The actual creation of the buffer objects for each part occurs in the function initArrayBufferForLaterUse() from line 189 to 193. This function is shown here:

```
211 function initArrayBufferForLaterUse(gl, data, num, type){
212   var buffer = gl.createBuffer();    // Create a buffer object
    ...
217   // Write data to the buffer object
218   gl.bindBuffer(gl.ARRAY_BUFFER, buffer);
219   gl.bufferData(gl.ARRAY_BUFFER, data, gl.STATIC_DRAW);
220
221   // Store information to assign it to attribute variable later
222   buffer.num = num;
223   buffer.type = type;
224
225   return buffer;
226 }
```

initArrayBufferForLaterUse() simply creates a buffer object at line 212 and writes data to it at lines 218 and 219. Notice that assigning it to an attribute variable (gl.vertex AttribPointer()) and enabling the assignment (gl.enableVertexAttribAray()) are not done within the function but later, just before drawing. To assign the buffer object to the attribute variable a_Position later, the data needed is stored as properties of the buffer object at lines 222 and 223.

Here you take advantage of an interesting feature of JavaScript that allows you to freely add new properties of an object and assign data to them. You can do this by simply appending the .property-name to the object name and assigning a value. Using this feature, you store the number of items in the num property (line 222), and the type in the type property (line 223). Of course, you can access the contents of the newly made properties using the same name. Note, you must be careful when referring to properties created in this way, because JavaScript gives no error indications even if you misspell only one character in the property name. Equally, be aware that, although convenient, appending properties has a performance overhead. A better approach, user-defined types, is explained in Chapter 10, "Advanced Techniques," but let's stick with this approach for now.

Finally, the `draw()` function, invoked at line 255, is the same as used in `MultiJointModel` in terms of drawing parts according to the hierarchical structure, but it's different in terms of using `drawSegment()` to draw each segment. In particular, the third argument of `drawSegment()`, shown next, is the buffer object in which the vertex coordinates of the parts are stored.

```
262    drawSegment(gl, n, g_baseBuffer, viewProjMatrix, u_MvpMatrix, u_NormalMatrix);
```

This function is defined at line 311 and operates as follows. It assigns a buffer object to the attribute variable `a_Position` and enables it at lines 312 to 316 before drawing at line 327. Here, `num` and `type`, which are just stored as buffer object properties, are used.

```
310  // Draw segments
311  function drawSegment(gl, n, buffer, viewProjMatrix, a_Position,
                                          ➥u_MvpMatrix, u_NormalMatrix) {
312    gl.bindBuffer(gl.ARRAY_BUFFER, buffer);
313    // Assign the buffer object to the attribute variable
314    gl.vertexAttribPointer(a_Position, buffer.num, buffer.type, false, 0, 0);
315    // Enable the assignment
316    gl.enableVertexAttribArray(a_Position);
317
318    // Calculate model view project matrix and set it to u_MvpMatrix
    ...
322    // Calculate transformation matrix for normal and set it to u_NormalMatrix
    ...
327    gl.drawElements(gl.TRIANGLES, n, gl.UNSIGNED_BYTE, 0);
328  }
```

This time you don't need to scale objects with the model matrix because you have prepared the vertex coordinates per part, so there is no need to store and retrieve the matrix. Therefore, `pushMatrix()` and `popMatrix()` are not necessary.

Shader and Program Objects: The Role of initShaders()

Finally, before we wrap up this chapter, let's examine one of the convenience functions defined for this book: `initShaders()`. This function has been used in all the sample programs and has hidden quite a lot of complex detail about setting up and using shaders. We have deliberately left this explanation to the end of this chapter to ensure you have a good understanding of the basics of WebGL before tackling some of these complex details. We should note that it's not actually necessary to master these details. For some readers it will be sufficient to simply reuse the `initShaders()` function we supply and skip this section. However, for those who are interested, let's take a look.

`initShaders()` carries out the routine work to make shaders available in WebGL. It consists of seven steps:

1. Create shader objects (`gl.createShader()`).

2. Store the shader programs (to avoid confusion, we refer to them as "source code") in the shader objects (`g.shaderSource()`).

3. Compile the shader objects (`gl.compileShader()`).

4. Create a program object (`gl.createProgram()`).

5. Attach the shader objects to the program object (`gl.attachShader()`).

6. Link the program object (`gl.linkProgram()`).

7. Tell the WebGL system the program object to be used (`gl.useProgram()`).

Each step is simple but when combined can appear complex, so let's take a look at them one by one. First, as you know from earlier, two types of objects are necessary to use shaders: shader objects and program objects.

Shader object   A shader object manages a vertex shader or a fragment shader. One shader object is created per shader.

Program object   A program object is a container that manages the shader objects. A vertex shader object and a fragment shader object (two shader objects in total) must be attached to a program object in WebGL.

The relationship between a program object and shader objects is shown in Figure 9.10.

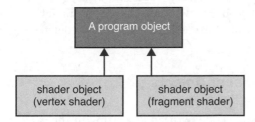

Figure 9.10   The relationship between a program object and shader objects

Using this information, let's discuss the preceding seven steps sequentially.

Create Shader Objects (gl.createShader())

All shader objects have to be created with a call to `gl.createShader()` before using them.

gl.createShader(type)

Create a shader of the specified *type*.

Parameters	type	Specifies the type of shader object to be created: either gl.VERTEX_SHADER (a vertex shader) or gl.FRAGMENT_SHADER (a fragment shader).
Return value	Non-null	The created shader object.
	null	The creation of the shader object failed.
Errors	INVALID_ENUM	The specified type is none of the above.

gl.createShader() creates a vertex shader or a fragment shader according to the specified *type*. If you do not need the shader any more, you can delete it with gl.deleteShader().

gl.deleteShader(shader)

Delete the shader object.

Parameters	shader	Specifies the shader object to be deleted.
Return value	None	
Errors	None	

Note that the specified shader object is not deleted immediately if it is still in use (that is, it is attached to a program object using gl.attachShader(), which is discussed in a few pages). The shader object specified as an argument of gl.deleteShader() will be deleted when a program object no longer uses it.

Store the Shader Source Code in the Shader Objects (g.shaderSource())

A shader object has storage to store the shader source code (written as a string in the JavaScript program or in the separate file; see Appendix F, "Loading Shader Programs from Files"). You use gl.shaderSource() to store the source code in a shader object.

`gl.shaderSource(shader, source)`		

Store the source code specified by *source* in the shader object specified by *shader*. If any source code was previously stored in the shader object, it is replaced by new source code.

Parameters	shader	Specifies the shader object in which the program is stored.
	source	Specifies the shader source code (string)
Return value	None	
Errors	None	

Compile Shader Objects (gl.compileShader())

After storing the shader source code in the shader object, you have to compile it so that it can be used in the WebGL system. Unlike JavaScript, and like C or C++, shaders need to be compiled before use. In this process, the source code stored in a shader object is compiled to executable format (binary) and kept in the WebGL system. Use `gl.compile-Shader()` to compile. Note, if you replace the source code in the shader object with a call to `gl.shaderSource()` after compiling, the compiled binary kept in the shader object is not replaced. You have to recompile it explicitly.

`gl.compileShader(shader)`		

Compile the source code stored in the shader object specified by *shader*.

Parameters	shader	Specifies the shader object in which the source code to be compiled is stored.
Return Value	None	
Errors	None	

When executing `gl.compileShader()`, it is possible a compilation error occurs due to mistakes in the source code. You can check for such errors, as well as the status of the shader object, using `gl.getShaderParameter()`.

---

gl.getShaderParameter(shader, pname)

Get the information specified by *pname* from the shader object specified by *shader*.

Parameters	shader	Specifies the shader object.
	pname	Specifies the information to get from the shader:
		gl.SHADER_TYPE, gl.DELETE_STATUS, or
		gl.COMPILE_STATUS.
Return value	The following depending on *pname*:	
	gl.SHADER_TYPE	The type of shader (gl.VERTEX_SHADER or gl.FRAGMENT_SHADER)
	gl.DELETE_STATUS	Whether the deletion has succeeded (true or false)
	gl.COMPILE_STATUS	Whether the compilation has succeeded (true or false)
Errors	INVALID_ENUM	*pname* is none of the above values.

To check whether the compilation succeeded, you can call gl.getShaderParameter() with gl.COMPILE_STATUS specified in *pname*.

If the compilation has failed, gl.getShaderParameter() returns false, and the error information is written in the **information log** for the shader in the WebGL system. This information can be retrieved with gl.getShaderInfoLog().

---

gl.getShaderInfoLog(shader)

Retrieve the information log from the shader object specified by *shader*.

Parameters	shader	Specifies the shader object from which the information log is retrieved.
Return value	non-null	The string containing the logged information.
	null	Any errors are generated.
Errors	None	

Although the exact details of the logged information is implementation specific, almost all WebGL systems return error messages containing the line numbers where the compiler has detected the errors in the program. For example, assume that you compiled a fragment shader program as follows:

```
var FSHADER_SOURCE =
  'void main() {\n' +
  '  gl.FragColor = vec4(1.0, 0.0, 0.0, 1.0);\n' +
  '}\n';
```

Because the second line is incorrect in this case (gl. must be gl_), the error messages displayed in the JavaScript console of Chrome will be similar to those shown in Figure 9.11.

Figure 9.11 A compile error in a shader

The first message indicates that gl at line 2 is undeclared.

```
failed to compile shader: ERROR: 0:2: 'gl' : undeclared identifier
                                               cuon-utils.js:88
```

The reference to cuon-utils.js:88 on the right means that the error has been detected in gl.getShaderInfoLog(), which was invoked at line 88 of the cuon-utils.js file, where initShaders() is defined.

Create a Program Object (gl.createProgram())

As mentioned before, a program object is a container to store the shader objects and is created by gl.createProgram(). You are already familiar with this program object because it is the object you pass as the first argument of gl.getAttribLocation() and gl.getUniformLocation().

gl.createProgram()		
Create a program object.		
Parameters	None	
Return value	non-null	The newly created program object.
	null	Failed to create a program object.
Errors	None	

A program object can be deleted by using `gl.deleteProgram()`.

`gl.deleteProgram(program)`

Delete the program object specified by *program*. If the program object is not referred to from anywhere, it is deleted immediately. Otherwise, it will be deleted when it is no longer referred to.

Parameters	program	Specifies the program object to be deleted.
Return value	None	
Errors	None	

Once the program object has been created, you attach the two shader objects to it.

Attach the Shader Objects to the Program Object (gl.attachShader())

Because you always need two shaders in WebGL—a vertex shader and a fragment shader—you must attach both of them to the program object with `gl.attachShader()`.

`gl.attachShader(program, shader)`

Attach the shader object specified by *shader* to the program object specified by *program*.

Parameters	program	Specifies the program object.
	shader	Specifies the shader object to be attached to *program*.
Return value	None	
Errors	INVALID_OPERATION	*Shader* had already been attached to *program*.

It is not necessary to compile or store any source code before it is attached to the program object. You can detach the shader object with `gl.detachShader()`.

```
gl.detachShader(program, shader)
```

Detach the shader object specified by *shader* from the program object specified by *program*.

Parameters	program	Specifies the program object.
	shader	Specifies the shader object to be detached from program.
Return value	None	
Errors	INVALID_OPERATION	*shader* is not attached to *program*.

Link the Program Object (gl.linkProgram())

After attaching shader objects to a program object, you need to link the shader objects. You use `gl.linkProgram()` to link the shader objects in the program object.

```
gl.linkProgram(program)
```

Link the program object specified by *program*.

Parameters	program	Specifies the program object to be linked.
Return value	None	
Errors	None	

During linking, various constraints of the WebGL system are checked: (1) when `varying` variables are declared in a vertex shader, whether `varying` variables with the same names and types are declared in a fragment shader, (2) whether a vertex shader has written data to `varying` variables used in a fragment shader, (3) when the same `uniform` variables are used in both a vertex shader and a fragment shader, whether their types and names match, (4) whether the numbers of `attribute` variables, `uniform` variables, and `varying` variables does not exceed an upper limit, and so on.

After linking the program object, it is always good programming practice to check whether it succeeded. The result of linking can be confirmed with `gl.getProgramParameters()`.

gl.getProgramParameter(program, pname)

Return information about *pname* for the program object specified by *program*. The return value differs depending on *pname*.

Parameters	program	Specifies the program object.
	pname	Specifies any one of gl.DELETE_STATUS, gl.LINK_STATUS, gl.VALIDATE_STATUS, gl.ATTACHED_SHADERS, gl.ACTIVE_ATTRIBUTES, or gl.ACTIVE_UNIFORMS.
Return value		Depending on *pname*, the following values can be returned:

gl.DELETE_STATUS	Whether the *program* has been deleted (true or false)
gl.LINK_STATUS	Whether the *program* was linked successfully (true or false)
gl.VALIDATE_STATUS	Whether the *program* was validated successfully (true or false)[1]
gl.ATTACHED_SHADERS	The number of attached shader objects
gl.ACTIVE_ATTRIBUTES	The number of attribute variables in the vertex shader
gl.ACTIVE_UNIFORMS	The number of uniform variables

Errors	INVALID_ENUM	*pname* is none of the above values.

If linking succeeded, you are returned an executable program object. Otherwise, you can get the information about the linking from the information log of the program object with gl.getProgramInfoLog().

gl.getProgramInfoLog(program)

Retrieve the information log from the program object specified by *program*.

Parameters	program	Specifies the program object from which the information log is retrieved.
Return value		The string containing the logged information
Errors		None

---

[1] A program object may fail to execute even if it was linked successfully, such as if no texture units are set for the sampler. This can only be detected when drawing, not when linking. Because this check takes time, check for these errors only when debugging and turn off otherwise.

Tell the WebGL System Which Program Object to Use (gl.useProgram())

The last step is to tell the WebGL system which program object to use when drawing by making a call to `gl.useProgram()`.

`gl.useProgram(program)`

Tell the WebGL system that the program object specified by *program* will be used.

Parameters	program Specifies the program object to be used.
Return value	None
Errors	None

One powerful feature of this function is that you can use it during drawing to switch between multiple shaders prepared in advance. This will be discussed and used in Chapter 10.

With this final step, the preparation for drawing with the shaders is finished. As you have seen, `initShaders()` hides quite a lot of detail and can be safely used without worrying about this detail. Essentially, once executed, the vertex and fragment shaders are set up and can be used with calls to `gl.drawArrays()` or `gl.drawElements()`.

Now that you have an understanding of the steps and appropriate WebGL functions used in `initShaders()`, let's take a look at the program flow of `initShaders()` as defined in `cuon-utils.js`.

The Program Flow of initShaders()

`initShaders()` is composed of two main functions: `createProgram()`, which creates a linked program object, and `loadShader()`, called from `createProgram()`, which creates the compiled shader objects. Both are defined in `cuon-utils.js`. Here, you will work through `initShader()` in order from the top (see Listing 9.5). Note that in contrast to the normal code samples used in the book, the comments in this code are in the JavaDoc form, which is used in the convenience libraries.

Listing 9.5 initShaders()

```
1 // cuon-utils.js
2 /**
3  * Create a program object and make current
4  * @param gl GL context
5  * @param vshader a vertex shader program (string)
6  * @param fshader a fragment shader program (string)
7  * @return true, if the program object was created and successfully made current
```

```
 8  */
 9  function initShaders(gl, vshader, fshader) {
10    var program = createProgram(gl, vshader, fshader);
      ...
16    gl.useProgram(program);
17    gl.program = program;
18
19    return true;
20  }
```

First, `initShaders()` creates a linked program object with `createProgram()` at line 10 and tells the WebGL system to use the program object at line 16. Then it sets the program object to the property named `program` of the `gl` object.

Next, look at `createProgram()` in Listing 9.6.

Listing 9.6   createProgram()

```
22  /**
23   * Create the linked program object
24   * @param gl GL context
25   * @param vshader a vertex shader program(string)
26   * @param fshader a fragment shader program(string)
27   * @return created program object, or null if the creation has failed.
28   */
29  function createProgram(gl, vshader, fshader) {
30    // Create shader objects
31    var vertexShader = loadShader(gl, gl.VERTEX_SHADER, vshader);
32    var fragmentShader = loadShader(gl, gl.FRAGMENT_SHADER, fshader);
      ...
37    // Create a program object
38    var program = gl.createProgram();
      ...
43    // Attach the shader objects
44    gl.attachShader(program, vertexShader);
45    gl.attachShader(program, fragmentShader);
46
47    // Link the program object
48    gl.linkProgram(program);
49
50    // Check the result of linking
51    var linked = gl.getProgramParameter(program, gl.LINK_STATUS);
      ...
60    return program;
61  }
```

The function `createProgram()` creates the shader objects for the vertex and the fragment shaders, which are loaded using `loadShader()` at lines 31 and 32. The shader object returned from `loadShader()` contains the stored shader source code and compiled versions.

The program object, to which the shader objects created here will be attached, is created at line 38, and the vertex and fragment shader objects are attached at lines 44 and 45.

Then `createProgram()` links the program object at line 48 and checks the result at line 51. If the linking has succeeded, it returns the program object at line 60.

Finally, let's look at `loadShader()` (Listing 9.7) which was invoked at lines 31 and 32 from within `createProgram()`.

Listing 9.7   loadShader()

```
63 /**
64  * Create a shader object
65  * @param gl GL context
66  * @param type the type of the shader object to be created
67  * @param source a source code of a shader (string)
68  * @return created shader object, or null if the creation has failed.
69  */
70 function loadShader(gl, type, source) {
71   // Create a shader object
72   var shader = gl.createShader(type);
     . . .
78   // Set source codes of the shader
79   gl.shaderSource(shader, source);
80
81   // Compile the shader
82   gl.compileShader(shader);
83
84   // Check the result of compilation
85   var compiled = gl.getShaderParameter(shader, gl.COMPILE_STATUS);
     . . .
93   return shader;
94 }
```

First `loadShader()` creates a shader object at line 72. It associates the source code to the object at line 79 and compiles it at line 82. Finally, it checks the result of compilation at line 85 and, if no errors have occurred, returns the shader object to `createShader()`, which attaches it to the program object.

Summary

This chapter is the final one to explore basic features of WebGL. It looked at how to draw and manipulate complex 3D objects composed of multiple segments organized in a hierarchical structure. This technique is important for understanding how to use simple 3D objects like cubes or blocks to build up more complex objects like robots or game characters. In addition, you looked at one of the most complex convenience functions we have provided for this book, `initShaders()`, which has been treated as a black box up until now. You saw the details of how shader objects are created and managed by program objects, so you have a better sense of the internal structure of shaders and how WebGL manages them through program objects.

At this stage you have a full understanding of WebGL and are capable of writing your own complex 3D scenes using the expressive power of WebGL. In the next chapter, we will outline various advanced techniques used in 3D graphics and leverage what you have learned so far to show how WebGL can support these techniques.

Chapter 10

Advanced Techniques

This chapter includes a "grab-bag" of interesting techniques that you should find useful for creating your WebGL applications. The techniques are mostly stand-alone, so you can select and read any section that interests you. Where there are dependencies, they are clearly identified. The explanations in this chapter are terse in order to include as many techniques as possible. However, the sample programs on the website include comprehensive comments, so please refer to them as well.

Rotate an Object with the Mouse

When creating WebGL applications, sometimes you want users to be able to control 3D objects with the mouse. In this section, you construct a sample program `RotateObject`, which allows users to rotate a cube by dragging it with the mouse. To make the program simple, it uses a cube, but the basic method is applicable to any object. Figure 10.1 shows a screen shot of the cube that has a texture image mapped onto it.

Figure 10.1   A screen shot of RotateObject

How to Implement Object Rotation

Rotating a 3D object is simply the application of a technique you've already studied for 2D objects—transforming the vertex coordinates by using the model view projection matrix. The process requires you to create a rotation matrix based on the mouse movement, change the model view projection matrix, and then transform the coordinates by using the matrix.

You can obtain the amount of mouse movement by simply recording the position where the mouse is initially clicked and then subtracting that position from the new position as the mouse moves. Clearly, an event handler will be needed to calculate the mouse movement, and then this will be converted into an angle that will rotate the object. Let's take a look at the sample program.

Sample Program (RotateObject.js)

Listing 10.1 shows the sample program. As you can see, the shaders do not do anything special. Line 9 in the vertex shader transforms the vertex coordinates by using the model view projection matrix, and line 10 maps the texture image onto the cube.

Listing 10.1   RotateObject.js

```
 1  // RotateObject.js
 2  // Vertex shader program
 3  var VSHADER_SOURCE =
    ...
 8    'void main() {\n' +
 9    '  gl_Position = u_MvpMatrix * a_Position;\n' +
10    '  v_TexCoord = a_TexCoord;\n' +
11    '}\n';
    ...
24  function main() {
    ...
42    var n = initVertexBuffers(gl);
    ...
61    viewProjMatrix.setPerspective(30.0, canvas.width / canvas.height,
                                                    ➥1.0, 100.0);
62    viewProjMatrix.lookAt(3.0, 3.0, 7.0, 0.0, 0.0, 0.0, 0.0, 1.0, 0.0);
63
64    // Register the event handler
65    var currentAngle = [0.0, 0.0]; // [x-axis, y-axis] degrees
66    initEventHandlers(canvas, currentAngle);
    ...
74    var tick = function() {                    // Start drawing
75      draw(gl, n, viewProjMatrix, u_MvpMatrix, currentAngle);
76      requestAnimationFrame(tick, canvas);
77    };
```

```
 78    tick();
 79  }

       ...

138  function initEventHandlers(canvas, currentAngle) {
139    var dragging = false;              // Dragging or not
140    var lastX = -1, lastY = -1;        // Last position of the mouse
141
142    canvas.onmousedown = function(ev) {  // Mouse is pressed
143      var x = ev.clientX, y = ev.clientY;
144      // Start dragging if a mouse is in <canvas>
145      var rect = ev.target.getBoundingClientRect();
146      if (rect.left <= x && x < rect.right && rect.top <= y && y < rect.bottom) {
147        lastX = x; lastY = y;
148        dragging = true;
149      }
150    };
151    // Mouse is released
152    canvas.onmouseup = function(ev) { dragging = false; };
153
154    canvas.onmousemove = function(ev) {      // Mouse is moved
155      var x = ev.clientX, y = ev.clientY;
156      if (dragging) {
157        var factor = 100/canvas.height; // The rotation ratio
158        var dx = factor * (x - lastX);
159        var dy = factor * (y - lastY);
160        // Limit x-axis rotation angle to -90 to 90 degrees
161        currentAngle[0] = Math.max(Math.min(currentAngle[0] + dy, 90.0), -90.0);
162        currentAngle[1] = currentAngle[1] + dx;
163      }
164      lastX = x, lastY = y;
165    };
166  }
167
168  var g_MvpMatrix = new Matrix4(); // The model view projection matrix
169  function draw(gl, n, viewProjMatrix, u_MvpMatrix, currentAngle) {
170    // Calculate the model view projection matrix
171    g_MvpMatrix.set(viewProjMatrix);
172    g_MvpMatrix.rotate(currentAngle[0], 1.0, 0.0, 0.0); // x-axis
173    g_MvpMatrix.rotate(currentAngle[1], 0.0, 1.0, 0.0); // y-axis
174    gl.uniformMatrix4fv(u_MvpMatrix, false, g_MvpMatrix.elements);
175
176    gl.clear(gl.COLOR_BUFFER_BIT | gl.DEPTH_BUFFER_BIT);
177    gl.drawElements(gl.TRIANGLES, n, gl.UNSIGNED_BYTE, 0);
178  }
```

At lines 61 and 62 of `main()` in JavaScript, the view projection matrix is calculated in advance. You will have to change the model matrix on-the-fly according to the amount of mouse movement.

The code from line 65 registers the event handlers, a key part of this sample program. The variable `currentAngle` is initialized at line 65 and used to hold the current rotation angle. Here, it is an array because it needs to handle two rotation angles around the x-axis and y-axis. The actual registration of the event handlers is done inside `initEventHandlers()`, called at line 66. It draws the cube using the function `tick()` that is defined from line 74.

`initEventHandlers()` is defined at line 138. The code from line 142 handles mouse down, the code from line 152 handles mouse up, and the code from line 154 handles the mouse movement.

The processing when the mouse button is first pushed at line 142 is simple. Line 146 checks whether the mouse has been pressed inside the `<canvas>` element. If it is inside the `<canvas>`, line 147 saves that position in `lastX` and `lastY`. Then the variable `dragging`, which indicates dragging has begun, is set to `true` at line 148.

The processing of the mouse button release at line 152 is simple. Because this indicates that dragging is done, the code simply sets the variable `dragging` back to `false`.

The processing from line 154 is the critical part and tracks the movement of the mouse. Line 156 checks whether dragging is taking place and, if it is, lines 158 and 159 calculate how long it has moved, storing the results to `dx` and `dy`. These values are scaled, using `factor`, which is a function of the canvas size. Once the distance dragged has been calculated, it can be used to determine the new angle by directly adding to the current angles at line 161 and 162. The code limits rotation from –90 to +90 degrees simply to show the technique; you are free to remove this. Because the mouse has moved, its position is saved in `lastX` and `lastY`.

Once you have successfully transformed the movement of the mouse into a rotation angle, you can let the rotation matrix handle the updates and draw the results using `tick()`. These operations are done at lines 172 and 173.

This quick review of a technique to calculate the rotation angle is only one approach. Others, such as placing virtual track balls around the object, are described in detail in the book *3D User Interfaces*.

Select an Object

When your application requires users to be able to control 3D objects interactively, you will need a technique to allow users to select objects. There are many uses of this technique, such as selecting a 3D button created by a 3D model instead of the conventional 2D GUI button, or selecting a photo among multiple photos in a 3D scene.

Selecting a 3D object is generally more complex than selecting a 2D one because of the mathematics required to determine if the mouse is over a nonregular shape. However, you can use a simple trick, shown in the sample program, to avoid that complexity. In this sample, PickObject, the user can click a rotating cube, which causes a message to be displayed (see Figure 10.2). First, run the sample program and experiment with it for a while to get the feeling of how it works.

Figure 10.2   PickObject

Figure 10.2 shows with the message displayed when clicking the cube. The message says, "The cube was selected!" Also check what happens when you click the black part of the background.

How to Implement Object Selection

This program goes through the following steps to check whether the cube was clicked:

1. When the mouse is pressed, draw the cube with a single color "red" (see the middle of Figure 10.3).

2. Read the pixel value (color) of the selected point.

3. Redraw the cube with its original color (right in Figure 10.3).

4. If the color of the pixel is red, display, "The cube was selected!"

When the cube is drawn with a single color (red in this case), you can quickly see which part of the drawing area the cube occupies. After reading the pixel value at the position of the mouse pointer when the mouse is clicked, you can determine that the mouse was above the cube if the pixel color is red.

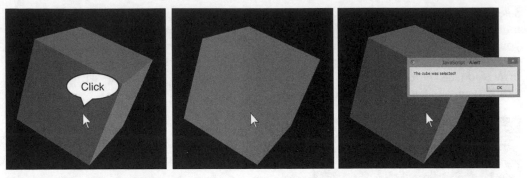

Figure 10.3 The object drawn at the point of mouse pressing

To ensure that the viewer doesn't see the cube flash red, you need to draw and redraw in the same function. Let's take a look at the actual sample program.

Sample Program (PickObject.js)

Listing 10.2 shows the sample program. The processing in this sample mainly takes place in the vertex shader. To implement step 1, you must inform the vertex shader that the mouse has been clicked so that it draws the cube red. The variable u_Clicked transmits this information and declared at line 7 in the vertex shader. When the mouse is pressed, u_Clicked is set to true in the JavaScript and tested at line 11. If true, the color red is assigned to v_Color; if not, the color of the cube (a_Color) is directly assigned to v_Color. This turns the cube red when the mouse is pressed.

Listing 10.2 PickObject.js

```
1   // PickObject.js
2   // Vertex shader program
3   var VSHADER_SOURCE =
    ...
6     'uniform mat4 u_MvpMatrix;\n' +
7     'uniform bool u_Clicked;\n' +    // Mouse is pressed
8     'varying vec4 v_Color;\n' +
9     'void main() {\n' +
10    '  gl_Position = u_MvpMatrix * a_Position;\n' +
11    '  if (u_Clicked) {\n' + // Draw in red if mouse is pressed          <- (1)
12    '    v_Color = vec4(1.0, 0.0, 0.0, 1.0);\n' +
13    '  } else {\n' +
14    '    v_Color = a_Color;\n' +
15    '  }\n' +
16    '}\n';
17
18  // Fragment shader program
```

```
       ...
25     '  gl_FragColor = v_Color;\n' +
       ...
30  function main() {
       ...
60     var u_Clicked = gl.getUniformLocation(gl.program, 'u_Clicked');
       ...
71     gl.uniform1i(u_Clicked, 0); // Pass false to u_Clicked
72
73     var currentAngle = 0.0; // Current rotation angle
74     // Register the event handler
75     canvas.onmousedown = function(ev) {   // Mouse is pressed
76       var x = ev.clientX, y = ev.clientY;
77       var rect = ev.target.getBoundingClientRect();
78       if (rect.left <= x && x < rect.right && rect.top <= y && y < rect.bottom) {
79         // Check if it is on object
80         var x_in_canvas = x - rect.left, y_in_canvas = rect.bottom - y;
81         var picked = check(gl, n, x_in_canvas, y_in_canvas, currentAngle,
                                    ➥u_Clicked, viewProjMatrix, u_MvpMatrix);
82         if (picked) alert('The cube was selected! ');                <-(4)
83       }
84     }
       ...
92  }
       ...
147 function check(gl, n, x, y, currentAngle, u_Clicked, viewProjMatrix,
                                                     ➥u_MvpMatrix) {
148    var picked = false;
149    gl.uniform1i(u_Clicked, 1);  // Draw the cube with red
150    draw(gl, n, currentAngle, viewProjMatrix, u_MvpMatrix);
151    // Read pixel at the clicked position
152    var pixels = new Uint8Array(4);  // Array for storing the pixels
153    gl.readPixels(x, y, 1, 1, gl.RGBA, gl.UNSIGNED_BYTE, pixels);         <-(2)
154
155    if (pixels[0] == 255)  // The mouse in on cube if pixels[0] is 255
156      picked = true;
157
158    gl.uniform1i(u_Clicked, 0); // Pass false to u_Clicked: redraw cube
159    draw(gl, n, currentAngle, viewProjMatrix, u_MvpMatrix); //           <-(3)
160
161    return picked;
162 }
```

Let's take a look from line 30 of main() in JavaScript. Line 60 obtains the storage location for u_Clicked, and line 71 assigns the initial value of u_Clicked to be false.

Line 75 registers the event handler to be called when the mouse has been clicked. This event handler function does a sanity check to see if the clicked position is inside the <canvas> element at line 78. Then it calls to check() at line 81 if it is. This function checks whether the position, specified by the third and fourth arguments, is on the cube (see next paragraph). If so, it returns true which causes a message to be displayed at line 82.

The function check() begins from line 147. This function processes steps (2) and (3) from the previous section together. Line 149 informs the vertex shader that the click event has occurred by passing 1 (true) to u_Clicked. Then line 150 draws the cube with the current rotation angle. Because u_Clicked is true, the cube is drawn in red. Then the pixel value of the clicked position is read from the color buffer at line 153. The following shows the gl.readPixels() function used here.

---

gl.readPixels(x, y, width, height, format, type, pixels)

Read a block of pixels from the color buffer[1] and store it to the array *pixels*. *x, y, width,* and *height* define the block as a rectangle.

Parameters	x, y	Specify the position of the first pixel that is read from the buffer.
	width, height	Specify the dimensions of the pixel rectangle.
	format	Specifies the format of the pixel data. gl.RGBA must be specified.
	type	Specifies the data type of the pixel data. gl.UNSIGNED_BYTE must be specified.
	pixels	Specifies the typed array (Uint8Array) for storing the pixel data.
Return value	None	
Errors		INVALID_VALUE: *pixels* is null. Either *width* or *height* is negative.
		INVALID_OPERATION: *pixels* is not large enough to store the pixel data.
		INVALID_ENUM: *format* or *type* is none of the above values.

The pixel value that was read is stored in the *pixels* array. This array is defined at line 152, and the R, G, B, and A values are stored in pixels[0], pixels[1], pixels[2], and pixels[3], respectively. Because, in this sample program, you know that the only colors used are red for the cube and black for the background, you can see if the mouse is on the cube by checking the values for pixels[0]. This is done at line 155, and if it is red, it changes picked to true.

---

[1] If a framebuffer object is bound to gl.FRAMEBUFFER, this method reads the pixel values from the object. We explain the object in the later section "Use What You've Drawn as a Texture Image."

Then line 158 sets u_Clicked to false and redraws the cube at line 159. This turns the cube back to its original color. Line 161 returns picked as the return value.

Note, if at this point you call any function that returns control to the browser, such as alert(), the content of the color buffer will be displayed on the <canvas> at that point. For example, if you execute alert('The cube was selected!') at line 156, the red cube will be displayed when you click the cube.

This approach, although simple, can handle more than one object by assigning different colors to each object. For example, red, blue, and green are enough if there are three objects. For larger numbers of objects, you can use individual bits. Because there are 8 bits for each component in RGBA, you can represent 255 objects just by using the R component. However, if the 3D objects are complex or the drawing area is large, it will take some time to process the selection of objects. To overcome this disadvantage, you can use simplified models to select objects or shrink the drawing area. In such cases, you can use the framebuffer object, which will be explained in the section "Use What You've Drawn as a Texture Image" later in this chapter.

Select the Face of the Object

You can also apply the method explained in the previous section to select a particular face of an object. Let's customize PickObject to build PickFace, a program that turns the selected face white. Figure 10.4 shows PickFace.

Figure 10.4　PickFace

PickFace is easy once you understand how PickObject works. PickObject drew the cube in red when the mouse was clicked, resulting in the object's display area in the color buffer being red. By reading the pixel value of the clicked point and seeing if the color of the pixel at the position was red, the program could determine if the object had been selected. PickFace goes one step further and inserts the information of which face has been selected into the color buffer. Here, you will insert the information in the alpha component of the RGBA value. Let's take a look at the sample program.

Sample Program (PickFace.js)

`PickFace.js` is shown in Listing 10.3. Some parts, such as the fragment shader, are omitted for brevity.

Listing 10.3 PickFace.js

```
1  // PickFace.js
2  // Vertex shader program
3  var VSHADER_SOURCE =
4    'attribute vec4 a_Position;\n' +
5    'attribute vec4 a_Color;\n' +
6    'attribute float a_Face;\n' +   // Surface number (Cannot use int)
7    'uniform mat4 u_MvpMatrix;\n' +
8    'uniform int u_PickedFace;\n' + // Surface number of selected face
9    'varying vec4 v_Color;\n' +
10   'void main() {\n' +
11   '  gl_Position = u_MvpMatrix * a_Position;\n' +
12   '  int face = int(a_Face);\n' +  // Convert to int
13   '  vec3 color = (face == u_PickedFace) ? vec3(1.0):a_Color.rgb;\n'+
14   '  if(u_PickedFace == 0) {\n' + // Insert face number into alpha
15   '    v_Color = vec4(color, a_Face/255.0);\n' +
16   '  } else {\n' +
17   '    v_Color = vec4(color, a_Color.a);\n' +
18   '  }\n' +
19   '}\n';
     ...
33 function main() {
     ...
50   // Set vertex information
51   var n = initVertexBuffers(gl);
     ...
74   // Initialize selected surface
75   gl.uniform1i(u_PickedFace, -1);
76
77   var currentAngle = 0.0; // Current rotation angle (degrees)
78   // Register event handlers
79   canvas.onmousedown = function(ev) {   // Mouse is pressed
80     var x = ev.clientX, y = ev.clientY;
81     var rect = ev.target.getBoundingClientRect();
82     if (rect.left <= x && x < rect.right && rect.top <= y && y < rect.bottom) {
83       // If clicked position is inside the <canvas>, update the face
84       var x_in_canvas = x - rect.left, y_in_canvas = rect.bottom - y;
85       var face = checkFace(gl, n, x_in_canvas, y_in_canvas,
                     ➡currentAngle, u_PickedFace, viewProjMatrix, u_MvpMatrix);
86       gl.uniform1i(u_PickedFace, face);  // Pass the surface number
87       draw(gl, n, currentAngle, viewProjMatrix, u_MvpMatrix);
```

```
88        }
89      }

        . . .

99   function initVertexBuffers(gl) {

        . . .

109     var vertices = new Float32Array([    // Vertex coordinates
110         1.0, 1.0, 1.0,   -1.0, 1.0, 1.0,   -1.0,-1.0, 1.0,   1.0,-1.0, 1.0,
111         1.0, 1.0, 1.0,    1.0,-1.0, 1.0,    1.0,-1.0,-1.0,   1.0, 1.0,-1.0,

        . . .

115         1.0,-1.0,-1.0,   -1.0,-1.0,-1.0,   -1.0, 1.0,-1.0,   1.0, 1.0,-1.0
116     ]);

        . . .

127     var faces = new Uint8Array([    // Surface number
128       1, 1, 1, 1,       // v0-v1-v2-v3 Front
129       2, 2, 2, 2,       // v0-v3-v4-v5 Right

        . . .

133       6, 6, 6, 6,       // v4-v7-v6-v5 Depth
134     ]);

        . . .

154     if (!initArrayBuffer(gl, faces, gl.UNSIGNED_BYTE, 1,
                               ➥'a_Face')) return -1;  // Surface Information
        . . .
164   }
165
166   function checkFace(gl, n, x, y, currentAngle, u_PickedFace, viewProjMatrix,
                                                    ➥u_MvpMatrix) {
167     var pixels = new Uint8Array(4); // Array for storing the pixel
168     gl.uniform1i(u_PickedFace, 0);  // Write surface number into alpha
169     draw(gl, n, currentAngle, viewProjMatrix, u_MvpMatrix);
170     // Read the pixels at (x, y). pixels[3] is the surface number
171     gl.readPixels(x, y, 1, 1, gl.RGBA, gl.UNSIGNED_BYTE, pixels);
172
173     return pixels[3];
174   }
```

Let's take a look from the vertex shader. a_Face at line 6 is the attribute variable used to pass the surface number, which is then "coded" into the alpha value when the mouse is clicked. The surface numbers are set up in initVertexBuffers() defined at line 99 and simply map vertices to a surface. Lines 127 onward define these mappings. So, for example, vertices v0-v1-v2-v3 define a surface that is numbered 1, vertices v0-v3-v4-v5 are numbered 2, and so on. Because each vertex needs a number to pass to the vertex shader, there are four 1s written at line 128 to represent the first face.

If a face is already selected, u_PickedFace at line 8 informs the vertex shader of the selected face number, allowing the shader to switch the way it draws the face based on this information.

Line 12 converts a_Face, the surface number that is a float type, into an int type because an int type cannot be used in the attribute variables (Chapter 6, "The OpenGL ES Shading Language [GLSL ES]"). If the selected surface number is the same as the surface number currently being manipulated, white is assigned to color at line 13. Otherwise, the original surface color is assigned. If the mouse has been clicked (that is, u_PickedFace is set to 0), the a_Face value is inserted into the alpha value and the cube is drawn (line 15).

Now, by passing 0 into u_PickedFace when the mouse is clicked, the cube is drawn with an alpha value set to the surface number. u_PickedFace is initialized to –1 at line 75. There is no surface with the number –1 (refer to the faces array at line 127), so the cube is initially drawn without surfaces selected.

Let's take a look at the essential processing of the event handler. u_PickedFace is passed as an argument to checkFace() at line 85, which returns the surface number of the picked face, checkFace(), at line 166. At line 168, 0 is passed to u_PickedFace to tell the vertex shader that the mouse has been clicked. When draw() is called in the next line, the surface number is inserted into the alpha value and the object is redrawn. Line 171 checks the pixel value of the clicked point, and line 173 retrieves the inserted surface number by using pixels[3]. (It is the alpha value, so the subscript is 3.) This surface number is returned to the main code and then used at lines 86 and 87 to draw the cube. The vertex shader handles the rest of the processing, as described earlier.

HUD (Head Up Display)

The Head Up Display, originally developed for aircraft, is a transparent display that presents data without requiring users to look away from their usual viewpoints. A similar effect can be achieved in 3D graphics and used to overlay textual information on the 3D scene. Here, you will construct a sample program that will display a diagram and some information on top of the 3D graphics (HUD), as you can see in Figure 10.5.

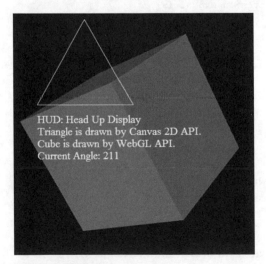

Figure 10.5 HUD

The goal of the program is to draw a triangle and some simple information about the 3D scene, including the current rotation angle of the cube (from `PickObject`) that will change as the cube rotates.

How to Implement a HUD

This HUD effect can be implemented using HTML and the canvas function without WebGL. This is done as follows:

1. In the HTML file, prepare a `<canvas>` to draw the 3D graphics using WebGL and another `<canvas>` to draw the HUD using the canvas function. In other words, prepare two `<canvas>` and place the HUD on top of the WebGL canvas.

2. Draw the 3D graphics using the WebGL API on the `<canvas>` for WebGL.

3. Draw the HUD using the canvas functions on the `<canvas>` for the HUD.

As you can see, this is extremely simple and shows the power of WebGL and its ability to mix 2D and 3D graphics within the browser. Let's take a look at the sample program.

Sample Program (HUD.html)

Because we need to make changes to the HTML file to add the extra canvas, we show HUD. html in Listing 10.4, with the additions in bold.

Listing 10.4   HUD.html

```
 1  <!DOCTYPE html>
 2  <html lang="ja">
      ...
 8    <body onload="main()">
 9      <canvas id="webgl" width="400" height="400" style="position:
                                         ➥absolute; z-index: 0">
10        Please use a browser that supports "canvas"
11      </canvas>
12      <canvas id="hud" width="400" height="400" style="position:
                                         ➥absolute;z-index: 1"></canvas>
      ...
18      <script src="HUD.js"></script>
19    </body>
20  </html>
```

The `style` attribute, used to define how an element looks or how it is arranged, allows you to place the HUD canvas on top of the WebGL canvas. Style information is composed of the property name and the value separated with a : as seen at line 9: `style="position: absolute"`. Multiple style elements are separated with `;`.

In this example, you use `position`, which specifies how the element is placed, and the `z-index`, which specifies the hierarchical relationship.

You can specify the position of the element in the absolute coordinate if you use `absolute` for the `position` value. Unless you specify the position, all the elements specified to this attribute will be place at the same position. `z-index` specifies the order in which elements are displayed when multiple elements are at the same position. The element with the larger number will be displayed over the one with a smaller number. In this case, the `z-index` of the `<canvas>` for the HUD at line 12 is 1.

The result of this code is two `<canvas>` elements, placed at the same location with the `<canvas>` that displays the HUD on top of the `<canvas>` that displays the WebGL. Conveniently, the background of the canvas element is transparent by default, so the WebGL canvas can be seen through the HUD canvas. Anything that is drawn on the HUD canvas will appear over the 3D objects and create the effect of a HUD.

Sample Program (HUD.js)

Next, let's take a look at `HUD.js` in Listing 10.5. There are two changes made compared to `PickObject.js`:

1. Retrieve the rendering context to draw in the `<canvas>` for the HUD and use it to draw.

2. Register the event handler when the mouse is clicked to the `<canvas>` for the HUD and not to the `<canvas>` for WebGL.

Step 1 simply uses the source code used in Chapter 2, "Your First Step with WebGL," to draw a triangle onto the `<canvas>`. Step 2 is required to ensure that mouse click information is passed to the HUD canvas rather than the WebGL canvas. The vertex shader and fragment shader are the same as `PickObject.js`.

Listing 10.5 HUD.js

```
 1  // HUD.js
    ...
30  function main() {
31    // Retrieve <canvas> element
32    var canvas = document.getElementById('webgl');
33    var hud = document.getElementById('hud');
      ...
40    // Get the rendering context for WebGL
41    var gl = getWebGLContext(canvas);
42    // Get the rendering context for 2DCG
43    var ctx = hud.getContext('2d');
      ...
82    // Register the event handler
83    hud.onmousedown = function(ev) {    // Mouse is pressed
```

```
          . . .
89            check(gl, n, x_in_canvas, y_in_canvas, currentAngle, u_Clicked,
                                              ➡viewProjMatrix, u_MvpMatrix);
          . . .
91        }
92
93        var tick = function() {    // Start drawing
94            currentAngle = animate(currentAngle);
95            draw2D(ctx, currentAngle); // Draw 2D
96            draw(gl, n, currentAngle, viewProjMatrix, u_MvpMatrix);
97            requestAnimationFrame(tick, canvas);
98        };
99        tick();
100   }

          . . .
184   function draw2D(ctx, currentAngle) {
185       ctx.clearRect(0, 0, 400, 400);              // Clear <hud>
186       // Draw triangle with white lines
187       ctx.beginPath();                            // Start drawing
188       ctx.moveTo(120, 10); ctx.lineTo(200, 150);  ctx.lineTo(40, 150);
189       ctx.closePath();
190       ctx.strokeStyle = 'rgba(255, 255, 255, 1)'; // Set the line color
191       ctx.stroke();                      // Draw triangle with white lines
192       // Draw white letters
193       ctx.font = '18px "Times New Roman"';
194       ctx.fillStyle = 'rgba(255, 255, 255, 1)';  // Set the letter color
195       ctx.fillText('HUD: Head Up Display', 40, 180);
196       ctx.fillText('Triangle is drawn by Hud API.', 40, 200);
197       ctx.fillText('Cube is drawn by WebGL API.', 40, 220);
198       ctx.fillText('Current Angle: '+ Math.floor(currentAngle), 40, 240);
199   }
```

Because the processing flow of the program is straightforward, let's take a look from main() at line 30. First, line 33 obtains the <canvas> element for the HUD. This is used to get the drawing context for the 2D graphics (Chapter 2) at line 43, which is used to draw the HUD. You register the mouse-click event handler for the HUD canvas (hud) instead of the WebGL canvas in PickObject.js. This is because the event goes to the HUD canvas, which is placed on top of the WebGL canvas.

The code from line 93 handles the animation and uses draw2D(), added at line 95, to draw the HUD information.

draw2D() is defined at line 184 and takes ctx parameters, the context to draw on the canvas, and the current rotation angle, currentAngle. Line 185 clears the HUD canvas using the clearRect() method, which takes the upper-left corner, the width, and the height of the rectangle to clear. Lines 187 to 191 draw the triangle which, unlike drawing a rectangle as explained in Chapter 2, requires that you define the path (outline) of a triangle to draw it. Lines 187 to 191 define the path, set the color, and draw the triangle. Lines 193 onward specify the text color and font and then use `fillText()`, which specifies the letters to draw as the first parameter and the x and y coordinates to draw as the second and third parameters, to actually write the text. Line 198 displays the current rotation angle and uses `Math.floor()` to truncate the numbers below the decimal point. Line 185 clears the canvas because the displayed value (rotation angle) changes at each drawing.

Display a 3D Object on a Web Page (3DoverWeb)

Displaying a 3D object on a web page is simple with WebGL and the inverse of the HUD example. In this case, the WebGL canvas is on top of the web page, and the canvas is set to transparent. Figure 10.6 shows 3DoverWeb.

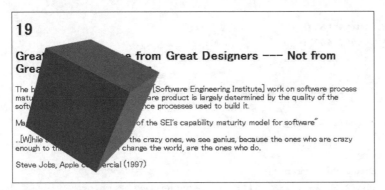

Figure 10.6 3DoverWeb[2]

`3DoverWeb.js` is based on `PickObject.js` with almost no changes. The only change is that the alpha value of the clear color is changed from 1.0 to 0.0 at line 55.

```
55    gl.clearColor(0.0, 0.0, 0.0, 0.0);
```

By making the alpha value 0.0, the background of the WebGL canvas becomes transparent, and you can see the web page behind the WebGL `<canvas>`. You can also experiment with the alpha value; any value other than 1.0 changes the transparency and makes the web page more or less visible.

Fog (Atmospheric Effect)

In 3D graphics, the term **fog** is used to describe the effect that makes a distant object seem hazy. The term describes objects in any medium, so objects underwater can also have a

---

[2] The sentences on the web page on the background are from the book *The Design of Design* (by Frederick P. Brooks Jr, Pearson).

fog effect applied. Here, you construct a sample program `Fog` that realizes the fog effect. Figure 10.7 shows a screen shot. You can adjust the density of the fog with the up/down arrow keys. Try running the sample program and experiment with the effect.

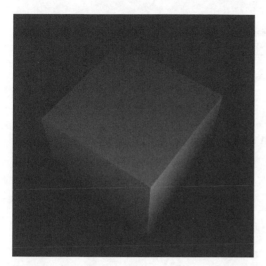

Figure 10.7 Fog

How to Implement Fog

There are various ways to calculate fog, but here you will use a linear computation (**linear fog**) because the calculation is easy. The linear fog method determines the density of the fog by setting the starting point (the distance where the object starts to become hazy) and the end point (where the object is completely obscured). The density of the fog between these points is changed linearly. Note that the end point is not where the fog ends; rather, it is where the fog becomes so dense that it obscures all objects. We will call how clearly we can see the object the **fog factor**; it is calculated, in the case of linear fog, as follows:

Equation 10.1

$$\langle fog\ factor \rangle = \frac{(\langle end\ point \rangle - \langle distance\ from\ eye\ point \rangle)}{(\langle end\ point \rangle - \langle starting\ point \rangle)}$$

Where

$$\langle starting\ point \rangle \le \langle distance\ from\ eye\ point \rangle \le \langle end\ point \rangle$$

When the fog factor is 1.0, you can see the object completely, and if it 0.0, you cannot see it at all (see Figure 10.8). The fog factor is 1.0 when the (distance from eye point) < (starting point), and 0.0 when (end point) < (distance from eye point).

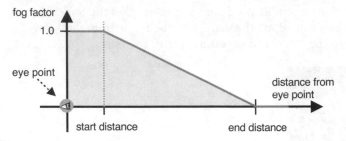

Figure 10.8 Fog factor

You can calculate the color of a fragment based on the fog factor, as follows in Equation 10.2.

Equation 10.2

$$\langle \textit{fragment color} \rangle =$$
$$\langle \textit{surface color} \rangle \times \langle \textit{fog factor} \rangle + \langle \textit{fog color} \rangle \times \left(1 - \langle \textit{fog factor} \rangle \right)$$

Now, let's take a look at the sample program.

Sample Program (Fog.js)

The sample program is shown in Listing 10.6. Here, you (1) calculate the distance of the object (vertex) from the eye point in the vertex shader, and based on that, you (2) calculate the fog factor and the color of the object based on the fog factor in the fragment shader. Note that this program specifies the position of the eye point with the world coordinate system (see Appendix G, "World Coordinate System Versus Local Coordinate System") so the fog calculation takes place in the world coordinate system.

Listing 10.6 Fog.js

```
 1  // Fog.js
 2  // Vertex shader program
 3  var VSHADER_SOURCE =
    ...
 7  'uniform mat4 u_ModelMatrix;\n' +
 8  'uniform vec4 u_Eye;\n' + // The eye point (world coordinates)
 9  'varying vec4 v_Color;\n' +
10  'varying float v_Dist;\n' +
11  'void main() {\n' +
12  '  gl_Position = u_MvpMatrix * a_Position;\n' +
13  '  v_Color = a_Color;\n' +
14     // Calculate the distance to each vertex from eye point      <-(1)
15  '  v_Dist = distance(u_ModelMatrix * a_Position, u_Eye);\n' +
16  '}\n';
17
```

```
18   // Fragment shader program
19   var FSHADER_SOURCE =
        ...
23   'uniform vec3 u_FogColor;\n' + // Color of Fog
24   'uniform vec2 u_FogDist;\n' +  // Fog starting point, end point)
25   'varying vec4 v_Color;\n' +
26   'varying float v_Dist;\n' +
27   'void main() {\n' +
28      // Calculate the fog factor                              <-(2)
29   '   float fogFactor = clamp((u_FogDist.y - v_Dist) / (u_FogDist.y -
                                            ➡u_FogDist.x), 0.0, 1.0);\n' +
30      // u_FogColor * (1 - fogFactor) + v_Color * fogFactor
31   '   vec3 color = mix(u_FogColor, vec3(v_Color), fogFactor);\n' +
32   '   gl_FragColor = vec4(color, v_Color.a);\n' +
33   '}\n';
34
35   function main() {
        ...
53      var n = initVertexBuffers(gl);
        ...
59      // Color of fog
60      var fogColor = new Float32Array([0.137, 0.231, 0.423]);
61      // Distance of fog [fog starts, fog completely covers object]
62      var fogDist = new Float32Array([55, 80]);
63      // Position of eye point (world coordinates)
64      var eye = new Float32Array([25, 65, 35]);
        ...
76      // Pass fog color, distances, and eye point to uniform variable
77      gl.uniform3fv(u_FogColor, fogColor); // Fog color
78      gl.uniform2fv(u_FogDist, fogDist);   // Starting point and end point
79      gl.uniform4fv(u_Eye, eye);           // Eye point
80
81      // Set clear color and enable hidden surface removal function
82      gl.clearColor(fogColor[0], fogColor[1], fogColor[2], 1.0);
        ...
93      mvpMatrix.lookAt(eye[0], eye[1], eye[2], 0, 2, 0, 0, 1, 0);
        ...
97      document.onkeydown = function(ev){ keydown(ev, gl, n, u_FogDist, fogDist); };
        ...
```

The calculation of the distance from the eye point to the vertex, done by the vertex shader, is straightforward. You simply transform the vertex coordinates to the world coordinates using the model matrix and then call the built-in function `distance()` with the position of the eye point (world coordinates) and the vertex coordinates. The `distance()`

function calculates the distance between two coordinates specified by the arguments. This calculation takes place at line 15, and the result is then written to the `v_Dist` variable and passed to the fragment shader.

The fragment shader calculates the fogged color of the object using Equations 10.1 and 10.2. The fog color, fog starting point, and fog end point, which are needed to calculate the fogged color, are passed in the uniform variables `u_FogColor` and `u_FogDist` at lines 23 and 24. `u_FogDist.x` is the starting point, and `u_FogDist.y` is the end point.

The fog factor is calculated at line 29 using Equation 10.1. The `clamp()` function is a built-in function; if the value specified by the first parameter is outside the range specified by the second and third parameter ([0.0 0.1] in this case), it will fix the value to one within the range. In other words, the value is fixed to 0.0 if the value is smaller than 0.0, and 1.0 if the value is larger than 1.0. If the value is within the range, the value is unchanged.

Line 31 is the calculation of the fragment color using the fog factor. This implements Equation 10.2 and uses a built-in function, `mix()`, which calculates x*(1–z)+y*z, where x is the first parameter, y is the second, and z is the third.

The processing in JavaScript's `main()` function from line 35 sets up the values necessary for calculating the fog in the appropriate uniform variables.

You should note that there are many types of fog calculations other than linear fog, for example exponential fog, used in OpenGL (see the book *OpenGL Programming Guide*). You can implement these fog calculations using the same approach, just changing the calculation method in the fragment shader.

Use the w Value (Fog_w.js)

Because the distance calculation within the shader can affect performance, an alternative method allows you to easily approximate the calculation of the distance from the eye point to the object (vertex) by using the w value of coordinates transformed by the model view projection conversion. In this case, the coordinates are substituted in `gl_Position`. The fourth component, w of `gl_Position` which you haven't used explicitly before, is the z value of each vertex in the view coordinate system multiplied by –1. The eye point is the origin in the view coordinates, and the view direction is the negative direction of z, so z is a negative value. The w value, which is the z value multiplied by –1, can be used as an approximation of the distance.

If you reimplement the calculation in the vertex shader using w, as shown in Listing 10.7, the fog effect will work as before.

Listing 10.7 Fog_w.js

```
1  // Fog_w.js
2  // Vertex shader program
3  var VSHADER_SOURCE =
     ...
```

```
7      'varying vec4 v_Color;\n' +
8      'varying float v_Dist;\n' +
9      'void main() {\n' +
10     '  gl_Position = u_MvpMatrix * a_Position;\n' +
11     '  v_Color = a_Color;\n' +
12        // Use the negative z value of vertex in view coordinate system
13     '  v_Dist = gl_Position.w;\n' +
14     '}\n';
```

Make a Rounded Point

In Chapter 2, you constructed a sample program that draws a point to help you understand the basics of shaders. However, to allow you to focus on the operation of the shaders, the point displayed wasn't "round" but actually "square," which is simpler to draw. In this section, you construct a sample program, RoundedPoint, which draws a round point (see Figure 10.9).

Figure 10.9 A screen shot of RoundedPoint

How to Implement a Rounded Point

To draw a "round" point, you just have to make the "rectangle" point round. This can be achieved using the rasterization process that takes place between the vertex shader and the fragment shader and was explained in Chapter 5, "Using Colors and Texture Images." This rasterization process generates a rectangle consisting of multiple fragments, and each fragment is passed to the fragment shader. If you draw these fragments as-is, a rectangle will be displayed. So you just need to modify the fragment shader to draw only the fragments inside the circle, as shown in Figure 10.10.

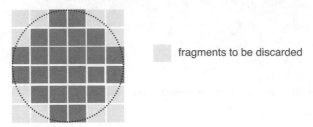

fragments to be discarded

Figure 10.10 Discarding fragments to turn a rectangle into a circle

To achieve this, you need to know the position of each fragment created during rasterization. In Chapter 5, you saw a sample program that uses the built-in variable `gl_FragCoord` to pass (input) the data to the fragment shader. In addition to this, there is one more built-in variable `gl_PointCoord`, which is suitable for drawing a round point (see Table 10.1).

Table 10.1 Built-In Variables of Fragment Shader (Input)

Type and Name of Variable	Description
`vec4 gl_FragCoord`	Window coordinates of fragment
`vec4 gl_PointCoord`	Position of fragment in the drawn point (0.0 to 1.0)

`gl_PointCoord` gives the position of each fragment taken from the range (0.0, 0.0) to (1.0, 1.0), as shown in Figure 10.11. To make the rectangle round, you simply have to discard the fragments outside the circle centered at (0.5, 0.5) with radius 0.5. You can use the `discard` statement to discard these fragments.

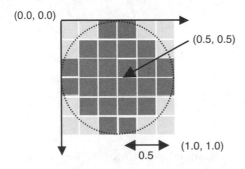

Figure 10.11 Coordinates of gl_PointCoord

Sample Program (RoundedPoints.js)

The sample program is shown in Listing 10.8. This is derived from `MultiPoint.js`, which was used in Chapter 4, "More Transformations and Basic Animation," to draw multiple points. The only difference is in the fragment shader. The vertex shader is also shown for reference.

Listing 10.8 RoundedPoint.js

```
 1  // RoundedPoints.js
 2  // Vertex shader program
 3  var VSHADER_SOURCE =
 4    'attribute vec4 a_Position;\n' +
 5    'void main() {\n' +
 6    '  gl_Position = a_Position;\n' +
 7    '  gl_PointSize = 10.0;\n' +
 8    '}\n';
 9
10  // Fragment shader program
11  var FSHADER_SOURCE =
      . . .
15    'void main() {\n' +          // Center coordinate is (0.5, 0.5)
16    '  float dist = distance(gl_PointCoord, vec2(0.5, 0.5));\n' +
17    '  if(dist < 0.5) {\n' +       // Radius is 0.5
18    '    gl_FragColor = vec4(1.0, 0.0, 0.0, 1.0);\n' +
19    '  } else { discard; }\n' +
20    '}\n';
21
22  function main() {
      . . .
53    gl.drawArrays(gl.POINTS, 0, n);
54  }
```

The key difference is the calculation, starting at line 16, which determines whether a fragment should be discarded. gl_PointCoord holds the fragment's position (specified in the range 0.0 to 0.1), and the center point is (0.5, 0.5). Therefore, to make a rectangle point round, you have to do the following:

1. Calculate the distance from the center (0.5, 0.5) to each fragment.

2. Draw those fragments for which the distance is less than 0.5.

In RoundedPoint.js, the distance calculation takes place at line 16. Here, you just have to calculate the distance between the center point (0.5, 0.5) and gl_PointCoord. Because the gl_PointCoord is a vec2 type, you need to pass (0.5, 0.5) to distance() as a vec2.

Once you have calculated the distance from the center, it is used at line 17 to check whether the distance is less than 0.5 (in other words, whether the fragment is in the circle). If the fragment is in circle, the fragment is drawn so line 18 uses gl_FragColor to set the draw color. Otherwise, at line 19, the discard statement causes WebGL to automatically throw away the fragment.

Alpha Blending

The alpha value controls the transparency of drawn objects. If you specify 0.5 as the alpha value, the object becomes semi-transparent, allowing anything drawn underneath it to be partially visible. As the alpha value approaches 0, more of the background objects appear. If you try this yourself, you'll actually see that as you decrease the alpha value, WebGL objects become white. This is because WebGL's default behavior is to use the same alpha value for both objects and the <canvas>. In the sample programs, the web page behind the <canvas> is white, so this shows through.

Let's construct a sample program that shows how to use alpha blending to get the desired effect. The function that allows the use of the alpha value is called an **alpha blending** (or simply **blending**) **function**. This function is already built into WebGL, so you just need to enable it to tell WebGL to start to use the alpha values supplied.

How to Implement Alpha Blending

You'll need the following two steps to enable and use the alpha blending function.

1. Enable the alpha blending function:

```
gl.enable(gl.BLEND);
```

2. Specify the blending function:

```
gl.blendFunc(gl.SRC_ALPHA, gl.ONE_MINUS_SRC_ALPHA);
```

The blending function will be explained later, so let's try using the sample program. Here, we will reuse LookAtTrianglesWithKey_ViewVolume described in Chapter 7, "Toward the 3D World." As shown in Figure 10.12, this program draws three triangles and allows the position of the eye point to be changed using the arrow key.

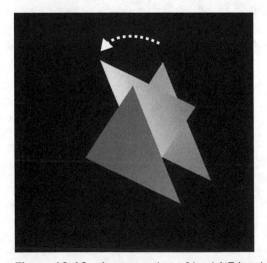

Figure 10.12   A screen shot of LookAtTrianglesWithKeys_ViewVolume

Let's add the code for steps 1 and 2, specify 0.4 as the alpha value of the color of the triangles, and call the resulting program LookAtBlendedTriangles. Figure 10.13 shows the effect when run. As you can see, all triangles became semitransparent, and you are able to see the triangles behind. When you move the eye point with the arrow key, you can see that the blending is continuously taking place.

Figure 10.13   A screen shot of LookAtBlendedTriangles

Let's look at the sample program.

Sample Program (LookAtBlendedTriangles.js)

LookAtBlendedTriangles.js is shown in Listing 10.9. The code that has changed is in lines 51 to 54, and the alpha value (0.4) is added to the definition of color information in initVertexBuffer() at lines 81 to 91. Accordingly, the *size* and *stride* parameters have changed for gl.vertexAttribPointer().

Listing 10.9   LookAtBlenderTriangles.js

```
 1  // LookAtBlendedTriangles.js
 2  // LookAtTrianglesWithKey_ViewVolume.js is the original
    ...
25  function main() {
    ...
43    var n = initVertexBuffers(gl);
    ...
51    // Enable alpha blending
52    gl.enable (gl.BLEND);
53    // Set blending function
54    gl.blendFunc(gl.SRC_ALPHA, gl.ONE_MINUS_SRC_ALPHA);
    ...
```

```
75      draw(gl, n, u_ViewMatrix, viewMatrix);
76  }
77
78  function initVertexBuffers(gl) {
79      var verticesColors = new Float32Array([
80          // Vertex coordinates and color(RGBA)
81          0.0,   0.5, -0.4,    0.4,  1.0,  0.4,  0.4,
82         -0.5,  -0.5, -0.4,    0.4,  1.0,  0.4,  0.4,
            ...
91          0.5,  -0.5,  0.0,    1.0,  0.4,  0.4,  0.4,
92      ]);
93      var n = 9;
            ...
127     return n;
128 }
```

Blending Function

Let's explore the blending function `gl.blendFunc()` to understand how this can be used to achieve the blending effect. You need two colors for blending: the color to blend (source color) and the color to be blended (destination color). For example, when you draw one triangle on top of the other, the color of the triangle already drawn is the destination color, and the color of the triangle drawn on top is the source color.

`gl.blendFunc(src_factor, dst_factor)`

Specify the method to blend the source color and the destination color. The blended color is calculated as follows:

$$\langle color(RGB) \rangle = \langle source\ color \rangle \times src\_factor + \langle destination\ color \rangle \times dst\_factor$$

Parameters	src_factor	Specifies the multiplier for the source color (Table 10.2).
	dst_factor	Specifies the multiplier for the destination color (Table 10.2).
Return value	None	
Errors	INVALID_ENUM	*src_factor* and *dst_factor* are none of the values in Table 10.2

Table 10.2 Constant Values that Can Be Specified as src_factor and dst_factor[3]

Constant	Multiplicand for R	Multiplicand for G	Multiplicand for B
gl.ZERO	0.0	0.0	0.0
gl.ONE	1.0	1.0	1.0

Constant	Multiplicand for R	Multiplicand for G	Multiplicand for B
gl.SRC_COLOR	Rs	Gs	Bs
gl.ONE_MINUS_SRC_COLOR	(1 − Rs)	(1 − Gs)	(1 − Bs)
gl.DST_COLOR	Rd	Gd	Bd
gl.ONE_MINUS_DST_COLOR	(1 − Rd)	(1 − Bd)	(1 − Gd)
gl.SRC_ALPHA	As	As	As
gl.ONE_MINUS_SRC_ALPHA	(1 − As)	(1 − As)	(1 − As)
gl.DST_ALPHA	Ad	Ad	Ad
gl.ONE_MINUS_DST_ALPHA	(1 − Ad)	(1 − Ad)	(1 − Ad)
gl.SRC_ALPHA_SATURATE	min(As, Ad)	min(As, Ad)	min(As, Ad)

[3] gl.CONSTANT_COLOR, gl.ONE_MINUSCONSTANT_COLOR, gl.CONSTANT_ALPHA, *and* gl.ONE_MINUS_CONSTANT_ALPHA *are removed from OpenGL.*

(Rs,Gs,Bs,As) is the source color and (Rd,Gd,Bd,Ad) is the destination color.

In the sample program, you used the following:

```
54      gl.blendFunc(gl.SRC_ALPHA, gl.ONE_MINUS_SRC_ALPHA);
```

For example, if the source color is semitransparent green (0.0, 1.0, 0.0, 0.4) and the destination color is yellow (1.0, 1.0, 0.0, 1.0), *src_factor* becomes the alpha value 0.4 and *dst_factor* becomes (1 − 0.4)=0.6. The calculation is shown in Figure 10.14.

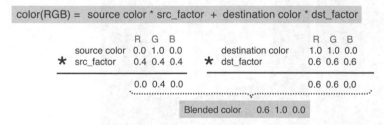

Figure 10.14   Calculation of gl.blendFunc(gl.SRC_ALPHA, gl.ONE_MINUS_SRC_ALPHA)

You can experiment with the other possible parameter values for *src_factor, dst_factor,* but one that is often used is additive blending. When used, the result will become brighter than the original value because it is a simple addition. It can be used for an indicator or the lighting effect resulting from an explosion.

```
glBlendFunc(GL_SRC_ALPHA, GL_ONE);
```

Alpha Blend 3D Objects (BlendedCube.js)

Let's now explore the effects of alpha blending on a representative 3D object, a cube, by making it semitransparent. You will reuse the ColoredCube sample program from Chapter 7 to create BlendedCube, which adds the two steps needed for blending (see Listing 10.10).

Listing 10.10 BlendedCube.js

```
 1    // BlendedCube.js
       ...
47    // Set the clear color and enable the depth test
48    gl.clearColor(0.0, 0.0, 0.0, 1.0);
49    gl.enable(gl.DEPTH_TEST);
50    // Enable alpha blending
51    gl.enable (gl.BLEND);
52    // Set blending function
53    gl.blendFunc(gl.SRC_ALPHA, gl.ONE_MINUS_SRC_ALPHA);
```

Unfortunately, if you run this program as-is, you won't see the expected result (right side of Figure 10.15); rather, you will see something similar to the left side, which is no different from the original ColoredCube used in Chapter 7.

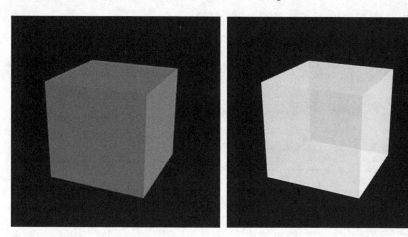

Figure 10.15 BlendedCube

This is because of the hidden surface removal function enabled at line 49. Blending only takes place on the drawn surfaces. When the hidden surface removal function is enabled, the hidden surfaces are not drawn, so there is no other surface to be blended with. Therefore, you don't see the blending effect as expected. To solve this problem, you can simply comment out line 49 that enables the hidden surface removal function.

```
48    gl.clearColor(0.0, 0.0, 0.0, 1.0);
49    // gl.enable(gl.DEPTH_TEST);
50    // Enable alpha blending
51    gl.enable (gl.BLEND);
```

How to Draw When Alpha Values Coexist

This is a quick solution, but it's not very satisfactory because, as we've seen in Chapter 7, hidden surface removal is often needed to correctly draw a 3D scene.

You can overcome this problem by drawing objects while turning the hidden surface removal function on and off.

1. Enable the hidden surface removal function.

   ```
   gl.enable(gl.DEPTH_TEST);
   ```

2. Draw all the opaque objects (whose alpha values are 1.0).

3. Make the depth buffer (Chapter 7), which is used in the hidden surface removal, read-only.

   ```
   gl.depthMask(false);
   ```

4. Draw all the transparent objects (whose alpha values are smaller than 1.0). Note, they should be sorted by the depth order and drawn back to front.

5. Make the depth buffer readable and writable.

   ```
   gl.depthMask(true);
   ```

If you completely disable the hidden surface removal function, when there are transparent objects behind opaque objects, the transparent object will not be hidden behind the opaque objects. So you need to control that with gl.depthMask(). gl.depthMask() has the following specification.

gl.depthMask(mask)		
Enable or disable writing into the depth buffer.		
Parameters	mask	Specifies whether the depth buffer is enabled for writing. If *mask* is false, depth buffer writing is disabled.
Return value	None	
Errors	None	

The depth buffer was briefly introduced in Chapter 7. The z values of fragments (which are normalized to a value between 0.0 and 1.0) are written into the buffer. For example, say there are two triangles on top of each other and you draw from the triangle on top. First, the z value of the triangle on top is written into the depth buffer. Then, when the triangle on bottom is drawn, the hidden surface removal function compares the z value of its fragment that is going to be drawn, with the z value already written in the depth buffer. Then only when the z value of the fragment that is going to be drawn is smaller than the existing value in the buffer (that is, when it's closer to the eye point) will the fragment be drawn into the color buffer. This approach ensures that hidden surface removal is achieved. Therefore, after drawing, the z value of the fragment of the surface that can be seen from the eye point is left in the depth buffer.

Opaque objects are drawn into the color buffer in the correct order by removing the hidden surfaces in the processing of steps 1 and 2, and the z value that represents the order is written in the depth buffer. Transparent objects are drawn into the color buffer using that z value in steps 3, 4, and 5, so the hidden surfaces of the transparent objects behind the opaque objects will be removed. This results in the correct image being shown where both objects coexist.

Switching Shaders

The sample programs in this book draw using a single vertex shader and a single fragment shader. If all objects can be drawn with the same shaders, there is no problem. However, if you want to change the drawing method for each object, you need to add significant complexity to the shaders to achieve multiple effects. A solution is to prepare more than one shader and then switch between these shaders as required. Here, you construct a sample program, ProgramObject, which draws a cube colored with a single color and another cube with a texture image. Figure 10.16 shows a screen shot.

Figure 10.16   A screen shot of ProgramObject

This program is also an example of the shading of an object with a texture image.

How to Implement Switching Shaders

The shaders can be switched easily by creating program objects, as explained in Chapter 8, "Lighting Objects," and switching them before drawing. Switching is carried out using the function gl.useProgram(). Because you are explicitly manipulating shader objects, you cannot use the convenience function initShaders(). However, you can use the function createProgram() in cuon-utils.js, which is called from initShaders().

The following is the processing flow of the sample program. It performs the same procedure twice, so it looks long, but the essential code is simple:

1. Prepare the shaders to draw an object shaded with a single color.

2. Prepare the shaders to draw an object with a texture image.

3. Create a program object that has the shaders from step 1 with createProgram().

4. Create a program object that has the shaders from step 2 with createProgram().

5. Specify the program object created by step 3 with gl.useProgram().

6. Enable the buffer object after assigning it to the attribute variables.

7. Draw a cube (drawn in a single color).

8. Specify the program object created in step 4 using gl.useProgram().

9. Enable the buffer object after assigning it to the attribute variables.

10. Draw a cube (texture is pasted).

Now let's look at the sample program.

Sample Program (ProgramObject.js)

The key program code for steps 1 to 4 is shown in Listing 10.11. Two types of vertex shader and fragment shader are prepared: SOLID_VSHADER_SOURCE (line 3) and SOLID_FSHADER_SOURCE (line 19) to draw an object in a single color, and TEXTURE_VSHADER_SOURCE (line 29) and TEXTURE_FSHADER_SOURCE (line 46) to draw an object with a texture image. Because the focus here is on how to switch the program objects, the contents of the shaders are omitted.

Listing 10.11   ProgramObject (Process for Steps 1 to 4)

```
 1  // ProgramObject.js
 2  // Vertex shader for single color drawing              <- (1)
 3  var SOLID_VSHADER_SOURCE =
      ...
18  // Fragment shader for single color drawing
```

```
19  var SOLID_FSHADER_SOURCE =
      ...
28  // Vertex shader for texture drawing                              <- (2)
29  var TEXTURE_VSHADER_SOURCE =
      ...
45  // Fragment shader for texture drawing
46  var TEXTURE_FSHADER_SOURCE =
      ...
58  function main() {
      ...
69    // Initialize shaders
70    var solidProgram = createProgram(gl, SOLID_VSHADER_SOURCE,
                                    ➡SOLID_FSHADER_SOURCE);   <- (3)
71    var texProgram = createProgram(gl, TEXTURE_VSHADER_SOURCE,
                                    ➡TEXTURE_FSHADER_SOURCE); <- (4)
      ...
77    // Get the variables in the program object for single color drawing
78    solidProgram.a_Position = gl.getAttribLocation(solidProgram, 'a_Position');
79    solidProgram.a_Normal = gl.getAttribLocation(solidProgram, 'a_Normal');
      ...
83    // Get the storage location of attribute/uniform variables
84    texProgram.a_Position = gl.getAttribLocation(texProgram, 'a_Position');
85    texProgram.a_Normal = gl.getAttribLocation(texProgram, 'a_Normal');
      ...
89    texProgram.u_Sampler = gl.getUniformLocation(texProgram, 'u_Sampler');
      ...
99    // Set vertex information
100   var cube = initVertexBuffers(gl, solidProgram);
      ...
106   // Set texture
107   var texture = initTextures(gl, texProgram);
      ...
122   // Start drawing
123   var currentAngle = 0.0; // Current rotation angle (degrees)
124   var tick = function() {
125     currentAngle = animate(currentAngle);  // Update rotation angle
      ...
128     // Draw a cube in single color
129     drawSolidCube(gl, solidProgram, cube, -2.0, currentAngle, viewProjMatrix);
130     // Draw a cube with texture
131     drawTexCube(gl, texProgram, cube, texture, 2.0, currentAngle,
                                                ➡viewProjMatrix);
132
133     window.requestAnimationFrame(tick, canvas);
```

```
134    };
135    tick();
136  }
137
138  function initVertexBuffers(gl, program) {
        ...
148    var vertices = new Float32Array([   // Vertex coordinates
149      1.0, 1.0, 1.0, -1.0, 1.0, 1.0, -1.0,-1.0, 1.0,  1.0,-1.0, 1.0,
150      1.0, 1.0, 1.0,  1.0,-1.0, 1.0,  1.0,-1.0,-1.0,  1.0, 1.0,-1.0,
        ...
154      1.0,-1.0,-1.0, -1.0,-1.0,-1.0, -1.0, 1.0,-1.0,  1.0, 1.0,-1.0
155    ]);
156
157    var normals = new Float32Array([   // Normal
        ...
164    ]);
165
166    var texCoords = new Float32Array([ // Texture coordinates
        ...
173    ]);
174
175    var indices = new Uint8Array([      // Indices for vertices
        ...
182    ]);
183
184    var o = new Object(); // Use Object to return buffer objects
185
186    // Write vertex information to buffer object
187    o.vertexBuffer = initArrayBufferForLaterUse(gl, vertices, 3, gl.FLOAT);
188    o.normalBuffer = initArrayBufferForLaterUse(gl, normals, 3, gl.FLOAT);
189    o.texCoordBuffer = initArrayBufferForLaterUse(gl, texCoords, 2, gl.FLOAT);
190    o.indexBuffer = initElementArrayBufferForLaterUse(gl, indices,
                                              ➥gl.UNSIGNED_BYTE);
        ...
193    o.numIndices = indices.length;
        ...
199    return o;
200  }
```

Starting with the main() function in JavaScript, you first create a program object for
each shader with createProgram() at lines 70 and 71. The arguments of the createPro-
gram() are the same as the initShaders(), and the return value is the program object.
You save each program object in solidProgram and texProgram. Then you retrieve the
storage location of the attribute and uniform variables for each shader at lines 78 to 89.
You will store them in the corresponding properties of the program object, as you did in

`MultiJointModel_segment.js`. Again, you leverage JavaScript's ability to freely append a new property of any type to an object.

The vertex information is then stored in the buffer object by `initVertexBuffers()` at line 100. You need (1) vertex coordinates, (2) the normals, and (3) indices for the shader to draw objects in a single color. In addition, for the shader to draw objects with a texture image, you need the texture coordinates. The processing in `initVertexBuffers()` handles this and binds the correct buffer object to the corresponding attribute variables when the program object is switched.

`initVertexBuffers()` prepares the vertex coordinates from line 148, normals from line 157, texture coordinates from line 166, and index arrays from line 175. Line 184 creates object (o) of type `Object`. Then you store the buffer object to the property of the object (lines 187 to 190). You can maintain each buffer object as a global variable, but that introduces too many variables and makes it hard to understand the program. By using properties, you can more conveniently manage all four buffer objects using one object o.[4]

You use `initArrayBufferForLaterUse()`, explained in `MultiJointModel_segment.js`, to create each buffer object. This function writes vertex information into the buffer object but does not assign it to the attribute variables. You use the buffer object name as its property name to make it easier to understand. Line 199 returns the object o as the return value.

Once back in `main()` in JavaScript, the texture image is set up in `initTextures()` at line 107, and then everything is ready to allow you to draw the two cube objects. First, you draw a single color cube using `drawSolidCube()` at line 129, and then you draw a cube with a texture image by using `drawTexCube()` at line 131. Listing 10.12 shows the latter half of the steps, steps 5 through 10.

Listing 10.12   ProgramObject.js (Processes for Steps 5 through 10)

```
236  function drawSolidCube(gl, program, o, x, angle, viewProjMatrix) {
237    gl.useProgram(program);   // Tell this program object is used          <-(5)
238
239    // Assign the buffer objects and enable the assignment                 <-(6)
240    initAttributeVariable(gl, program.a_Position, o.vertexBuffer);
241    initAttributeVariable(gl, program.a_Normal, o.normalBuffer);
242    gl.bindBuffer(gl.ELEMENT_ARRAY_BUFFER, o.indexBuffer);
243
244    drawCube(gl, program, o, x, angle, viewProjMatrix);     // Draw        <-(7)
245  }
246
247  function drawTexCube(gl, program, o, texture, x, angle, viewProjMatrix) {
```

---

[4] To keep the explanation simple, the object (o) was used. However, it is better programming practice to create a new user-defined type for managing the information about a buffer object and to use it to manage the four buffers.

```
248    gl.useProgram(program);    // Tell this program object is used <-(8)
249
250    // Assign the buffer objects and enable the assignment        <-(9)
251    initAttributeVariable(gl, program.a_Position, o.vertexBuffer);
252    initAttributeVariable(gl, program.a_Normal, o.normalBuffer);
253    initAttributeVariable(gl, program.a_TexCoord, o.texCoordBuffer);
254    gl.bindBuffer(gl.ELEMENT_ARRAY_BUFFER, o.indexBuffer);
255
256    // Bind texture object to texture unit 0
257    gl.activeTexture(gl.TEXTURE0);
258    gl.bindTexture(gl.TEXTURE_2D, texture);
259
260    drawCube(gl, program, o, x, angle, viewProjMatrix); // Draw  <-(10)
261  }
262
263  // Assign the buffer objects and enable the assignment
264  function initAttributeVariable(gl, a_attribute, buffer) {
265    gl.bindBuffer(gl.ARRAY_BUFFER, buffer);
266    gl.vertexAttribPointer(a_attribute, buffer.num, buffer.type, false, 0, 0);
267    gl.enableVertexAttribArray(a_attribute);
268  }
       ...
275  function drawCube(gl, program, o, x, angle, viewProjMatrix) {
276    // Calculate a model matrix
       ...
281    // Calculate transformation matrix for normal
       ...
286    // Calculate a model view projection matrix
       ...
291    gl.drawElements(gl.TRIANGLES, o.numIndices, o.indexBuffer.type, 0);
292  }
```

drawSolidCube() is defined at line 236 and uses gl.useProgram() at line 237 to tell the WebGL system that you will use the program (program object, solidProgram) specified by the argument. Then you can draw using solidProgram. The buffer objects for vertex coordinates and normals are assigned to attribute variables and enabled by initAttributeVariable() at lines 240 and 241. This function is defined at line 264. Line 242 binds the buffer object for the indices to gl.ELEMENT_ARRAY_BUFFER. With everything set up, you then call drawCube() at line 244, which uses gl.drawElements() at line 291 to perform the draw operation.

drawTexCube(), defined at line 247, follows the same steps as drawSolidCube(). Line 253 is added to assign the buffer object for texture coordinates to the attribute variables, and lines 257 and 258 are added to bind the texture object to the texture unit 0. The actual drawing is performed in drawCube(), just like drawSolidCube().

Once you've mastered this basic technique, you can use it to switch between any number of shader programs. This way you can use a variety of different drawing effects in a single scene.

Use What You've Drawn as a Texture Image

One simple but powerful technique is to draw some 3D objects and then use the resulting image as a texture image for another 3D object. Essentially, if you can use the content you've drawn as a texture image, you are able to generate images on-the-fly. This means you do not need to download images from the network, and you can apply special effects (such as motion blur and depth of field) before displaying the image. You can also use this technique for shadowing, which will be explained in the next section. Here, you will construct a sample program, FramebufferObject, which maps a rotating cube drawn with WebGL to a rectangle as a texture image. Figure 10.17 shows a screen shot.

Figure 10.17 FramebufferObject

If you actually run the program, you can see a rotating cube with a texture image of a summer sky pasted to the rectangle as its texture. Significantly, the image of the cube that is pasted on the rectangle is not a movie prepared in advance but a rotating cube drawn by WebGL in real time. This is quite powerful, so let's take a look at what WebGL must do to achieve this.

Framebuffer Object and Renderbuffer Object

By default, the WebGL system draws using a color buffer and, when using the hidden surface removal function, a depth buffer. The final image is kept in the color buffer.

The **framebuffer object** is an alternative mechanism you can use instead of a color buffer or a depth buffer (Figure 10.18). Unlike a color buffer, the content drawn in a framebuffer object is not directly displayed on the `<canvas>`. Therefore, you can use it if you want to perform different types of processing before displaying the drawn content. Or you can use it as a texture image. Such a technique is often referred to as **offscreen drawing**.

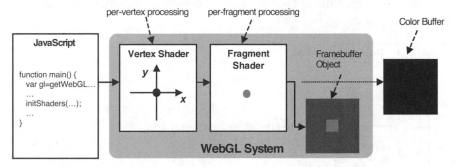

Figure 10.18   Framebuffer object

The framebuffer object has the structure shown in Figure 10.19 and supports substitutes for the color buffer and the depth buffer. As you can see, drawing is not carried out in the framebuffer itself, but in the drawing areas of the objects that the framebuffer points to. These objects are attached to the framebuffer using its **attachment** function. A **color attachment** specifies the destination for drawing to be a replacement for the color buffer. A **depth attachment** and a **stencil attachment** specify the replacements for the depth buffer and stencil buffer.

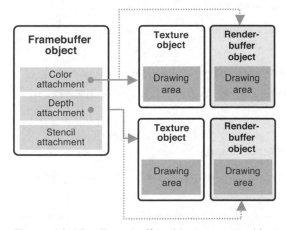

Figure 10.19   Framebuffer object, texture object, renderbuffer object

WebGL supports two types of objects that can be used to draw objects within: the texture object that you saw in Chapter 5, and the **renderbuffer object**. With the texture object, the content drawn into the texture object can be used as a texture image. The renderbuffer object is a more general-purpose drawing area, allowing a variety of data types to be written.

How to Implement Using a Drawn Object as a Texture

When you want to use the content drawn into a framebuffer object as a texture object, you actually need to use the content drawn into the color buffer for the texture object. Because you also want to remove the hidden surfaces for drawing, you will set up the framebuffer object as shown in Figure 10.20.

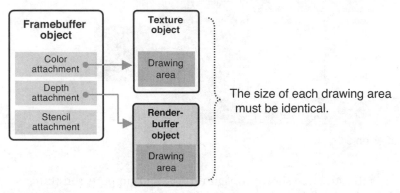

Figure 10.20 Configuration of framebuffer object when using drawn content as a texture

The following eight steps are needed for realizing this configuration. These processes are similar to the process for the buffer object. Step 2 was explained in Chapter 5, so there are essentially seven new processes:

1. Create a framebuffer object (gl.createFramebuffer()).

2. Create a texture object and set its size and parameters (gl.createTexture(), gl.bindTexture(), gl.texImage2D(), gl.Parameteri()).

3. Create a renderbuffer object (gl.createRenderbuffer()).

4. Bind the renderbuffer object to the target and set its size (gl.bindRenderbuffer(), gl.renderbufferStorage()).

5. Attach the texture object to the color attachment of the framebuffer object (gl.bindFramebuffer(), gl.framebufferTexture2D()).

6. Attach the renderbuffer object to the depth attachment of the framebuffer object (gl.framebufferRenderbuffer()).

7. Check whether the framebuffer object is configured correctly (gl.checkFramebuffer-Status()).

8. Draw using the framebuffer object (gl.bindFramebuffer()).

Now let's look at the sample program. The numbers in the sample program indicate the code used to implement the steps.

Sample Program (FramebufferObjectj.js)

Steps 1 to 7 of `FramebufferObject.js` are shown in Listing 10.13.

Listing 10.13   FramebufferObject.js (Processes for Steps 1 to 7)

```
  1  // FramebufferObject.js
     ...
 24  // Size of offscreen
 25  var OFFSCREEN_WIDTH = 256;
 26  var OFFSCREEN_HEIGHT = 256;
 27
 28  function main() {
     ...
 55    // Set vertex information
 56    var cube = initVertexBuffersForCube(gl);
 57    var plane = initVertexBuffersForPlane(gl);
     ...
 64    var texture = initTextures(gl);
     ...
 70    // Initialize framebuffer object (FBO)
 71    var fbo = initFramebufferObject(gl);
     ...
 80    var viewProjMatrix = new Matrix4();// For color buffer
 81    viewProjMatrix.setPerspective(30, canvas.width/canvas.height, 1.0, 100.0);
 82    viewProjMatrix.lookAt(0.0, 0.0, 7.0, 0.0, 0.0, 0.0, 0.0, 1.0, 0.0);
 83
 84    var viewProjMatrixFBO = new Matrix4();   // For FBO
 85    viewProjMatrixFBO.setPerspective(30.0, OFFSCREEN_WIDTH/OFFSCREEN_HEIGHT,
                                          ➥1.0, 100.0);
 86    viewProjMatrixFBO.lookAt(0.0, 2.0, 7.0, 0.0, 0.0, 0.0, 0.0, 1.0, 0.0);
     ...
 92      draw(gl, canvas, fbo, plane, cube, currentAngle, texture, viewProjMatrix,
                                          ➥viewProjMatrixFBO);
     ...
 96  }
     ...
263  function initFramebufferObject(gl) {
264    var framebuffer, texture, depthBuffer;
     ...
274    // Create a framebuffer object (FBO)                              <-(1)
275    framebuffer = gl.createFramebuffer();
     ...
281    // Create a texture object and set its size and parameters        <-(2)
282    texture = gl.createTexture(); // Create a texture object
     ...
```

```
287     gl.bindTexture(gl.TEXTURE_2D, texture);
288     gl.texImage2D(gl.TEXTURE_2D, 0, gl.RGBA, OFFSCREEN_WIDTH,
                      ➥OFFSCREEN_HEIGHT, 0, gl.RGBA, gl.UNSIGNED_BYTE, null);
289     gl.texParameteri(gl.TEXTURE_2D, gl.TEXTURE_MIN_FILTER, gl.LINEAR);
290     framebuffer.texture = texture;          // Store the texture object
291
292     // Create a renderbuffer object and set its size and parameters
293     depthBuffer = gl.createRenderbuffer();// Create a renderbuffer       <-(3)
        ...
298     gl.bindRenderbuffer(gl.RENDERBUFFER, depthBuffer);                   <-(4)
299     gl.renderbufferStorage(gl.RENDERBUFFER, gl.DEPTH_COMPONENT16,
                      ➥OFFSCREEN_WIDTH, OFFSCREEN_HEIGHT);
300
301     // Attach the texture and the renderbuffer object to the FBO
302     gl.bindFramebuffer(gl.FRAMEBUFFER, framebuffer);
303     gl.framebufferTexture2D(gl.FRAMEBUFFER, gl.COLOR_ATTACHMENT0,
                      ➥gl.TEXTURE_2D, texture, 0);      <-(5)
304     gl.framebufferRenderbuffer(gl.FRAMEBUFFER, gl.DEPTH_ATTACHMENT,
                      ➥gl.RENDERBUFFER, depthBuffer);    <-(6)
305
306     // Check whether FBO is configured correctly                         <-(7)
307     var e = gl.checkFramebufferStatus(gl.FRAMEBUFFER);
308     if (e !== gl.FRAMEBUFFER_COMPLETE) {
309       console.log('Framebuffer object is incomplete: ' + e.toString());
310       return error();
311     }
312
        ...
319     return framebuffer;
320   }
```

The vertex shader and fragment shader are omitted because this sample program uses the
same shaders as TexturedQuad.js in Chapter 5, which pasted a texture image on a rectangle. The sample program in this section draws two objects: a cube and a rectangle. Just
as you did in ProgramObject.js in the previous section, you assign multiple buffer objects
needed for drawing each object as properties of an Object object. Then you store the
object to the variables cube and plane. You will use them for drawing by assigning each
buffer in the object to the attribute variable.

The key point of this program is the initialization of the framebuffer object by init-
FramebufferObject() at line 71. The initialized framebuffer object is stored in a variable
fbo and passed as the third argument of draw() at line 92. You'll return to the function
draw() later. For now let's examine initFramebufferObject(), at line 263, step by step.
This function performs steps 1 to 7. The view projection matrix for the framebuffer object
is prepared separately at line 84 because it is different from the one used for a color buffer.

Create Frame Buffer Object (gl.createFramebuffer())

You must create a framebuffer object before you can use it. The sample program creates it at line 275:

```
275 framebuffer = gl.createFramebuffer();
```

You will use `gl.createFramebuffer()` to create the framebuffer object.

---

gl.createFramebuffer()

Create a framebuffer object.

Parameters	None	
Return value	non-null	The newly created framebuffer object.
	null	Failed to create a framebuffer object.
Errors	None	

You use `gl.deleteFramebuffer()` to delete the created framebuffer object.

---

gl.deleteFramebuffer(framebuffer)

Delete a framebuffer object.

Parameters	framebuffer	Specifies the framebuffer object to be deleted.
Return value	None	
Errors	None	

Once you have created the framebuffer object, you need to attach a texture object to the color attachment and a renderbuffer object to the depth attachment in the framebuffer object. Let's start by creating the texture object for the color attachment.

Create Texture Object and Set Its Size and Parameters

You have already seen how to create a texture object and set up its parameters (gl.TEXTURE_MIN_FILTER) in Chapter 5. You should note that its width and height are OFFSCREEN_WIDTH and OFFSCREEN_HEIGHT, respectively. The size is smaller than that of the `<canvas>` to make the drawing process faster.

```
282    texture = gl.createTexture(); // Create a texture object
       ...
287    gl.bindTexture(gl.TEXTURE_2D, texture);
```

```
288   gl.texImage2D(gl.TEXTURE_2D, 0, gl.RGBA, OFFSCREEN_WIDTH, OFFSCREEN_HEIGHT, 0,
                                     ↪gl.RGBA, gl.UNSIGNED_BYTE, null);
289   gl.texParameteri(gl.TEXTURE_2D, gl.TEXTURE_MIN_FILTER, gl.LINEAR);
290   framebuffer.texture = texture; // Store the texture object
```

The `gl.texImage2D()` at line 288 allocates a drawing area in a texture object. You can allocate a drawing area by specifying `null` to the last argument, which is used to specify an `Image` object. You will use this texture object later, so store it in `framebuffer.texture` at line 290.

That completes the preparation for a texture object that is attached to the color attachment. Next, you need to create a renderbuffer object for the depth buffer.

Create Renderbuffer Object (gl.createRenderbuffer())

Like texture buffers, you need to create a renderbuffer object before using it. The sample program does this at line 293.

```
293   depthBuffer = gl.createRenderbuffer();  // Create a renderbuffer
```

You use `gl.createRenderbuffer()` to create the renderbuffer object.

gl.createRenderbuffer()		
Create a renderbuffer object.		
Parameters	None	
Return value	Non-null	The newly created renderbuffer object.
	Null	Failed to create a renderbuffer object.
Errors	None	

You use `gl.deleteRenderbuffer()` to delete the created renderbuffer object.

gl.deleteRenderbuffer(renderbuffer)		
Delete a renderbuffer object.		
Parameters	renderbuffer	Specifies the renderbuffer object to be deleted.
Return value	None	
Errors	None	

The created renderbuffer object is used as a depth buffer here, so you store it in a variable named depthBuffer.

Bind Renderbuffer Object to Target and Set Size (gl.bindRenderbuffer(), gl.renderbufferStorage())

When using the created renderbuffer object, you need to bind the renderbuffer object to a target and perform the operation on that target.

```
298    gl.bindRenderbuffer(gl.RENDERBUFFER, depthBuffer);
299    gl.renderbufferStorage(gl.RENDERBUFFER, gl.DEPTH_COMPONENT16,
                              ➡OFFSCREEN_WIDTH, OFFSCREEN_HEIGHT);
```

The renderbuffer object is bound to a target with gl.bindRenderbuffer().

---

gl.bindRenderbuffer(target, renderbuffer)

Bind the renderbuffer object specified by *renderbuffer* to *target*. If null is specified as *renderbuffer*, the *renderbuffer* is unbound from the *target*.

Parameters	target	Must be gl.RENDERBUFFER.
	renderbuffer	Specifies the renderbuffer object.
Return value	None	
Errors	INVALID_ENUM	*target* is not gl.RENDERBUFFER

When the binding is complete, you can set the format, width, and height of the renderbuffer object by using gl.renderbufferStorage(). You must set the same width and height as the texture object that is used as the color attachment.

---

gl.renderbufferStorage(target, internalformat, width, height)

Create and initialize a renderbuffer object's data store.

Parameters	target	Must be gl.RENDERBUFFER.
	internalformat	Specifies the format of the renderbuffer.
	gl.DEPTH_COMPONENT16	The renderbuffer is used as a depth buffer.
	gl.STENCIL_INDEX8	The renderbuffer is used as a stencil buffer.

	gl.RGBA4	The renderbuffer is used as a color buffer. gl.RGBA4 (each RGBA component has 4, 4, 4, and 4 bits, respectively), gl.RGB5_A1 (each RGB component has 5 bits, and A has 1 bit), gl.RGB565 (each RGB component has 5, 6, and 5 bits, respectively)
	gl.RGB5_A1	
	gl.RGB565	
	width, height	Specifies the width and height of the renderbuffer in pixels.
Return value	None	
Errors	INVALID_ENUM	Target is not gl.RENDERBUFFER or *internalformat* is none of the preceding values.
	INVALID_OPERATION	No renderbuffer is bound to *target*.

The preparations of the texture object and renderbuffer object of the framebuffer object are now complete. At this stage, you can use the object for offscreen drawing.

Set Texture Object to Framebuffer Object (gl.bindFramebuffer(), gl.framebufferTexture2D())

You use a framebuffer object in the same way you use a renderbuffer object: You need to bind it to a target and operate on the target, not the framebuffer object itself.

```
302    gl.bindFramebuffer(gl.FRAMEBUFFER, framebuffer);  // Bind to target
303    gl.framebufferTexture2D(gl.FRAMEBUFFER, gl.COLOR_ATTACHMENT0, gl.TEXTURE_2D,
                                                              ➥texture, 0);
```

A framebuffer object is bound to a target with gl.bindFramebuffer().

---

gl.bindFramebuffer(target, framebuffer)

Bind a framebuffer object to a target. If *framebuffer* is null, the binding is broken.

Parameters	target	Must be gl.FRAMEBUFFER.
	framebuffer	Specify the framebuffer object.
Return value	None	
Errors	INVALID_ENUM	*target* is not gl.FRAMEBUFFER

Once the framebuffer object is bound to *target*, you can use the *target* to write a texture object to the framebuffer object. In this sample, you will use the texture object instead of a color buffer so you attach the texture object to the color attachment of the framebuffer.

You can assign the texture object to the framebuffer object with `gl.framebufferTexture2D()`.

---

gl.framebufferTexture2D(target, attachment, textarget, texture, level)

Attach a texture object specified by *texture* to the framebuffer object bound by *target*.

Parameters	target	Must be `gl.FRAMEBUFFER`.
	attachment	Specifies the attachment point of the framebuffer.
	`gl.COLOR_ATTACHMENT0`	*texture* is used as a color buffer
	`gl.DEPTH_ATTACHMENT`	*texture* is used as a depth buffer
	textarget	Specifies the first argument of `gl.texImage2D()` (`gl.TEXTURE_2D` or `gl.CUBE_MAP_TEXTURE`).
	texture	Specifies a texture object to attach to the framebuffer attachment point.
	level	Specifies 0 (if you use a MIPMAP in *texture*, you should specify its level).
Return value	None	
Errors	INVALID_ENUM	*target* is not `gl.FRAMEBUFFER`. *attachment* or *textarget* is none of the preceding values.
	INVALID_VALUE	*level* is not valid.
	INVALID_OPERATION	No framebuffer object is bound to *target*.

The 0 in the `gl.COLOR_ATTACHMENT0` used for the *attachment* parameter is because a framebuffer object in OpenGL, the basis of WebGL, can hold multiple color attachments (`gl.COLOR_ATTACHMENT0`, `gl.COLOR_ATTACHMENT1`, `gl.COLOR_ATTACHMENT2`...). However, WebGL can use just one of them.

Once the color attachment has been attached to the framebuffer object, you need to assign a renderbuffer object as a depth attachment. This follows a similar process.

Set Renderbuffer Object to Framebuffer Object (gl.framebufferRenderbuffer())

You will use `gl.framebufferRenderbuffer()` to attach a renderbuffer object to a framebuffer object. You need a depth buffer because this sample program will remove hidden surfaces. So the depth attachment needs to be attached.

```
304     gl.framebufferRenderbuffer(gl.FRAMEBUFFER, gl.DEPTH_ATTACHMENT,
gl.RENDERBUFFER, depthBuffer);
```

---

gl.framebufferRenderbuffer(target, attachment, renderbuffertarget, renderbuffer)

Attach a renderbuffer object specified by *renderbuffer* to the framebuffer object bound by *target*.

Parameters	target	Must be gl.FRAMEBUFFER.
	attachment	Specifies the attachment point of the framebuffer.
	gl.COLOR_ATTACHMENT0	*renderbuffer* is used as a color buffer.
	gl.DEPTH_ATTACHMENT	*renderbuffer* is used as a depth buffer.
	gl.STENCIL_ATTACHMENT	*renderbuffer* is used as a stencil buffer.
	renderbuffertarget	Must be gl.RENDERBUFFER.
	renderbuffer	Specifies a renderbuffer object to attach to the framebuffer attachment point
Return value	None	
Errors	INVALID_ENUM	*target* is not a gl.FRAMEBUFFER. *attachment* is none of the above values. *renderbuffertarget* is not gl.RENDERBUFFER.

Now that you've completed the preparation of the color attachment and depth attachment to the framebuffer object, you are ready to draw. But before that, let's check that the configuration of the framebuffer object is correct.

Check Configuration of Framebuffer Object (gl.checkFramebufferStatus())

Obviously, when you use a framebuffer that is not correctly configured, an error occurs. As you have seen in the past few sections, preparing a texture object and renderbuffer object that are needed to configure the framebuffer object is a complex process that sometimes generates mistakes. You can check whether the created framebuffer object is configured correctly and is available with gl.checkFramebufferStatus().

```
307     var e = gl.checkFramebufferStatus(gl.FRAMEBUFFER);          <- (7)
308     if (gl.FRAMEBUFFER_COMPLETE !== e) {
309       console.log('Frame buffer object is incomplete:' + e.toString());
310       return error();
311     }
```

The following shows the specification of gl.checkFramebufferStatus().

gl.checkFramebufferStatus(target)		
Check the completeness status of a framebuffer bound to *target*.		
Parameters	target	Must be gl.FRAMEBUFFER.
Return value	0	*Target* is not gl.FRAMEBUFFER.
	Others	
	gl.FRAMEBUFFER_COMPLETE	The framebuffer object is configured correctly.
	gl.FRAMEBUFFER_INCOMPLETE_ ATTACHMENT	One of the framebuffer attachment points is incomplete. (The attachment is not sufficient. The texture object or the renderbuffer object is invalid.)
	gl.FRAMEBUFFER_INCOMPLETE_ DIMENSIONS	The width or height of the texture object or renderbuffer object of the attachment is different.
	gl.FRAMEBUFFER_INCOMPLETE_ MISSING_ATTACHMENT	The framebuffer does not have at least one valid attachment.
Errors	INVALID_ENUM	*target* is not gl.FRAMEBUFFER.

That completes the preparation of the framebuffer object. Let's now take a look at the draw() function.

Draw Using the Framebuffer Object

Listing 10.14 shows draw(). It switches the drawing destination to fbo (the framebuffer) and draws a cube in the texture object. Then drawTexturedPlane() uses the texture object to draw a rectangle to the color buffer.

Listing 10.14 FramebufferObject.js (Process of (8))

```
321  function draw(gl, canvas, fbo, plane, cube, angle, texture, viewProjMatrix,
                                                  ➥viewProjMatrixFBO) {
322    gl.bindFramebuffer(gl.FRAMEBUFFER, fbo);                          <-(8)
323    gl.viewport(0, 0, OFFSCREEN_WIDTH, OFFSCREEN_HEIGHT); // For FBO
324
325    gl.clearColor(0.2, 0.2, 0.4, 1.0); // Color is slightly changed
326    gl.clear(gl.COLOR_BUFFER_BIT | gl.DEPTH_BUFFER_BIT);  // Clear FBO
```

```
327    // Draw the cube
328    drawTexturedCube(gl, gl.program, cube, angle, texture, viewProjMatrixFBO);
329    // Change the drawing destination to color buffer
330    gl.bindFramebuffer(gl.FRAMEBUFFER, null);
331    // Set the size of view port back to that of <canvas>
332    gl.viewport(0, 0, canvas.width, canvas.height);
333    gl.clearColor(0.0, 0.0, 0.0, 1.0);
334    gl.clear(gl.COLOR_BUFFER_BIT | gl.DEPTH_BUFFER_BIT);
335    // Draw the plane
336    drawTexturedPlane(gl, gl.program, plane, angle, fbo.texture, viewProjMatrix);
337  }
```

Line 322 switches the drawing destination to the framebuffer object using `gl.bindFrame-buffer()`. As a result, draw operations using `gl.drawArrays()` or `gl.drawElements()` are performed for the framebuffer object. Line 332 uses `gl.viewport()` to specify the draw area in the buffer (an offscreen area).

---

gl.viewport(x, y, width, height)

Set the viewport where `gl.drawArrays()` or `gl.drawElements()` draws. In WebGL, x and y are specified in the `<canvas>` coordinate system.

Parameters	x, y	Specify the lower-left corner of the viewport rectangle (in pixels).
	width, height	Specify the width and height of the viewport (in pixels).
Return value	None	
Errors	None	

Line 326 clears the texture image and the depth buffer bound to the framebuffer object. When a cube is drawn at line 328, it is drawn in the texture image. To make it easier to see the result, the clear color at line 325 is changed to a purplish blue from black. The result of this is that the cube has been drawn into the texture buffer and is now available for use as a texture image. The next step is to draw a rectangle (`plane`) using this texture image. In this case, because you want to draw in the color buffer, you need to set the drawing destination back to the color buffer. This is done at line 330 by specifying `null` for the second argument of `gl.bindFramebuffer()` (that is, cancelling the binding). Then line 336 draws the `plane`. You should note that `fbo.texture` is passed as the texture argument and used to map the drawn content to the rectangle. You will notice that in this sample program, the texture image is mapped onto the back side of the rectangle. This is because WebGL, by default, draws both sides of a polygon. You can eliminate the back face drawing by enabling the **culling function** using `gl.enable(gl.CULL_FACE)`, which increases the drawing speed (ideally making it twice as fast).

Display Shadows

Chapter 8 explained shading, which is one of the phenomena when light hits an object. We briefly mentioned shadowing, another phenomena, but didn't explain how to implement it. Let's take a look at that now. There are several methods to realize shadowing, but we will explain a method that uses a **shadow map** (depth map). This method is quite expressive and used in a variety of computer graphics situations and even in special effects in movies.

How to Implement Shadows

The shadow map method is based on the idea that the sun cannot see the shadow of objects. Essentially, it works by considering the viewer's eye point to be at the same position as the light source and determining what can be seen from that point. All the objects you can see would appear to be in the light. Anything behind those objects would be in shadow. With this method, you can use the distance to the objects (in fact, you will use the z value, which is the depth value) from the light source to judge whether the objects are visible. As you can see in Figure 10.21, where there are two points on the same line, P1 and P2, P2 is in the shadow because the distance from the light source to P2 is longer than P1.

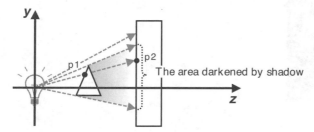

Figure 10.21   Theory of shadow map

You need two pairs of shaders for this process: (1) a pair of shaders that calculate the distance from the light source to the objects, and (2) a pair of shaders that draws the shadow using the calculated distance. Then you need a method to pass the distance data from the light source calculated in the first pair of shaders to the second pair of shaders. You can use a texture image for this purpose. This texture image is called the **shadow map**, so this method is called **shadow mapping**. The shadow mapping technique consists of the following two processes:

1. Move the eye point to the position of the light source and draw objects from there. Because the fragments drawn from the position are hit by the light, you write the distances from the light source to each fragment in the texture image (shadow map).

2. Move the eye point back to the position from which you want to view the objects and draw them from there. Compare the distance from the light source to the fragments drawn in this step and the distance recorded in the shadow map from step

1. If the former distance is greater, you can draw the fragment as in shadow (in the darker color).

You will use the framebuffer object in step 1 to save the distance in the texture image. Therefore, the configurations of the framebuffer object used here is the same as that of FramebufferObject.js in Figure 10.20. You also need to switch pairs of shaders between steps 1 and 2 using the technique you learned in the section "Switching Shaders," earlier in this chapter. Now let's take a look at the sample program Shadow. Figure 10.22 shows a screen shot where you can see a shadow of the red triangle cast onto the slanted white rectangle.

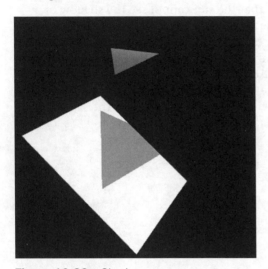

Figure 10.22 Shadow

Sample Program (Shadow.js)

The key aspects of shadowing take place in the shaders, which are shown in Listing 10.15.

Listing 10.15 Shadow.js (Shader part)

```
1  // Shadow.js
2  // Vertex shader program to generate a shadow map
3  var SHADOW_VSHADER_SOURCE =
   ...
6    'void main() {\n' +
7    '  gl_Position = u_MvpMatrix * a_Position;\n' +
8    '}\n';
9
10 // Fragment shader program for creating a shadow map
11 var SHADOW_FSHADER_SOURCE =
```

```
      . . .
15    'void main() {\n' +
16    '  gl_FragColor = vec4(gl_FragCoord.z, 0.0, 0.0, 0.0);\n' +          <-(1)
17    '}\n';

18
19    // Vertex shader program for regular drawing
20    var VSHADER_SOURCE =
      . . .
23    'uniform mat4 u_MvpMatrix;\n' +
24    'uniform mat4 u_MvpMatrixFromLight;\n' +
25    'varying vec4 v_PositionFromLight;\n' +
26    'varying vec4 v_Color;\n' +
27    'void main() {\n' +
28    '  gl_Position = u_MvpMatrix * a_Position;\n' +
29    '  v_PositionFromLight = u_MvpMatrixFromLight * a_Position;\n' +
30    '  v_Color = a_Color;\n' +
31    '}\n';

32
33    // Fragment shader program for regular drawing
34    var FSHADER_SOURCE =
      . . .
38    'uniform sampler2D u_ShadowMap;\n' +
39    'varying vec4 v_PositionFromLight;\n' +
40    'varying vec4 v_Color;\n' +
41    'void main() {\n' +
42    '  vec3 shadowCoord = (v_PositionFromLight.xyz/v_PositionFromLight.w)
                                                ➥/ 2.0 + 0.5;\n' +
43    '  vec4 rgbaDepth = texture2D(u_ShadowMap, shadowCoord.xy);\n' +
44    '  float depth = rgbaDepth.r;\n' +  // Retrieve the z value from R
45    '  float visibility = (shadowCoord.z > depth + 0.005) ? 0.7:1.0;\n'+   <-(2)
46    '  gl_FragColor = vec4(v_Color.rgb * visibility, v_Color.a);\n' +
47    '}\n';
```

Step 1 is performed in the shader responsible for the shadow map, defined from lines 3 to 17. You just switch the drawing destination to the framebuffer object, pass a model view projection matrix in which an eye point is located at a light source to u_MvpMatrix, and draw the objects. This results in the distance from the light source to the fragments being written into the texture map (shadow map) attached to the framebuffer object. The vertex shader at line 7 just multiplies the model view projection matrix by the vertex coordinates to calculate this distance. The fragment shader is more complex and needs to calculate the distance from the light source to the drawn fragments. For this purpose, you can utilize the built-in variable gl_FragCoord of the fragment shader used in Chapter 5.

gl_FragCoord is a vec4 type built-in variable that contains the coordinates of each fragment. gl_FragCoord.x and gl_FragCoord.y represents the position of the fragment on the screen, and `gl_FragCoord.z` contains the normalized z value in the range of [0, 1]. This is calculated using (`gl_Position.z/gl.Position.w`)`/2.0+0.5`. (See Section 2.12 of *OpenGL ES 2.0 specification* for further details.) `gl_FragCoord.z` is specified in the range of 0.0 to 1.0, with 0.0 representing the fragments on the near clipping plane and 1.0 representing those on the far clipping plane. This value is written into the R (red) component value (any component could be used) in the shadow map at line 16.

```
16      '  gl_FragColor = vec4(gl_FragCoord.z, 0.0, 0.0, 0.0);\n'  +    <-(1)
```

Subsequently, the z value for each fragment drawn from the eye point placed at the light source is written into the shadow map. This shadow map is passed to `u_ShadowMap` at line 38.

For step 2, you need to draw the objects again after resetting the drawing destination to the color buffer and moving the eye point to its original position. After drawing the objects, you decide a fragment color by comparing the z value of the fragment with that stored in the shadow map. This is done in the normal shaders from lines 20 to 47. `u_MvpMatrix` is the model view projection matrix where the eye point is placed at the original position and `uMvpMatrixFromLight`, which was used to create the shadow map, is the model view projection matrix where the eye point is moved to the light source. The main task of the vertex shader defined at line 20 is calculating the coordinates of each fragment from the light source and passing them to the fragment shader (line 29) to obtain the z value of each fragment from the light source.

The fragment shader uses the coordinates to calculate the z value (line 42). As mentioned, the shadow map contains the value of (`gl_Position.z/gl.Position.w`)`/2.0+0.5`. So you could simply calculate the z value to compare with the value in the shadow map by (`v_PositionFromLight.z/v_PositionFromLight.w`)`/2.0+0.5`. However, because you need to get the texel value from the shadow map, line 42 performs the following extra calculation using the same operation. To compare to the value in the shadow map, you need to get the texel value from the shadow map whose texture coordinates correspond to the coordinates (`v_PositionFromLight.x, v_PositionFromLight.y`). As you know, `v_PositionFromLight.x` and `v_PositionFromLight.y` are the x and y coordinates in the WebGL coordinate system (see Figure 2.18 in Chapter 2), and they range from −1.0 to 1.0. On the other hand, the texture coordinates s and t in the shadow map range from 0.0 to 1.0 (see Figure 5.20 in Chapter 5). So, you need to convert the x and y coordinates to the s and t coordinates. You can also do this with the same expression to calculate the z value. That is:

The texture coordinate s is (`v_PositionFromLight.x/v_PositionFromLight.w`)`/2.0 + 0.5`.

The texture coordinate t is (`v_PositionFromLight.y/v_PositionFromLight.w`)`/2.0 + 0.5`.

See also Section 2.12 of the *OpenGL ES 2.0 specification*[5] for further details about this calculation. These are carried out using the same type of calculation and can be achieved in one line, as shown at line 42:

---

[5] www.khronos.org/registry/gles/specs/2.0/es_full_spec_2.0.25.pdf

```
42    '   vec3 shadowCoord =(v_PositionFromLight.xyz/v_PositionFromLight.w)
                                                        ↪/ 2.0 + 0.5;\n' +
43    '   vec4 rgbaDepth = texture2D(u_ShadowMap, shadowCoord.xy);\n' +
44    '   float depth = rgbaDepth.r;\n' +   // Retrieve the z value from R
```

You retrieve the value from the shadow map at lines 43 and 44. Only the R value is retrieved using rgbaDepth.r at line 44 because you wrote it into the R component at line 16. Line 45 checks whether that fragment is in the shadow. When the position of the fragment is determined to be greater than the depth (that is, shadowCoord.z > depth), a value of 0.7 is stored in visibility. The visibility is used at line 46 to draw the shadow with a darker color:

```
45    '   float visibility = (shadowCoord.z > depth + 0.005) ? 0.7:1.0;\n'+
46    '   gl_FragColor = vec4(v_Color.rgb * visibility, v_Color.a);\n' +
```

Line 45 adds a small offset of 0.005 to the depth value. To understand why this is needed, try running the sample program without this number. You will see a striped pattern as shown in Figure 10.23, referred to as the **Mach band**.

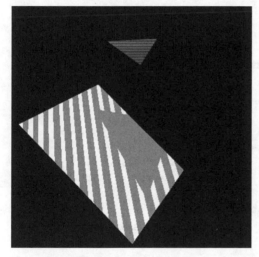

Figure 10.23 Striped pattern

The value of 0.005 is added to suppress the stripe pattern. The stripe pattern occurs because of the precision of the numbers you can store in the RGBA components. It's a little complex, but it's worth understanding because this problem occurs elsewhere in 3D graphics. The z value of the shadow map is stored in the R component of RGBA in the texture map, which is an 8-bit number. This means that the precision of R is lower than its comparison target (shadowCoord.z), which is of type float. For example, let the z value simply be 0.1234567. If you represent the value using 8 bits, in other words using 256 possibilities, you can represent the value in a precision of 1/256 (=0.0390625). So you can represent 0.1234567 as follows:

```
0.1234567 / (1 / 256) = 31.6049152
```

Numbers below the decimal point cannot be used in 8 bits, so only 31 can be stored in 8 bits. When you divide 31 by 256, you obtain 0.12109375 which, as you can see, is smaller than the original value (0.1234567). This means that even if the fragment is at the same position, its z value stored in the shadow map becomes smaller than its z value in shadowCoord.z. As a result, the z value in shadowCoord.z becomes larger than that in the shadow map according to the position of the fragment resulting in the stripe patterns. Because this happens because the precision of the R value is 1/256 (=0.00390625), by adding a small offset, such as 0.005, to the R value, you can stop the stripe pattern from appearing. Note that any offset greater than 1/256 will work; 0.005 was chosen because it is 1/256 plus a small margin.

Next, let's look at the JavaScript program that passes the data to the shader (see Listing 10.16) with a focus on the type of transformation matrices passed. To draw a shadow clearly, the size of a texture map for the offscreen rendering defined at line 49 is larger than that of the <canvas>.

Listing 10.16   Shadow.js (JavaScript Part)

```
49   var OFFSCREEN_WIDTH = 1024, OFFSCREEN_HEIGHT = 1024;
50   var LIGHT_X = 0, LIGHT_Y = 7, LIGHT_Z = 2;
51
52   function main() {
       ...
63     // Initialize shaders for generating a shadow map
64     var shadowProgram = createProgram(gl, SHADOW_VSHADER_SOURCE,
                                               ➥SHADOW_FSHADER_SOURCE);
       ...
72     // Initialize shaders for regular drawing
73     var normalProgram = createProgram(gl, VSHADER_SOURCE, FSHADER_SOURCE);
       ...
85     // Set vertex information
86     var triangle = initVertexBuffersForTriangle(gl);
87     var plane = initVertexBuffersForPlane(gl);
       ...
93     // Initialize a framebuffer object (FBO)
94     var fbo = initFramebufferObject(gl);
       ...
99     gl.activeTexture(gl.TEXTURE0); // Set a texture object to the texture unit
100    gl.bindTexture(gl.TEXTURE_2D, fbo.texture);
       ...
106    var viewProjMatrixFromLight = new Matrix4(); // For the shadow map
```

```
107    viewProjMatrixFromLight.setPerspective(70.0,
                                   ➥OFFSCREEN_WIDTH/OFFSCREEN_HEIGHT, 1.0, 100.0);
108    viewProjMatrixFromLight.lookAt(LIGHT_X, LIGHT_Y, LIGHT_Z, 0.0, 0.0, 0.0, 0.0,
                                   ➥1.0, 0.0);
109
110    var viewProjMatrix = new Matrix4(); // For regular drawing
111    viewProjMatrix.setPerspective(45, canvas.width/canvas.height, 1.0, 100.0);
112    viewProjMatrix.lookAt(0.0, 7.0, 9.0, 0.0, 0.0, 0.0, 0.0, 1.0, 0.0);
113
114    var currentAngle = 0.0; // Current rotation angle [degrees]
115    var mvpMatrixFromLight_t = new Matrix4();  // For triangle
116    var mvpMatrixFromLight_p = new Matrix4();  // For plane
117    var tick = function() {
118      currentAngle = animate(currentAngle);
119      // Change the drawing destination to FBO
120      gl.bindFramebuffer(gl.FRAMEBUFFER, fbo);
       ...
124      gl.useProgram(shadowProgram); // For generating a shadow map
125      // Draw the triangle and the plane (for generating a shadow map)
126      drawTriangle(gl, shadowProgram, triangle, currentAngle,
                                   ➥viewProjMatrixFromLight);
127      mvpMatrixFromLight_t.set(g_mvpMatrix);  // Used later
128      drawPlane(gl, shadowProgram, plane, viewProjMatrixFromLight);
129      mvpMatrixFromLight_p.set(g_mvpMatrix);  // Used later
130      // Change the drawing destination to color buffer
131      gl.bindFramebuffer(gl.FRAMEBUFFER, null);
       ...
135      gl.useProgram(normalProgram); // For regular drawing
136      gl.uniform1i(normalProgram.u_ShadowMap, 0); // Pass gl.TEXTURE0
137      // Draw the triangle and plane (for regular drawing)
138      gl.uniformMatrix4fv(normalProgram.u_MvpMatrixFromLight, false,
                                   ➥mvpMatrixFromLight_t.elements);
139      drawTriangle(gl, normalProgram, triangle, currentAngle, viewProjMatrix);
140      gl.uniformMatrix4fv(normalProgram.u_MvpMatrixFromLight, false,
                                   ➥mvpMatrixFromLight_p.elements);
141      drawPlane(gl, normalProgram, plane, viewProjMatrix);
142
143      window.requestAnimationFrame(tick, canvas);
144    };
145    tick();
146  }
```

Let's look at the main() function from line 52 in the JavaScript program. Line 64
initializes the shaders for generating the shadow map. Line 73 initializes the shaders
for normal drawing. Lines 86 and 87, which set up the vertex information and

initFramebufferObject() at line 94, are the same as the FramebufferObject.js. Line 94 prepares a framebuffer object, which contains the texture object for a shadow map. Lines 99 and 100 enable texture unit 0 and bind it to the target. This texture unit is passed to u_ShadowMap in the shaders for normal drawing.

Lines 106 to 108 prepare a view projection matrix to generate a shadow map. The key point is that the first three arguments (that is, the position of an eye point) at line 108 are specified as the position of the light source. Lines 110 to 112 prepare the view projection matrix from the eye point where you want to view the scene.

Finally, you draw the triangle and plane using all the preceding information. First you generate the shadow map, so you switch the drawing destination to the framebuffer object at line 120. You draw the objects by using the shaders for generating a shadow map (shadowProgram) at lines 126 and 128. You should note that lines 127 and 129 save the model view projection matrices from the light source. Then the shadow map is generated, and you use it to draw shadows with the code from line 135. Line 136 passes the map to the fragment shader. Lines 138 and 140 pass the model view projection matrices saved at line 127 and 129, respectively, to u_MvpMatrixFromLight.

Increasing Precision

Although you've successfully calculated the shadow and drawn the scene with the shadow included, the example code is only able to handle situations in which the light source is close to the object. To see this, let's change the y coordinate of the light source position to 40:

```
50  var LIGHT_X = 0, LIGHT_Y = 40, LIGHT_Z = 2;
```

If you run the modified sample program, you can see that the shadow is not displayed—as in the left side of Figure 10.24. Obviously, you want the shadow to be displayed correctly, as in the figure on the right.

The reason the shadow is no longer displayed when the distance from the light source to the object is increased is that the value of gl_FragCoord.z could not be stored in the R component of the texture map because it has only an 8-bit precision. A simple solution to this problem is to use not just the R component but the B, G, and A components. In other words, you save the value separately in 4 bytes. There is a routine procedure to do this, so let's see the sample program. Only the fragment shader is changed.

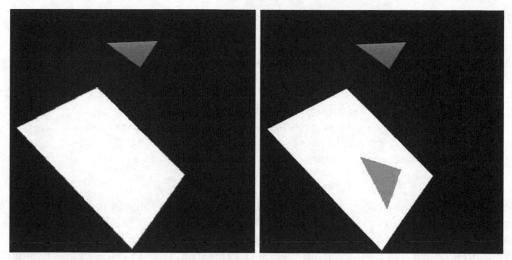

Figure 10.24 The shadow is not displayed

Sample Program (Shadow_highp.js)

Listing 10.17 shows the fragment shader of Shadow_highp.js. You can see that the processing to handle the z value is more complex than that in Shadow.js.

Listing 10.17 Shadow_highp.js

```
 1   // Shadow_highp.js
         ...
10   // Fragment shader program for creating a shadow map
11   var SHADOW_FSHADER_SOURCE =
         ...
15     'void main() {\n' +
16     '  const vec4 bitShift = vec4(1.0, 256.0, 256.0 * 256.0, 256.0 * 256.0 *
                                                    ➥256.0);\n' +
17     '  const vec4 bitMask = vec4(1.0/256.0, 1.0/256.0, 1.0/256.0, 0.0);\n' +
18     '  vec4 rgbaDepth = fract(gl_FragCoord.z * bitShift);\n' +
19     '  rgbaDepth -= rgbaDepth.gbaa * bitMask;\n' +
20     '  gl_FragColor = rgbaDepth;\n' +
21     '}\n';
         ...
37   // Fragment shader program for regular drawing
38   var FSHADER_SOURCE =
         ...
45     // Recalculate the z value from the rgba
46     'float unpackDepth(const in vec4 rgbaDepth) {\n' +
47     '  const vec4 bitShift = vec4(1.0, 1.0/256.0, 1.0/(256.0 * 256.0),
                                       ➥1.0/(256.0 * 256.0 * 256.0));\n' +
```

```
48      '    float depth = dot(rgbaDepth, bitShift);\n' +
49      '    return depth;\n' +
50      '}\n' +
51      'void main() {\n' +
52      '    vec3 shadowCoord = (v_PositionFromLight.xyz /
                              ➥v_PositionFromLight.w)/2.0 + 0.5;\n' +
53      '    vec4 rgbaDepth = texture2D(u_ShadowMap, shadowCoord.xy);\n' +
54      '    float depth = unpackDepth(rgbaDepth);\n' +    // Recalculate the z
55      '    float visibility = (shadowCoord.z > depth + 0.0015)? 0.7:1.0;\n'+
56      '    gl_FragColor = vec4(v_Color.rgb * visibility, v_Color.a);\n' +
57      '}\n';
```

The code that splits `gl_FragCoord.z` into 4 bytes (RGBA) is from lines 16 to 19. Because 1 byte can represent up to 1/256, you can store the value greater than 1/256 in R, the value less than 1/256 and greater than 1/(256*256) in G, the value less than 1/(256*256) and greater than 1/(256*256*256) in B, and the rest of value in A. Line 18 calculates each value and stores it in the RGBA components, respectively. It can be written in one line using a `vec4` data type. The function `fract()` is a built-in one that discards numbers below the decimal point for the value specified as its argument. Each value in `vec4`, calculated at line 18, has more precision than 1 byte, so line 19 discards the value that does not fit in 1 byte. By substituting this result to `gl_FragColor` at line 20, you can save the z value using all four components of the RGBA type and achieve higher precision.

`unpackDepth()` at line 54 reads out the z value from the RGBA. This function is defined at line 46. Line 48 performs the following calculation to convert the RGBA value to the original z value. As you can see, the calculation is the same as the inner product, so you use `dot()` at line 48.

$$depth = rgbDepth.r \times 1.0 + \frac{rgbaDepth.g}{256.0} + \frac{rgbaDepth.b}{(256.0 \times 256.0)} + \frac{rgbaDepth.a}{(256.0 \times 256.0 \times 256.0)}$$

Now you have retrieved the distance (z value) successfully, so you just have to draw the shadow by comparing the distance with `shadowCoord.z` at line 55. In this case, 0.0015 is used as the value for adjusting the error (the stripe pattern), instead of 0.005. This is because the precision of the z value stored in the shadow map is a `float` type of `medium` precision (that is, its precision is $2^{-10} = 0.000976563$, as shown in Table 6.15 in Chapter 6). So you add a little margin to it and chose 0.0015 as the value. After that, the shadow can be drawn correctly.

Load and Display 3D Models

In the previous chapters, you drew 3D objects by specifying their vertex coordinates and color information by hand and stored them in arrays of type `Float32Array` in the JavaScript program. However, as mentioned earlier in the book, in most cases you will actually read the vertex coordinates and color information from 3D model files constructed by a 3D modeling tool.

In this section, you construct a sample program that reads a 3D model constructed using a 3D modeling tool. For this example, we use the Blender[6] modeling tool, which is a popular tool with a free version available. Blender is able to export 3D model files using the well-known OBJ format, which is text based and easy to read, understand, and parse. OBJ is a geometry definition file format originally developed by Wavefront Technologies. This file format is open and has been adopted by other 3D graphics vendors. Although this means it is reasonably well known and used, it also means that there are a number of variations in the format. To simplify the example code, we have made a number of assumptions, such as not using textures. However, the example gives you a good understanding of how to read model data into your programs and provides a basis for you to begin experimentation. The approach taken in the example code is designed to be reasonably generic and can be used for other text-based formats.

Start Blender and create a cube like that shown in Figure 10.25. The color of one face of this cube is orange, and the other faces are red. Then export the model to a file named cube.obj. (You can find an example of it in the resources directory with the sample programs.) Let's take a look at cube.obj, which, because it is a text file, can be opened with a simple text editor.

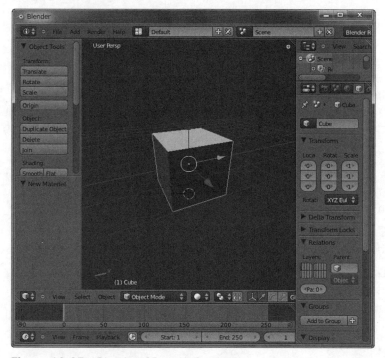

Figure 10.25   Blender, 3D modeling tool

[6.] www.blender.org/

Figure 10.26 shows the contents of `cube.obj`. Line numbers have been added to help with the explanation and would not normally be in the file.

```
1   # Blender v2.60 (sub 0) OBJ File: "
2   # www.blender.org
3   mtllib cube.mtl
4   o Cube
5   v 1.000000 -1.000000 -1.000000
6   v 1.000000 -1.000000 1.000000
7   v -1.000000 -1.000000 1.000000
8   v -1.000000 -1.000000 -1.000000
9   v 1.000000 1.000000 -1.000000
0   v 1.000000 1.000000 1.000001
1   v -1.000000 1.000000 1.000000
2   v -1.000000 1.000000 -1.000000
3   usemtl Material
4   f 1 2 3 4
5   f 5 8 7 6
6   f 2 6 7 3
7   f 3 7 8 4
8   f 5 1 4 8
9   usemtl Material.001
0   f 1 5 6 2
```

Figure 10.26   cube.obj

Once the model file has been created by the modeling tool, your program needs to read the data and store it in the same type of data structures that you've used before. The following steps are required:

1. Prepare the array (`vertices`) of type `Float32Array` and read the vertex coordinates of the model from the file into the array.

2. Prepare the array (`colors`) of type `Float32Array` and read the colors of the model from the file into the array.

3. Prepare the array (`normals`) of type `Float32Array` and read the normals of the model form the file into the array.

4. Prepare the array (`indices`) of type `Uint16Array` (or `Uint8Array`) and read the indices of the vertices that specify the triangles that make up the model from the file into the array.

5. Write the data read during steps 1 through 4 into the buffer object and then draw the model using `gl.drawElements()`.

So in this case, you read the data described in `cube.obj` (shown in Figure 10.26) in the appropriate arrays and then draw the model in step 5. Reading data from the file requires understanding the format of the file `cube.obj` (referred to as the OBJ file).

The OBJ File Format

An OBJ file is made up of several sections,[7] including vertex positions, face definitions, and material definitions. There may be multiple vertices, normals, and faces within their sections:

- Lines beginning with a hash character (#) are comments. Lines 1 and 2 in Figure 10.26 are comments generated by Blender describing its version number and origin. The remaining lines define the 3D model.

- Line 3 references an external materials file. The OBJ format maintains the material information of the model in an external material file called an MTL file.

  `mtllib` <external mtl filename>

  specifies that the materials file is `cube.mtl`.

- Line 4 specifies the named object in the following format:

  <object name>

  This sample program does not use this information.

- Lines 5 to 12 define vertex positions in the following format using (x,y,z[,w]) coordinates, where w is optional and defaults to 1.0.

  `v` x y z [w]

  In this example, it has eight vertices because the model is a standard cube.

- Lines 13 to 20 specify a material and the faces that use the material. Line 13 specifies the material name, as defined in the MTL file referenced at line 4, and the specific material using the following format:

  `usemtl` <material name>

- The following lines, 14 to 18, define faces of the model and the material to be applied to them. Faces are defined using lists of vertex, texture, and normal indices.

  `f` v1 v2 v3 v4 ...

  v1, v2, v3, ... are the vertex indices starting from 1 and matching the corresponding vertex elements of a previously defined vertex list. This sample program handles vertex and normals. Figure 10.26 does not contain normals, but if a face has a normal, the following format would be used:

  `f` v1//vn1 v2//vn2 v3//vn3 ...

  vn1, vn2, vn3, ... are the normal indices starting from 1.

---

[7] See http://en.wikipedia.org/wiki/Wavefront_.obj_file

The MTL File Format

The MTL file may define multiple materials. Figure 10.27 shows `cube.mtl`.

```
 1  # Blender MTL File: "
 2  # Material Count: 2
 3  newmtl Material
 4  Ka 0.000000 0.000000 0.000000
 5  Kd 1.000000 0.000000 0.000000
 6  Ks 0.000000 0.000000 0.000000
 7  Ns 96.078431
 8  Ni 1.000000
 9  d 1.000000
10  illum 0
11  newmtl Material.001
12  Ka 0.000000 0.000000 0.000000
13  Kd 1.000000 0.450000 0.000000
14  Ks 0.000000 0.000000 0.000000
15  Ns 96.078431
16  Ni 1.000000
17  d 1.000000
18  illum 0
```

Figure 10.27   cube.mtl

- Lines 1 and 2 are comments that Blender generates.

- Each new material (from line 3) starts with the `newmtl` command:

  `newmtl <material name>`

  This is the material name that is used in the OBJ file.

- Lines 4 to 6 define the ambient, diffuse, and specular color using `Ka`, `Kd`, and `Ks`, respectively. Color definitions are in RGB format, where each component is between 0 and 1. This sample program uses only diffuse color.

- Line 7 specifies the weight of the specular color using `Ns`. Line 8 specifies the optical density for the surface using `Ni`. Line 9 specifies transparency using `d`. Line 10 specifies illumination models using `illum`. The sample program does not use this item of information.

Given this understanding of the structure of the OBJ and MTL files, you have to extract the vertex coordinates, colors, normals, and indices describing a face from the file, write them into the buffer objects, and draw with `gl.drawElements()`. The OBJ file may not have the information on normals, but you can calculate them from the vertex coordinates that make up a face by using a "cross product."[8]

Let's look at the sample program.

---

[8] If the vertices of a triangle are v0, v1, and v2, the vector of v0 and v1 is (x1, y1, z1), and the vector of v1 and v2 is (x2, y2, z2), then the cross product is defined as (y1*z2 – z1*y2, z1*x2 – x1*z2, x1*y2 – y1*z2). The result will be the normal for the triangle. (See the book *3D Math Primer for Graphics and Game Development*.)

Sample Program (OBJViewer.js)

The basic steps are as follows: (1) prepare an empty buffer object, (2) read an OBJ file (an MTL file), (3) parse it, (4) write the results into the buffer object, and (5) draw. These steps are implemented as shown in Listing 10.18.

Listing 10.18 OBJViewer.js

```
 1 // OBJViewer.js (
   ...
28 function main() {
   ...
40   if (!initShaders(gl, VSHADER_SOURCE, FSHADER_SOURCE)) {
41     console.log('Failed to initialize shaders.');
42     return;
43   }
   ...
49   // Get the storage locations of attribute and uniform variables
50   var program = gl.program;
51   program.a_Position = gl.getAttribLocation(program, 'a_Position');
52   program.a_Normal = gl.getAttribLocation(program, 'a_Normal');
53   program.a_Color = gl.getAttribLocation(program, 'a_Color');
   ...
63   // Prepare empty buffer objects for vertex coordinates, colors, and normals
64   var model = initVertexBuffers(gl, program);
   ...
75   // Start reading the OBJ file
76   readOBJFile('../resources/cube.obj', gl, model, 60, true);
   ...
81     draw(gl, gl.program, currentAngle, viewProjMatrix, model);
   ...
85 }
86
87 // Create a buffer object and perform the initial configuration
88 function initVertexBuffers(gl, program) {
89   var o = new Object();
90   o.vertexBuffer = createEmptyArrayBuffer(gl, program.a_Position, 3, gl.FLOAT);
91   o.normalBuffer = createEmptyArrayBuffer(gl, program.a_Normal, 3, gl.FLOAT);
92   o.colorBuffer = createEmptyArrayBuffer(gl, program.a_Color, 4, gl.FLOAT);
93   o.indexBuffer = gl.createBuffer();
   ...
98   return o;
99 }
100
101 // Create a buffer object, assign it to attribute variables, and enable the
```
➥assignment

```
102 function createEmptyArrayBuffer(gl, a_attribute, num, type) {
103   var buffer = gl.createBuffer();  // Create a buffer object
    ...
108   gl.bindBuffer(gl.ARRAY_BUFFER, buffer);
109   gl.vertexAttribPointer(a_attribute, num, type, false, 0, 0);
110   gl.enableVertexAttribArray(a_attribute);  // Enable the assignment
111
112   return buffer;
113 }
114
115 // Read a file
116 function readOBJFile(fileName, gl, model, scale, reverse) {
117   var request = new XMLHttpRequest();
118
119   request.onreadystatechange = function() {
120     if (request.readyState === 4 && request.status !== 404) {
121       onReadOBJFile(request.responseText, fileName, gl, model, scale, reverse);
122     }
123   }
124   request.open('GET', fileName, true); // Create a request to get file
125   request.send();                      // Send the request
126 }
127
128 var g_objDoc = null;      // The information of OBJ file
129 var g_drawingInfo = null; // The information for drawing 3D model
130
131 // OBJ file has been read
132 function onReadOBJFile(fileString, fileName, gl, o, scale, reverse) {
133   var objDoc = new OBJDoc(fileName);  // Create a OBJDoc object
134   var result = objDoc.parse(fileString, scale, reverse);
135   if (!result) {
136     g_objDoc = null; g_drawingInfo = null;
137     console.log("OBJ file parsing error.");
138     return;
139   }
140   g_objDoc = objDoc;
141 }
```

Within the JavaScript, the processing in `initVertexBuffers()`, called at line 64, has been changed. The function simply prepares an empty buffer object for the vertex coordinates, colors, and normals for the 3D model to be displayed. After parsing the OBJ file, the information corresponding to each buffer object will be written in the object.

The `initVertexBuffers()` function at line 88 creates the appropriate empty buffer objects at lines 90 to 92 using `createEmptyArrayBuffer()` and assigns them to an attribute variable. This function is defined at line 102 and, as you can see, creates a buffer object (line 103), assigns it to an attribute variable (line 109), and enables the assignment (line 110), but it does not write the data. After storing these buffer objects to `model` at line 64, the preparations of the buffer object are completed. The next step is to read the OBJ file contents into this buffer, which takes place at line 76 using `readOBJFile()`. The first argument is the location of the file (URL), the second one is `gl`, and the third one is the `Object` object (`model`) that packages the buffer objects. The tasks carried out by this function are similar to those when loading a texture image using the `Image` object and are shown here:

(2.1) Create an `XMLHttpRequest` object (line 117).

(2.2) Register the event handler to be called when the loading of the file is completed (line 119).

(2.3) Create a request to acquire the file using the `open()` method (line 124).

(2.4) Send the request to acquire the file (line 125).

Line 117 creates the `XMLHttpRequest` object, which sends an HTTP request to a web server. Line 119 is the registration of the event handler that will be called after the browser has loaded the file. Line 124 creates the request to acquire the file using the `open()` method. Because you are requesting a file, the first argument is `GET`, and the second one is the URL for the file. The last one specifies whether or not the request is asynchronous. Finally, line 125 uses the `send()` method to send the request to the web server to get the file.[9]

Once the browser has loaded the file, the event handler at line 119 is called. Line 120 checks for any errors returned by the load request. If the `readyState` property is 4, it indicates that the loading process is completed. However, if the `readyState` is not 4 and the `status` property is 404, it indicates that the specified file does not exist. The 404 error is the same as "404 Not Found," which is displayed when you try to display a web page that does not exist. When the file has been loaded successfully, `onReadOBJFile()` is called, which is defined at line 132 and takes five arguments. The first argument, `responseText`, contains the contents of the loaded file as one string. An `OBJDoc` object is created at line 133, which will be used, via the `parse()` method, to extract the results in a form that WebGL can easily use. The details will be explained next. Line 140 assigns the `objDoc`, which contains the parsing result in `g_objDoc` for rendering the model later.

---

[9] Note: When you want to run the sample programs that use external files in Chrome from your local disk, you should add the option `--allow-file-access-from-files` to Chrome. This is for security reasons. Chrome, by default, does not allow access to local files such as `../resources/cube.obj`. For Firefox, the equivalent parameter, set via `account:config`, is `security.fileuri.strict_origin_policy`, which should be set to `false`. Remember to set it back as you open a security loophole if local file access is enabled.

User-Defined Object

Before proceeding to the explanation of the remaining code of OBJViewer.js, you need to understand how to create your own (user-defined) objects in JavaScript. OBJViewer.js uses user-defined objects to parse an OBJ file. In JavaScript, you can create user-defined objects which, once created, are treated in the same way as built-in objects like Array and Date.

The following is the StringParser object used in OBJViewer.js. The key aspects are how to define a **constructor** to create a user-defined object and how to add methods to the object. The constructor is a special method that is called when creating an object with new. The following is the constructor for the StringParser object:

```
595   // Constructor
596   var StringParser = function(str) {
597     this.str;    // Store the string specified by the argument
598     this.index; // Position in the string to be processed
599     this.init(str);
600   }
```

You can define the constructor with the anonymous function (see Chapter 2). Its parameter is the one that will be specified when creating the object with new. Lines 597 and 598 are the declaration of properties that can be used for this new object type, similar to properties like the length property of Array. You can define the property by writing the keyword this followed by . and the property name. Line 599 then calls init(), an initialization method that has been defined for this user-defined object.

Let's take a look at init(). You can add a method to the object by writing the method name after the keyword prototype. The body of the method is also defined using an anonymous function:

```
601   // Initialize StringParser object
602   StringParser.prototype.init = function(str) {
603     this.str = str;
604     this.index = 0;
605   }
```

What is convenient here is that you can access the property that is defined in the constructor from the method. The this.str at line 603 refers to this.str defined at line 597 in the constructor. The this.index at line 604 refers to this.index at line 598 in the constructor. Let's try using this StringParse object:

```
var sp = new StringParser('Tomorrow is another day.');
alert(sp.str);        // "Tomorrow is another day." is displayed.
sp.str = 'Quo Vadis'; // The content of str is changed to "Quo Vadis".
alert(sp.str);        // "Quo Vadis" is displayed
sp.init('Cinderella, tonight?');
alert(sp.str);        // "Cinderella, tonight?" is displayed
```

Let's look at another method, `skipDelimiters()`, that skips the delimiters (tab, space, (,), or ") in a string:

```
608  StringParser.prototype.skipDelimiters = function() {
609    for(var i = this.index, len = this.str.length; i < len; i++) {
610      var c = this.str.charAt(i);
611      // Skip TAB, Space, (, ), and "
612      if (c == '\t'|| c == ' ' || c == '(' || c == ')' || c == '"') continue;
613      break;
614    }
615    this.index = i;
616  }
```

The `charAt()` method at line 610 is supported by the `String` object that manages a string and retrieves the character specified by the argument from the string.

Now let's look at the parser code in `OBJViewer.js`.

Sample Program (Parser Code in OBJViewer.js)

`OBJViewer.js` parses the content of an OBJ file line by line and converts it to the structure shown in Figure 10.28. Each box in Figure 10.28 is a user-defined object. Although the parser code in `OBJViewer.js` looks quite complex, the core parsing process is simple. The complexity comes because it is repeated several times. Let's take a look at the core processing, which once you understand will allow you to understand the whole process.

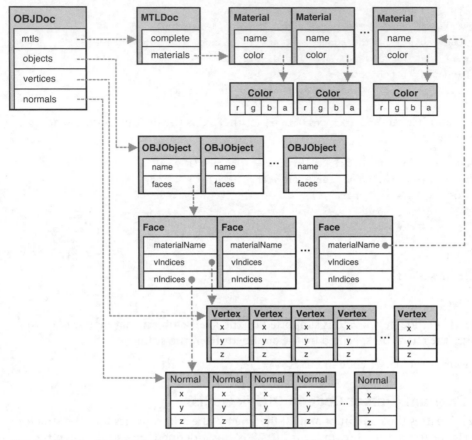

Figure 10.28 The internal structure after parsing an OBJ file

Listing 10.19 shows the basic code of OBJViewer.js.

Listing 10.19 OBJViewer.js (Parser Part)

```
214 // OBJDoc object
215 // Constructor
216 var OBJDoc = function(fileName) {
217   this.fileName = fileName;
218   this.mtls = new Array(0);      // Initialize the property for MTL
219   this.objects = new Array(0);   // Initialize the property for Object
220   this.vertices = new Array(0);  // Initialize the property for Vertex
221   this.normals = new Array(0);   // Initialize the property for Normal
222 }
223
224 // Parsing the OBJ file
225 OBJDoc.prototype.parse = function(fileString, scale, reverseNormal) {
```

```
226    var lines = fileString.split('\n');   // Break up into lines
227    lines.push(null); // Append null
228    var index = 0;      // Initialize index of line
229
230    var currentObject = null;
231    var currentMaterialName = "";
232
233    // Parse line by line
234    var line;           // A string in the line to be parsed
235    var sp = new StringParser();   // Create StringParser
236    while ((line = lines[index++]) != null) {
237      sp.init(line);                        // init StringParser
238      var command = sp.getWord();      // Get command
239      if(command == null)      continue;   // check null command
240
241      switch(command){
242      case '#':
243        continue;  // Skip comments
244      case 'mtllib':      // Read Material chunk
245        var path = this.parseMtllib(sp, this.fileName);
246        var mtl = new MTLDoc();   // Create MTL instance
247        this.mtls.push(mtl);
248        var request = new XMLHttpRequest();
249        request.onreadystatechange = function() {
250          if (request.readyState == 4) {
251            if (request.status != 404) {
252              onReadMTLFile(request.responseText, mtl);
253            }else{
254              mtl.complete = true;
255            }
256          }
257        }
258        request.open('GET', path, true); // Create a request to get file
259        request.send();                  // Send the request
260        continue; // Go to the next line
261      case 'o':
262      case 'g':   // Read Object name
263        var object = this.parseObjectName(sp);
264        this.objects.push(object);
265        currentObject = object;
266        continue; // Go to the next line
267      case 'v':   // Read vertex
268        var vertex = this.parseVertex(sp, scale);
269        this.vertices.push(vertex);
270        continue; // Go to the next line
```

```
271    case 'vn':    // Read normal
272      var normal = this.parseNormal(sp);
273      this.normals.push(normal);
274      continue; // Go to the next line
275    case 'usemtl': // Read Material name
276      currentMaterialName = this.parseUsemtl(sp);
277      continue; // Go to the next line
278    case 'f': // Read face
279      var face = this.parseFace(sp, currentMaterialName, this.vertices,
                                                        ➥reverse);
280      currentObject.addFace(face);
281      continue; // Go to the next line
282    }
283  }
284
285  return true;
286 }
```

Lines 216 to 222 define the constructor for the OBJDoc object, which consists of five properties that will be parsed and set up. The actual parsing is done in the parse() method at line 225. The content of the OBJ file is passed as one string to the argument *fileString* of the parse() method and then split into manageable pieces using the split() method. This method splits a string into pieces delimited by the characters specified as the argument. As you can see at line 226, the argument specifies "\n" (new line), so each line is stored in this.lines as an array. null is appended at the end of the array at line 227 to make it easy to find the end of the array. this.index indicates how many lines have been parsed and is initialized to 0 at line 228.

You have already seen the StringParser object, which is created at line 235, in the previous section. This object is used for parsing the content of the line.

Now you are ready to start parsing the OBJ file. Each line is stored in line using this.lines[this.index++] at line 236. Line 237 writes the line to sp (StringParser). Line 238 gets the first word of the line using sp.getWord() and stores it in command. You use the methods shown in Table 10.3, where "word" in the table indicates a string surrounded by a delimiter (tab, space, (,), or ").

Table 10.3 Method that StringParser Supports

Method	Description
StringParser.init(str)	Initialize StringParser to be able to parse *str*.
StringParser.getWord()	Get a word.
StringParser.skipToNext-Word()	Skip to the beginning of the next word.

Method	Description
`StringParser.getInt()`	Get a word and convert it to an integer number.
`StringParser.getFloat()`	Get a word and convert it to a floating point number.

The `switch` statement at line 241 checks the command to determine how to process the following lines in the OBJ file.

If the command is # (line 242), the line is a comment. Line 243 skips it using `continue`.

If the command is `mtllib` (line 241), the line is a reference to an MTL file. Line 245 generates the path to the file. Line 246 creates an MTLDoc object for storing the material information in the MTL file, and line 247 stores it in `this.mtls`. Then lines 248 to 259 read the file in the same way that you read an OBJ file. The MTL file is parsed by `onReadMTLfile()`, which is called when it is loaded.

If the command is `o` (line 261) or `g` (line 262), it indicates a named object or group. Line 263 parses the line and returns the results in `OBJObject`. This object is stored in `this.objects` at line 264 and `currentObject`.

If the command is `v`, the line is a vertex position. Line 268 parses (x, y, z) and returns the result in `Vertex` object. This object is stored in `this.vertices` at line 269.

If the command is `f`, it indicates that the line is a face definition. Line 279 parses it and returns the result in the `Face` object. This object is stored in the `currentObject`. Let's take a look at `parseVertex()`, which is shown in Listing 10.20.

Listing 10.20   OBJViewer.js (parseVertex())

```
302 OBJDoc.prototype.parseVertex = function(sp, scale) {
303   var x = sp.getFloat() * scale;
304   var y = sp.getFloat() * scale;
305   var z = sp.getFloat() * scale;
306   return (new Vertex(x, y, z));
307 }
```

Line 303 retrieves the x value from the line using `sp.getFloat()`. A scaling factor is applied when the model is too small or large. After retrieving the three coordinates, line 306 creates a `Vertex` object using x, y, and z and returns it.

Once the OBJ file and MTL files have been fully parsed, the arrays for the vertex coordinates, colors, normals, and indices are created from the structure shown in Figure 10.28. Then `onReadComplete()` is called to write them into the buffer object (see Listing 10.21).

Listing 10.21 OBJViewer.js (onReadComplete())

```
176 // OBJ File has been read completely
177 function onReadComplete(gl, model, objDoc) {
178   // Acquire the vertex coordinates and colors from OBJ file
179   var drawingInfo = objDoc.getDrawingInfo();
180
181   // Write date into the buffer object
182   gl.bindBuffer(gl.ARRAY_BUFFER, model.vertexBuffer);
183   gl.bufferData(gl.ARRAY_BUFFER, drawingInfo.vertices,gl.STATIC_DRAW);
184
185   gl.bindBuffer(gl.ARRAY_BUFFER, model.normalBuffer);
186   gl.bufferData(gl.ARRAY_BUFFER, drawingInfo.normals, gl.STATIC_DRAW);
187
188   gl.bindBuffer(gl.ARRAY_BUFFER, model.colorBuffer);
189   gl.bufferData(gl.ARRAY_BUFFER, drawingInfo.colors, gl.STATIC_DRAW);
190
191   // Write the indices to the buffer object
192   gl.bindBuffer(gl.ELEMENT_ARRAY_BUFFER, model.indexBuffer);
193   gl.bufferData(gl.ELEMENT_ARRAY_BUFFER, drawingInfo.indices, gl.STATIC_DRAW);
194
195   return drawingInfo;
196 }
```

This method is straightforward and starts at Line 178, which retrieves the drawing information from objDoc that contains the results from parsing the OBJ file. Lines 183, 186, 189, and 193 write vertices, normals, colors, and indices into the respective buffer objects.

The function getDrawingInfo() at line 451 retrieves the vertices, normals, colors, and indices from the objDoc and is shown in Listing 10.22.

Listing 10.22 OBJViewer.js (Retrieving the Drawing Information)

```
450 // Retrieve the information for drawing 3D model
451 OBJDoc.prototype.getDrawingInfo = function() {
452   // Create an array for vertex coordinates, normals, colors, and indices
453   var numIndices = 0;
454   for (var i = 0; i < this.objects.length; i++){
455     numIndices += this.objects[i].numIndices;
456   }
457   var numVertices = numIndices;
458   var vertices = new Float32Array(numVertices * 3);
459   var normals = new Float32Array(numVertices * 3);
460   var colors = new Float32Array(numVertices * 4);
461   var indices = new Uint16Array(numIndices);
462
463   // Set vertex, normal, and color
```

```
464    var index_indices = 0;
465    for (var i = 0; i < this.objects.length; i++){
466      var object = this.objects[i];
467      for (var j = 0; j < object.faces.length; j++){
468         var face = object.face[j];
469        var color = this.findColor(face.materialName);
470        var faceNormal = face.normal;
471        for (var k = 0; k < face.vIndices.length; k++){
472           // Set index
473           indices[index_indices] = index_indices;
474           // Copy vertex
475           var vIdx = face.vIndices[k];
476           var vertex = this.vertices[vIdx];
477           vertices[index_indices * 3 + 0] = vertex.x;
478           vertices[index_indices * 3 + 1] = vertex.y;
479           vertices[index_indices * 3 + 2] = vertex.z;
480           // Copy color
481           colors[index_indices * 4 + 0] = color.r;
482           colors[index_indices * 4 + 1] = color.g;
483           colors[index_indices * 4 + 2] = color.b;
484           colors[index_indices * 4 + 3] = color.a;
485           // Copy normal
486           var nIdx = face.nIndices[k];
487           if(nIdx >= 0){
488              var normal =  this.normals[nIdx];
489              normals[index_indices * 3 + 0] = normal.x;
490              normals[index_indices * 3 + 1] = normal.y;
491              normals[index_indices * 3 + 2] = normal.z;
492           }else{
493              normals[index_indices * 3 + 0] = faceNormal.x;
494              normals[index_indices * 3 + 1] = faceNormal.y;
495              normals[index_indices * 3 + 2] = faceNormal.z;
496           }
497           index_indices ++;
498        }
499      }
500    }
501
502    return new DrawingInfo(vertices, normals, colors, indices);
503 };
```

Line 454 calculates the number of indices using a for loop. Then lines 458 to 461 create typed arrays for storing vertices, normals, colors, and indices that are assigned to the appropriate buffer objects. The size of each array is determined by the number of indices at line 454.

The program traverses the `OBJObject` objects and its `Face` objects in the order shown in Figure 10.28 and stores the information in the arrays `vertices`, `colors`, and `indices`.

The `for` statement at line 465 loops, extracting each `OBJObject` one by one from the result of the earlier parsing. The `for` statement at line 467 does the same for each `Face` object that makes up the `OBJObject` and performs the following steps for each `Face`:

1. Lines 469 finds the color of the `Face` using `materialName` and stores the color in `color`. Line 468 stores the normal of the face in `faceNomal` for later use.

2. The `for` statement at line 471 loops, extracting vertex indices from the face, storing its vertex position in `vertices` (lines 477 to 479), and storing the r, g, and b components of the color in `colors` (lines 482 to 484). The code from line 486 handles normals. OBJ files may or may not contain normals, so line 487 checks for that. If normals are found in the OBJ file, lines 487 to 489 store them in `normals`. Lines 492 to 494 then store the normals this program generates.

Once you complete these steps for all `OBJObjects`, you are ready to draw. Line 502 returns the information for drawing the model in a `DrawingInfo` object, which manages the vertex information that has to be written in the buffer object, as described previously.

Although this has been, by necessity, a rapid explanation, at this stage you should understand how the contents of the OBJ file can be read in, parsed, and displayed with WebGL. If you want to read multiple model files in a single scene, you would repeat the preceding processes. There are several other models stored as OBJ files in the `resources` directory of the sample programs, which you can look at and experiment with to confirm your understanding (see Figure 10.29).

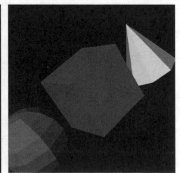

Figure 10.29   Various 3D models

Handling Lost Context

WebGL uses the underlying graphics hardware, which is a shared resource managed by the operating system. There are several situations where this resource can be "taken away," resulting in information stored within the graphics hardware being lost. These include situations when another program takes over the hardware or when the machine hibernates. When this happens, information that WebGL uses to draw correctly, its "context," can be lost. A good example is when you run a WebGL program on a notebook PC or smart phone and it enters hibernation mode. Often, an error message is displayed before the machine hibernates. When the machine awakes after you press the power button, the system returns to the original state, but browser that is running the WebGL program may display nothing on the screen, as on the right side of Figure 10.30. Because the background color of the web page that this sample program draws is white, the web browser shows a completely white screen.

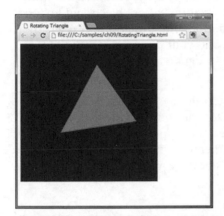 

Before Hibernation   After Hibernation

Figure 10.30 WebGL program stops after returning from a hibernation mode

For example, if you are running `RotatingTriangle`, the following message may be displayed on the console:

```
WebGL error CONTEXT_LOST_WEBGL in uniformMatrix4fv([object WebGLUniformLocation,
false, [object Float32Array]]
```

This indicates that the error occurred when the program performed the `gl.uniformMatrix4fv()` either before the system entered the hibernation mode or on return from hibernation. The error message will differ slightly depending on what the program was trying to do at the time of hibernation. In this section, we will explain how to deal with this problem.

How to Implement Handling Lost Context

As previously discussed, context can be lost for any number of reasons. However, WebGL supports two events to indicate state changes within the system: a **context lost event** (`webglcontextlost`) and a **context restore event** (`webglcontextrestored`). See Table 10.4.

Table 10.4 The Context Events

Event	Description
Webglcontextlost	Occurs when the rendering context for WebGL is lost
webglcontextrestored	Occurs when the browser completes a reset of the WebGL system

When the context lost event occurs, the rendering context acquired by `getWebGLContext()` (that is `gl` in the sample programs) becomes invalid, and any operations carried out using the `gl` context are invalidated. These processes include creating buffer objects and texture objects, initializing shaders, setting the clear color, and more. After the browser resets the WebGL system, the context restore event is generated, and your program needs to redo these operations. The other variables in your JavaScript program are not affected and can be used as normal.

Before taking a look at the sample program, you need to use the `addEventListener()` method of the `<canvas>` to register the event handlers for the context lost event and the context restore event. This is because the `<canvas>` does not support a specific property that you can use to register context event handlers. Remember that in previous examples you used the `onmousedown` property of `<canvas>` to register the event handler for the mouse event.

`canvas.addEventListener(type, handler, useCapture)`

Register the event handler specified by *handler* to the `<canvas>` element.

Parameters	type	Specifies the name of the event to listen for (string).
	handler	Specifies the event handler to be called when the event occurs. This function is called with one argument (event object).
	useCapture	Specifies whether the event needs to be captured or not (boolean). If `true`, the event is not dispatched to other elements. If `false`, the event is dispatched to others.
Return value	None	

Sample Program (RotatingTriangle_contextLost.js)

In this section, you will construct a sample program, `RotatingTriangle_contextLost`, which modifies `RotatingTriangle` to make it possible to deal with the context lost event (shown in Figure 10.30). The sample program is shown in Listing 10.23.

Listing 10.23   RotatingTriangle_contextLost.js

```
 1   // RotatingTriangle_contextLost.js
     ...
16   function main() {
17     // Retrieve <canvas> element
18     var canvas = document.getElementById('webgl');
19
20     // Register event handler for context lost and restored events
21     canvas.addEventListener('webglcontextlost', contextLost, false);
22     canvas.addEventListener('webglcontextrestored', function(ev)
                                            ➥{ start(canvas); }, false);
23
24     start(canvas);    // Perform WebGL-related processes
25   }
       ...
29   // Current rotation angle
30   var g_currentAngle = 0.0;  // Changed from local variable to global
31   var g_requestID;           // The return value of requestAnimationFrame()
32
33   function start(canvas) {
34     // Get the rendering context for WebGL
35     var gl = getWebGLContext(canvas);
       ...
41     // Initialize shaders
42     if (!initShaders(gl, VSHADER_SOURCE, FSHADER_SOURCE)) {
       ...
45     }
46
47     var n = initVertexBuffers(gl);   // Set vertex coordinates
       ...
55     // Get storage location of u_ModelMatrix
56     var u_ModelMatrix = gl.getUniformLocation(gl.program, 'u_ModelMatrix');
       ...
62     var modelMatrix = new Matrix4();   // Create a model matrix
63
64     var tick = function() {   // Start drawing
65       g_currentAngle = animate(g_currentAngle); // Update rotation angle
66       draw(gl, n, g_currentAngle, modelMatrix, u_ModelMatrix);
67       g_requestID = requestAnimationFrame(tick, canvas);
68     };
69     tick();
70   }
71
72   function contextLost(ev) {   // Event handler for context lost event
```

```
73    cancelAnimationFrame(g_requestID);  // Stop animation
74    ev.preventDefault();                // Prevent the default behavior
75  }
```

The processing of the context lost event has no implications for the shaders, so let's focus on the `main()` function in the JavaScript program starting at line 16. Line 21 registers the event handler for the context lost event, and line 22 registers the event handler for the context restore event. The `main()` function ends by calling the function `start()` at line 24.

The `start()` function, defined at line 33, contains the same steps as in `RotatingTriangle.js`. They are the processes you have to redo when the context lost event occurs. There are two changes from `RotatingTriangle.js` to handle lost context.

First, the current rotation angle, at line 65, is stored in a global variable `g_currentAngle` (line 30) instead of a local variable. This allows you to draw the triangle using the angle held in the global variable when a context restore event occurs. Line 67 stores the return value of `requestAnimationFrame()` in the global variable `g_requestID` (line 31). This is used to cancel the registration of the function when the context lost event occurs.

Let's take a look at the actual event handlers. The event handler for the context lost event, `contextLost()`, is defined at line 72 and has only two lines. Line 73 cancels the registration of the function used to carry out the animation, ensuring no further attempt at drawing is made until the context is correctly restored. Then at Line 74 you prevent the browser's default behavior for this event. This is because, by default, the browser doesn't generate the context restore event. However, in our case, the event is needed, so you must prevent this default behavior.

The event handler for the context restore event is straightforward and makes a call to `start()`, which rebuilds the WebGL context. This is carried out by registering the event handler at line 22, which calls `start()` by using an anonymous function.

Note that when a context lost event occurs, the following alert is always displayed on the console:

```
WARNING: WebGL content on the page might have caused the graphics card to reset
```

By implementing these handlers for the lost context events, your WebGL applications will be able to deal with situations where the WebGL context is lost.

Summary

This chapter explained a number of miscellaneous techniques that are useful to know when creating WebGL applications. Due to space limitations, the explanations have been kept brief but contain sufficient information for you to master and use the techniques in your own WebGL applications. Although there are many more techniques you could learn, we have chosen these because they will help you begin to apply the lessons in this book to building your own 3D applications.

As you have seen, WebGL is a powerful tool for creating 3D applications and one that is capable of creating sophisticated and visually stunning 3D graphics. Our aim in this book has been to provide you with a step-by-step introduction to the basics of WebGL and give you a strong enough foundation on which to begin building your own WebGL applications and exploring further. There are many other resources available to help you in that exploration. However, our hope is that as you begin to venture out and explore WebGL yourself, you will return to this book and find it valuable as a reference and guide as you build your knowledge.

No Need to Swap Buffers in WebGL

For those of you with some experience in developing OpenGL applications on PCs, you may have noticed that none of the examples in this book seem to swap color buffers, which is something that most OpenGL implementations require.

As you know, OpenGL uses two buffers: a "front" color buffer and a "back" color buffer with the contents of the front color buffer being displayed on the screen. Usually, when you draw something using OpenGL, it is drawn into the back color buffer. When you want to actually display something, you need to copy the contents of the back buffer to the front buffer to cause it to be displayed. If you were to draw directly into the front buffer, you would see visual artifacts (such as flickers) because the screen was being updated before you had finalized the data in the buffer.

To support this dual-buffer approach, OpenGL provides a mechanism to swap the back buffer and the front buffer. In some systems this is automatic; in others, explicit calls to swap buffers, such as `glutSwapBuffers()` or `eglSwapBuffers()`, are needed after drawing into the back buffer. For example, a typical OpenGL application has the following user-defined "display" function:

```
void display(void) {
 // Clear color buffer and depth buffer
  glClear(GL_COLOR_BUFFER_BIT | GL_DEPTH_BUFFER_BIT);
  draw();              // Draw something
  glutSwapBuffers(); // Swap color buffers
}
```

In contrast, WebGL relies on the browser to automatically manage the display update, relieving you of the need to do it explicitly in your applications. Referring to Figure A.1 (which is the same as Figure 2.10), when WebGL applications draw something in the color buffer, the browser detects the drawing and displays the content on the screen. Therefore, WebGL supports only one color buffer.

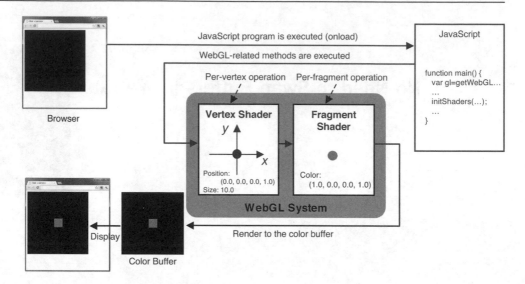

Figure A.1 The processing flow from executing a JavaScript program to displaying the result in a browser

This approach works, because as seen in the sample programs in this book, all WebGL programs are executed in the browser by executing the JavaScript in the form of a method invocation from the browser.

Because the programs are not independently executed, the browser has a chance to check whether the content of the color buffer was modified after the JavaScript program executes and exits. If the contents have been modified, the browser is responsible for ensuring it is displayed on the screen.

For example, in HelloPoint1, we execute the JavaScript function (main()) from the HTML file (HelloPoint1.html) as follows:

```
<body onload="main()">
```

This causes the browser to execute the JavaScript function main() after loading the <body> element. Within main(), the draw operation modifies the color buffer.

```
main(){
  ...
  // Draw a point
  gl.drawArrays(gl.POINTS, 0, 1);
}
```

When main() exits, the control returns to the browser that called the function. The browser then checks the content of the color buffer, and if anything has been changed, causes it to be displayed. One useful side effect of this approach is that the browser handles combining the color buffer with the rest of the web page, allowing you to combine 3D graphics with your web pages. Note that `HelloPoint1` shows only the `<canvas>` element on the page, because `HelloPoint1.html` contains no other elements than the `<canvas>` element.

This implies that if you call methods that return control to the browser, such as `alert()` or `confirm()`, the browser may then display the contents of the color buffer to the screen. This may not be what you expect, so take care when using these methods in your WebGL programs.

The browser behaves in the same way when JavaScript draws something in an event handler. This is because the event handler is also called from the browser, and then the control is returned to the browser after the handler exits.

Built-In Functions of GLSL ES 1.0

This appendix details all embedded functions supported by GLSL ES 1.0, including many that are not explained in this book but which are often used in programming shaders.

Note that, in all but texture lookup functions, the operations on vector or matrix arguments are carried out component-wise. For example,

```
vec2 deg = vec2(60, 80);
vec2 rad = radians(deg);
```

In these examples, the components of the variable rad are assigned values converted from 60 and 80 degrees, respectively.

Angle and Trigonometry Functions

Syntax	Description
float radians(float *degree*)	Converts degrees to radians; that is, $\pi * degree/180$.
vec2 radians(vec2 *degree*)	
vec3 radians(vec3 *degree*)	
vec4 radians(vec4 *degree*)	
float degrees(float *radian*)	Converts radians to degrees; that is, $180 * radian/\pi$.
vec2 degrees(vec2 *radian*)	
vec3 degrees(vec3 *radian*)	
vec4 degrees(vec4 *radian*)	

Syntax	Description

`float sin(float `*`angle`*`)`
 	
`vec2 sin(vec2 `*`angle`*`)`
 	
`vec3 sin(vec3 `*`angle`*`)`
 	
`vec4 sin(vec4 `*`angle`*`)`
	The standard trigonometric sine function. *angle* is in radians.
	
	The range of the return value is [–1, 1].

`float cos(float `*`angle`*`)`
 	
`vec2 cos(vec2 `*`angle`*`)`
 	
`vec3 cos(vec3 `*`angle`*`)`
 	
`vec4 cos(vec4 `*`angle`*`)`
	The standard trigonometric cosine function. *angle* is in radians.
	
	The range of the return value is [–1, 1].

`float tan(float `*`angle`*`)`
 	
`vec2 tan(vec2 `*`angle`*`)`
 	
`vec3 tan(vec3 `*`angle`*`)`
 	
`vec4 tan(vec4 `*`angle`*`)`
	The standard trigonometric tangent function. *angle* is in radians.

`float asin(float `*`x`*`)`
 	
`vec2 asin(vec2 `*`x`*`)`
 	
`vec3 asin(vec3 `*`x`*`)`
 	
`vec4 asin(vec4 `*`x`*`)`
	Arc sine. Returns an angle (in radians) whose sine is *x*. The range of the return value is $[-\pi/2, \pi/2]$. Results are undefined if x > –1 or x > +1.

`float acos(float `*`x`*`)`
 	
`vec2 acos(vec2 `*`x`*`)`
 	
`vec3 acos(vec3 `*`x`*`)`
 	
`vec4 acos(vec4 `*`x`*`)`
	Arc cosine. Returns an angle (in radians) whose cosine is *x*. The range of the return value is $[0, \pi]$. Results are undefined if x > –1 or x > +1.

`float atan(float `*`y`*`, float `*`x`*`)`
 	
`vec2 atan(vec2 `*`y`*`, vec2 `*`x`*`)`
 	
`vec3 atan(vec3 `*`y`*`, vec3 `*`x`*`)`
 	
`vec4 atan(vec4 `*`y`*`, vec4 `*`x`*`)`
	Arc tangent. Returns an angle (in radians) whose tangent is *y*/*x*. The signs of *x* and *y* are used to determine what quadrant the angle is in. The range of the return value is $[-\pi, \pi]$. Results are undefined if *x* and *y* are both 0.
	
	Note, for vectors, this is a component-wise operation.

`float atan(float `*`y_over_x`*`)`
 	
`vec2 atan(vec2 `*`y_over_x`*`)`
 	
`vec3 atan(vec3 `*`y_over_x`*`)`
 	
`vec4 atan(vec4 `*`y_over_x`*`)`
	Arc tangent. Returns an angle whose tangent is *y_over_x*. The range of the return value is $[-\pi/2, \pi/2]$.
	
	Note, for vectors, this is a component-wise operation.

Exponential Functions

Syntax	Description
`float pow(float x, float y)`	Returns x raised to the y power; that is, x^y.
`vec2 pow(vec2 x, vec2 y)`	Results are undefined if $x < 0$.
`vec3 pow(vec3 x, vec3 y)`	Results are undefined if $x = 0$ and $y \leq 0$.
`vec4 pow(vec4 x, vec4 y)`	Note, for vectors, this is a component-wise operation.
`float exp(float x)`	Returns the natural exponentiation of x; that is, e^x.
`vec2 exp(vec2 x)`	
`vec3 exp(vec3 x)`	
`vec4 exp(vec4 x)`	
`float log(float x)`	Returns the natural logarithm of x; that is, returns the value y, which satisfies the equation $x = e^y$. Results are undefined if $x \leq 0$.
`vec2 log(vec2 x)`	
`vec3 log(vec3 x)`	
`vec4 log(vec4 x)`	
`float exp2(float x)`	Returns 2 raised to the x power; that is, 2^x.
`vec2 exp2(vec2 x)`	
`vec3 exp2(vec3 x)`	
`vec4 exp2(vec4 x)`	
`float log2(float x)`	Returns the base 2 logarithm of x; that is, returns the value y, which satisfies the equation $x = 2^y$.
`vec2 log2(vec2 x)`	
`vec3 log2(vec3 x)`	Results are undefined if $x \leq 0$.
`vec4 log2(vec4 x)`	
`float sqrt(float x)`	
`vec2 sqrt(vec2 x)`	Returns $\sqrt{x}$.
`vec3 sqrt(vec3 x)`	Results are undefined if $x < 0$.
`vec4 sqrt(vec4 x)`	
`float inversesqrt(float x)`	
`vec2 inversesqrt(vec2 x)`	Returns $1/\sqrt{x}$.
`vec3 inversesqrt(vec3 x)`	Results are undefined if $x \leq 0$.
`vec4 inversesqrt(vec4 x)`	

Common Functions

Syntax	Description
float abs(float x) vec2 abs(vec2 x) vec3 abs(vec3 x) vec4 abs(vec4 x)	Returns the non-negative value of x without regard to its sign; that is, x if $x \geq 0$, otherwise it returns $-x$.
float sign(float x) vec2 sign(vec2 x) vec3 sign(vec3 x) vec4 sign(vec4 x)	Returns 1.0 if $x > 0$, 0.0 if $x = 0$, or -1.0 if $x < 0$.
float floor(float x) vec2 floor(vec2 x) vec3 floor(vec3 x) vec4 floor(vec4 x)	Returns a value equal to the nearest integer that is less than or equal to x.
float ceil(float x) vec2 ceil(vec2 x) vec3 ceil(vec3 x) vec4 ceil(vec4 x)	Returns a value equal to the nearest integer that is greater than or equal to x.
float fract(float x) vec2 fract(vec2 x) vec3 fract(vec3 x) vec4 fract(vec4 x)	Returns the fractional part of x; that is, $x - \text{floor}(x)$.
float mod(float x, float y) vec2 mod(vec2 x, vec2 y) vec3 mod(vec3 x, vec3 y) vec4 mod(vec4 x, vec4 y) vec2 mod(vec2 x, float y) vec3 mod(vec3 x, float y) vec4 mod(vec4 x, float y)	Modulus (modulo). Returns the remainder of the division of x by y; that is, $(x - y * \text{floor}(x/y))$. Given two positive numbers x and y, mod(x, y) is the remainder of the division of x by y. Note, for vectors, this is a component-wise operation.

Syntax	Description

`float min(float x, float y)`
 	
`vec2 min(vec2 x, vec2 y)`
 	
`vec3 min(vec3 x, vec3 y)`
 	
`vec4 min(vec4 x, vec4 y)`
 	
`vec2 min(vec2 x, float y)`
 	
`vec3 min(vec3 x, float y)`
 	
`vec4 min(vec4 x, float y)`
	Returns the smallest value; that is, y if $y < x$, otherwise it returns x.
	
	Note, for vectors, this is a component-wise operation.

`float max(float x, float y)`
 	
`vec2 max(vec2 x, vec2 y)`
 	
`vec3 max(vec3 x, vec3 y)`
 	
`vec4 max(vec4 x, vec4 y)`
 	
`vec2 max(vec2 x, float y)`
 	
`vec3 max(vec3 x, float y)`
 	
`vec4 max(vec4 x, float y)`
	Returns the largest value; that is, y if $x < y$, otherwise it returns x.
	
	Note, for vectors, this is a component-wise operation.

`float clamp(float x, float minVal,`
`        float maxVal)`
 	
`vec2 clamp(vec2 x, vec2 minVal,`
`        vec2 maxVal)`
 	
`vec3 clamp(vec3 x, vec3 minVal,`
`        vec3 maxVal)`
 	
`vec4 clamp(vec4 x, vec4 minVal,`
`        vec4 maxVal)`
 	
`vec2 clamp(vec2 x, float minVal,`
`        float maxVal)`
 	
`vec3 clamp(vec3 x, float minVal,`
`        float maxVal)`
 	
`vec4 clamp(vec4 x, float minVal,`
`        float maxVal)`
	Constrains x to lie between minVal and maxVal; that is, returns min (max (x, $minVal$), $maxVal$).
	
	Results are undefined if $minVal > maxVal$.

Syntax	Description
`float mix(float x, float y, float a)`	Returns the linear blend of x and y; that is, $x * (1-a) + y * a$.
`vec2 mix(vec2 x, vec2 y, float a)`	
`vec3 mix(vec3 x, vec3 y, float a)`	
`vec4 mix(vec4 x, vec4 y, float a)`	
`vec2 mix(vec2 x, float y, vec2 a)`	
`vec3 mix(vec3 x, float y, vec3 a)`	
`vec4 mix(vec4 x, float y, vec4 a)`	
`vec2 mix(vec2 x, vec2 y, vec2 a)`	
`vec3 mix(vec3 x, vec3 y, vec3 a)`	
`vec4 mix(vec4 x, vec4 y, vec4 a)`	
`float step(float edge, float x)`	Generates a step function by comparing two values; that is, returns 0.0 if $x < edge$, otherwise it returns 1.0.
`vec2 step(vec2 edge, vec2 x)`	
`vec3 step(vec3 edge, vec3 x)`	
`vec4 step(vec4 edge, vec4 x)`	
`vec2 step(float edge, vec2 x)`	
`vec3 step(float edge, vec3 x)`	
`vec4 step(float edge, vec4 x)`	
`float smoothstep(float edge0, float edge1, float x)`	Hermite interpolation. Returns 0.0 if $x \leq edge0$ and 1.0 if $x \geq edge1$ and performs smooth Hermite interpolation between 0 and 1 when $edge0 < x < edge1$. This is equivalent to:
`vec2 smoothstep(vec2 edge0, vec2 edge1, vec2 x)`	`// genType is float, vec2, vec3, or vec4` `genType t;` `t = clamp ((x - edge0) / (edge1 - edge0), 0, 1);` `return t * t * (3 - 2 * t);`
`vec3 smoothstep(vec3 edge0, vec3 edge1, vec3 x)`	
`vec4 smoothstep(vec4 edge0, vec4 edge1, vec4 x)`	Results are undefined if $edge0 \geq edge1$.

The following functions determine which components of their arguments will be used depending on the functionality of the function.

Geometric Functions

Syntax	Description
`float length(float x)`	Returns the length of vector x.
`float length(vec2 x)`	
`float length(vec3 x)`	
`float length(vec4 x)`	
`float distance(float p0, float p1)`	Returns the distance between p0 and p1; that is, length (p0 − p1).
`float distance(vec2 p0, vec2 p1)`	
`float distance(vec3 p0, vec3 p1)`	
`float distance(vec4 p0, vec4 p1)`	
`float dot(float x, float y)`	Returns the dot product of x and y, in case of vec3, x[0]*y [0]+x [1]*y[1]+x[2]*y[2].
`float dot(vec2 x, vec2 y)`	
`float dot(vec3 x, vec3 y)`	
`float dot(vec4 x, vec4 y)`	
`vec3 cross(vec3 x, vec3 y)`	Returns the cross product of x and y, in case of vec3, result[0] = x[1]*y[2] - y[1]*x[2] result[1] = x[2]*y[0] - y[2]*x[0] result[2] = x[0]*y[1] - y[0]*x[1]
`float normalize(float x)`	Returns a vector in the same direction as x but with a length of 1; that is, x/length(x).
`vec2 normalize(vec2 x)`	
`vec3 normalize(vec3 x)`	
`vec4 normalize(vec4 x)`	
`float faceforward(float N, float I,` `              float Nref)`	Reverse the normal. Adjust the vector N according to the incident vector I and the reference vector Nref.
`vec2 faceforward(vec2 N, vec2 I,` `              vec2 Nref)`	If dot(Nref, I) < 0 return N, otherwise return −N.
`vec3 faceforward(vec3 N, vec3 I,` `              vec3 Nref)`	
`vec4 faceforward(vec4 N, vec4 I,` `              vec4 Nref)`	

Syntax	Description

`float reflect(float I, float N)`
 	
 `vec2 reflect(vec2 I, vec2 N)`
 	
 `vec3 reflect(vec3 I, vec3 N)`
 	
 `vec4 reflect(vec4 I, vec4 N)`
	Calculate reflection vector. For the incident vector I and surface orientation N, returns the reflection direction: $I - 2 * dot(N, I) * N$
	
	 N must already be normalized to achieve the desired result.

`float refract(float I, float N,`
 `                      float eta)`
 	
 `vec2 refract(vec2 I, vec2 N, float`
 `                      eta)`
 	
 `vec3 refract(vec3 I, vec3 N, float`
 `                      eta)`
 	
 `vec4 refract(vec4 I, vec4 N, float`
 `                      eta)`
	Calculate the change in direction of light due to its medium by calculating the incident vector using the ratio of indices of refraction. For the incident vector I and surface normal N, and the ratio of indices of refraction *eta*, return the refraction vector using the following:
	
	 k = 1.0 – *eta* * *eta* * (1.0 – dot(N, I) * dot(N, I))
	 if (k < 0.0)
	     // genTyp is float, vec2, vec3, or vec4
	     return genType(0.0)
	 else
	     return *eta* * I - (*eta* * dot(N, I) + sqrt(k)) * N
	
	 The input parameters for the incident vector I and the surface normal N must already be normalized.

Matrix Functions

Syntax	Description

`mat2 matrixCompMult(mat2 x, mat2 y)`
 	
 `mat3 matrixCompMult(mat3 x, mat3 y)`
 	
 `mat4 matrixCompMult(mat4 x, mat4 y)`
	Multiply matrix x by matrix y component-wise; that is, if result = matrixCompMatrix(x, y) then result[i][j] = x[i][j] * y[i][j].

Vector Functions

Syntax	Description

`bvec2 lessThan(vec2 `x`, vec2 `y`)`
 	
`bvec3 lessThan(vec3 `x`, vec3 `y`)`
 	
`bvec4 lessThan(vec4 `x`, vec4 `y`)`
 	
`bvec2 lessThan(ivec2 `x`, ivec2 `y`)`
 	
`bvec3 lessThan(ivec3 `x`, ivec3 `y`)`
 	
`bvec4 lessThan(ivec4 `x`, ivec4 `y`)`
	Return the component-wise comparison of $x < y$.

`bvec2 lessThanEqual(vec2 `x`, vec2 `y`)`
 	
`bvec3 lessThanEqual(vec3 `x`, vec3 `y`)`
 	
`bvec4 lessThanEqual(vec4 `x`, vec4 `y`)`
 	
`bvec2 lessThanEqual(ivec2 `x`, ivec2 `y`)`
 	
`bvec3 lessThanEqual(ivec3 `x`, ivec3 `y`)`
 	
`bvec4 lessThanEqual(ivec4 `x`, ivec4 `y`)`
	Return the component-wise comparison of $x \leq y$.

`bvec2 greaterThan(vec2 `x`, vec2 `y`)`
 	
`bvec3 greaterThan(vec3 `x`, vec3 `y`)`
 	
`bvec4 greaterThan(vec4 `x`, vec4 `y`)`
 	
`bvec2 greaterThan(ivec2 `x`, ivec2 `y`)`
 	
`bvec3 greaterThan(ivec3 `x`, ivec3 `y`)`
 	
`bvec4 greaterThan(ivec4 `x`, ivec4 `y`)`
	Return the component-wise comparison of $x > y$.

`bvec2 greaterThanEqual(vec2 `x`, vec2 `y`)`
 	
`bvec3 greaterThanEqual(vec3 `x`, vec3 `y`)`
 	
`bvec4 greaterThanEqual(vec4 `x`, vec4 `y`)`
 	
`bvec2 greaterThanEqual(ivec2 `x`, ivec2 `y`)`
 	
`bvec3 greaterThanEqual(ivec3 `x`, ivec3 `y`)`
 	
`bvec4 greaterThanEqual(ivec4 `x`, ivec4 `y`)`
	Return the component-wise comparison of $x \geq y$.

Syntax	Description
bvec2 equal(vec2 *x*, vec2 *y*) bvec3 equal(vec3 *x*, vec3 *y*) bvec4 equal(vec4 *x*, vec4 *y*) bvec2 equal(ivec2 *x*, ivec2 *y*) bvec3 equal(ivec3 *x*, ivec3 *y*) bvec4 equal(ivec4 *x*, ivec4 *y*)	Return the component-wise comparison of *x* == *y*.
bvec2 notEqual(vec2*x*, vec2 *y*) bvec3 notEqual(vec3 *x*, vec3 *y*) bvec4 notEqual(vec4 *x*, vec4 *y*) bvec2 notEqual(ivec2 *x*, ivec2 *y*) bvec3 notEqual(ivec3 *x*, ivec3 *y*) bvec4 notEqual(ivec4 *x*, ivec4 *y*)	Return the component-wise comparison of *x* != *y*.
bool any(bvec2 *x*) bool any(bvec3 *x*) bool any(bvec4 *x*)	Return true if any component of *x* is true.
bool all(bvec2 *x*) bool all(bvec3 *x*) bool all(bvec4 *x*)	Return true only if all components of *x* are true.
bvec2 not(bvec2 *x*) bvec3 not(bvec3 *x*) bvec4 not(bvec4 *x*)	Return the component-wise logical complement of *x*.

Texture Lookup Functions

Syntax	Description

vec4 texture2D(
    sampler2D *sampler*, vec2 *coord*)
 	
vec4 texture2D(
    sampler2D *sampler*, vec2 *coord*,
    float *bias*)
 	
vec4 texture2DProj(
    sampler2D *sampler*, vec3 *coord*)
 	
vec4 texture2DProj(
    sampler2D *sampler*, vec3 *coord*,
    float *bias*)
 	
vec4 texture2DProj(
    sampler2D *sampler*, vec4 *coord*)
 	
vec4 texture2DProj(
    sampler2D *sampler*, vec4 *coord*,
    float *bias*)
 	
vec4 texture2DLod(
    sampler2D *sampler*, vec2 *coord*,
    float *lod*)
 	
vec4 texture2DProjLod(
    sampler2D *sampler*, vec3 *coord*,
    float *lod*)
 	
vec4 texture2DProjLod(
    sampler2D *sampler*, vec4 *coord*,
    float *lod*)
	Use the texture coordinate *coord* to read out texel values in the 2D texture currently bound to *sampler*. For the projective (Proj) versions, the texture coordinate (*coord*.s, *coord*.t) is divided by the last component of *coord*. The third component of *coord* is ignored for the vec4 *coord* variant. The *bias* parameter is only available in fragment shaders. It specifies the value to add the current *lod* when a MIPMAP texture is bound to *sampler*.

vec4 textureCube(
    samplerCube *sampler*, vec3 *coord*)
 	
vec4 textureCube(
    samplerCube *sampler*, vec3 *coord*,
    float *bias*)
 	
vec4 textureCubeLod(
    samplerCube *sampler*, vec3 *coord*,
    float *lod*)
	Use the texture coordinate *coord* to read out a texel from the cube map texture currently bound to *sampler*. The direction of *coord* is used to select the face from the cube map texture.

Projection Matrices

Orthogonal Projection Matrix

The following matrix is created by `Matrix4.setOrtho(left, right, bottom, top, near, far)`.

$$
\begin{bmatrix}
\dfrac{2}{right - left} & 0 & 0 & -\dfrac{right + left}{right - left} \\[2.2ex]
0 & \dfrac{2}{top - bottom} & 0 & -\dfrac{top + bottom}{top - bottom} \\[2.2ex]
0 & 0 & -\dfrac{2}{far - near} & \dfrac{far + near}{far - near} \\[2.2ex]
0 & 0 & 0 & 1
\end{bmatrix}
$$

Perspective Projection Matrix

The following matrix is created by `Matrix4.setPerspective(fov, aspect, near, far)`.

$$
\begin{bmatrix}
\dfrac{1}{aspect * \tan(\frac{fov}{2})} & 0 & 0 & 0 \\[3ex]
0 & \dfrac{1}{\tan(\frac{fov}{2})} & 0 & 0 \\[3ex]
0 & 0 & -\dfrac{far + near}{far - near} & -\dfrac{2 * far * near}{far - near} \\[3ex]
0 & 0 & -1 & 0
\end{bmatrix}
$$

WebGL/OpenGL: Left or Right Handed?

In Chapter 2, "Your First Step with WebGL," the coordinate system of WebGL was introduced as a right-handed system. However, you will probably come across tutorials and other material on the web that contradict this. In this appendix, you'll learn the "real" coordinate systems used by WebGL by examining what will happen when something is drawn using WebGL's default settings. Because WebGL is based on OpenGL, what you learn is equally applicable to OpenGL. You should read this appendix after reading Chapter 7, "Toward the 3D World," because it refers back to sample programs and explanations in that chapter.

Let's start by referring to the "font of all knowledge": the original specification. Specifically, the authorized specification of OpenGL ES 2.0, which is the base specification of WebGL, published by the Khronos group,[1] states in Appendix B:

7. The GL does not force left- or right-handedness on any of its coordinate systems.

If this is the case, and WebGL is agnostic about handedness, then why do many books and tutorials, and in fact this book, describe WebGL as right handed? Essentially, it's a convention. When you are developing your applications, you need to decide which coordinate system you are using and stick with it. That's true for your applications, but it's also true for the many libraries that have been developed to help people use WebGL (and OpenGL). Many of those libraries choose to adopt the right-handed convention, so over time it becomes the accepted convention and then becomes synonymous with the GL itself, leading people to believe that the GL is right handed.

So why the confusion? If everybody accepts the same convention, there shouldn't be a problem. That's true, but the complication arises because WebGL (and OpenGL) at certain times requires the GL to choose a handedness to carry out its operations, a default behavior if you will, and that default isn't always right handed!

[1] www.khronos.org/registry/gles/specs/2.0/es_cm_spec_2.0.24.pdf

In this appendix, we explore the default behavior of WebGL to give you a clearer understanding of the issue and how to factor this into your own applications.

To begin the exploration of WebGL's default behavior, let's construct a sample program CoordinateSystem as a test bed for experimentation. We'll use this program to go back to first principals, starting with the simplest method of drawing triangles and then adding features to explore how WebGL draws multiple objects. The goal of our sample program is to draw a blue triangle at –0.1 on the z-axis and then a red triangle at –0.5 on the z-axis. Figure D.1 shows the triangles, their z coordinates, and colors.

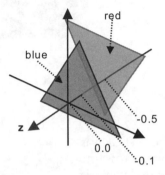

Figure D.1   The triangles used in this appendix and their colors

As this appendix will show, to achieve our relatively modest goal, we actually have to get a number of interacting features to work together, including the basic drawing, hidden surface removal, and viewing volume. Unless all three are set up correctly, you will get unexpected results when drawing, which can lead to confusion about left and right handedness.

Sample Program CoordinateSystem.js

Listing D.1 shows CoordinateSystem.js. The code for error processing and some comments have been removed to allow all lines in the program to be shown in a limited space, but as you can see, it is a complete program.

Listing D.1   CoordinateSystem

```
1 // CoordinateSystem.js
2 // Vertex shader program
3 var VSHADER_SOURCE =
4   'attribute vec4 a_Position;\n' +
5   'attribute vec4 a_Color;\n' +
6   'varying vec4 v_Color;\n' +
7   'void main() {\n' +
8   ' gl_Position = a_Position;\n' +
9   ' v_Color = a_Color;\n' +
```

```
10    '}\n';
11
12  // Fragment shader program
13  var FSHADER_SOURCE =
14    '#ifdef GL_ES\n' +
15    'precision mediump float;\n' +
16    '#endif\n' +
17    'varying vec4 v_Color;\n' +
18    'void main() {\n' +
19    '  gl_FragColor = v_Color;\n' +
20    '}\n';
21
22  function main() {
23    var canvas = document.getElementById('webgl'); // Retrieve <canvas>
24    var gl = getWebGLContext(canvas); // Get the context for WebGL
25    initShaders(gl, VSHADER_SOURCE, FSHADER_SOURCE);// Initialize shaders
26    var n = initVertexBuffers(gl);    // Set vertex coordinates and colors
27
28    gl.clearColor(0.0, 0.0, 0.0, 1.0);  // Specify the clear color
29    gl.clear(gl.COLOR_BUFFER_BIT);      // Clear <canvas>
30    gl.drawArrays(gl.TRIANGLES, 0, n);  // Draw the triangles
31  }
32
33  function initVertexBuffers(gl) {
34    var pc = new Float32Array([  // Vertex coordinates and color
35       0.0,  0.5,  -0.1,  0.0,  0.0,  1.0,  // The blue triangle in front
36      -0.5, -0.5,  -0.1,  0.0,  0.0,  1.0,
37       0.5, -0.5,  -0.1,  1.0,  1.0,  0.0,
38
39       0.5,  0.4,  -0.5,  1.0,  1.0,  0.0,  // The red triangle behind
40      -0.5,  0.4,  -0.5,  1.0,  0.0,  0.0,
41       0.0, -0.6,  -0.5,  1.0,  0.0,  0.0,
42    ]);
43    var numVertex = 3; var numColor = 3; var n = 6;
44
45    // Create a buffer object and write data to it
46    var pcbuffer = gl.createBuffer();
47    gl.bindBuffer(gl.ARRAY_BUFFER, pcbuffer);
48    gl.bufferData(gl.ARRAY_BUFFER, pc, gl.STATIC_DRAW);
49
50    var FSIZE = pc.BYTES_PER_ELEMENT; // The number of byte
51    var STRIDE = numVertex + numColor; // Calculate the stride
52
53    // Assign the vertex coordinates to attribute variable and enable it
54    var a_Position = gl.getAttribLocation(gl.program, 'a_Position');
```

```
55    gl.vertexAttribPointer(a_Position, numVertex, gl.FLOAT, false, FSIZE *
                                                    ➥STRIDE, 0);
56    gl.enableVertexAttribArray(a_Position);
57
58    // Assign the vertex colors to attribute variable and enable it
59    var a_Color = gl.getAttribLocation(gl.program, 'a_Color');
60    gl.vertexAttribPointer(a_Color, numColor, gl.FLOAT, false, FSIZE *
                                                    ➥STRIDE, FSIZE * numVertex);
61    gl.enableVertexAttribArray(a_Color);
62
63    return n;
64 }
```

When the sample program is run, it produces the output shown in Figure D.2. Although it's not easy to see in black and white (remember, you can run these examples in your browser from the book's website), the red triangle is in front of the blue triangle. This is the opposite of what you might expect because lines 32 to 42 specify the vertex coordinates of the blue triangle before the red triangle.

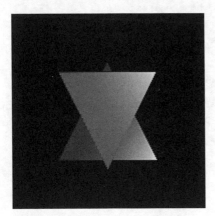

Figure D.2   CoordinateSystem

However, as explained in Chapter 7, this is actually correct. What is happening is that WebGL is first drawing the blue triangle, because its vertex coordinates are specified first, and then it's drawing the red triangle *over* the blue triangle. This is a little like oil painting; once you lay down a layer of paint, anything painted on top has to overwrite the paint below.

For many newcomers to WebGL, this can be counterintuitive. Because WebGL is a system for drawing 3D graphics, you'd expect it to "do the right thing" and draw the red triangle behind the blue one. However, by default WebGL draws in the order specified in the application code, regardless of the position on the z-axis. If you want WebGL to "do the right thing," you are required to enable the Hidden Surface Removal feature discussed in

Chapter 7. As you saw in Chapter 7, Hidden Surface Removal tells WebGL to be smart about the 3D scene and to remove surfaces that are actually hidden. In our case, this should deal with the red triangle problem because in the 3D scene, most of the red triangle is hidden behind the blue one.

Hidden Surface Removal and the Clip Coordinate System

Let's turn on Hidden Surface Removal in our sample program and examine its effect. To do that, enable the function using `gl.enable(gl.DEPTH_TEST)`, clear the depth buffer, and then draw the triangles. First, you add the following at line 27.

```
27 gl.enable(gl.DEPTH_TEST);
```

Then you modify line 29 as follows:

```
29 gl.clear(gl.COLOR_BUFFER_BIT | gl.DEPTH_BUFFER_BIT);
```

Now if you rerun the program after making these changes, you'd expect to see the problem resolved and the blue triangle in front of the red one. However, what you actually see is that the red triangle is still in front. Again, although it's difficult to see in black and white, Figure D.3 shows the result.

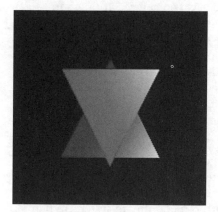

Figure D.3 CoordinateSystem using the hidden surface removal function

This is unexpected and is part of the confusion surrounding WebGL's left versus right handedness. We have correctly programmed our example based on the belief that WebGL is right handed, but it seems to be that WebGL is either telling us that –0.5 is located in front of –0.1 on the z-axis or that WebGL does in fact use the left-handed coordinate system, where the positive direction of the z-axis points into the screen (Figure D.4).

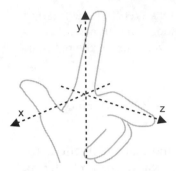

Figure D.4 The left-handed coordinate system

The Clip Coordinate System and the Viewing Volume

So our application example follows the convention that WebGL is right handed, but our program clearly shows a left-handed system is in place. What's the explanation? Essentially, hidden surface removal, when enabled, uses the **clip coordinate system** (see Figure G.5 in Appendix G), which itself uses the "left-handed" coordinate system, not the right-handed one.

In WebGL (OpenGL), hidden surface removal is performed using the value of `gl_Position`, the coordinates produced by the vertex shader. As you can see at line 8 in the vertex shader in Listing D.1, `a_Position` is directly assigned to `gl_Position` in `CoordinateSystem.js`. This means that the z coordinate of the red triangle is passed as –0.5 and that of the blue one is passed as –0.1 to the clip coordinate system (the left-handed coordinate system). As you know, the positive direction of the z-axis in the left-handed coordinate system points into the screen, so the smaller value of the z coordinate (–0.5) is located in front of the bigger one (–0.1). Therefore, it is the right behavior for the WebGL system to display the red triangle in front of the blue one in this situation.

This obviously contradicts the explanation in Chapter 3 (that WebGL uses the right-handed coordinate system). So how do we achieve our goal of having the red triangle displayed behind the blue triangle, and what does this tell us about WebGL's default behaviors? Until now, the program hasn't considered the viewing volume that needs to be set up correctly for Hidden Surface Removal to work with our coordinate system. When used correctly, the viewing volume requires that the near clipping plane be located in front of the far clipping plane (that is *near* < *far*). However, the values of *near* and *far* are the distance from the eye point toward the direction of line of sight and can take any value. Therefore, it is possible to specify a value of *far* that is actually smaller than that of *near* or even use negative values. (The negative values means the distance from the eye point toward the opposite direction of line of sight.) Obviously, the values set for *near* and *far* depend on whether we are assuming a right- or left-handed coordinate system.

Returning to the sample program, after setting the viewing volume correctly, let's carry out the hidden surface removal. Listing D.2 shows only the differences from `CoordinateSystem.js`.

Listing D.2   CoordinateSystem_viewVolume.js

```
 1 // CoordinateSystem_viewVolume.js
 2 // Vertex shader program
 3 var VSHADER_SOURCE =
 4 'attribute vec4 a_Position;\n' +
 5 'attribute vec4 a_Color;\n' +
 6 'uniform mat4 u_MvpMatrix;\n' +
 7 'varying vec4 v_Color;\n' +
 8 'void main() {\n' +
 9 'gl_Position = u_MvpMatrix * a_Position;\n' +
10 'v_Color = a_Color;\n' +
11 '}\n';
...
23 function main() {
...
29   gl.enable(gl.DEPTH_TEST); // Enable hidden surface removal function
30   gl.clearColor(0.0, 0.0, 0.0, 1.0); // Set the clear color
31   // Get the storage location of u_MvpMatrix
32   var u_MvpMatrix = gl.getUniformLocation(gl.program, 'u_MvpMatrix');
33
34   var mvpMatrix = new Matrix4();
35   mvpMatrix.setOrtho(-1, 1, -1, 1, 0, 1); // Set the viewing volume
36   // Pass the view matrix to u_MvpMatrix
37   gl.uniformMatrix4fv(u_MvpMatrix, false, mvpMatrix.elements);
38
39   gl.clear(gl.COLOR_BUFFER_BIT | gl.DEPTH_BUFFER_BIT);
40   gl.drawArrays(gl.TRIANGLES, 0, n); // Draw the triangle
41 }
```

Once you run this sample program, you can see the result shown in Figure D.5, in which the blue triangle is displayed in front of the red one.

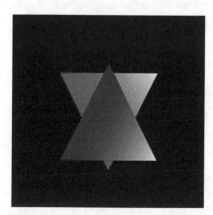

Figure D.5   CoordinateSystem_viewVolume

The critical change is that the uniform variable (u_MvpMatrix) for passing a view matrix was added to the vertex shader. It was multiplied by a_Position, and then its result was assigned to gl_Position. Although we used the setOrtho() method to specify the viewing volume, setPerspective() has the same result.

What Is Correct?

Let's compare the process of the vertex shader in CoordinateSystem.js with that in CoordinateSystem_viewVolume.js.

Line 8 in CoordinateSystem.js:

```
8 ' gl_Position = a_Position;\n' +
```

became line 9 in CoordinateSystem_viewVolume.js:

```
9 ' gl_Position = u_MvpMatrix * a_Position;\n' +
```

As you can see, in CoordinateSystem_viewVolume.js, which displays the order of triangles as was intended, the transformation matrix (in this case, a view matrix) is multiplied by a vertex coordinate. To understand this operation, let's examine how to rewrite line 8 in CoordinateSystem.js into the form <matrix> * <vertex coordinate> just like line 9 in CoordinateSystem_viewVolume.js.

Line 8 assigns the vertex coordinate (a_Position) to gl_Position directly. To ensure that the matrix multiplication operation has no effect the <matrix> must have the following elements (that is, the identity matrix):

$$\begin{bmatrix} 1 & 0 & 0 & 0 \\ 0 & 1 & 0 & 0 \\ 0 & 0 & 1 & 0 \\ 0 & 0 & 0 & 1 \end{bmatrix}$$

Therefore, line 8 in CoordinateSystem.js actually has the same effect as passing the identity matrix to u_MvpMatrix in line 9 in CoordinateSystem_viewVolume.js. In essence, this matrix is controlling the default behavior of WebGL.

To understand this behavior better, let's clarify what is happening if the projection matrix is the identity matrix. You can understand this by using the matrix in Appendix C (see Figure D.6) and the identify matrix to find *left*, *right*, *top*, *bottom*, *near*, and *far*.

$$\begin{bmatrix} \dfrac{2}{right-left} & 0 & 0 & -\dfrac{right+left}{right-left} \\[2ex] 0 & \dfrac{2}{top-bottom} & 0 & -\dfrac{top+bottom}{top-bottom} \\[2ex] 0 & 0 & -\dfrac{2}{far-near} & -\dfrac{far+near}{far-near} \\[2ex] 0 & 0 & 0 & 1 \end{bmatrix}$$

Figure D.6 The projection matrix generated by setOrtho()

In this case, *right – left* = 2 and *right + left* = 0, which resolves to *left* = –1, *right* = 1. Equally, *far – near* =–2 and *far + near* = 0, resolving to *near* = 1 and *far* = –1. That is:

```
left = -1, right = 1, bottom = -1, top = 1, near = 1, and far = -1
```

Using these parameters to setOrtho() as follows:

```
mvpMatrix.setOrtho(-1, 1, -1, 1, 1, -1);
```

results in *near* being greater than *far*. This means that the far clipping plane is placed in front of the near clipping plane along the direction of the line of sight (see Figure D.7).

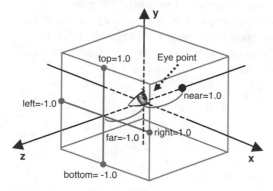

Figure D.7 The viewing volume created by the identity matrix

If you specify the viewing volume by yourself, you will observe the same phenomenon when you specify *near* > *far* to setOrtho(). That is, WebGL (OpenGL) follows the right-handed coordinate system when you specify the viewing volume in this way.

Then look at the matrix representing the viewing volume in which the objects are displayed correctly:

```
mvpMatrix.setOrtho(-1, 1, -1, 1, -1, 1);
```

This method generates the following projection matrix:

$$\begin{bmatrix} 1 & 0 & 0 & 0 \\ 0 & 1 & 0 & 0 \\ 0 & 0 & -1 & 0 \\ 0 & 0 & 0 & 1 \end{bmatrix}$$

You will recognize that this matrix is a scaling matrix described in Chapter 4, "More Transformations and Basic Animation." That is the matrix generated by `setScale(1, 1, -1)`. You should note that the scaling factor of the z-axis is –1, meaning that the sign of the z coordinates will be reversed. So this matrix transforms the conventional right-handed coordinate system used in this book (and assumed by most WebGL libraries) to the left-handed coordinate system used in the clip coordinate system by reversing the z coordinates.

Summary

In summary, we know from the specification that WebGL doesn't enforce either right or left handedness. We have seen that many WebGL libraries and applications adopt the convention that WebGL is right handed, as do we in this book. When WebGL's default behavior contradicts this (for example, when working in clip-space where it uses a left-handed coordinate system), we can compensate programmatically, by reversing, for example, the z coordinates. This allows us to continue to follow the convention that WebGL is right handed. However, as previously stated, it's only a convention. It's one that most people follow, but one that will occasionally trip you up if you aren't aware of WebGL's default behaviors and how to handle them.

The Inverse Transpose Matrix

The inverse transpose matrix, previously introduced in Chapter 8, "Lighting Objects," is a matrix that determines the inverse of a given matrix and then transposes it. As shown in Figure E.1, the direction of the normal vector of an object is subject to change depending on the type of the coordinate transformation. However, if you use the inverse transpose of the model matrix, you can safely ignore this in calculations.

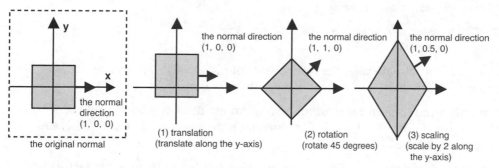

Figure E.1   The direction of normal vector changes along with the coordinate transformation

In Chapter 8, you saw how to use the inverse transpose of the model matrix to transform normals. However, there are actually some cases where you can also determine the normal vector direction with the model matrix. For instance, when rotating, you can determine the direction of the normal vector by multiplying the normal vector by the rotation matrix. When calculating the direction of the normal vector, whether you resort to the model matrix itself or its inverse transpose depends on which transformation (translation, rotation, and scaling) is already integrated inside the model matrix.

If the model matrix already includes a translation and you multiply the normal by the model matrix, the normal is translated, resulting in a modification of its orientation. For example, the normal (1, 0, 0), when translated by 2.0 along the y-axis, is repositioned to the location (1, 2, 0). You can avoid this problem by using the 3×3 submatrix extracted from the top left area of the 4×4 model matrix. For example:

```
attribute vec4 a_Normal; // normal
uniform mat4 u_ModelMatrix; // model matrix
void main() {
  ...
  vec3 normal = normalize(mat3(u_ModelMatrix) * a_Normal.xyz);
  ...
}
```

The values located in the rightmost column determine the scale of the displacement produced by the translation matrix, as illustrated in Figure E.2.

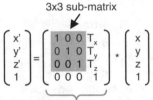

Transformation Matrix (4x4 Translation Matrix)

Figure E.2   The transformation matrix and its 3×3 submatrix

Because this submatrix also includes the components of the rotation and scaling matrices, you need to consider rotation and scaling on a case-by-case basis:

- **If you only want to perform a rotation:** You can use the 3×3 submatrix of the model matrix. If the normal is already normalized, the transformed normal does not have to be normalized.

- **If you want to perform a scaling transformation (with a uniform scale factor):** You can use the 3×3 submatrix of the model matrix. However, the transformed normal has to be normalized.

- **If you want to perform a scaling transformation (with a nonuniform scale factor):** You need to use the inverse transpose matrix of the model matrix. The transformed normal has to be normalized.

The second case, where you want to perform a scaling transformation with a uniform scale factor, implies that you perform a scaling with an identical scaling factor along the x-, y-, and z-axes. For example, if you scale by a factor of 2.0 along the x-, y-, and z-axes, you will set the same value to each of the arguments of `Matrix4.scale()`: `Matrix4`.

`scale(2.0, 2.0, 2.0)`. In this situation, even if the size of the object is modified, its shape is left unchanged. Alternatively, those cases involving a scaling transformation with a nonuniform scale factor require that you use a different scaling factor for each axis. For instance, if you limit the scaling to the y-axis direction, you will use `Matrix4.scale(1.0, 2.0,1.0)`.

You have to resort to the inverse transpose matrix in case (3) because, if the scaling is nonuniform, the direction of the normal vector is incorrectly modified when multiplying it with the model matrix that incorporates the scaling transformation. Figure E.3 shows this.

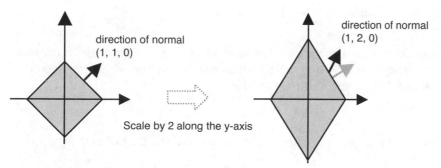

Figure E.3   Simply multiplying the normal vector with the model matrix results in a modification of the normal direction

Performing a nonuniform scaling of the object (left side of the figure), with a scaling factor of 2.0 limited to the y-axis, results in the shape on the right. Here, to determine the normal direction after the transformation, you multiply the model matrix with the normal (1. 1, 0) of the left side object. However, then the direction of the normal is changed to (1, 2, 0) and is no longer at a right angle (90 degrees) to the line.

The solution to this requires a little math. We will call the model matrix M, the original normal n, the transformation matrix M', which transforms n without changing the direction of n, and the vector perpendicular to n, s. In addition, we define n' and s', as shown in Equations E.1 and E.2:

Equation E.1 $n' = M' \times n$

Equation E.2 $s' = M \times s$

See Figure E.4.

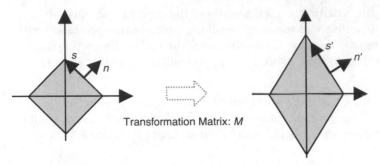

Transformation Matrix: *M*

Figure E.4 The relationship between n and s, and, n' and s'.

Here, you can calculate M' so that the two vectors n' and s' form a right angle. If the two vectors form a right angle, their dot product is equal to 0. Using the "·" notation for a dot product, you can derive the following equation:

```
n' . s' = 0
```

You can now rewrite this expression using the equations E.1 and E.2 (M^T is the transpose matrix of M):

```
(M ' × n)  ·  (M × s)  = 0

(M ' × n)^T × (M × s)  = 0  A. B = A^T × B

n^T × M '^T × M × s = 0  (A × B)^T = B^T × A^T
```

Because n and s form a right angle, their dot product is also 0 ($ns = 0$). Therefore, as already stated, $A \cdot B = A^T \times B$, so substituting n for A and s for B will result in $n \cdot s = n^T \times s = 0$. Comparing this expression with the equation E.3, if the goal is for the products $M'^T \times M^T$ between n^T and s to be equal to the identity matrix (I), this can be reformulated as follows:

```
M '^T × M^T = I
```

Resolving this equation provides us with the following result (M^{-1} is the inverse matrix of M):

```
M ' = (M^{-1})^T
```

From this equation, you can see that M' is the transpose matrix of the inverse matrix of M or, in other words, the inverse transpose of M. Because M can include cases (1), (2), and (3) enumerated earlier, if you calculate the inverse transpose matrix of M and multiply it with the normal vector, you will get the correct result. Thus, this provides the solution for transforming the normal vector.

Obviously, the calculation of the inverse transpose matrix can be time consuming, but if you can confirm the model matrix fits criteria (1) or (2), you can simply use the 3×3 submatrix for increased efficiency.

Load Shader Programs from Files

All the sample programs in this book embed the shader programs in the JavaScript program, which increases the readability of the sample programs but makes it hard to construct and maintain the shader programs.

As an alternative, you can load the shader programs from files by using the same methods described in the section "Load and Display 3D Models" in Chapter 10, "Advanced Techniques." To see how that's done, let's modify ColoredTriangle from Chapter 5, "Using Colors and Texture Images," to add support for loading shaders from a file. The new program is called LoadShaderFromFiles, which is shown in Listing F.1.

Listing F.1 LoadShaderFromFiles

```
 1 // LoadShaderFromFiles.js based on ColoredTriangle.js
 2 // Vertex shader program
 3 var VSHADER_SOURCE = null;
 4 // Fragment shader program
 5 var FSHADER_SOURCE = null;
 6
 7 function main() {
 8   // Retrieve <canvas> element
 9   var canvas = document.getElementById('webgl');
10
11   // Get the rendering context for WebGL
12   var gl = getWebGLContext(canvas);
   ...
17   // Load the shaders from files
18   loadShaderFile(gl, 'ColoredTriangle.vert', gl.VERTEX_SHADER);
19   loadShaderFile(gl, 'ColoredTriangle.frag', gl.FRAGMENT_SHADER);
20 }
```

```
21
22 function start(gl) {
23   // Initialize shaders
24   if (!initShaders(gl, VSHADER_SOURCE, FSHADER_SOURCE)) {
     ...
43   gl.drawArrays(gl.TRIANGLES, 0, n);
44 }
     ...
88 function loadShaderFile(gl, fileName, shader) {
89   var request = new XMLHttpRequest();
90
91   request.onreadystatechange = function() {
92     if (request.readyState === 4 && request.status !== 404) {
93       onLoadShader(gl, request.responseText, shader);
94     }
95   }
96   request.open('GET', fileName, true);
97   request.send();                       // Send the request
98 }
99
100 function onLoadShader(gl, fileString, type) {
101   if (type == gl.VERTEX_SHADER) { // The vertex shader is loaded
102     VSHADER_SOURCE = fileString;
103   } else
104   if (type == gl.FRAGMENT_SHADER) { // The fragment shader is loaded
105     FSHADER_SOURCE = fileString;
106   }
107   // Start rendering, after loading both shaders
108   if (VSHADER_SOURCE && FSHADER_SOURCE) start(gl);
109 }
```

Unlike ColoredTriangle.js, this sample program initializes the VSHADER_PROGRAM (line 3) and FSHADER_PROGRAM (line 5) to null to allow them to be loaded from files later. The function main() defined at line 7 loads the shader programs at lines 18 and line 19 by using loadShaderFile(). This function is defined at line 88, and its second argument specifies the filename (URL) that contains the shader program. The third argument specifies the type of the shader program.

The function loadShaderFile() creates a request of type XMLHttpRequest to get the file specified by *fileName* and then registers an event handler (onLoadShader()) at line 91 to handle the file when it is loaded. After that, it sends the request at line 97. Once the file is acquired, onLoadShader() is called. This function is defined at line 100.

The onLoadShader() checks the third parameter *type* and uses it to store the *fileString* containing the shader program to VSHADER_PROGRAM or FSHADER_PROGRAM. Once you load both shader programs, call start(gl) at line 108 to draw the triangle using the shaders.

World Coordinate System Versus Local Coordinate System

In Chapter 7, "Toward the 3D World," you used and displayed your first 3D object (a cube), allowing the sample program to begin to feel more like a "real" 3D application. However, to do so, you had to manually set up the vertex coordinates and the index information of the cube, which was quite time consuming. Although you will do the same manual setup throughout this book, this is not something you will generally do when creating your own WebGL applications. Usually you will use a dedicated 3D modeling tool to create 3D objects. This allows you to create elaborate 3D objects through the manipulation (combination, deformation, vertex population adjustment, vertex interval tuning, and so on) of elementary 3D shapes, such as cubes, cylinders, or spheres. The 3D modeling tool Blender (www.blender.org/) is shown in Figure G.1.

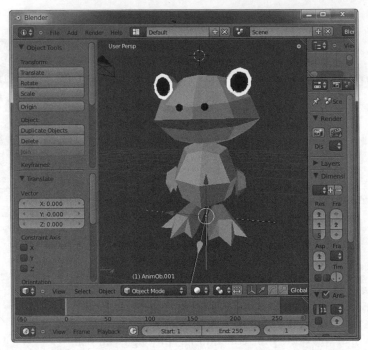

Figure G.1 Creation of a 3D object with a 3D modeling tool

The Local Coordinate System

When creating the model of a 3D object, it is necessary to decide where the origin (that is, (0, 0, 0)) is placed for the model. You can choose the origin of the model so that the model can be easily built, or alternatively so that the created model can be handled easily in a 3D scene. The cube introduced in the previous section was created with its center set at the origin (0, 0, 0). Sphere-shaped objects, like the sun or the moon, are usually modeled with their center at the origin.

On the other hand, in the case of game character models, such as the one shown in Figure G.1, most of the models are built with the origin positioned at their feet level, and the y-axis running through the center of the body. By doing so, if you place the character at the y coordinate = 0 height (at the ground level), the character looks like it is standing on the ground—neither floating above the ground nor sinking down into the ground. In this configuration, if you translate the model along the z-axis or x-axis, the character will appear to be walking or gliding along the ground. Additionally, you can turn the character using a simple rotation around the y-axis.

In such cases, the coordinates of the vertices that constitute objects or characters configured in this fashion are expressed with respect to this origin. Such a coordinate system is called the **local coordinate system**. Using modeling tools (like Blender), the components (vertex coordinates, colors, indices, and so on) of models designed this way can be exported to a file. You can then import this information into the buffer object in WebGL, and using `gl.drawElements()`, you can draw and display the model created with the 3D modeling tool.

The World Coordinate System

Let's consider the case of a game where multiple characters would appear in a single space. The goal is to use the characters illustrated in Figure G.2 (right side) in the 3D scene shown on the left side. All three characters and the world have their own origin.

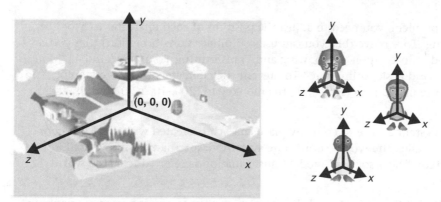

Figure G.2   Disposition of several characters inside a single world

When you want to display the characters as they are, you are faced with a problem. Because all the characters are built with their origin positioned at their feet level, they eventually are displayed on top of each other at the same location: the origin (0, 0, 0) of the 3D scene (Figure G.3).[1] That's not something that generally happens in the real world and certainly not what you want here.

---

[1] To keep the figure understandable, the characters are placed at slightly shifted positions.

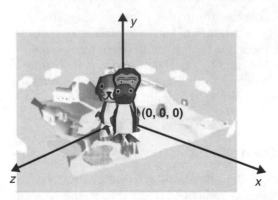

Figure G.3 All the characters are displayed at the origin.

To address this problem, you need to adjust the position of each character to avoid them overlapping. To achieve this, you can use coordinate transformations that you originally looked at in Chapter 3, "Drawing and Transforming Triangles," and 4, "More Transformations and Basic Animation." To prevent the characters from overlapping, you could translate the penguin to (100, 0, 0), the monkey to (200, 10, 120), and the dog to (10, 0, 200).

The coordinate system we use to correctly place characters created within a **local coordinate system** is called the **world coordinate system**, or alternatively the **global coordinate system**. The associated model transformation is referred to as the **world transformation**.

Of course, to prevent the characters of the penguin, monkey, and dog from overlapping, you can build them using the world coordinate system. For example, if you model the penguin in a tool such as Blender with its origin set to (100, 0, 0), when you insert the penguin into the world, it will be displayed at position (100, 0, 0), so you don't need a coordinate transformation to avoid overlapping. However, this approach creates its own difficulties. For example, it becomes difficult to make the penguin spin like a ballerina because, if you perform a rotation around the y-axis, you generate a circular motion of radius 100. You could, of course, first translate the penguin back to the origin, rotate it, and then translate it again to the original position, but that is quite a lot of work.

You actually already dealt with a similar case in Chapter 7. Using the coordinates of one set of triangles, the vertices of which were determined with respect to the origin set at the center, `PerspectiveView_mvp` draws a second set of triangles. Here is the figure we referred to in that program (see Figure G.4).

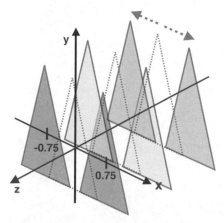

Figure G.4 Triangles group in PerspectiveView_mvp

Here, the local coordinate system expresses the vertex coordinates of the triangles shown with the dotted lines, whereas the world coordinate system is used to describe their translation along the x-axis.

Transformations and the Coordinate Systems

So far, we have not considered local and world coordinate systems so that you can focus on the core aspects of each example. However, for reference, Figure G.5 shows the relationship between the transformations and the coordinate systems and is something to bear in mind as you deepen your knowledge of 3D graphics and experiment with modeling tools.

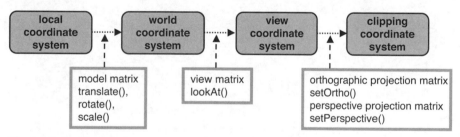

Figure G.5 Transformation and the coordinate system

Web Browser Settings for WebGL

This appendix explains how to use advanced web browser settings to ensure that WebGL is displayed correctly and what to do if it isn't.

If your graphics board isn't compatible with WebGL, you may see the message shown in Figure H.1.

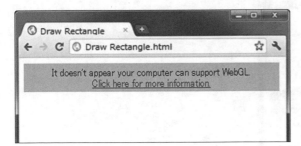

Figure H.1   Loading a WebGL application results in an error message

If this happens, you may still be able to get WebGL to work in your browser with a little bit of tweaking:

1. If you are using Chrome, start the browser with the option `--ignore-gpu-black-list`. To specify this option, right-click the Chrome browser shortcut icon and select Properties from the menu. You'll see a pop-up window similar to that in Figure H.2. Then add the option string at the end of the command string in the Target column on the window. After that, Chrome is always started with the option. If this solves your problem, leave this option enabled.

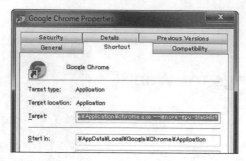

Figure H.2 Specifying an option in the Google Chrome Properties window

2. If you are using Firefox, enter `about:config` in the address bar. Firefox shows "This might void your warranty!" Click the button labeled "I'll be careful, I promise!" Type `webgl` in the text field labeled by Search or Filter, and then Firefox will display the WebGL-related setting names (see Figure H.3). Double-click `webgl.force-enabled` in the list to change its value from `false` to `true`. Again, if this solves your problem, leave this option enabled.

Figure H.3 WebGL-related settings in Firefox

If neither solution works, you will have to find another machine that has better support for WebGL. Again, look at the Khronos wiki for more information: www.khronos.org/webgl/wiki.

A

alpha blending   The process of using the alpha value ("A") in RGBA to blend the colors of two or more objects.

alpha value   The value used to indicate the transparency (0.0 is transparent and 1.0 is opaque) of an object. Alpha blending uses this value.

ambient light   Indirect light. Light that illuminates an object from all directions and with the same intensity.

attach   The process of establishing a connection between two existing objects. Compare to *bind*.

attribute variable   The variable used to pass data to a vertex shader.

B

bind   The process of creating a new object and then establishing a connection (the binding) between that object and a rendering context. Compare to *attach*.

buffer   A block of memory allocated and dedicated to storing a specific kind of data, such as color or depth values.

buffer object   WebGL object used to store multiple items of vertex information.

C

canvas   The HTML5 element and features to draw graphics on a web page.

clipping   An operation that identifies the area (or region) within a 3D scene that will be drawn. Anything not in the clipping region is not drawn.

color buffer   The memory area into which WebGL draws. Once drawn, the contents are displayed on the screen.

column major   A convention describing the way a matrix is stored in an array. In column major, the columns are listed in sequence in the array.

completeness   Used in the context of a framebuffer, indicates the state whether a framebuffer object meets all the requirements for drawing.

context   JavaScript object that implements the methods used to draw onto a canvas.

D

depth (value)   The z value of a fragment when viewing the fragment from the eye point along the line of sight.

depth buffer   The memory area used for hidden surface removal. It stores the depth value (z value) of all fragments.

directional light   A light source that emits parallel light rays.

F

far clipping plane   The farther clipping plane of the planes comprising the viewing volume from the eye point.

fog   The effect seen when fading colors to a background color based on the distance from the observer. Fog is often used to provide depth cues to the observer.

fragment   The pixel generated by the rasterization process and which has color, depth value, texture coordinates, and more.

fragment shader   The shader program to process the fragment information.

framebuffer object   WebGL object used for offscreen drawing.

G

GLSL ES   OpenGL ES Shading Language. ES stands for Embedded System.

H

hidden surface removal   The process to determine and hide the surfaces and parts of surfaces that are not visible from a certain viewpoint.

I

image   A rectangular array of pixels.

index (vertex)   See *vertex index*.

L

local coordinates   The vertex coordinates that are defined in the local coordinate system (the coordinate system that relates specifically to the selected object). (Also see *world coordinates*.)

M

model matrix   The matrix used to translate, rotate, or scale objects. It is also known as a modeling matrix.

model view matrix   The matrix that multiplies the view matrix by the model matrix.

model view projection matrix   The matrix that multiplies the projection matrix by the model view matrix.

N

near clipping plane   The nearer clipping plane of the planes comprising the viewing volume from the eye point.

normal   An imaginary line that is perpendicular to the surface of a polygon and represented by a vec3 number. It is also called the normal vector.

O

orthographic projection matrix   The matrix used to define a box-shaped viewing volume—left, right, bottom, top, near, far—that defines the clipping planes of the box. Objects located closer to the far clipping plane are not scaled.

P

perspective projection matrix   The matrix used to define a pyramid-shaped viewing volume. Objects located closer to the far clipping plane are scaled appropriately to give perspective.

pixel   Picture element. It has an RGBA or RGB value.

point light   Light source that emits light in all directions from one point.

program object   WebGL object to manage shader objects.

projection matrix   The generic term for the orthographic projection matrix and the perspective projection matrix.

R

rasterization process   The process to convert shapes, defined in a vector format into fragments (pixels or dots) for display on a video screen.

renderbuffer object   WebGL object that supports a general two-dimensional drawing area.

RGBA   A color format: R (red), G (green), B (blue), and A (alpha).

S

sampler   A data type used to access a texture image from within a fragment shader.

shader   The computer program that implements the fundamental drawing function used in WebGL. WebGL supports vertex shaders and fragment shaders.

shader object   WebGL object to manage shaders.

shading   The process of applying shading to each face of an object.

shadowing   The process to determine and draw shadows cast by objects.

T

texel   The basic element (**texture element**) that makes up a texture image. It has RGB or RGBA value.

texture coordinates   Two-dimensional coordinates to be used to access a texture image.

texture image   The image used in texture mapping. It is also simply called texture.

texture mapping   The process of applying (mapping) a texture image to the surface of an object.

texture object   WebGL object to manage a texture image.

texture unit   The mechanism to manage multiple texture objects.

transformation   The process of converting the vertex coordinates of an object to new vertex coordinates as a result of applying a transformation (translation, scaling, and so on).

U

uniform variable   The variable used to pass data to the vertex shader or fragment shader.

V

varying variable   The variable used to pass data from the vertex shader to the fragment shader.

vertex index   The number assigned to the vertex information elements stored in a buffer object. It starts from 0 and is increased by 1 for each new element stored.

vertex shader   The shader program that processes the vertex information.

view coordinate system   The coordinate system that has the eye point at its origin, the line of sight along the negative z-axis, and the up direction in the positive y-axis.

view matrix   The matrix to transform the vertex coordinates to the coordinates that are viewed from the eye point toward the line of sight.

view projection matrix   The matrix that multiplies the projection matrix by the view matrix.

viewing volume   The subspace that is displayed on the screen. The objects outside the volume are not displayed.

W

world coordinates   The coordinates that are obtained by multiplying the model matrix by the local vertex coordinates of the 3D model.

References

Bowman, Doug A., Ernst Kruijff, Joseph J. LaViola Jr, and Ivan Poupyrev. *3D User Interfaces: Theory and Practice*. Addison-Wesley Professional (July 26, 2004).

Dunn, Fletcher, and Ian Parberry. *3D Math Primer for Graphics and Game Development*, 2nd Edition. A K Peters/CRC Press (November 2, 2011).

Foley, James D., Andries van Dam, Steven K. Feiner, and John F. Hughes. *Computer Graphics: Principles and Practice in C*, 2nd Edition. Addison-Wesley Professional (August 4, 1995).

Munshi, Aaftab, Dan Ginsburg, and Dave Shreiner. *OpenGL ES 2.0 Programming Guide*. Addison-Wesley Professional (July 24, 2008).

Shreiner, Dave. The Khronos OpenGL ARB Working Group. *OpenGL Programming Guide: The Official Guide to Learning OpenGL, Versions 3.0 and 3.1*, 7th Edition. Addison-Wesley Professional (July 21, 2009).

Index

Symbols

array indexing ([ ]) operator, 203-204

arrays

    in GLSL ES, 208-209

    interleaving, 141-145

    typed arrays, 78-79

asin() function, 442

assigning

    buffer objects to attribute variables, 79-81

    texture images to texture objects, 177-179

    values

        in GLSL ES structures, 207

        in GLSL ES variables, 196-197

        in matrix data types, 199-201

        in vector data types, 199-201

asynchronous loading of texture images, 169-170

atan() function, 442

atmospheric effects, fog, 372-373

attaching shader objects to program objects, 350-351

attribute variables, 217-218

    assiging buffer objects to, 79-81

    declaring, 43

    enabling assignment, 81-82

    explained, 41-42

    for point size (MultiAttributeSize.js), 139-140

    setting value, 45-49

    storage location, 44-45

B

back color buffer, 437

background objects, 267-269

    z fighting, 273-275

binding

    buffer objects to targets, 75-76

    renderbuffer objects, 399-400

    texture objects to targets, 173-174

BlendedCube.js, 384

Blender 3D modeling tool, 415, 473-475

blending function, alpha blending, 382-383

<body> element, 12

bool data type, 196

Boolean values in GLSL ES, 194

boxed-shape viewing volume

    defining, 243-244

    OrthoView.html, 245-246

    OrthoView.js, 246-247

break statement in GLSL ES, 212-213

browsers

    <canvas> element support, 12

    console, viewing, 14

    enabling local file access, 161

    functionality in 3D graphics applications, 5

    JavaScript to WebGL processing flow, 27, 438

    WebGL settings, 479-480

buffer objects

    assigning to attribute variables, 79-81

    binding to targets, 75-76

    creating, 74-75

D

data, passing

  to fragment shaders with varying variable, 146-151

  to vertex shaders, 137-151. *See also* drawing; rectangles; shapes; triangles

    color changes, 146-151

    creating multiple buffer objects, 140-141

    interleaving, 141-145

    MultiAttributeSize.js, 139-140

data types

  in GLSL ES, 34, 194-196

    arrays, 208-209

    operators on, 197-198

    precision qualifiers, 219-221

    samplers, 209-210

    structures, 207-208

    type conversion, 196-197

    type sensitivity, 195

    vector and matrix types, 198-206

  typed arrays, 78-79

#define preprocessor directive, 222

degrees() function, 441

deleting

  shader objects, 346

  texture objects, 167

depth buffer, 22

DepthBuffer.js, 272-273

diffuse reflection, 294-295

  calculating, 297-299

  shading, 296-297

Direct3D, 5

directional light, 293

  shading, 296-297

discard statement in GLSL ES, 212-213

displaying 3D objects on web pages (3DoverWeb), 372

distance() function, 447

document.getElementById() function, 14, 19

dot() function, 447

dot (.) operator, 201-202

draw() function, 129-131

  objects composed of other objects, 332-334

  processing flow of, 249

drawArrays() function, 284

drawbox() function, 339-340

drawing

  to color buffers, 437-439

  Hello Cube with indices and vertices coordinates, 277-278

  multiple points/vertices, 68-85

    assigning buffer objects to attribute variables, 79-81

    binding buffer objects to targets, 75-76

    buffer object usage, 72-74

    creating buffer objects, 74-75

    enabling attribute variable assignments, 81-82

    gl.drawArrays() function, 82-83

    writing data to buffer objects, 76-78

  objects composed of other objects, 324-325

  points

    assigning uniform variable values, 63-66

    attribute variables, 41-42

execution order in GLSL ES, 193

exp2() function, 443

exp() function, 443

exponential functions, 216, 443

eye point, 228

    changing using keyboard, 238

    LookAtTrianglesWithKeys.js, 238-241

    visible range, 241

F

faceforward() function, 447

face of objects, selecting, 365

    PickFace.js, 366-368

files, loading shader programs from, 471-472

fill color, setting, 15

Firefox

    console, viewing, 14

    enabling local file access, 161

    WebGL browser settings, 480

flipping image y-axis, 170-171

Float32Array object, 78

float data type, 196

floor() function, 444

flow of vertex shaders, processing, 248-249

fog, 372-373

    implementing, 373-374

    w value, 376-377

Fog.js, 374-376

Fog_w.js, 376-377

foreground objects, 267-269

    DepthBuffer.js, 272-273

    hidden surface removal, 270-271

    z fighting, 273-275

for statement in GLSL ES, 211-212

fract() function, 444

fragments, 27, 35

fragment shaders, 27

    drawing points, 35-36

    example of, 192

    geometric shape assembly and rasterization, 151-155

    invoking, 155

    passing

        data to, 61-62, 146-151

        texture coordinates to, 180-181

        texture units to, 179-180

    program structure, 29-30

    retrieving texel color in, 181-182

    varying variables and interpolation process, 157-160

    verifying invocation, 156-157

FramebufferObject.js, 395-396, 403

framebuffer objects, 392-393

    checking configurations, 402-403

    creating, 397

    drawing with, 403-404

    renderbuffer objects set to, 401-402

    setting to renderbuffer objects, 400-401

front color buffer, 437

functions

    abs() function, 444

    acos() function, 442

J–K

L

origin

    in coordinate systems, 55

    in local coordinate system, 474-475

    in world coordinate system, 475-477

origins of WebGL, 5-6

orthographic projection matrix, 252-253, 261, 453

OrthoView.html, 245-246

OrthoView.js, 246-247

P

parameter qualifiers in GLSL ES functions, 214-215

parameters of texture objects, setting, 174-177

parser code (OBJViewer.js), 423-430

passing data

    to fragment shaders

        texture units, 179-180

        with varying variable, 146-151

    to vertex shaders, 137-151. *See also* drawing; rectangles; shapes; triangles

        color changes, 146-151

        creating multiple buffer objects, 140-141

        interleaving, 141-145

        MultiAttributeSize.js, 139-140

pasting images on rectangles, 160-183

    activating texture units, 171-172

    assigning texture images to texture objects, 177-179

    binding texture objects to target, 173-174

    changing texture coordinates, 182-183

flipping image y-axis, 170-171

mapping texture and vertex coordinates, 162-163, 166

multiple texture mapping, 183-190

passing coordinates from vertex to fragment shader, 180-181

passing texture unit to fragment shader, 179-180

retrieving texel color in fragment shader, 181-182

setting texture object parameters, 174-177

setting up and loading images, 166-170

texture coordinates, explained, 162

TexturedQuad.js, 163-166

perspective projection matrix, 257, 453

PerspectiveView.js, 255, 260-263

    model matrix, 262, 265

PerspectiveView_mvp.js, 263-266

per-vertex operations, 93

PickFace.js, 365-368

PickObject.js, 362-365

point light, 293

point light objects, 314-315

PointLightedCube.js, 315-319

PointLightedCube_perFragment.js, 319-321

points, drawing, 23-50

    attribute variables, 41-42

        setting value, 45-49

        storage location, 44-45

    changing point color, 58-66

    ClickedPoints.js, 50-52

    ColoredPoints.js, 59-61

    gl.drawArrays() function, 36-37

    HelloPoint1.html, 25